池田晃久
AKIHISA IKEDA

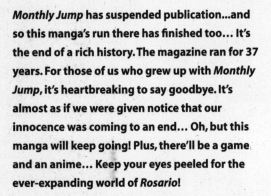

Monthly Jump has suspended publication...and so this manga's run there has finished too... It's the end of a rich history. The magazine ran for 37 years. For those of us who grew up with *Monthly Jump*, it's heartbreaking to say goodbye. It's almost as if we were given notice that our innocence was coming to an end... Oh, but this manga will keep going! Plus, there'll be a game and an anime... Keep your eyes peeled for the ever-expanding world of *Rosario*!

Akihisa Ikeda was born in 1977 in Miyazaki. He debuted as a mangaka with the four-volume magical warrior fantasy series *Kiruto* in 1999, which was serialized in *Monthly Shonen Jump*. *Rosario+Vampire* debuted in *Monthly Shonen Jump* in March of 2002, and is continuing in the new magazine *Jump Square* (Jump SQ). In Japan, *Rosario+Vampire* is also available as a drama CD. In 2008, the story was released as an anime.

Ikeda has been a huge fan of vampires and monsters since he was a little kid.

He says one of the perks of being a manga artist is being able to go for walks during the day when everybody else is stuck in the office.

ROSARIO+VAMPIRE 10
SHONEN JUMP ADVANCED Manga Edition

STORY AND ART BY AKIHISA IKEDA

Translation/Kaori Inoue
English Adaptation/Gerard Jones
Touch-up Art & Lettering/Stephen Dutro
Design/Ronnie Casson
Editor/Annette Roman

VP, Production/Alvin Lu
VP, Sales & Product Marketing/Gonzalo Ferreyra
VP, Creative/Linda Espinosa
Publisher/Hyoe Narita

ROSARIO TO VAMPIRE © 2004 by Akihisa Ikeda
All rights reserved. First published in Japan in 2004 by SHUEISHA Inc.,
Tokyo. English translation rights arranged by SHUEISHA Inc.

The rights of the author(s) of the work(s) in this publication to be so
identified have been asserted in accordance with the Copyright, Designs
and Patents Act 1988. A CIP catalogue record of this book is available
from the British Library.

Printed in the U.S.A.

Published by VIZ Media, LLC
P.O. Box 77010
San Francisco, CA 94107

10 9 8 7 6 5 4 3 2
First printing, November 2009
Second printing, December 2009

www.viz.com www.shonenjump.com

ROSARIO+VAMPIRE

MAGIC MIRROR

10

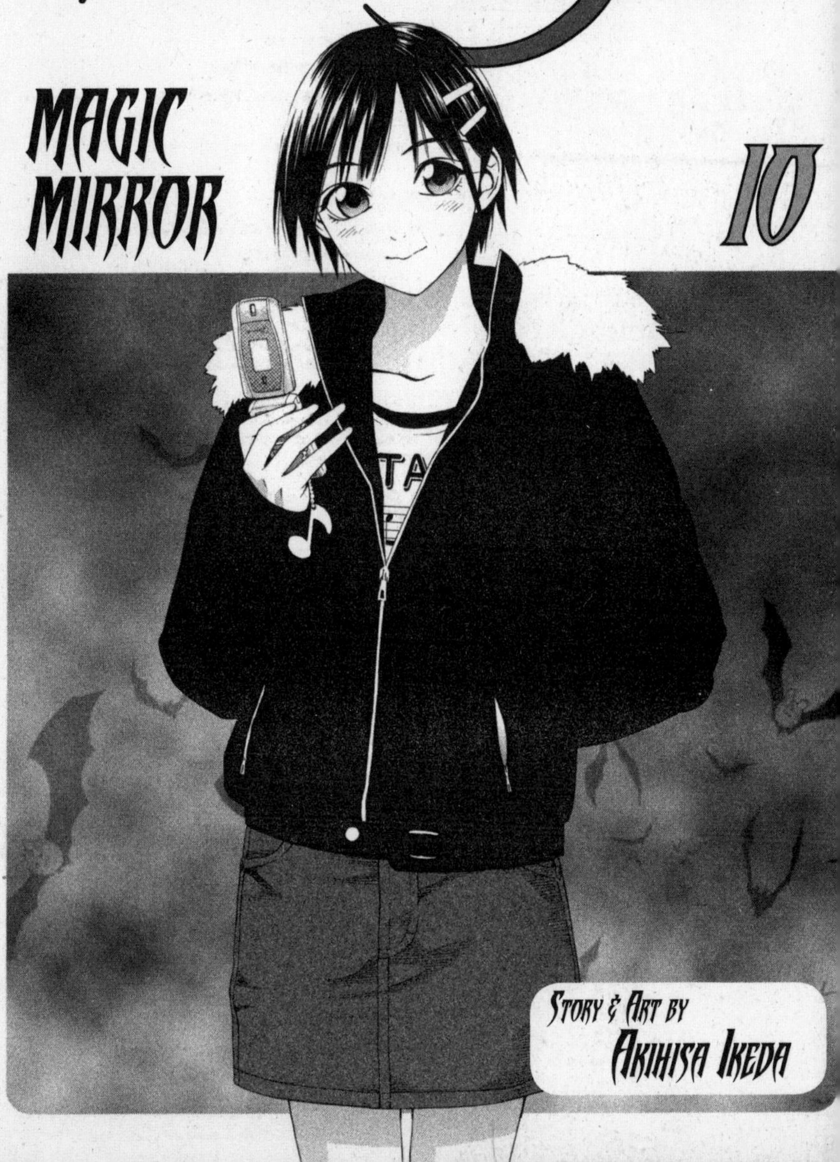

STORY & ART BY
AKIHISA IKEDA

Horror Story Thus Far

Tsukune Aono unsuspectingly enrolls in Yokai Academy—a private school for monsters. When beautiful Moka Akashiya befriends him, Tsukune is determined to stay...despite the rule that any humans who learn of Yokai's existence will be slain! Moka must save Tsukune's life repeatedly by infusing him with her blood, which briefly transforms him into a butt-kicking vampire!

Now it's the 2nd quarter of the school year... Tsukune borrows Moka's vampiric powers once too often and turns into a rampaging ghoul! The headmaster restores his humanity by chaining a "spirit lock" to his wrist, then pressures him into joining the school's Festival Committee. Unfortunately, the leader of the committee, charismatic Hokuto, turns out to be hell-bent on destroying the Great Barrier that separates Yokai from the human world!

Tsukune and friends defeat Hokuto and return the school to normal just in time for the School Festival. Then Tsukune's cousin Kyoko pays him a surprise visit...!

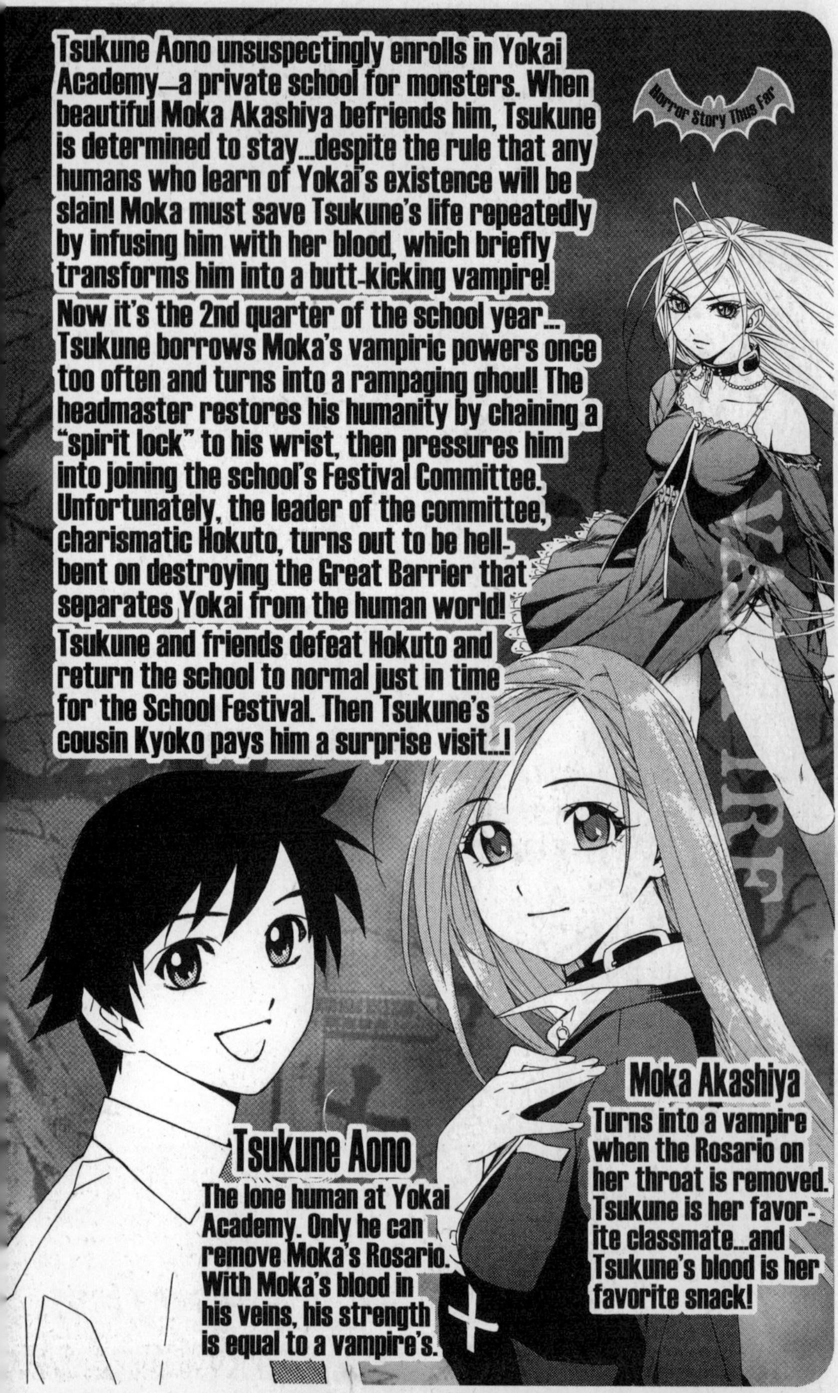

Moka Akashiya

Turns into a vampire when the Rosario on her throat is removed. Tsukune is her favorite classmate...and Tsukune's blood is her favorite snack!

Tsukune Aono

The lone human at Yokai Academy. Only he can remove Moka's Rosario. With Moka's blood in his veins, his strength is equal to a vampire's.

Yukari Sendo

An 11-year-old witch with a crush on everybody. Although smart enough to skip several grades, she is quite a pest—like a little sister.

Kurumu Kurono

SUCCUBUS

A succubus who believes Tsukune is her destiny.

WITCH

Ruby

A witch who hated humans until Tsukune was kind to her. Now the headmaster's right hand. (not literally)

SNOW WOMAN

Kyoko Aono

Tsukune's cousin grew up with him. She has come to Yokai Academy to check up on him. A bit dense.

Bus Driver

Crosses freely between the human and monster worlds. Pops up to impart advice at critical moments.

Mizore Shirayuki

Quietly stalking Tsukune. Able to manipulate ice.

CONTENTS

Volume 10: Magic Mirror

37: The Lilith Mirror

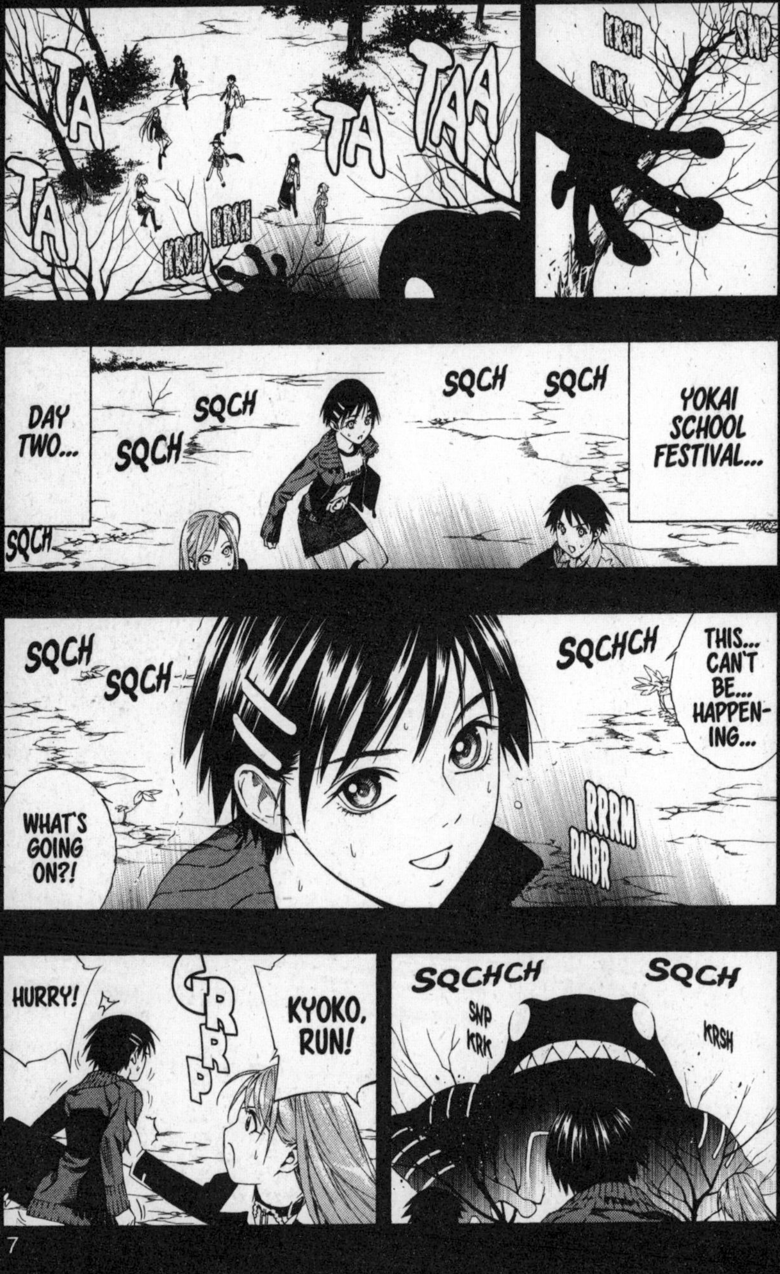
SNP
KRSH
KRRK
TAA
TA
TA
TA
KRSH
KRSH
YOKAI SCHOOL FESTIVAL...
SQCH
SQCH
SQCH
DAY TWO...
SQCH
SQCH
THIS... CAN'T BE... HAPPEN-ING...
SQCHCH
RRRM
RMBR
SQCH
SQCH
WHAT'S GOING ON?!
SQCH
KRSH
SQCHCH
SNP
KRK
KYOKO, RUN!
GRRP
HURRY!

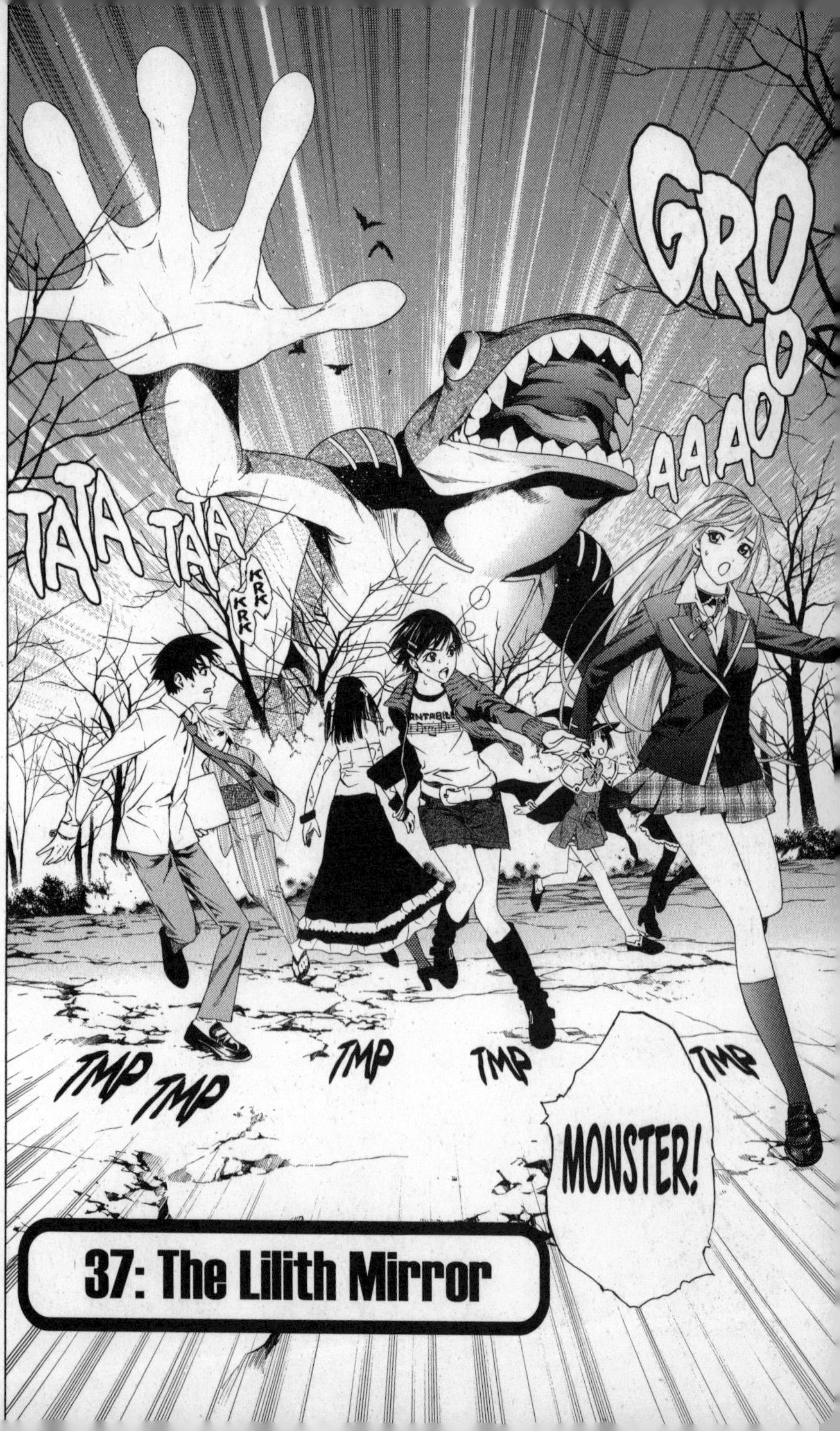
GROOO
AAAO
TATA TATA
KRK KRK
MONSTER!
TMP
TMP
TMP
TMP TMP
37: The Lilith Mirror

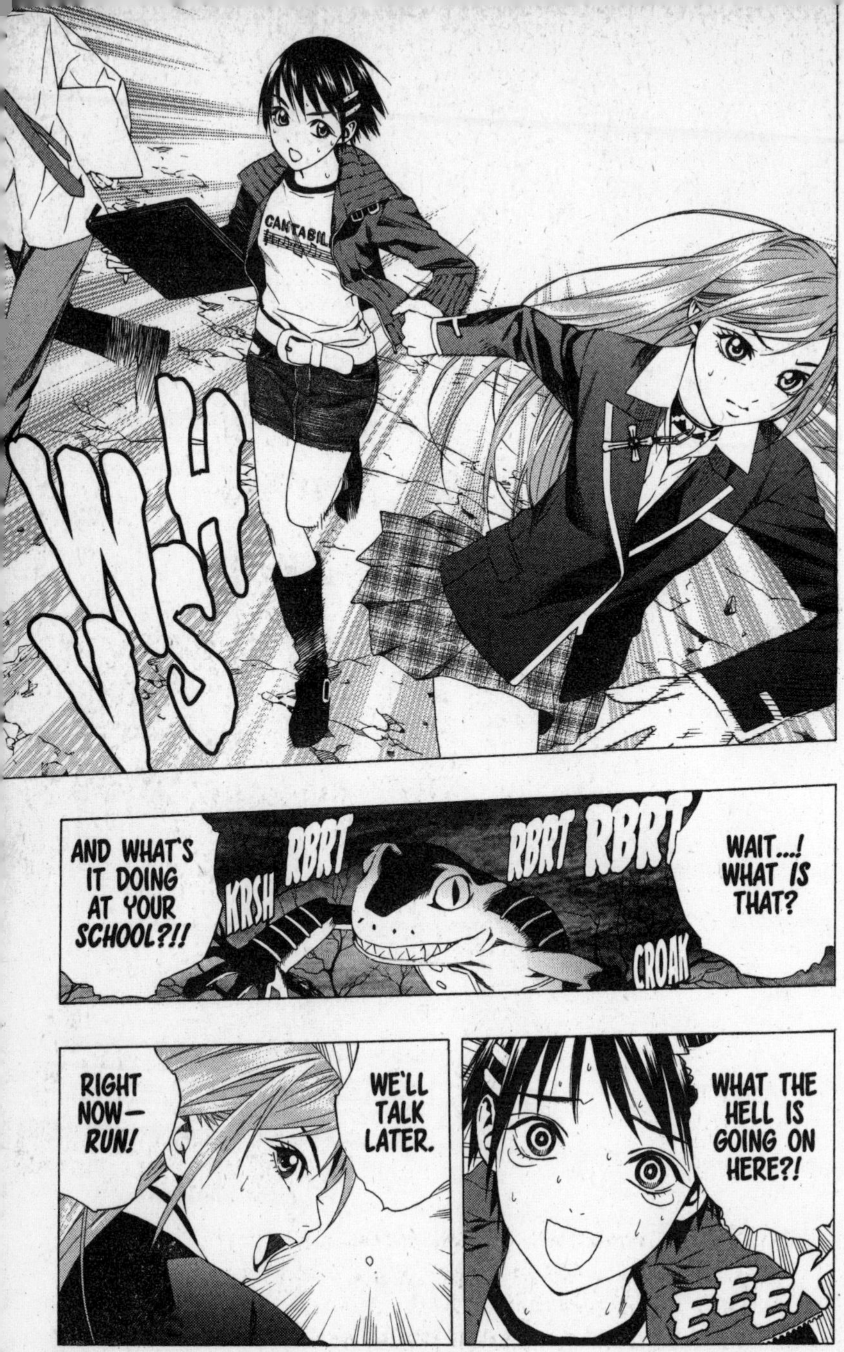
WHSH
WAIT...! WHAT IS THAT?
CROAK
RBRT RBRT
RBRT
KRSH
AND WHAT'S IT DOING AT YOUR SCHOOL?!!
WHAT THE HELL IS GOING ON HERE?!
EEEK
WE'LL TALK LATER.
RIGHT NOW— RUN!

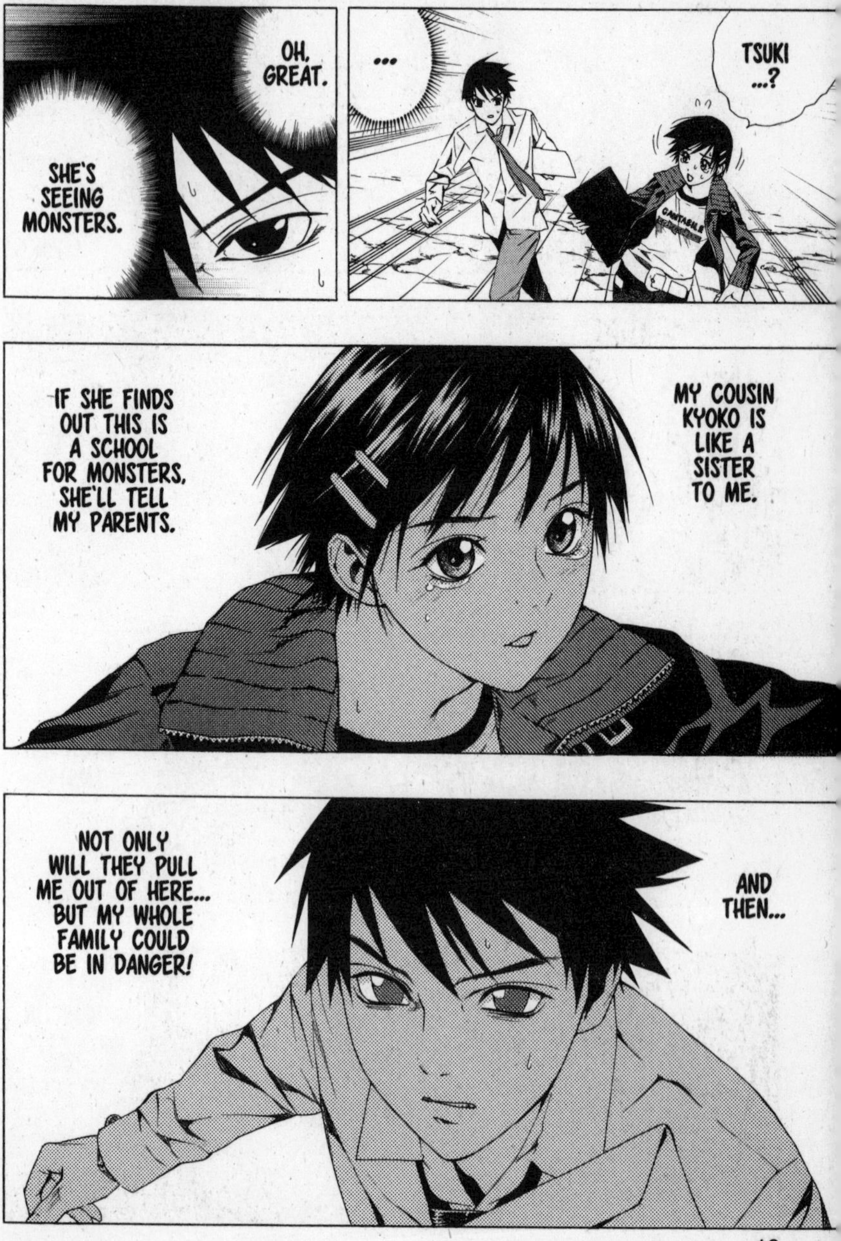
TSUKI ...?
...
OH, GREAT.
SHE'S SEEING MONSTERS.
MY COUSIN KYOKO IS LIKE A SISTER TO ME.
IF SHE FINDS OUT THIS IS A SCHOOL FOR MONSTERS, SHE'LL TELL MY PARENTS.
NOT ONLY WILL THEY PULL ME OUT OF HERE... BUT MY WHOLE FAMILY COULD BE IN DANGER!
AND THEN...

READ THIS WAY

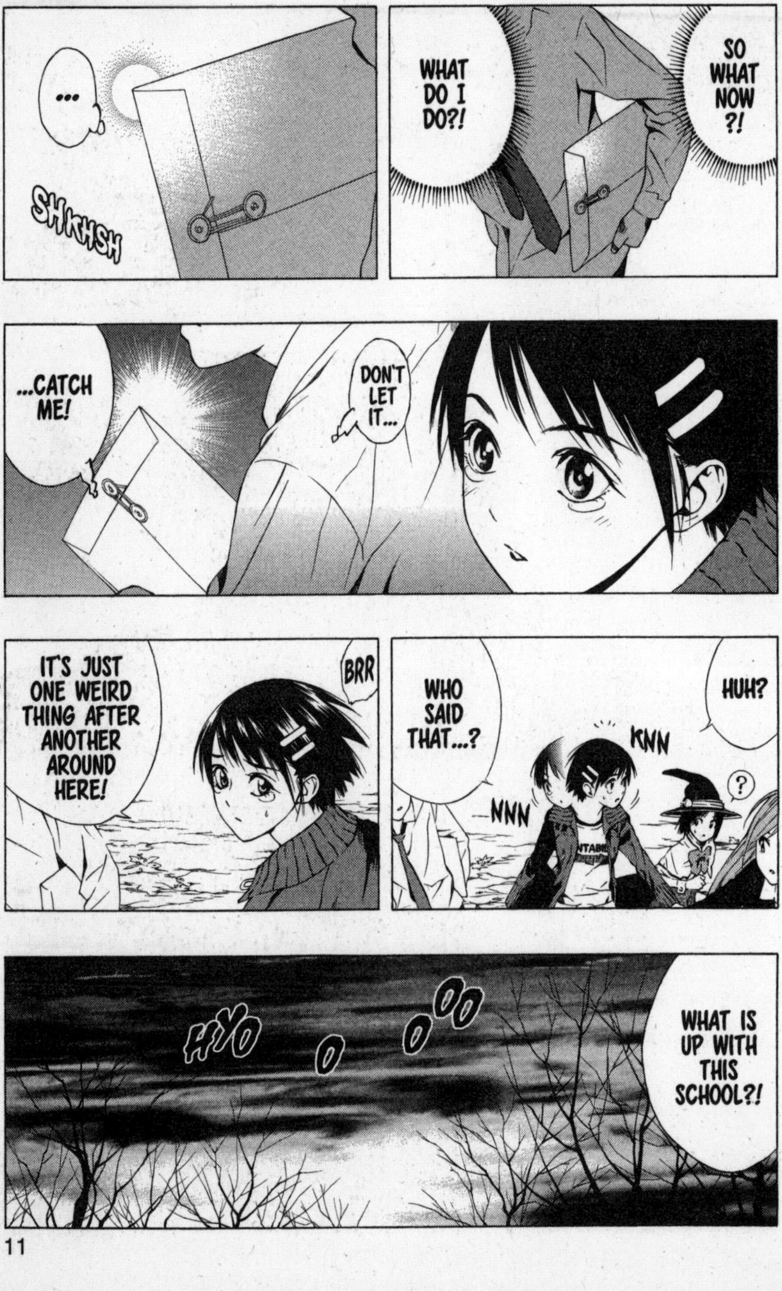

SO WHAT NOW?!
WHAT DO I DO?!
...
SHKHSH
DON'T LET IT...
...CATCH ME!
HUH?
KNN
?
WHO SAID THAT...?
NNN
BRR
IT'S JUST ONE WEIRD THING AFTER ANOTHER AROUND HERE!
WHAT IS UP WITH THIS SCHOOL?!
HYO O O OO

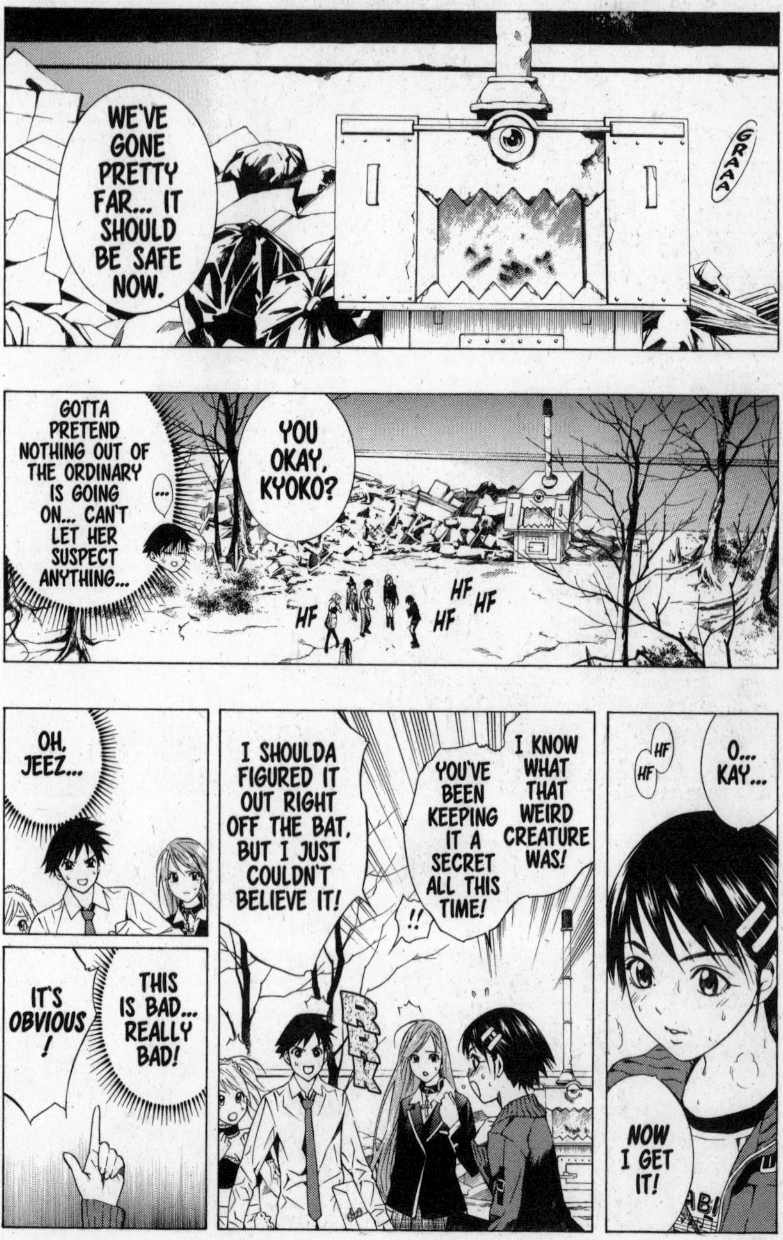

GRAAA
WE'VE GONE PRETTY FAR... IT SHOULD BE SAFE NOW.
YOU OKAY, KYOKO?
...
GOTTA PRETEND NOTHING OUT OF THE ORDINARY IS GOING ON... CAN'T LET HER SUSPECT ANYTHING...
HF HF HF HF
HF HF
O... KAY...
NOW I GET IT!
I KNOW WHAT THAT WEIRD CREATURE WAS!
YOU'VE BEEN KEEPING IT A SECRET ALL THIS TIME!
I SHOULDA FIGURED IT OUT RIGHT OFF THE BAT, BUT I JUST COULDN'T BELIEVE IT!
!!
RRR
OH, JEEZ...
THIS IS BAD... REALLY BAD!
IT'S OBVIOUS!

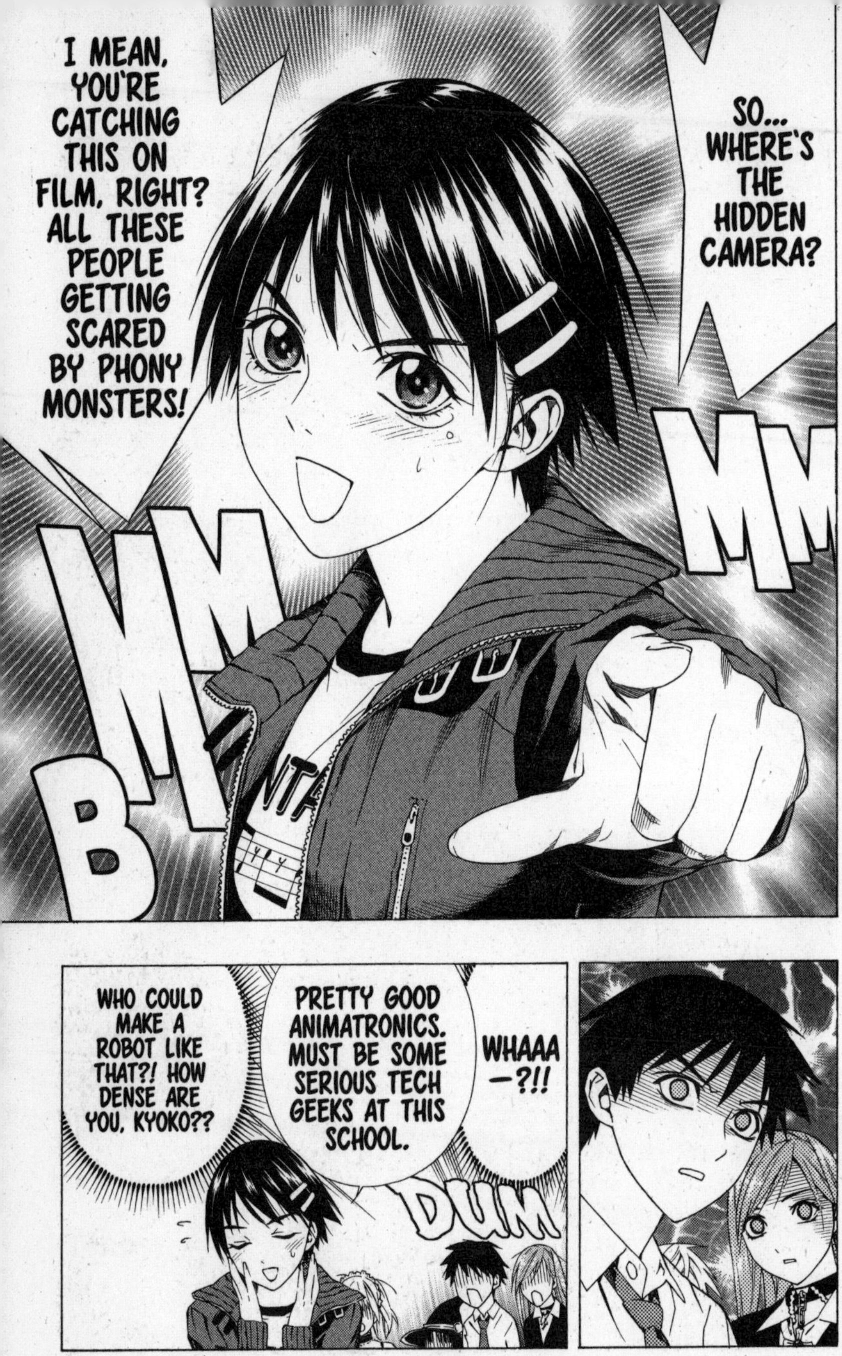
SO... WHERE'S THE HIDDEN CAMERA?
I MEAN, YOU'RE CATCHING THIS ON FILM, RIGHT? ALL THESE PEOPLE GETTING SCARED BY PHONY MONSTERS!
BAMMMM
WHAAA —?!!
PRETTY GOOD ANIMATRONICS. MUST BE SOME SERIOUS TECH GEEKS AT THIS SCHOOL.
WHO COULD MAKE A ROBOT LIKE THAT?! HOW DENSE ARE YOU, KYOKO??
DUM

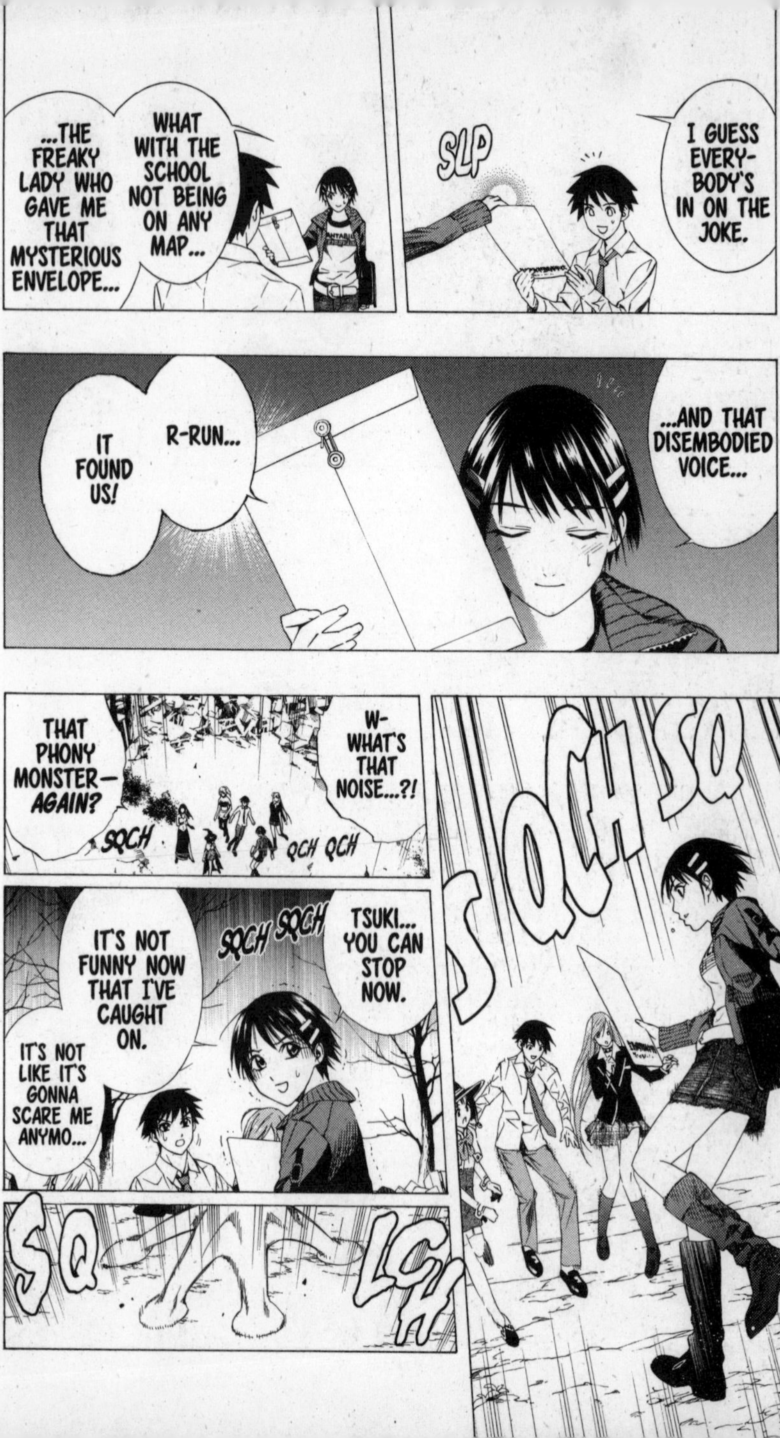

SLP
I GUESS EVERYBODY'S IN ON THE JOKE.
WHAT WITH THE SCHOOL NOT BEING ON ANY MAP...
...THE FREAKY LADY WHO GAVE ME THAT MYSTERIOUS ENVELOPE...
...AND THAT DISEMBODIED VOICE...
R-RUN...
IT FOUND US!
SQCH SQ
SQCH
W-WHAT'S THAT NOISE...?!
QCH QCH
THAT PHONY MONSTER—*AGAIN?*
SQCH
TSUKI... YOU CAN STOP NOW.
SQCH SQCH
IT'S NOT FUNNY NOW THAT I'VE CAUGHT ON.
IT'S NOT LIKE IT'S GONNA SCARE ME ANYMO...
SQ LCH

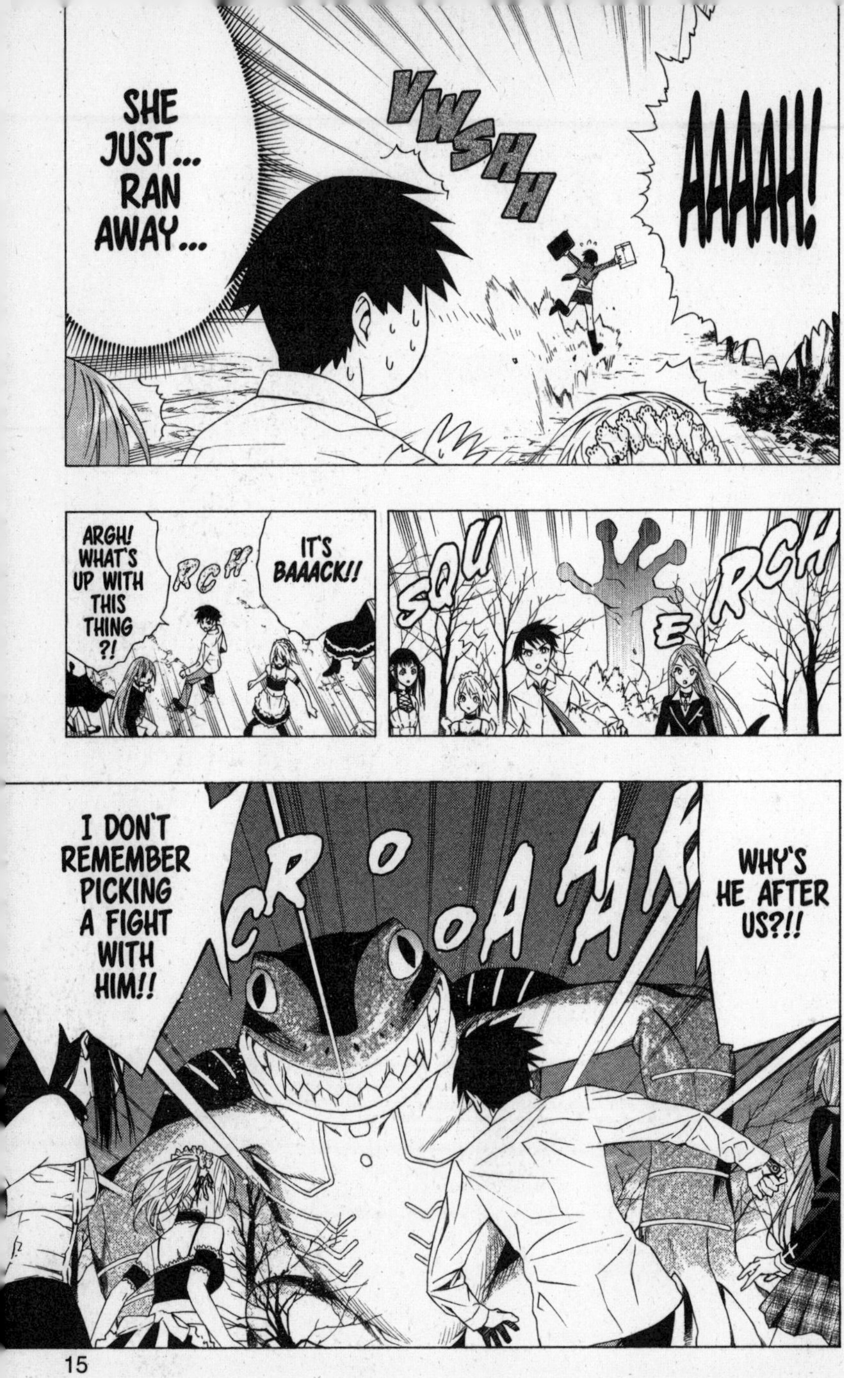
AAAAH!
VWSHH
SHE JUST... RAN AWAY...
SQUERCH
IT'S BAAACK!!
RCH
ARGH! WHAT'S UP WITH THIS THING ?!
WHY'S HE AFTER US?!!
CROOAAK
I DON'T REMEMBER PICKING A FIGHT WITH HIM!!

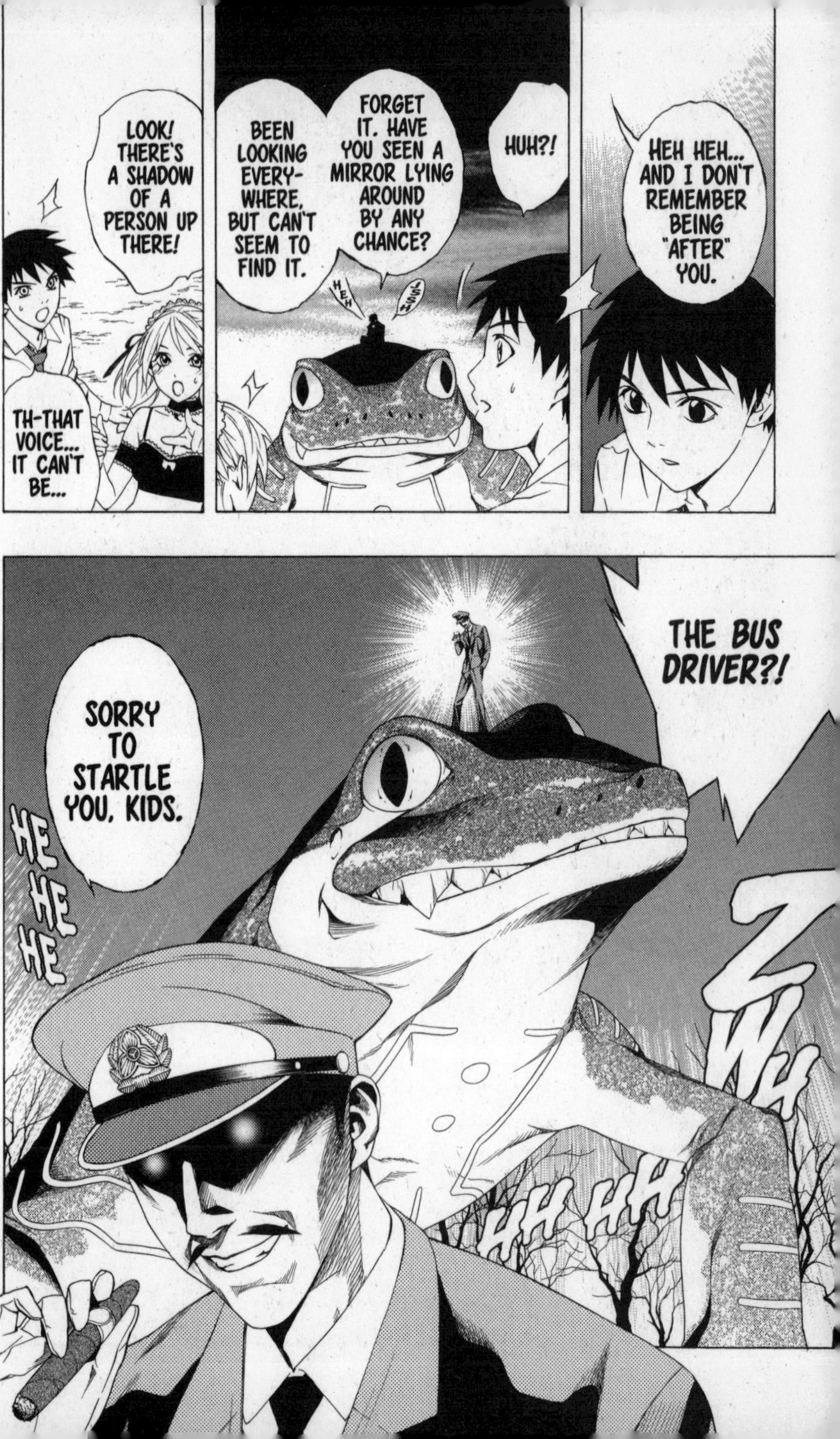
HEH HEH... AND I DON'T REMEMBER BEING "AFTER" YOU.
HUH?!
FORGET IT. HAVE YOU SEEN A MIRROR LYING AROUND BY ANY CHANCE?
BEEN LOOKING EVERY-WHERE, BUT CAN'T SEEM TO FIND IT.
ISSH
HEH
LOOK! THERE'S A SHADOW OF A PERSON UP THERE!
TH-THAT VOICE... IT CAN'T BE...
THE BUS DRIVER?!
SORRY TO STARTLE YOU, KIDS.
HE HE HE

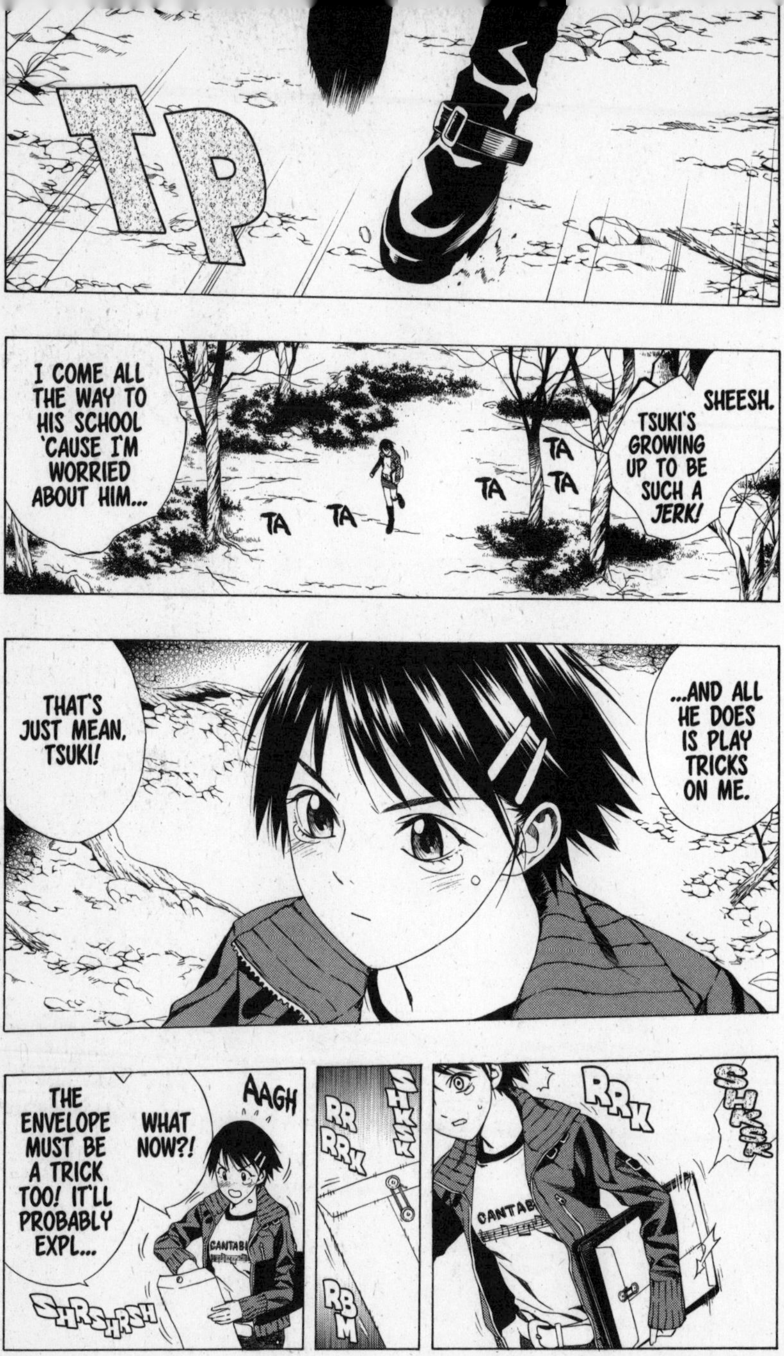
TP
SHEESH. TSUKI'S GROWING UP TO BE SUCH A JERK!
TA TA
TA
TA
TA
I COME ALL THE WAY TO HIS SCHOOL 'CAUSE I'M WORRIED ABOUT HIM...
...AND ALL HE DOES IS PLAY TRICKS ON ME.
THAT'S JUST MEAN, TSUKI!
SHKSK
RRRK
CANTAB
SHKSK
RRRRRK
RBM
AAGH
WHAT NOW?!
THE ENVELOPE MUST BE A TRICK TOO! IT'LL PROBABLY EXPL...
CANTABI
SHRSHRSH

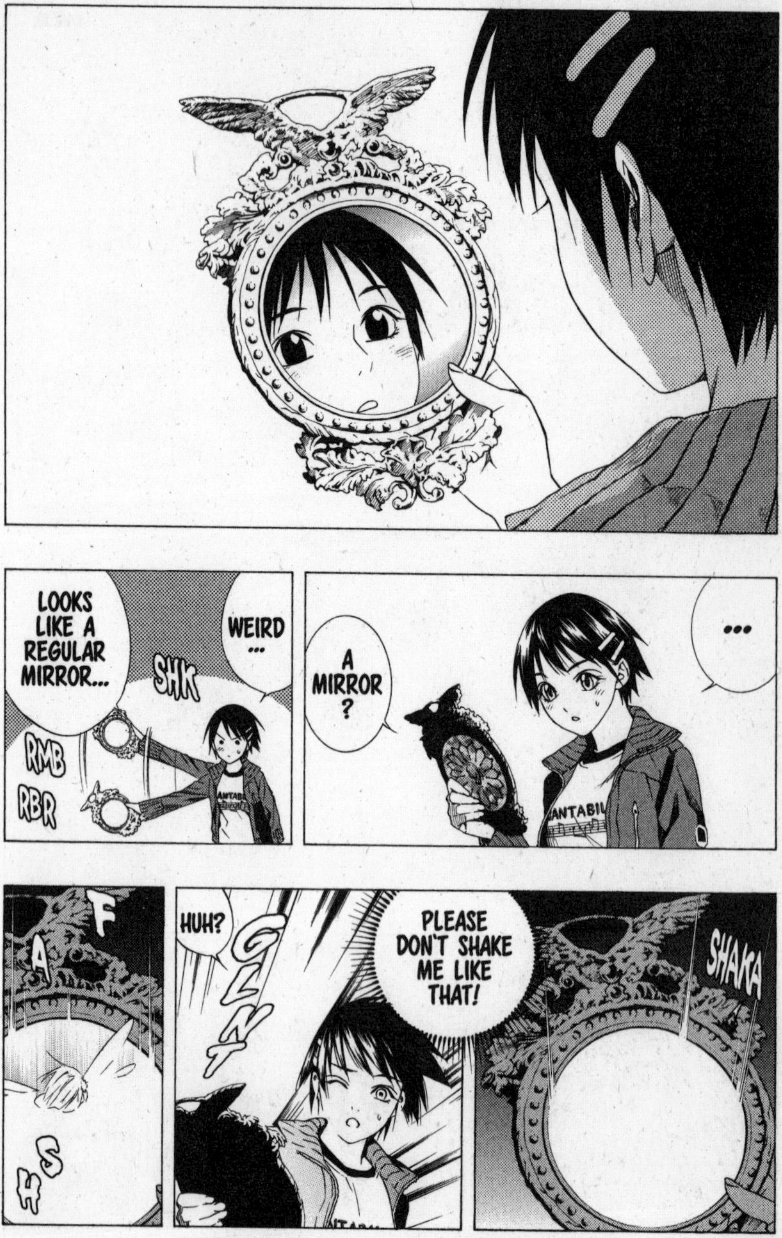
...
A MIRROR ?
WEIRD ...
LOOKS LIKE A REGULAR MIRROR...
SHK
RMB
RBR
SHAKA
PLEASE DON'T SHAKE ME LIKE THAT!
HUH?
GLNT
F A
S H

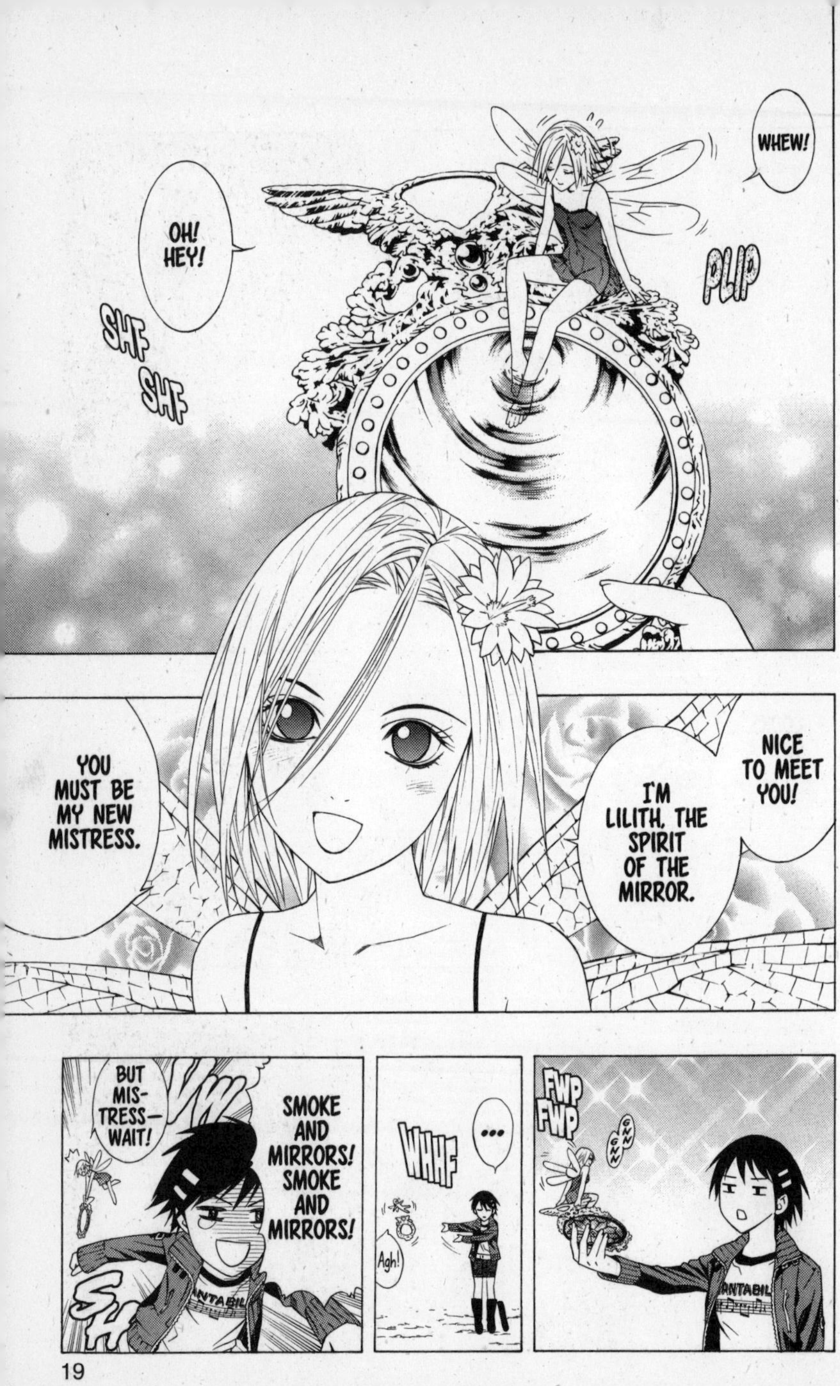
WHEW!
PLIP
OH! HEY!
SHF SHF
NICE TO MEET YOU!
I'M LILITH, THE SPIRIT OF THE MIRROR.
YOU MUST BE MY NEW MISTRESS.
FWP FWP
GNN GNN
...
WHHF
Agh!
SMOKE AND MIRRORS! SMOKE AND MIRRORS!
BUT MIS-TRESS—WAIT!
SH

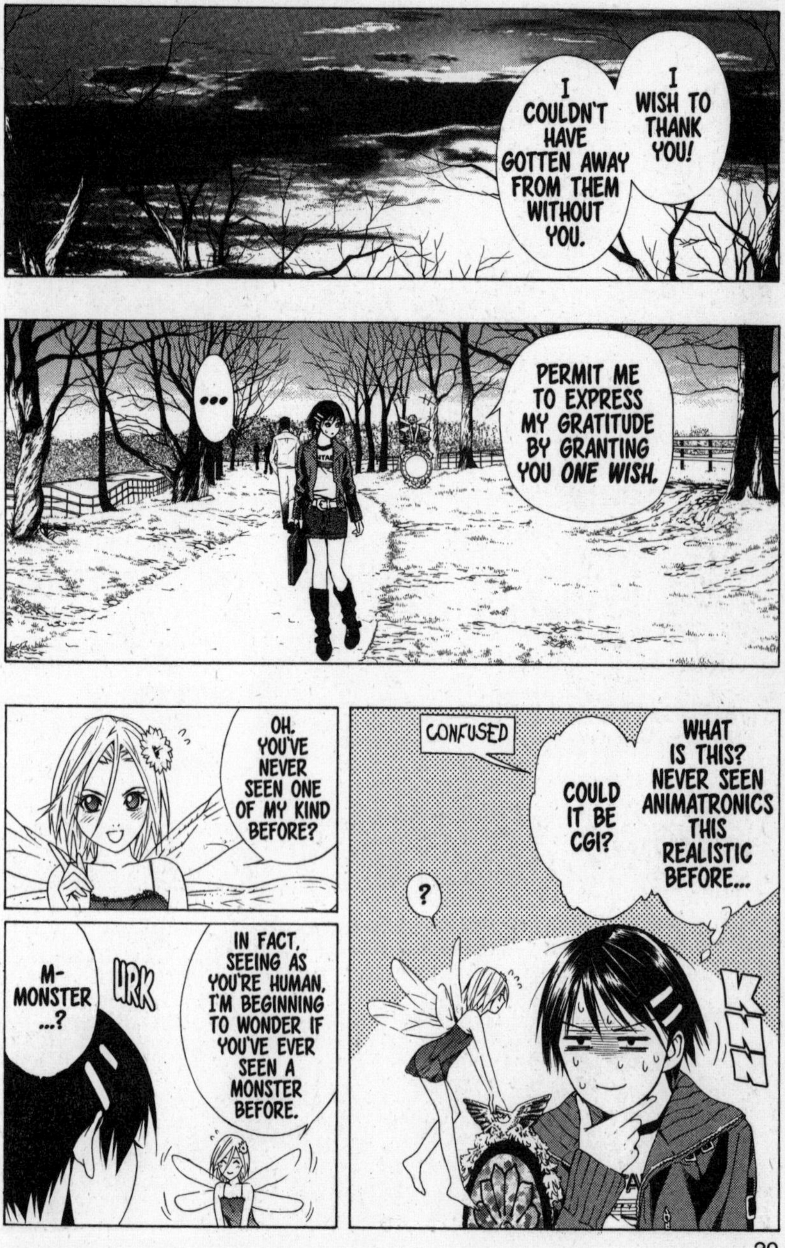
I WISH TO THANK YOU!
I COULDN'T HAVE GOTTEN AWAY FROM THEM WITHOUT YOU.
PERMIT ME TO EXPRESS MY GRATITUDE BY GRANTING YOU *ONE WISH.*
...
WHAT IS THIS? NEVER SEEN ANIMATRONICS THIS REALISTIC BEFORE...
CONFUSED
COULD IT BE CGI?
?
KNN
OH. YOU'VE NEVER SEEN ONE OF MY KIND BEFORE?
IN FACT, SEEING AS YOU'RE HUMAN, I'M BEGINNING TO WONDER IF YOU'VE EVER SEEN A MONSTER BEFORE.
URK
M-MONSTER ...?

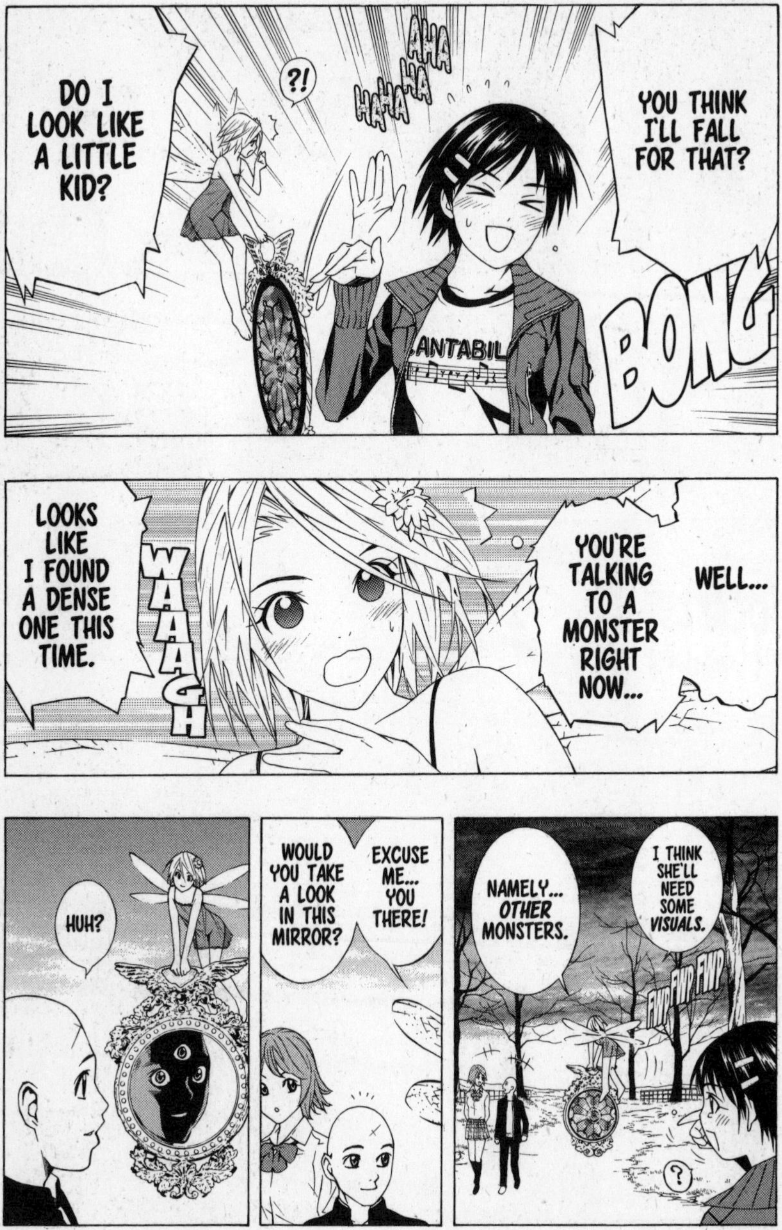
YOU THINK I'LL FALL FOR THAT?
AHAHA HAHA
?!
DO I LOOK LIKE A LITTLE KID?
BONG
WELL...
YOU'RE TALKING TO A MONSTER RIGHT NOW...
LOOKS LIKE I FOUND A DENSE ONE THIS TIME.
WAAAGH
I THINK SHE'LL NEED SOME *VISUALS.*
NAMELY... *OTHER* MONSTERS.
FWIP FWIP FWIP
?
EXCUSE ME... YOU THERE!
WOULD YOU TAKE A LOOK IN THIS MIRROR?
HUH?

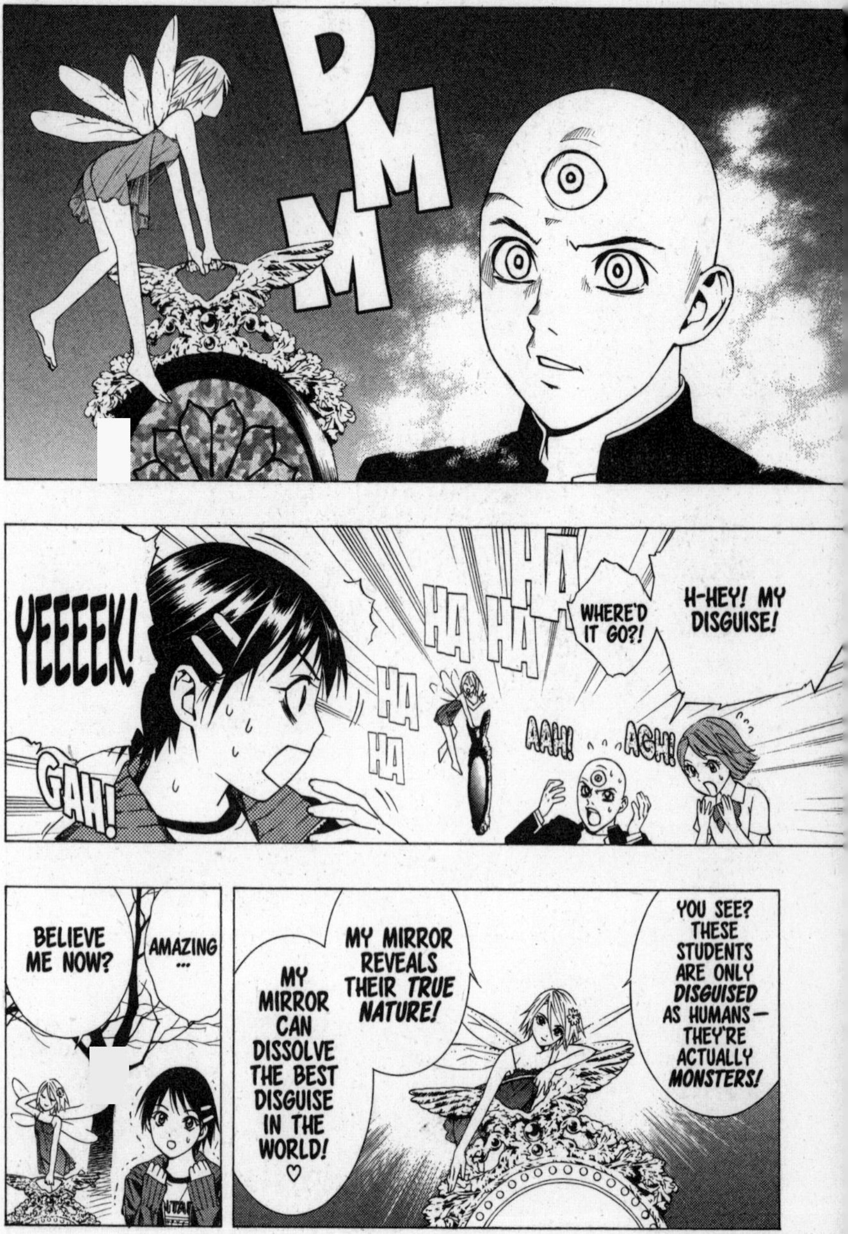
DMMM
H-HEY! MY DISGUISE!
WHERE'D IT GO?!
HA HA HA
HA HA HA
AGH!
AAH!
YEEEEK!
GAH!
YOU SEE? THESE STUDENTS ARE ONLY *DISGUISED* AS HUMANS—THEY'RE ACTUALLY *MONSTERS!*
MY MIRROR REVEALS THEIR *TRUE NATURE!*
MY MIRROR CAN DISSOLVE THE BEST DISGUISE IN THE WORLD! ♡
AMAZING...
BELIEVE ME NOW?

READ THIS WAY

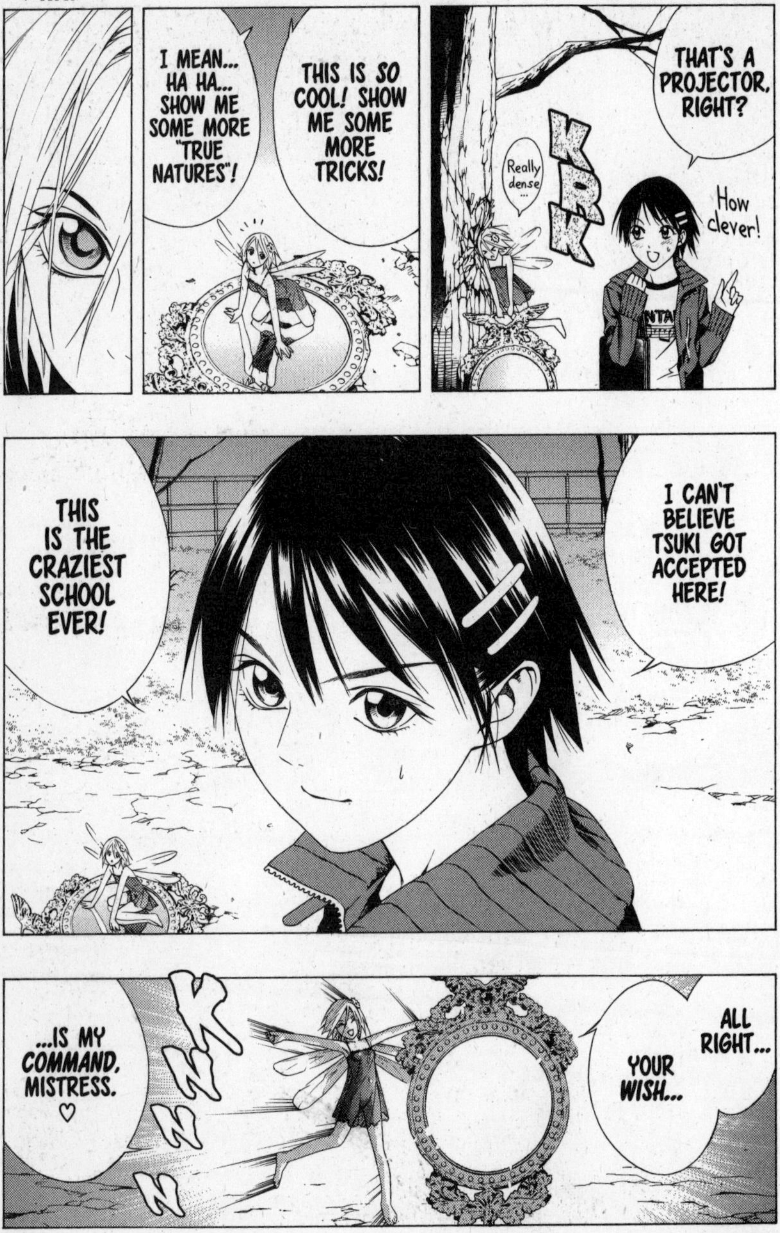
THAT'S A PROJECTOR, RIGHT?
How clever!
KRK
Really dense...
THIS IS SO COOL! SHOW ME SOME MORE TRICKS!
I MEAN... HA HA... SHOW ME SOME MORE "TRUE NATURES"!
I CAN'T BELIEVE TSUKI GOT ACCEPTED HERE!
THIS IS THE CRAZIEST SCHOOL EVER!
ALL RIGHT...
YOUR WISH...
...IS MY COMMAND, MISTRESS. ♡

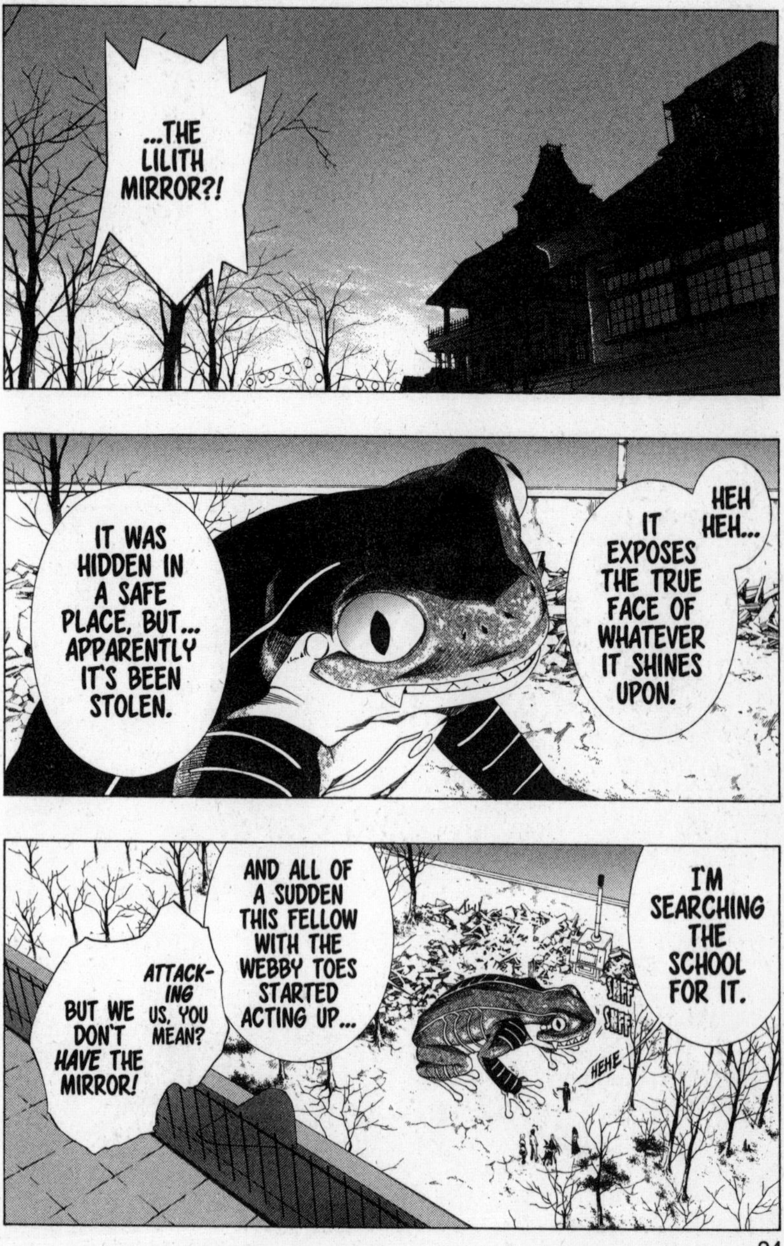

...THE LILITH MIRROR?!
HEH HEH... IT EXPOSES THE TRUE FACE OF WHATEVER IT SHINES UPON.
IT WAS HIDDEN IN A SAFE PLACE, BUT... APPARENTLY IT'S BEEN STOLEN.
I'M SEARCHING THE SCHOOL FOR IT.
SNFF
SNFF
HEHE
AND ALL OF A SUDDEN THIS FELLOW WITH THE WEBBY TOES STARTED ACTING UP...
ATTACKING US, YOU MEAN?
BUT WE DON'T HAVE THE MIRROR!

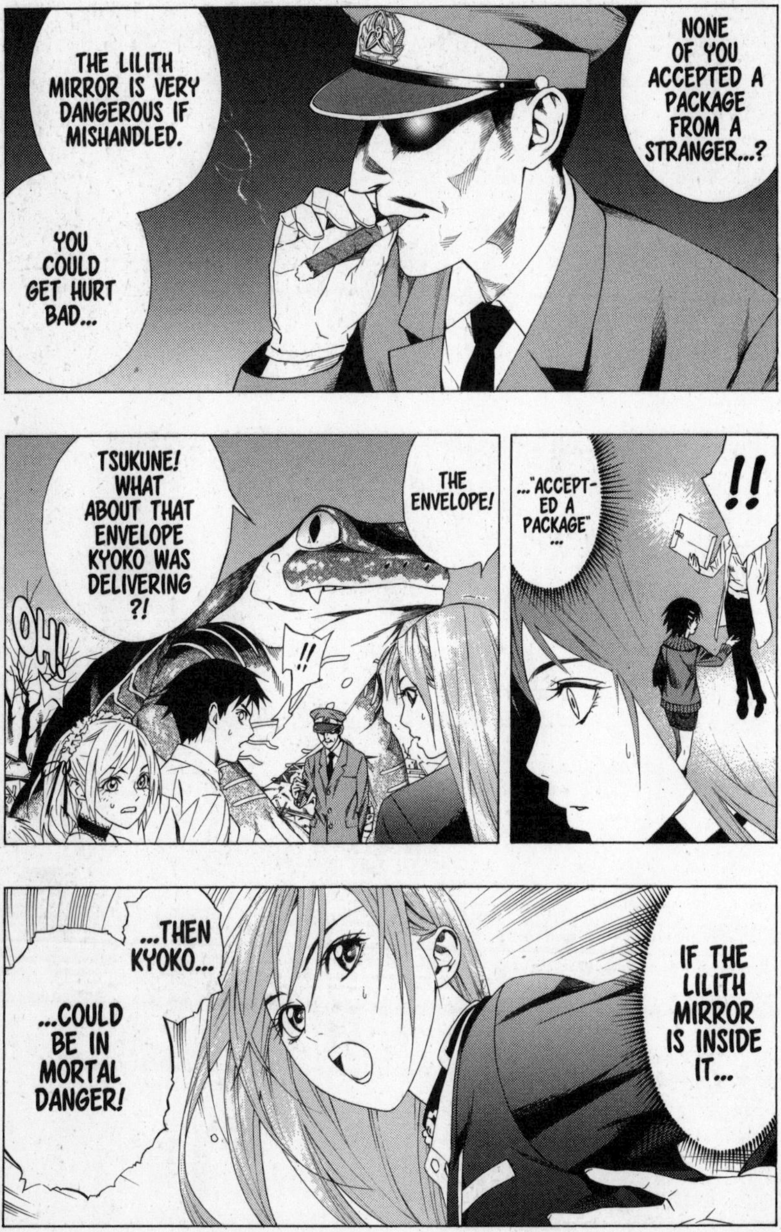
NONE OF YOU ACCEPTED A PACKAGE FROM A STRANGER...?
THE LILITH MIRROR IS VERY DANGEROUS IF MISHANDLED.
YOU COULD GET HURT BAD...
!!
..."ACCEPTED A PACKAGE"...
THE ENVELOPE!
TSUKUNE! WHAT ABOUT THAT ENVELOPE KYOKO WAS DELIVERING?!
!!
OH!
IF THE LILITH MIRROR IS INSIDE IT...
...THEN KYOKO...
...COULD BE IN MORTAL DANGER!

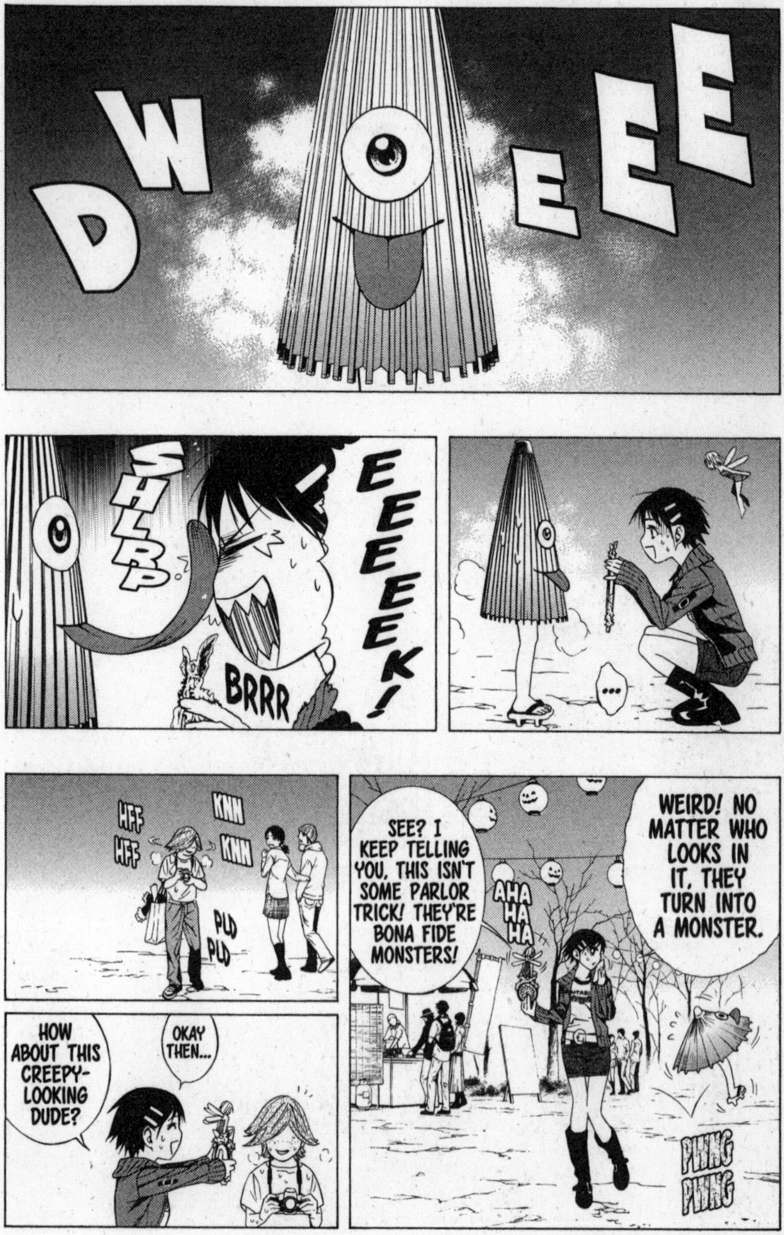
DWEEEE
...
SHLRP
EEEEEEK!
BRRR
WEIRD! NO MATTER WHO LOOKS IN IT, THEY TURN INTO A MONSTER.
SEE? I KEEP TELLING YOU, THIS ISN'T SOME PARLOR TRICK! THEY'RE BONA FIDE MONSTERS!
AHA HA HA
PWNG PWNG
HFF HFF
KNN KNN
PLD PLD
OKAY THEN...
HOW ABOUT THIS CREEPY-LOOKING DUDE?

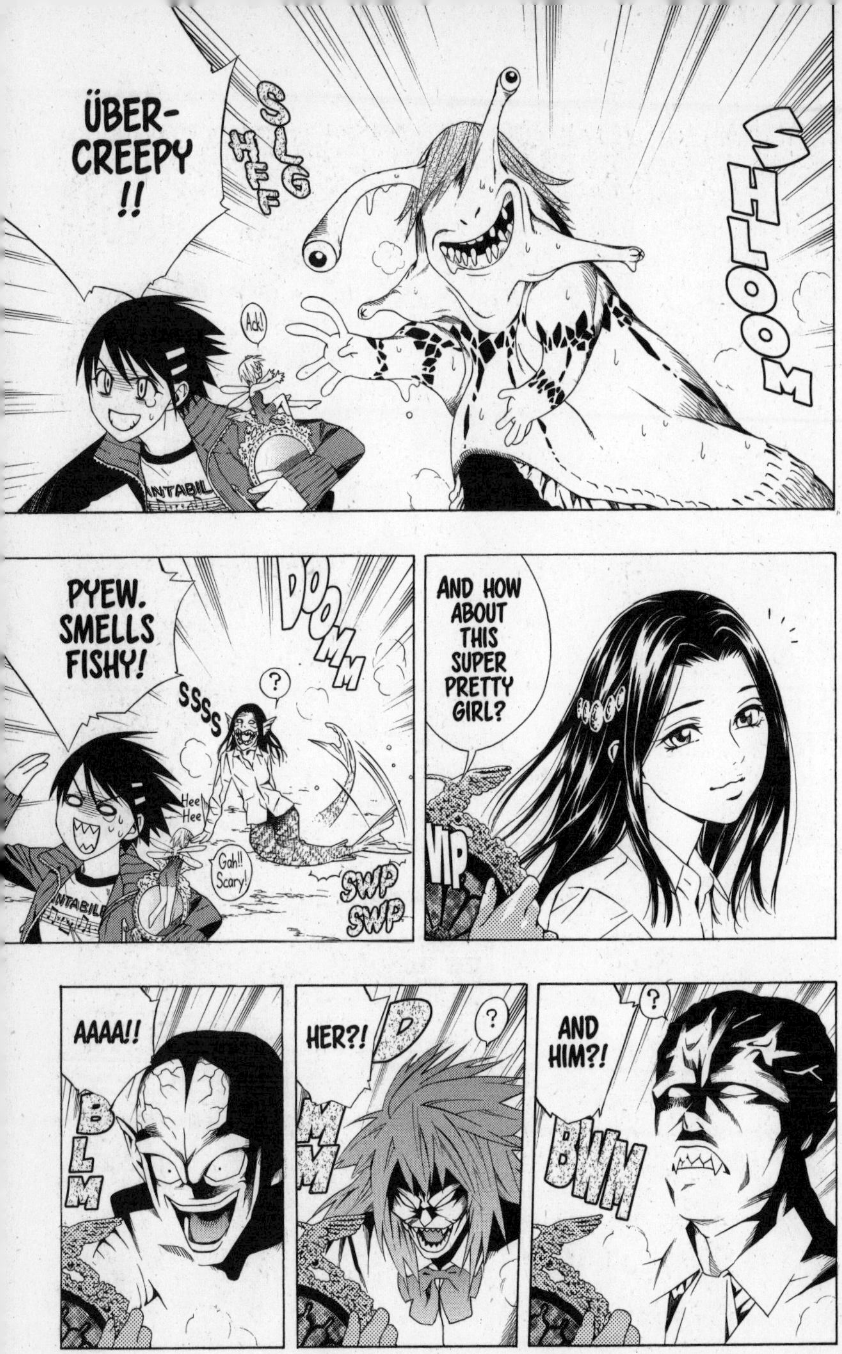
SHLOOM
SLG
HFF
ÜBER-CREEPY!!
Ack!
AND HOW ABOUT THIS SUPER PRETTY GIRL?
VIP
DOOMM
PYEW. SMELLS FISHY!
?
SSSS
Hee Hee
Gah!! Scary!
SWP SWP
?
AND HIM?!
BWM
?
D
HER?!
M M M
AAAA!!
BLM

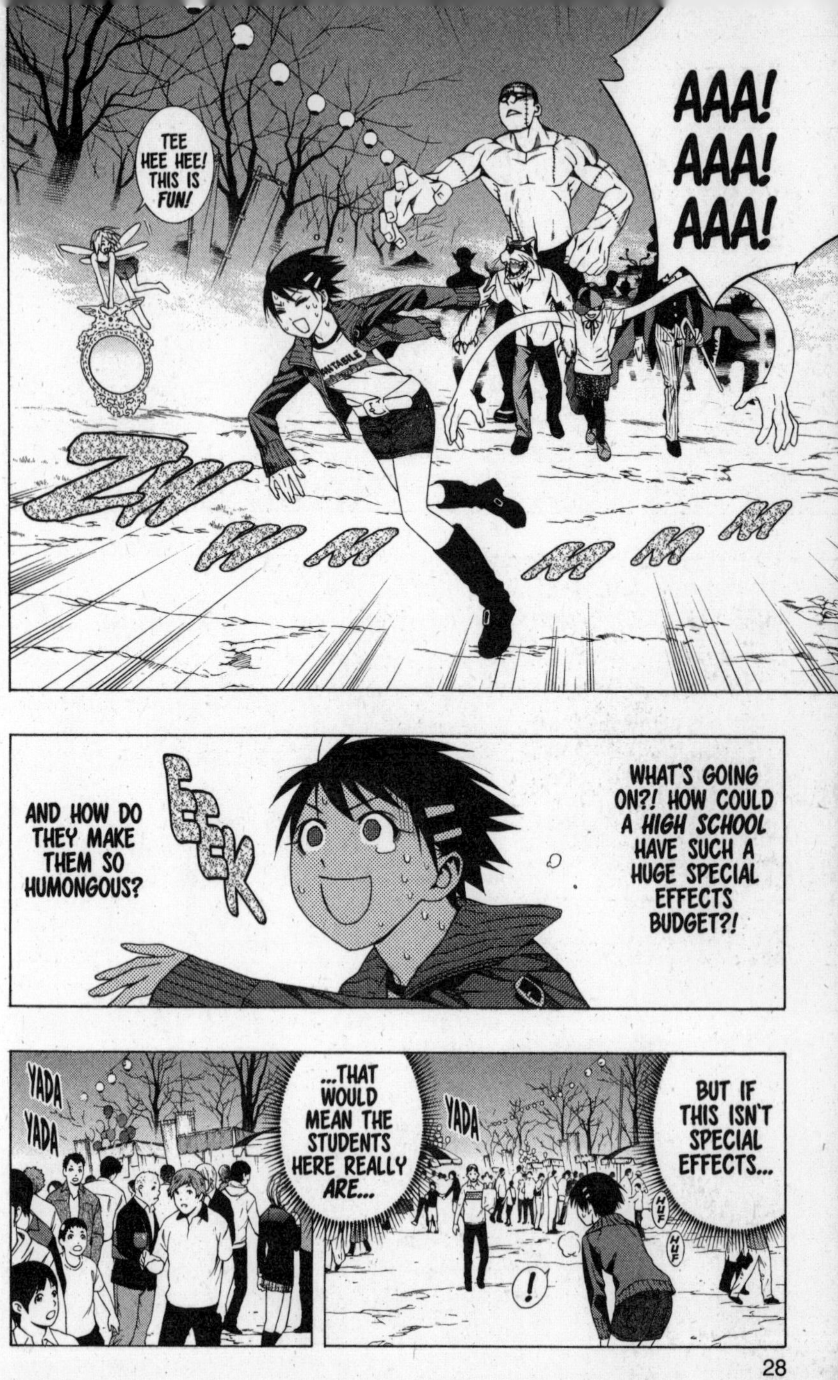
AAA! AAA! AAA!
TEE HEE HEE! THIS IS FUN!
ZWWMMMM
WHAT'S GOING ON?! HOW COULD A HIGH SCHOOL HAVE SUCH A HUGE SPECIAL EFFECTS BUDGET?!
EEEK
AND HOW DO THEY MAKE THEM SO HUMONGOUS?
BUT IF THIS ISN'T SPECIAL EFFECTS...
HUF
HUF
!
YADA
...THAT WOULD MEAN THE STUDENTS HERE REALLY ARE...
YADA
YADA

READ THIS WAY

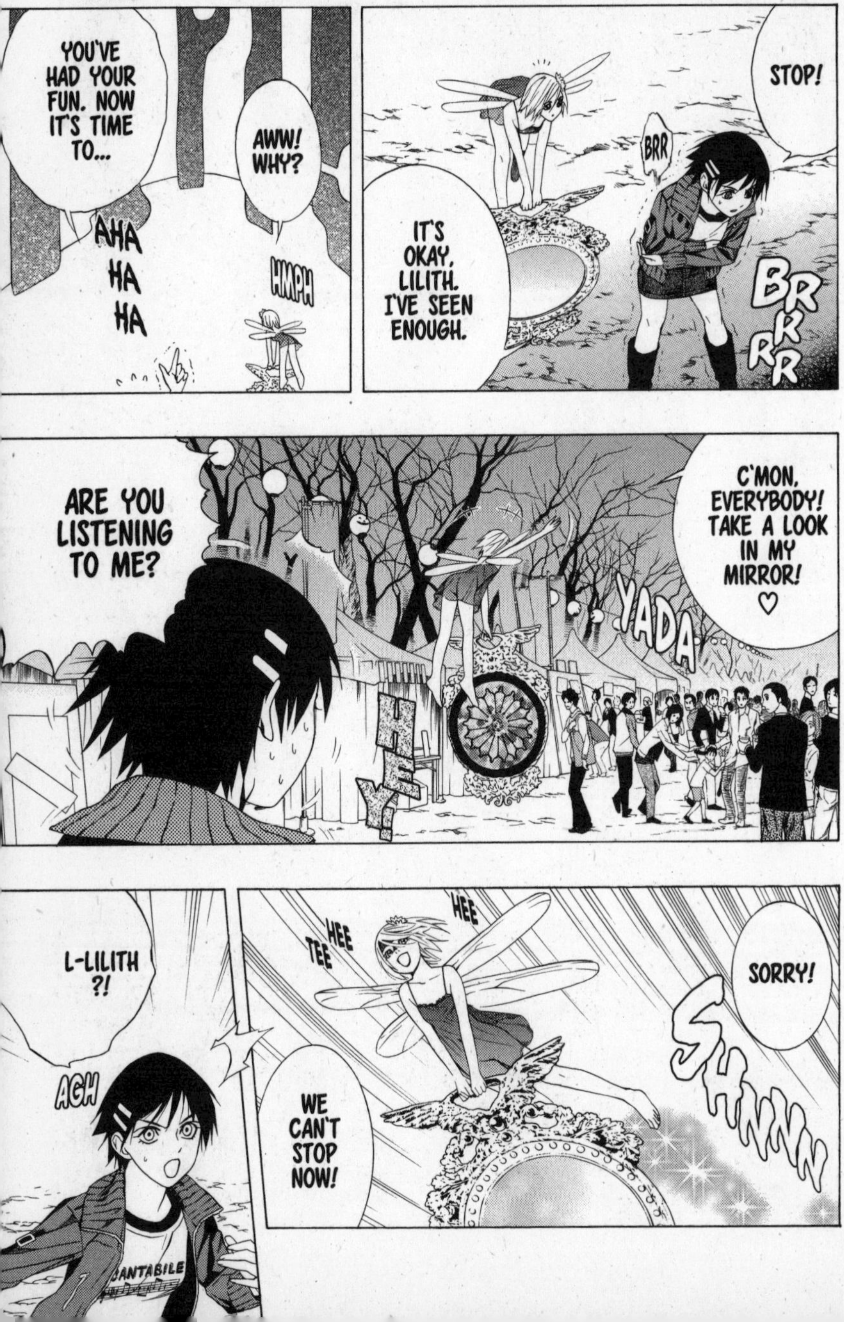
STOP!
BRR
BRRRRR
IT'S OKAY, LILITH. I'VE SEEN ENOUGH.
AWW! WHY?
HMPH
YOU'VE HAD YOUR FUN. NOW IT'S TIME TO...
AHA HA HA
C'MON, EVERYBODY! TAKE A LOOK IN MY MIRROR! ♡
YADA
HEY
ARE YOU LISTENING TO ME?
HEE
TEE HEE
SORRY!
SHNNNN
WE CAN'T STOP NOW!
L-LILITH ?!
AGH

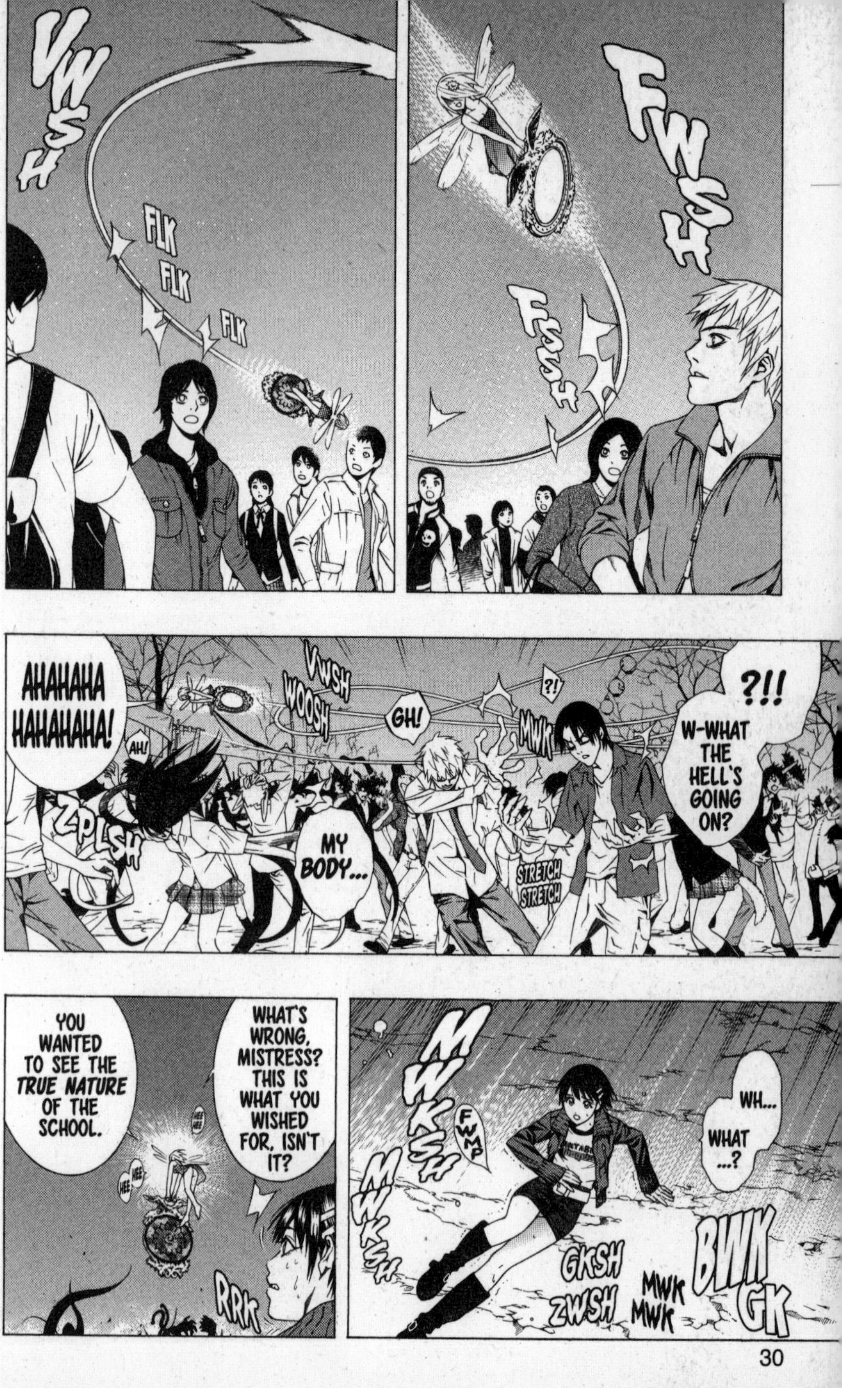
FWSH
FSSH
VWSH
FLK
FLK
FLK
?!!
W-WHAT THE HELL'S GOING ON?
?!
MWK
GH!
VWSH
WOOSH
STRETCH STRETCH
MY BODY...
AH!
AHAHAHA HAHAHAHA!
ZPLSH
WH... WHAT ...?
MWKSH
FWMP
MWKSH
BWK
GK
MWK MWK
GKSH
ZWSH
WHAT'S WRONG, MISTRESS? THIS IS WHAT YOU WISHED FOR, ISN'T IT?
YOU WANTED TO SEE THE TRUE NATURE OF THE SCHOOL.
HEE HEE
HEE
HEE
RRK

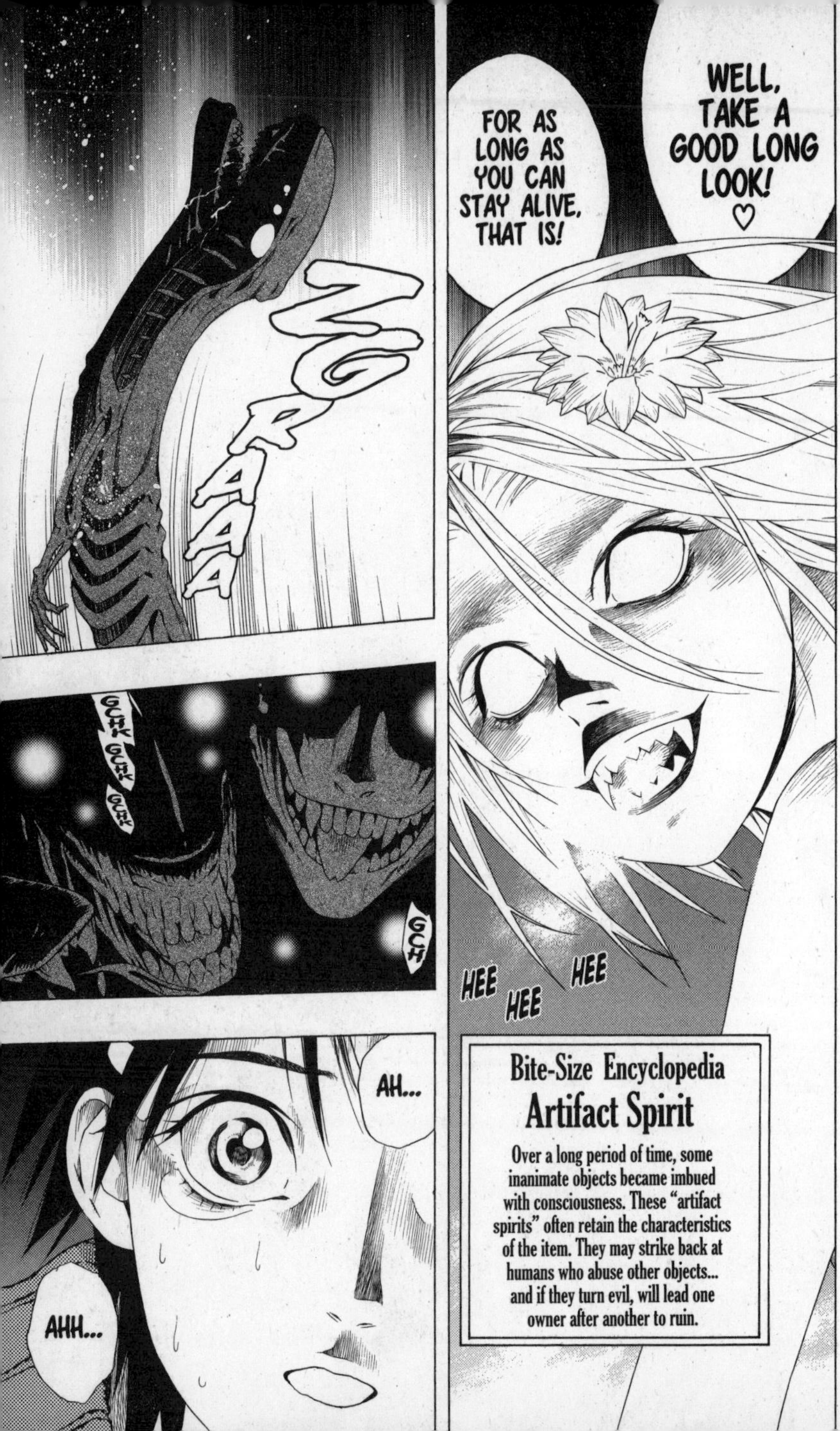
WELL, TAKE A GOOD LONG LOOK! ♡
FOR AS LONG AS YOU CAN STAY ALIVE, THAT IS!
HEE HEE HEE
Bite-Size Encyclopedia
Artifact Spirit
Over a long period of time, some inanimate objects became imbued with consciousness. These "artifact spirits" often retain the characteristics of the item. They may strike back at humans who abuse other objects... and if they turn evil, will lead one owner after another to ruin.
ZGRAAA
GCHK GCHK GCHK
GCH
AH...
AHH...

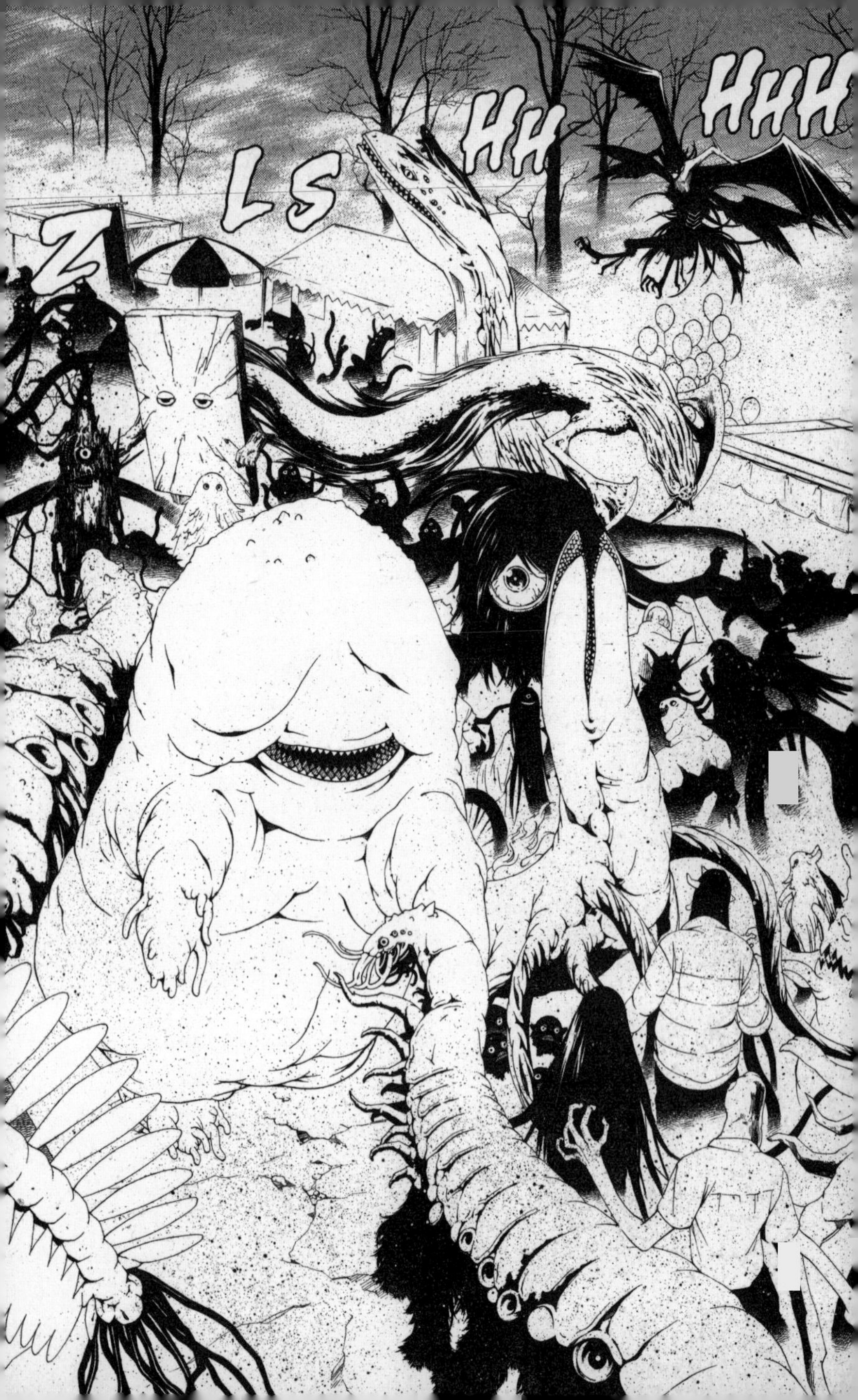
ZLSHHHHH

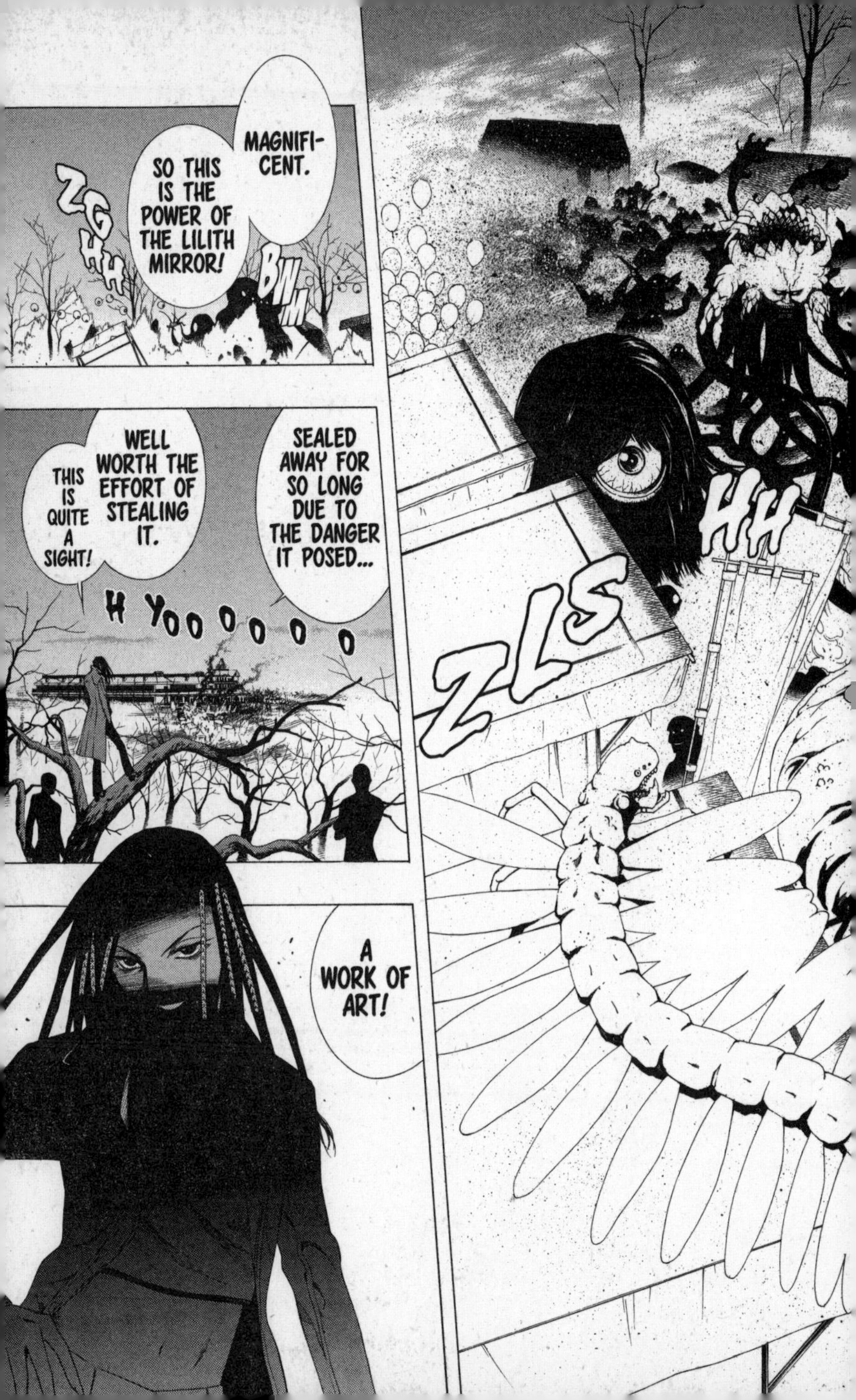
ZLS
HH
MAGNIFI-CENT.
SO THIS IS THE POWER OF THE LILITH MIRROR!
ZGHH
BWMM
SEALED AWAY FOR SO LONG DUE TO THE DANGER IT POSED...
WELL WORTH THE EFFORT OF STEALING IT.
THIS IS QUITE A SIGHT!
H YOOOOOO
A WORK OF ART!

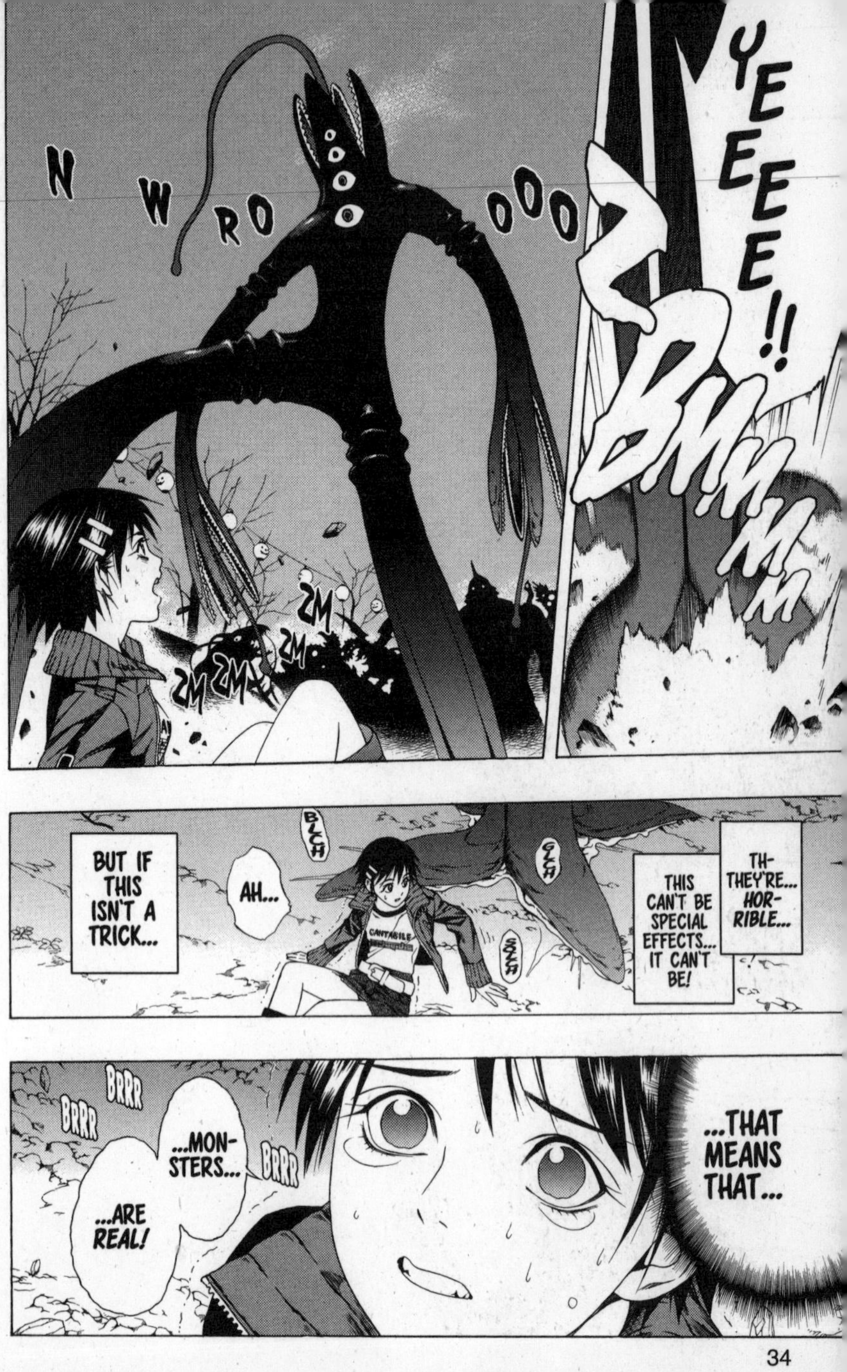
YEEEEE!!
ZBMMMMM
NWROOOO
ZM ZM ZM ZM ZM
TH-THEY'RE... HORRIBLE...
THIS CAN'T BE SPECIAL EFFECTS... IT CAN'T BE!
GLCH
BLCH
AH...
BUT IF THIS ISN'T A TRICK...
...THAT MEANS THAT...
BRRR BRRR BRRR
...MONSTERS...
...ARE REAL!

READ THIS WAY

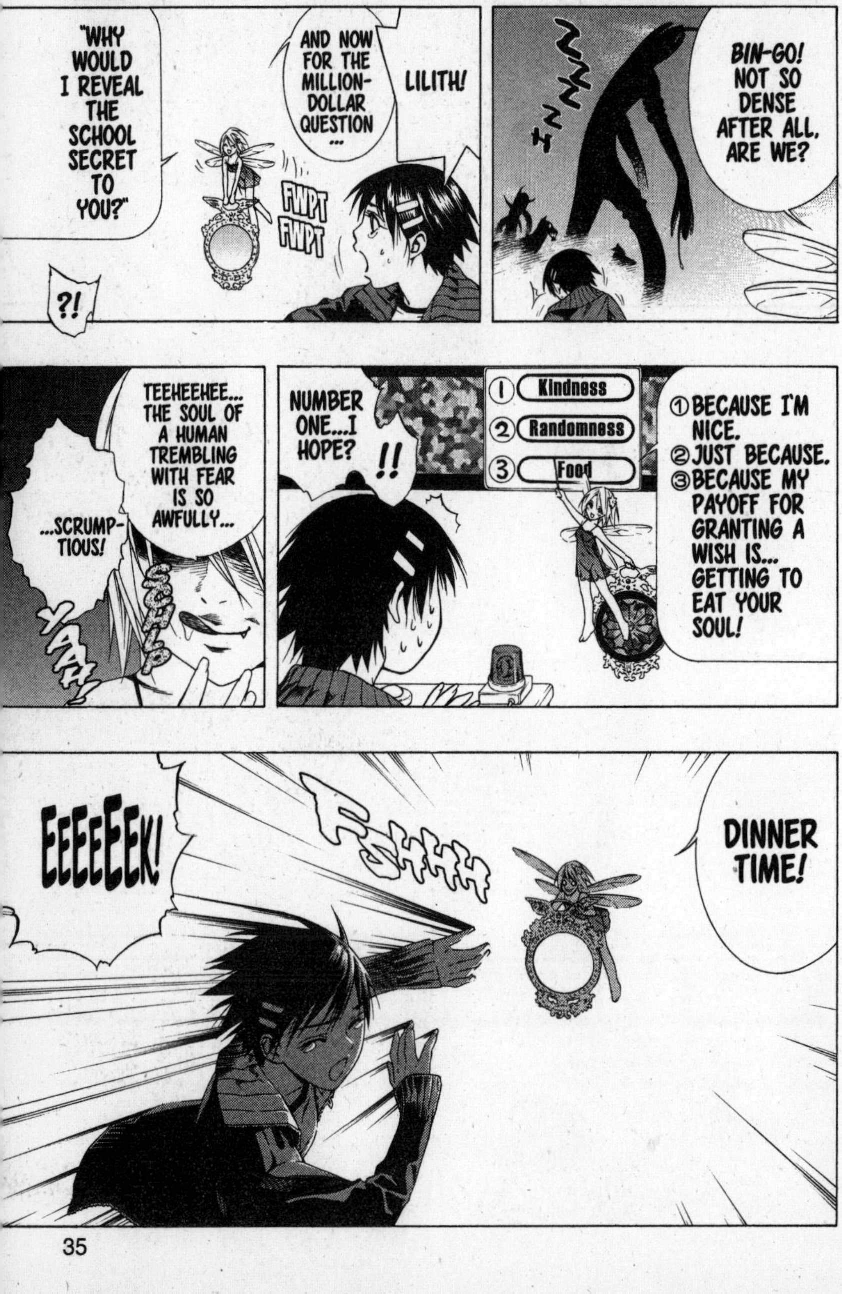
BIN-GO! NOT SO DENSE AFTER ALL, ARE WE?
LILITH!
AND NOW FOR THE MILLION-DOLLAR QUESTION...
FWPT FWPT
"WHY WOULD I REVEAL THE SCHOOL SECRET TO YOU?"
?!
① BECAUSE I'M NICE. ② JUST BECAUSE. ③ BECAUSE MY PAYOFF FOR GRANTING A WISH IS... GETTING TO EAT YOUR SOUL!
① Kindness
② Randomness
③ Food
!!
NUMBER ONE...I HOPE?
TEEHEEHEE... THE SOUL OF A HUMAN TREMBLING WITH FEAR IS SO AWFULLY...
...SCRUMPTIOUS!
DINNER TIME!
FSHHH
EEEEEEK!

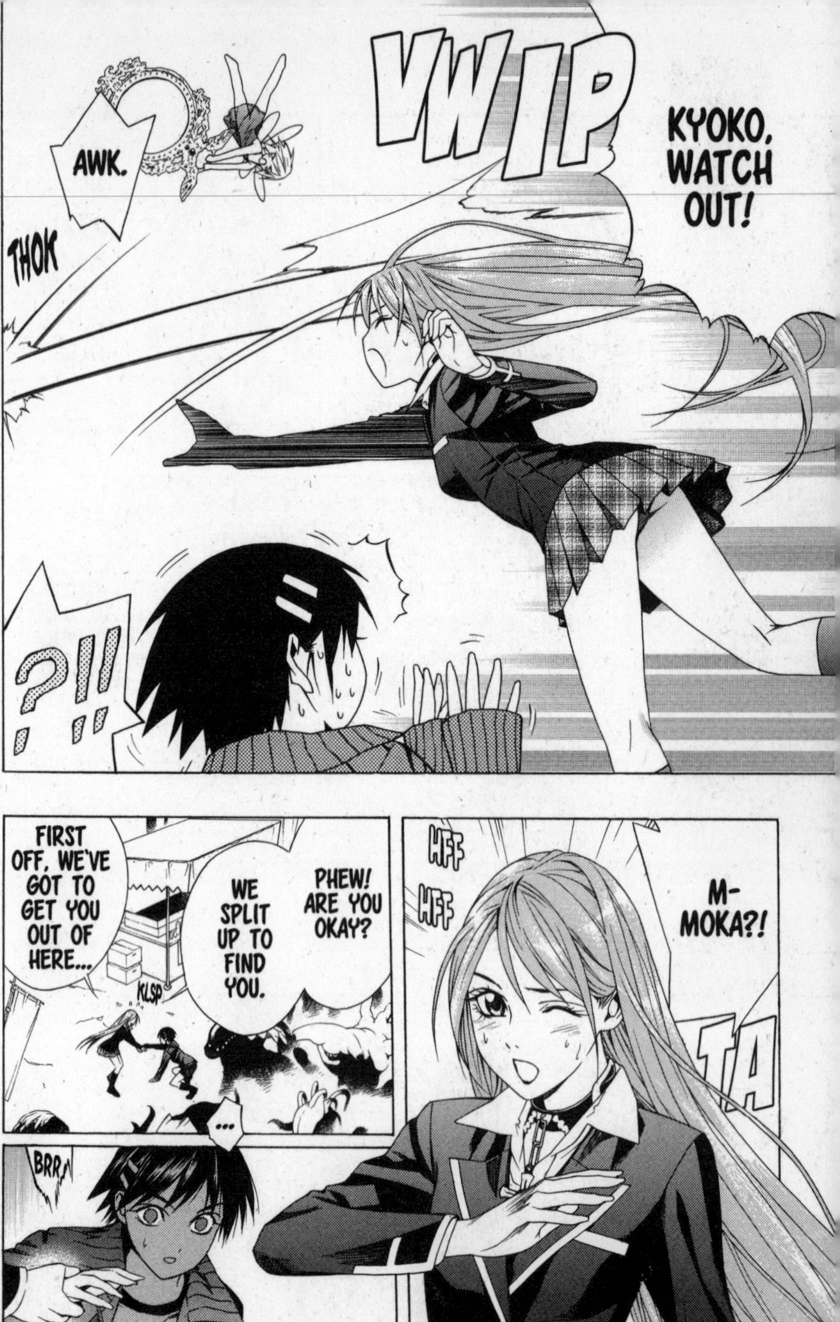
KYOKO, WATCH OUT!
VWIP
AWK.
THOK
?!!
M-MOKA?!
HFF
HFF
TA
PHEW! ARE YOU OKAY?
WE SPLIT UP TO FIND YOU.
FIRST OFF, WE'VE GOT TO GET YOU OUT OF HERE...
KLSP
...
BRR

READ THIS WAY

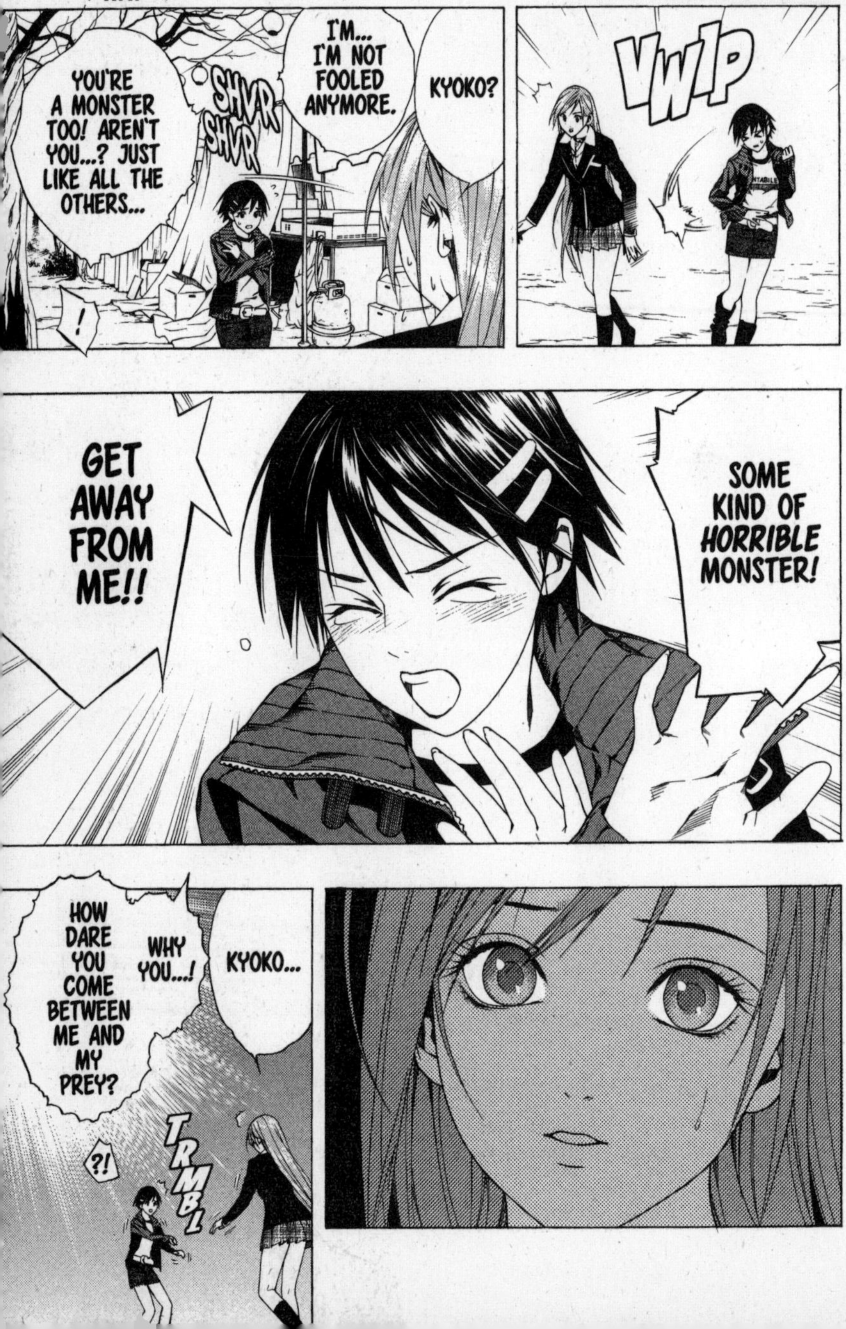
VWIP
KYOKO?
I'M... I'M NOT FOOLED ANYMORE.
SHVR SHVR
YOU'RE A MONSTER TOO! AREN'T YOU...? JUST LIKE ALL THE OTHERS...
!
SOME KIND OF *HORRIBLE* MONSTER!
GET AWAY FROM ME!!
KYOKO...
WHY YOU...!
HOW DARE YOU COME BETWEEN ME AND MY PREY?
TRMBL
?!

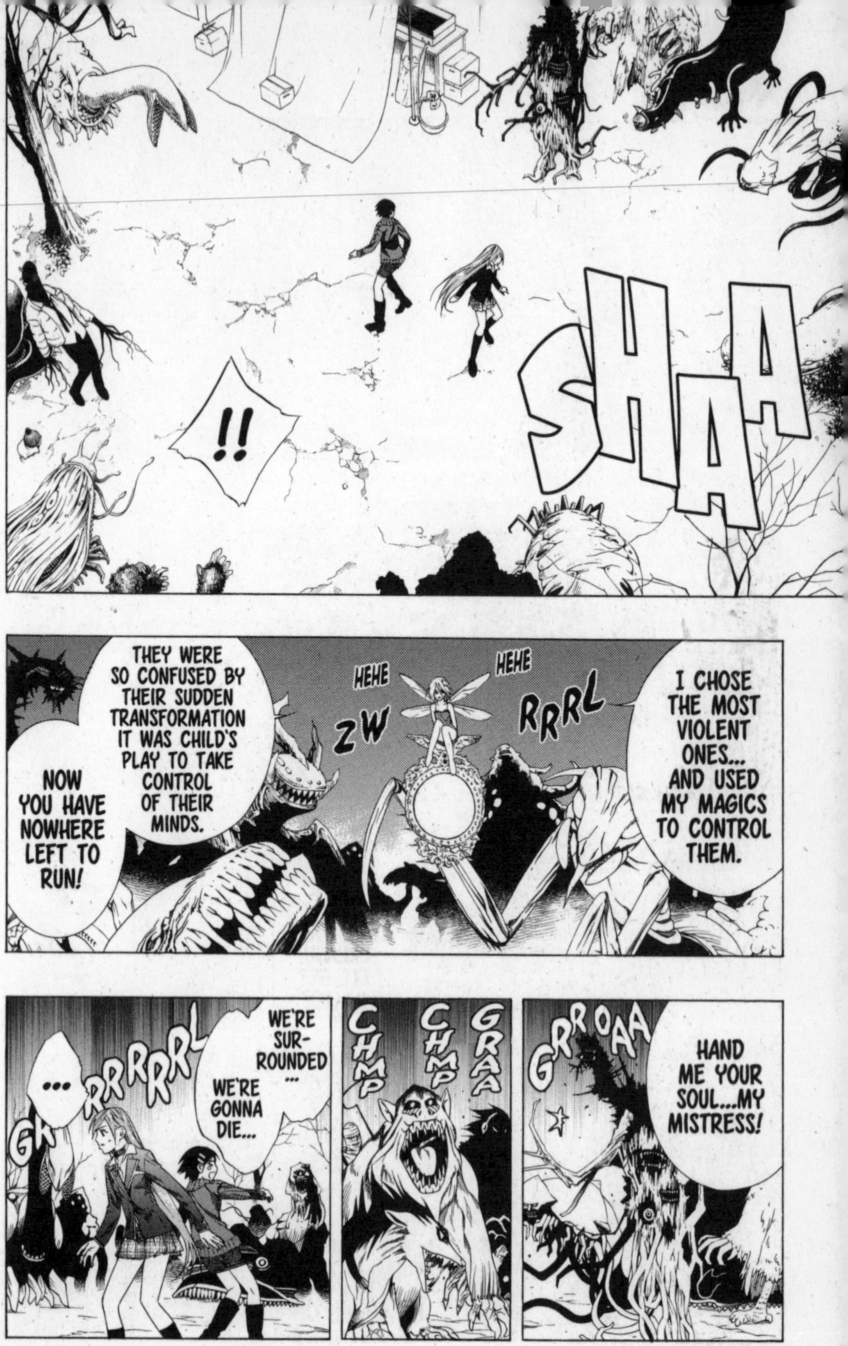
SHAA
!!
I CHOSE THE MOST VIOLENT ONES... AND USED MY MAGICS TO CONTROL THEM.
RRRL
HEHE
ZW
HEHE
THEY WERE SO CONFUSED BY THEIR SUDDEN TRANSFORMATION IT WAS CHILD'S PLAY TO TAKE CONTROL OF THEIR MINDS.
NOW YOU HAVE NOWHERE LEFT TO RUN!
GRROAA
HAND ME YOUR SOUL...MY MISTRESS!
GRAA
CHMP
CHMP
WE'RE SUR-ROUNDED...
WE'RE GONNA DIE...
GRRRRRL
...

READ THIS WAY

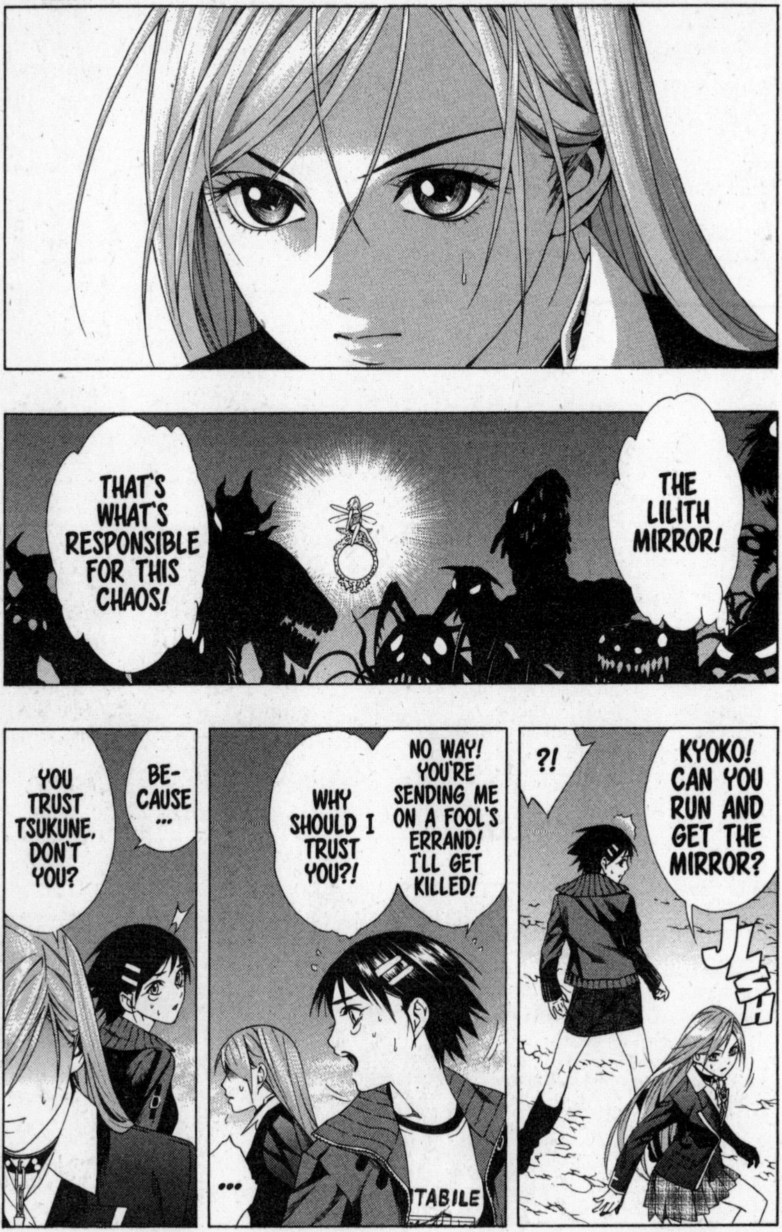
THE LILITH MIRROR!
THAT'S WHAT'S RESPONSIBLE FOR THIS CHAOS!
KYOKO! CAN YOU RUN AND GET THE MIRROR?
?!
JLSH
NO WAY! YOU'RE SENDING ME ON A FOOL'S ERRAND! I'LL GET KILLED!
WHY SHOULD I TRUST YOU?!
...
BE-CAUSE ...
YOU TRUST TSUKUNE, DON'T YOU?

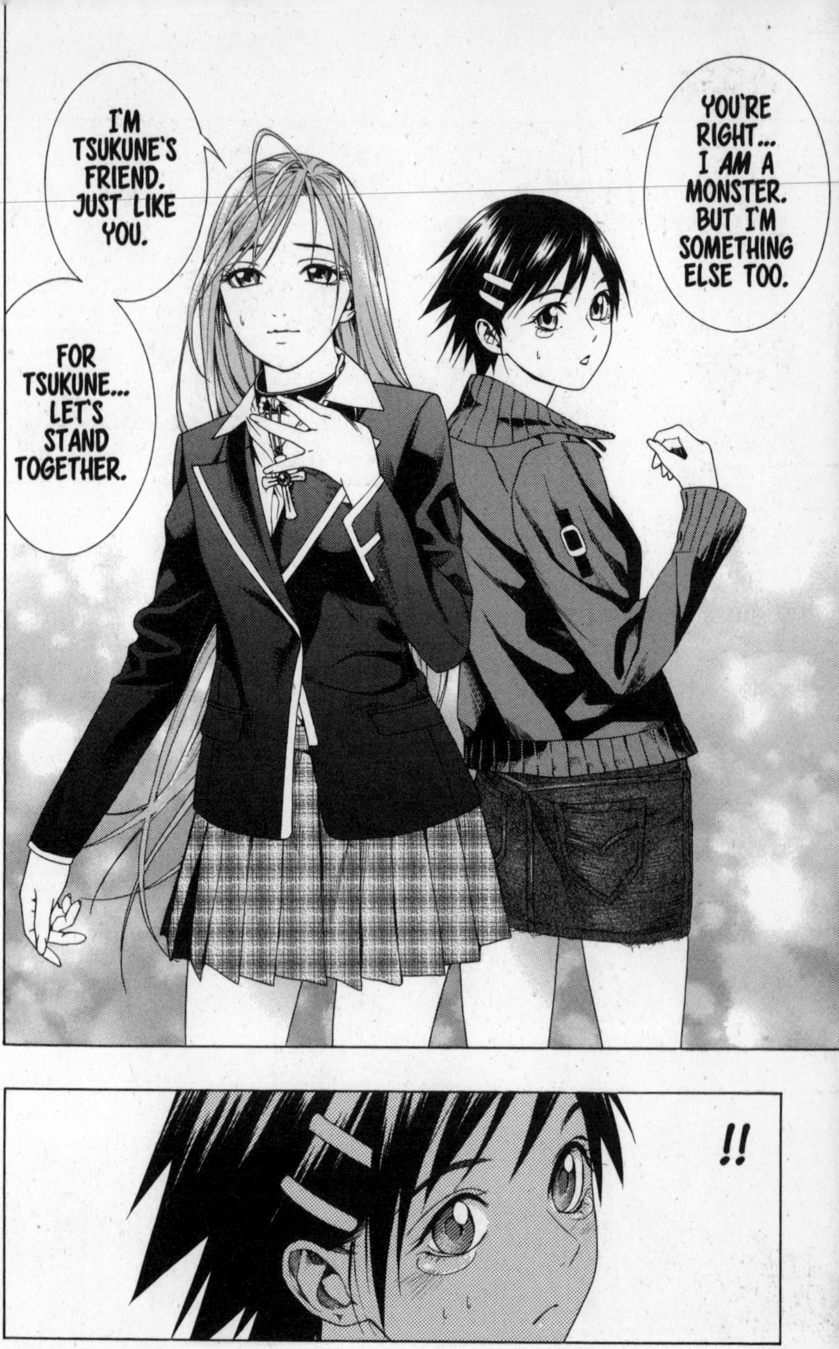
YOU'RE RIGHT... I *AM* A MONSTER. BUT I'M SOMETHING ELSE TOO.
I'M TSUKUNE'S FRIEND. JUST LIKE YOU.
FOR TSUKUNE... LET'S STAND TOGETHER.
!!

I'M HUNGRY!

NOW, MY PETS! GET THEM!

I'LL TAKE CARE OF THESE!

RUN, KYOKO!

RRRRG

M- MOKA...

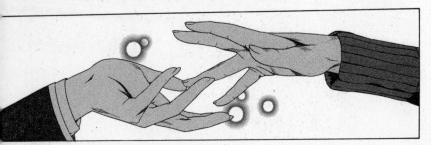

41

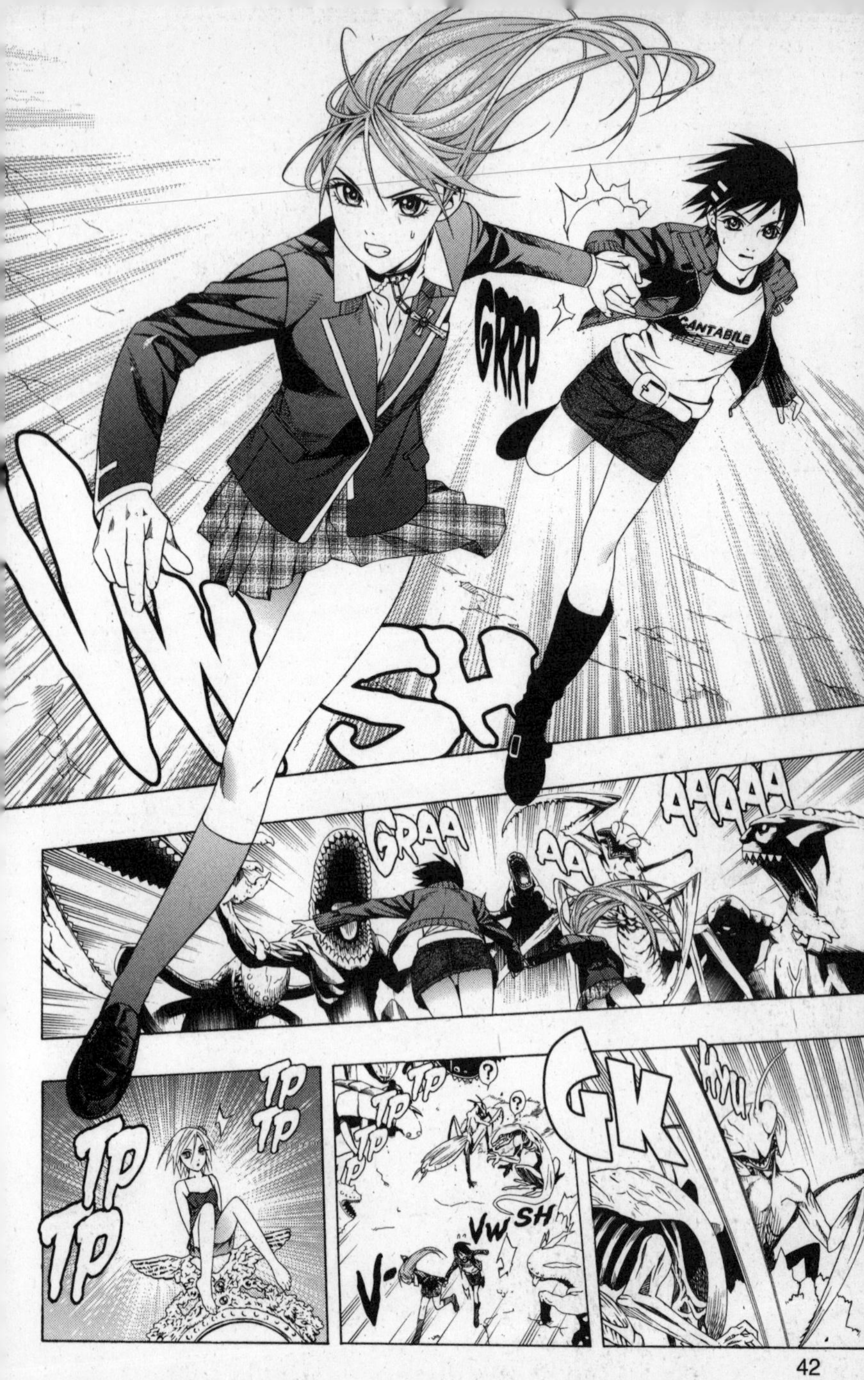
GRRP
VWSH
AAAAA
AA
GRAA
HYU
GK
TP TP TP TP
?
?
VWSH
V-
TP TP
TP TP

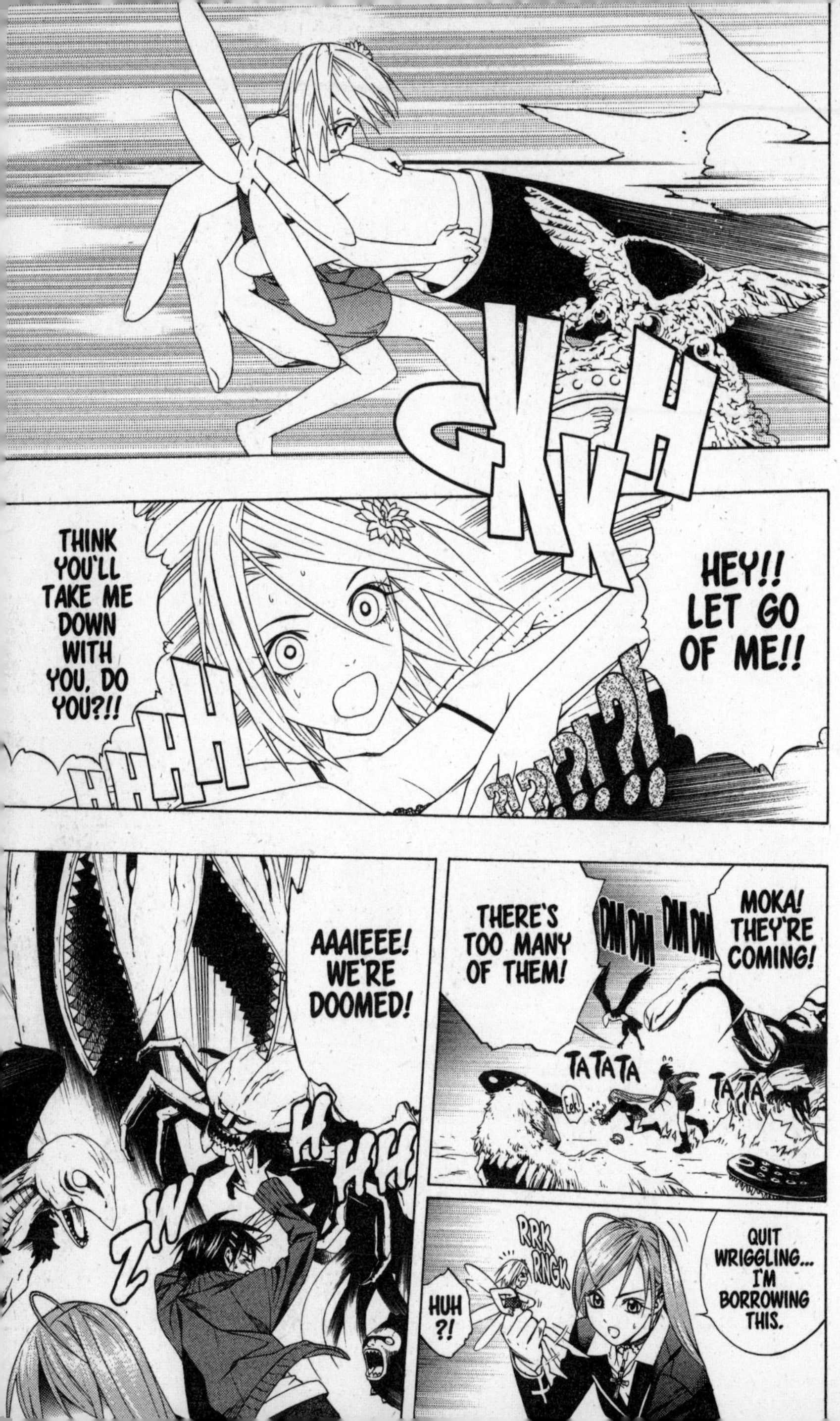

GKKH
HEY!! LET GO OF ME!!
?!!?!?!!
THINK YOU'LL TAKE ME DOWN WITH YOU, DO YOU?!!
HHHH
MOKA! THEY'RE COMING!
DM DM DM DM
THERE'S TOO MANY OF THEM!
TATATA
TA TA
Eek!
QUIT WRIGGLING... I'M BORROWING THIS.
RRK RNGK
HUH ?!
AAAIEEE! WE'RE DOOMED!
HHHH
ZW

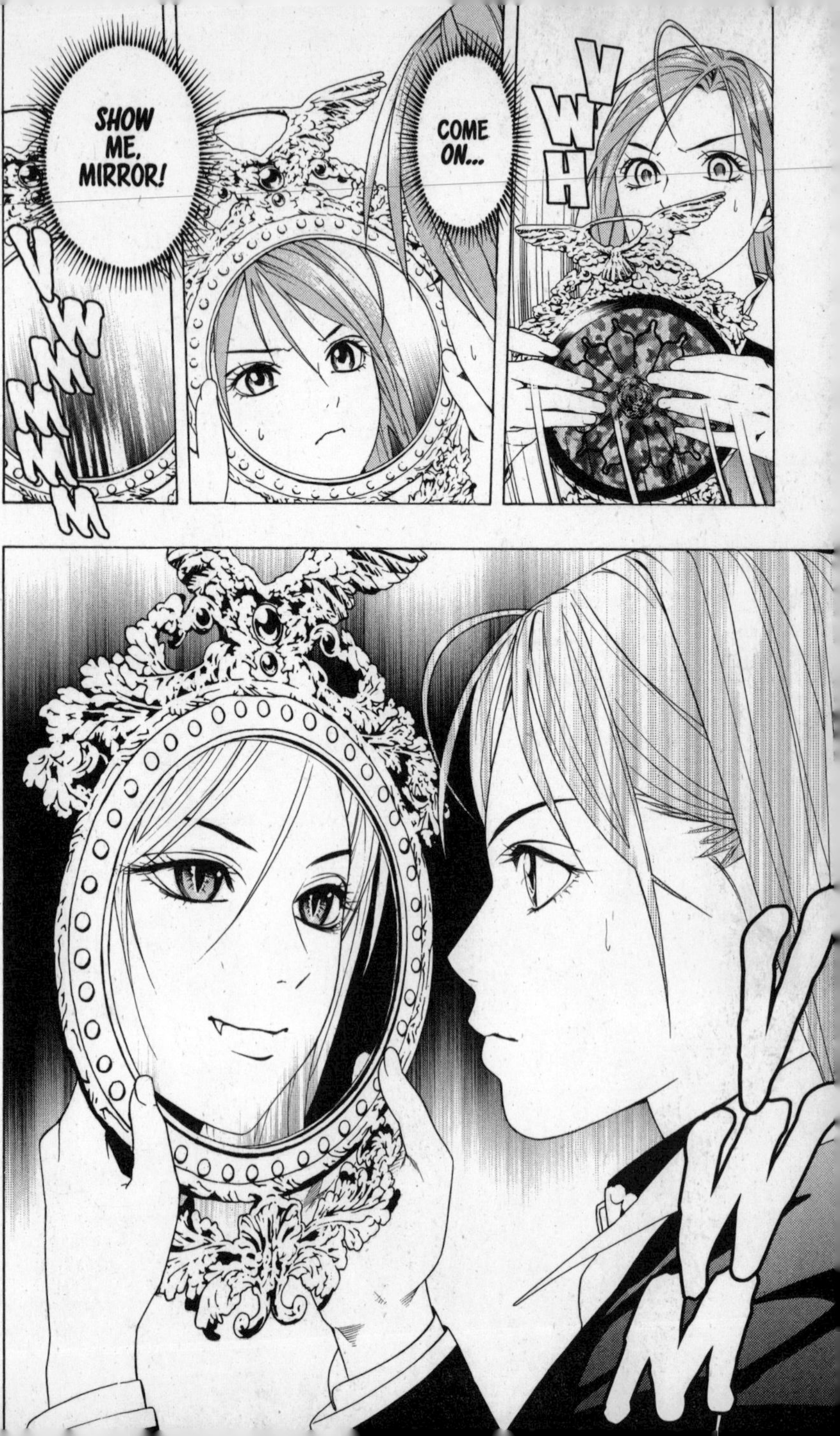
VWH
COME ON...
SHOW ME, MIRROR!
VWMMMM
VWM

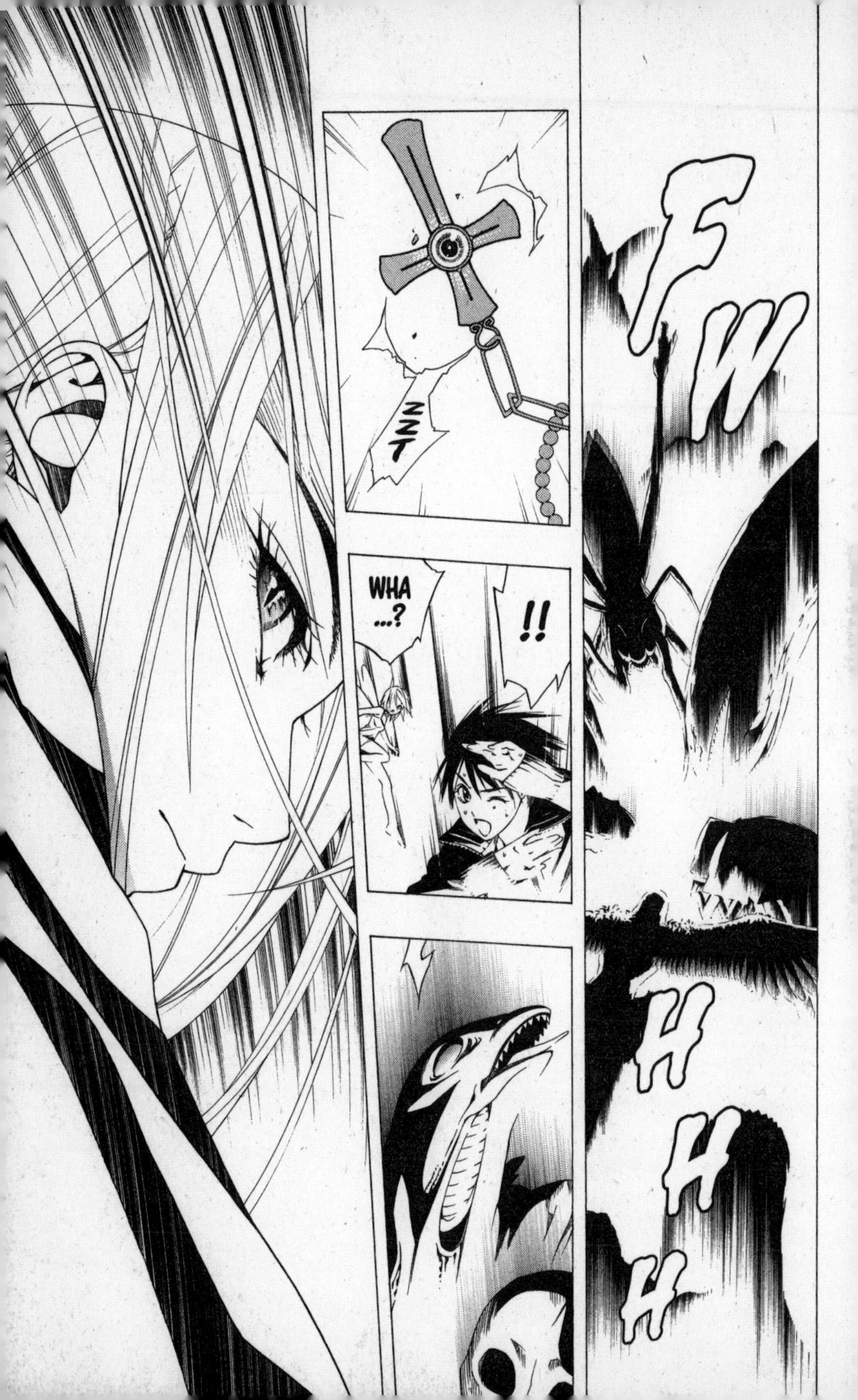
FWHHH
ZZT
!!
WHA ...?

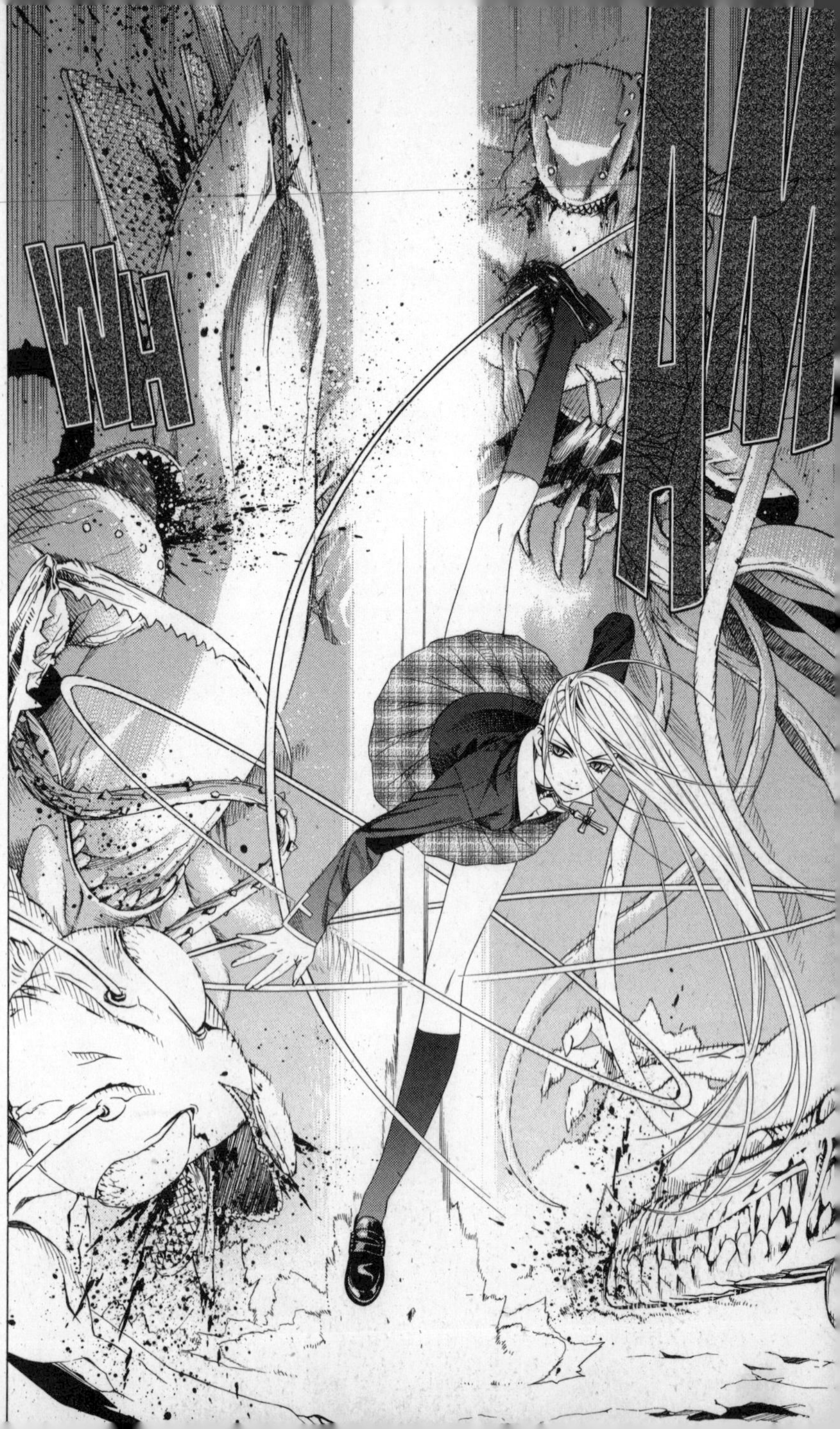
WH

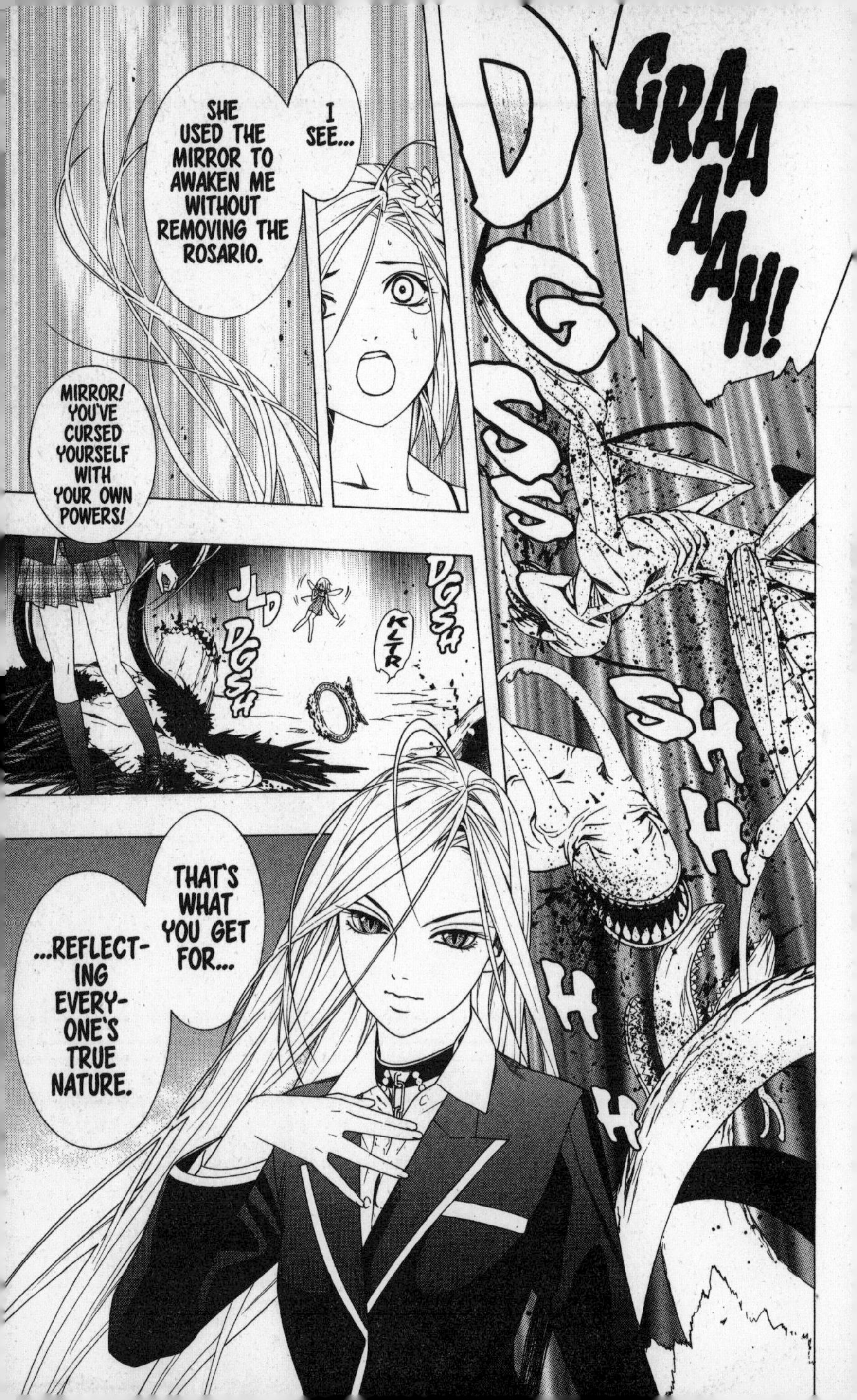
GRAAAAH!
DGSSSHHHHH
I SEE...
SHE USED THE MIRROR TO AWAKEN ME WITHOUT REMOVING THE ROSARIO.
MIRROR! YOU'VE CURSED YOURSELF WITH YOUR OWN POWERS!
DGSH
KLTR
JLD
DGSH
THAT'S WHAT YOU GET FOR...
...REFLECTING EVERYONE'S TRUE NATURE.

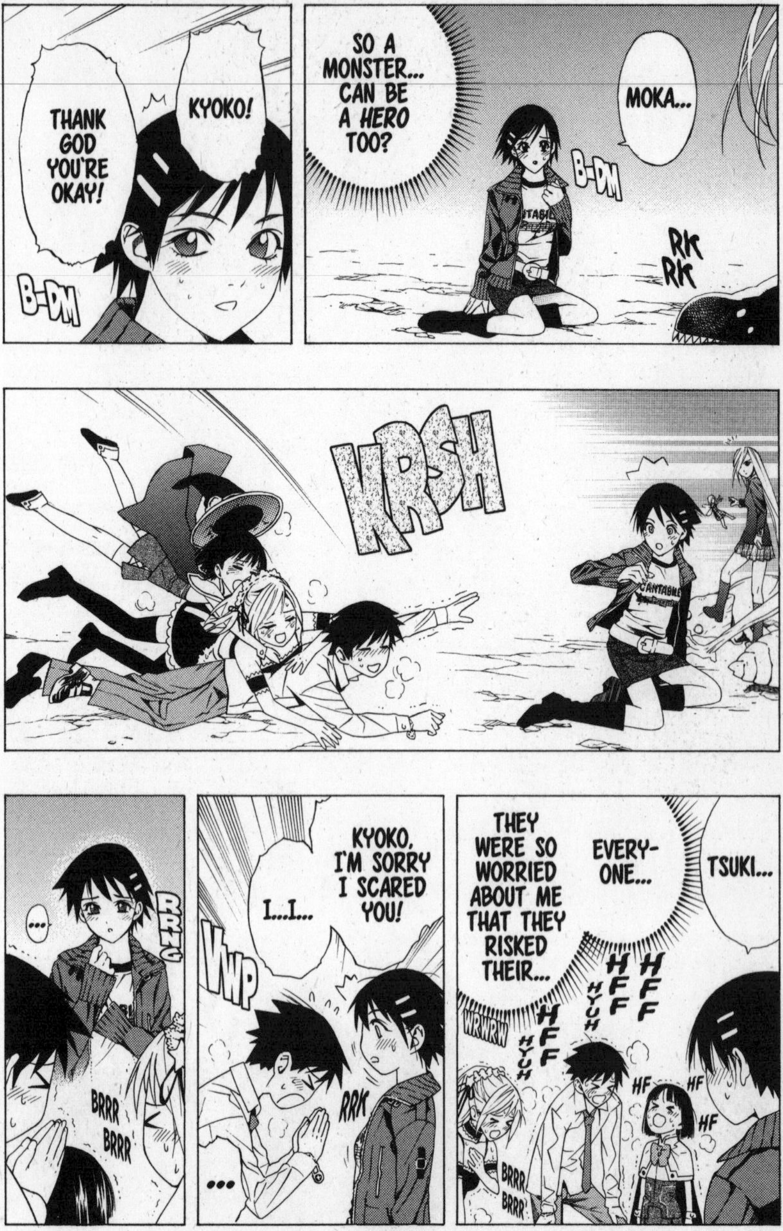
MOKA...
SO A MONSTER... CAN BE A HERO TOO?
B-DM
RK RK
KYOKO!
THANK GOD YOU'RE OKAY!
B-DM
KRSH
TSUKI...
EVERY-ONE...
THEY WERE SO WORRIED ABOUT ME THAT THEY RISKED THEIR...
HFF HFF
HYUH
HFF HFF
HYUH
HFF
WRWRW
HF HF
HF
BRRR BRRR
KYOKO, I'M SORRY I SCARED YOU!
I...I...
VWP
RRK
...
...
RRNG
BRRR BRRR

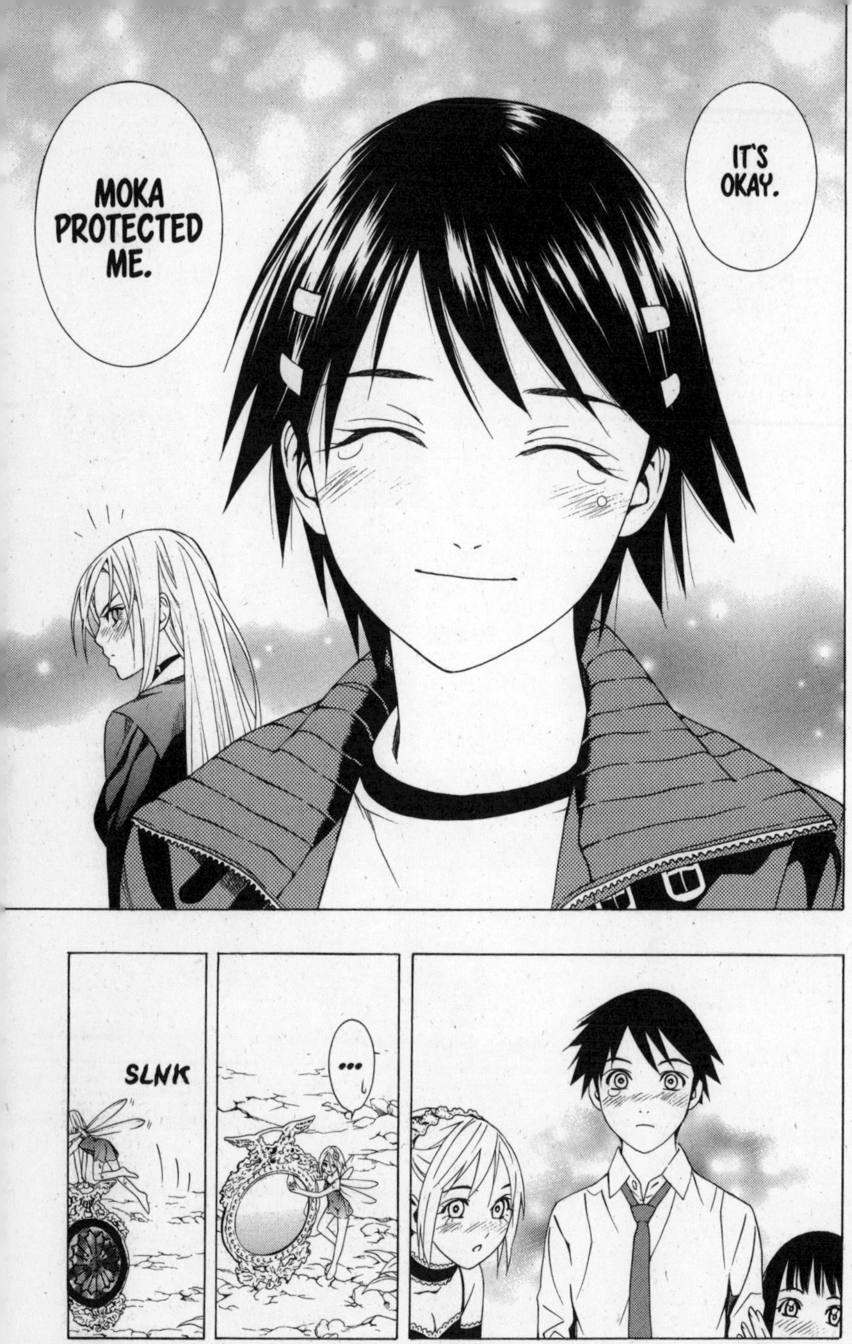
IT'S OKAY.
MOKA PROTECTED ME.
...
SLNK

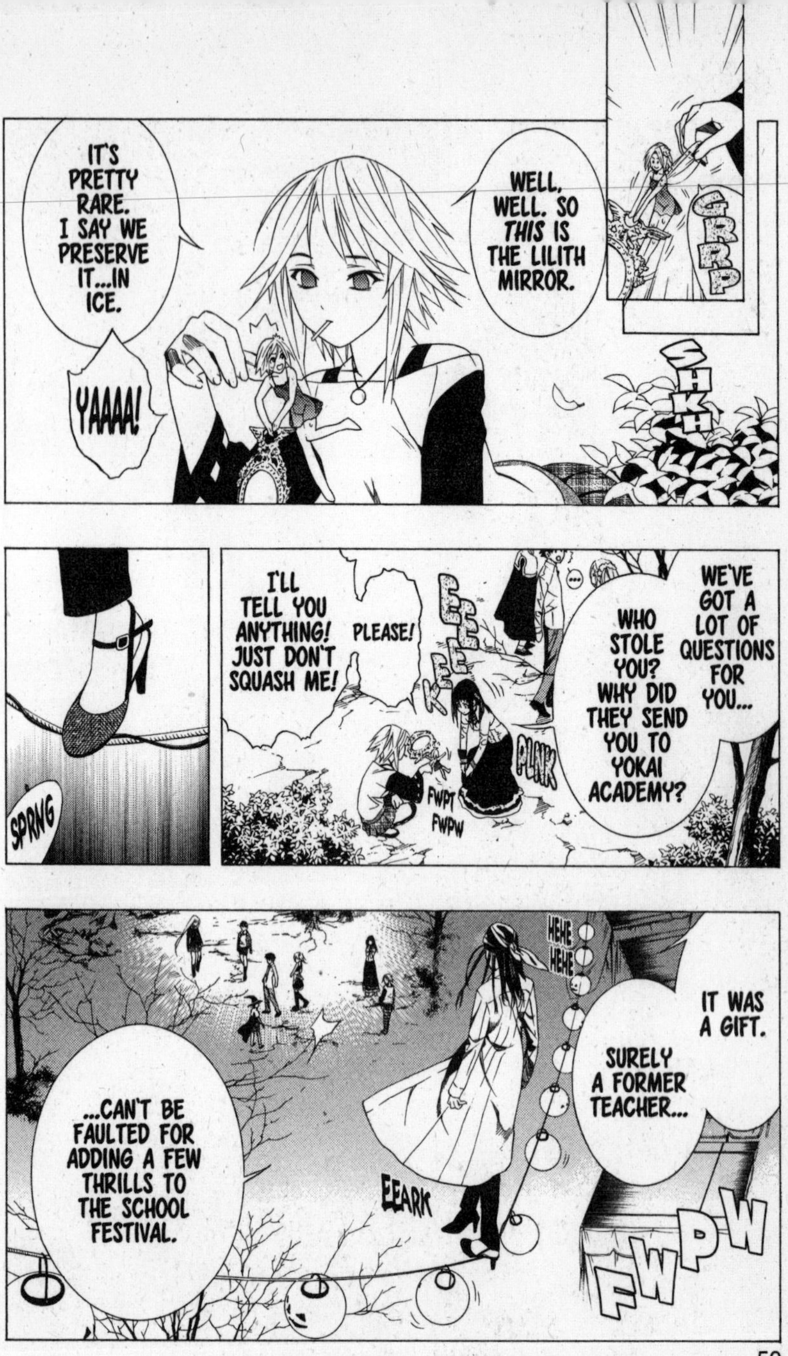
GRRP
WELL, WELL. SO *THIS* IS THE LILITH MIRROR.
IT'S PRETTY RARE. I SAY WE PRESERVE IT...IN ICE.
YAAAA!
SHKH
WE'VE GOT A LOT OF QUESTIONS FOR YOU...
WHO STOLE YOU? WHY DID THEY SEND YOU TO YOKAI ACADEMY?
...
EEEEK
PLINK
PLEASE!
I'LL TELL YOU ANYTHING! JUST DON'T SQUASH ME!
FWPT FWPW
SPRNG
HEHE HEHE
IT WAS A GIFT.
SURELY A FORMER TEACHER...
...CAN'T BE FAULTED FOR ADDING A FEW THRILLS TO THE SCHOOL FESTIVAL.
FWPW
EEARK

READ THIS WAY

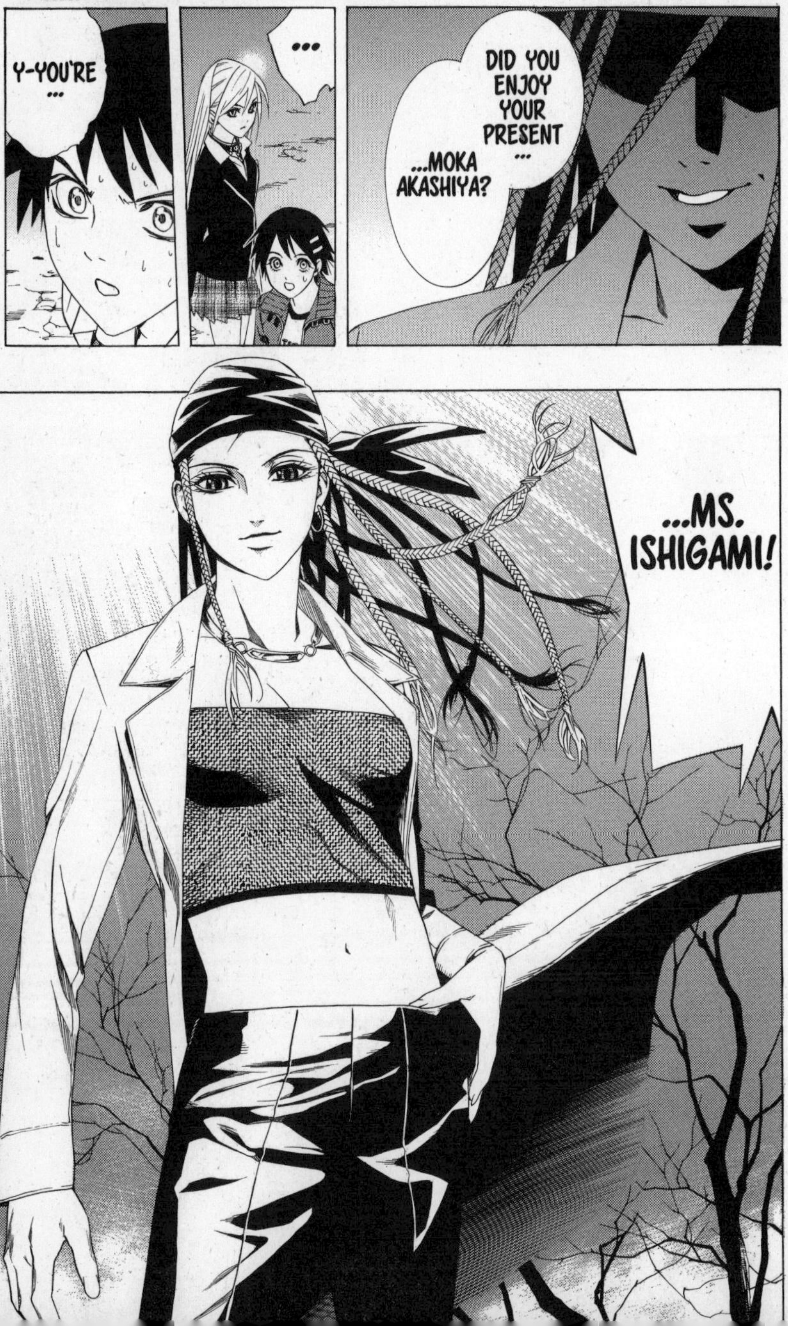

DID YOU ENJOY YOUR PRESENT ...
...MOKA AKASHIYA?
...
Y-YOU'RE ...
...MS. ISHIGAMI!

ROSARIO+VAMPIRE

38: Snapshot of the Future

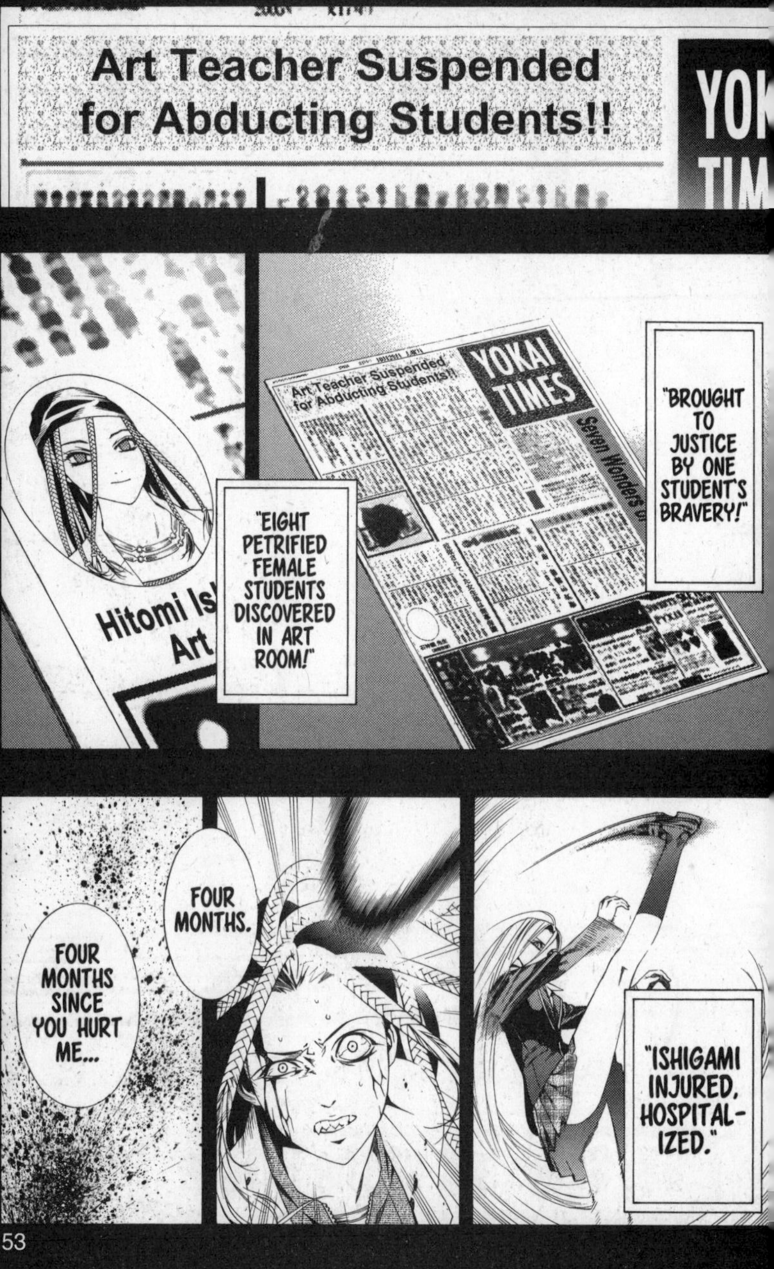
Art Teacher Suspended for Abducting Students!!
"BROUGHT TO JUSTICE BY ONE STUDENT'S BRAVERY!"
YOKAI TIMES
Art Teacher Suspended for Abducting Students!!
"EIGHT PETRIFIED FEMALE STUDENTS DISCOVERED IN ART ROOM!"
"ISHIGAMI INJURED, HOSPITAL-IZED."
FOUR MONTHS.
FOUR MONTHS SINCE YOU HURT ME...

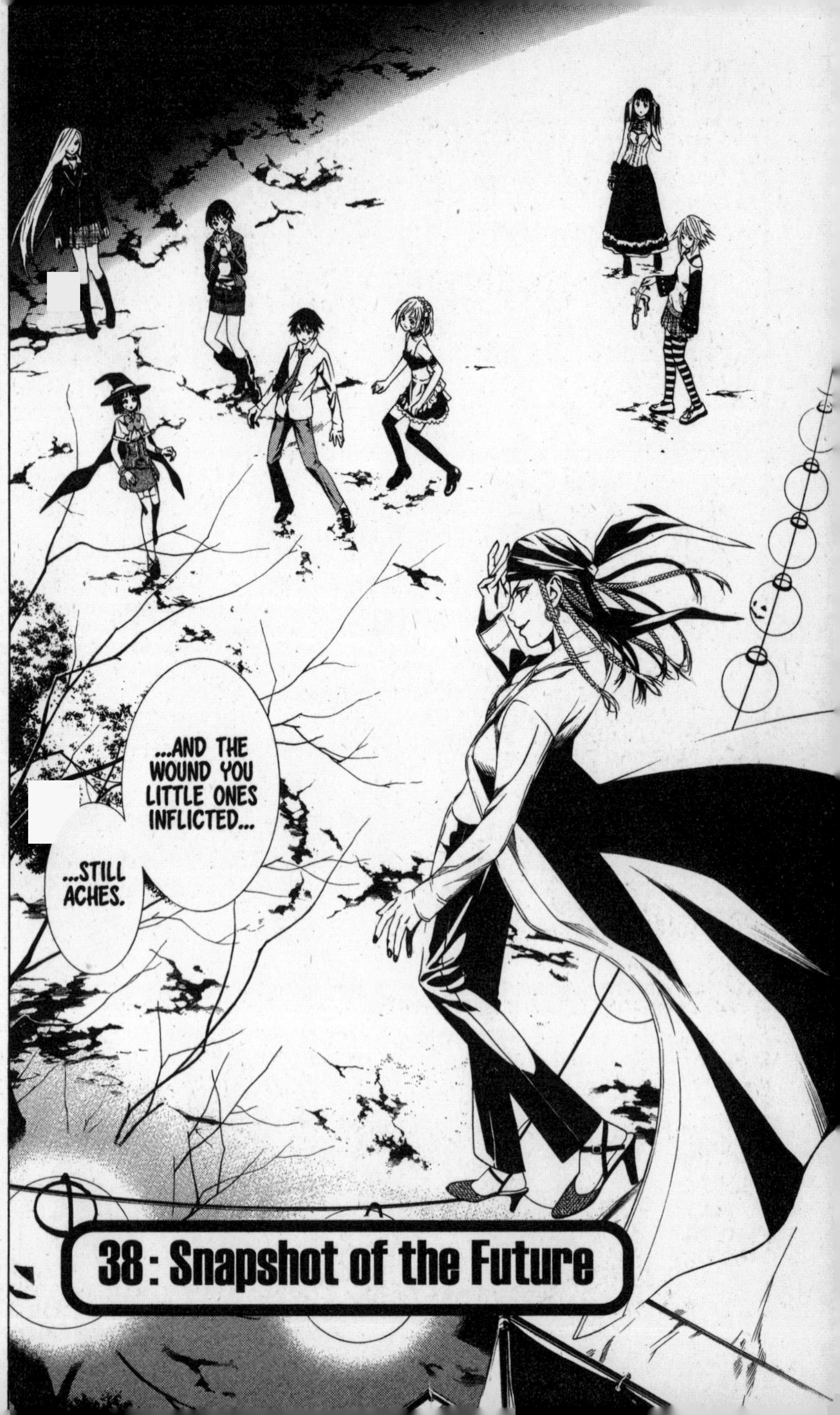
...AND THE WOUND YOU LITTLE ONES INFLICTED...
...STILL ACHES.
38 : Snapshot of the Future

READ THIS WAY

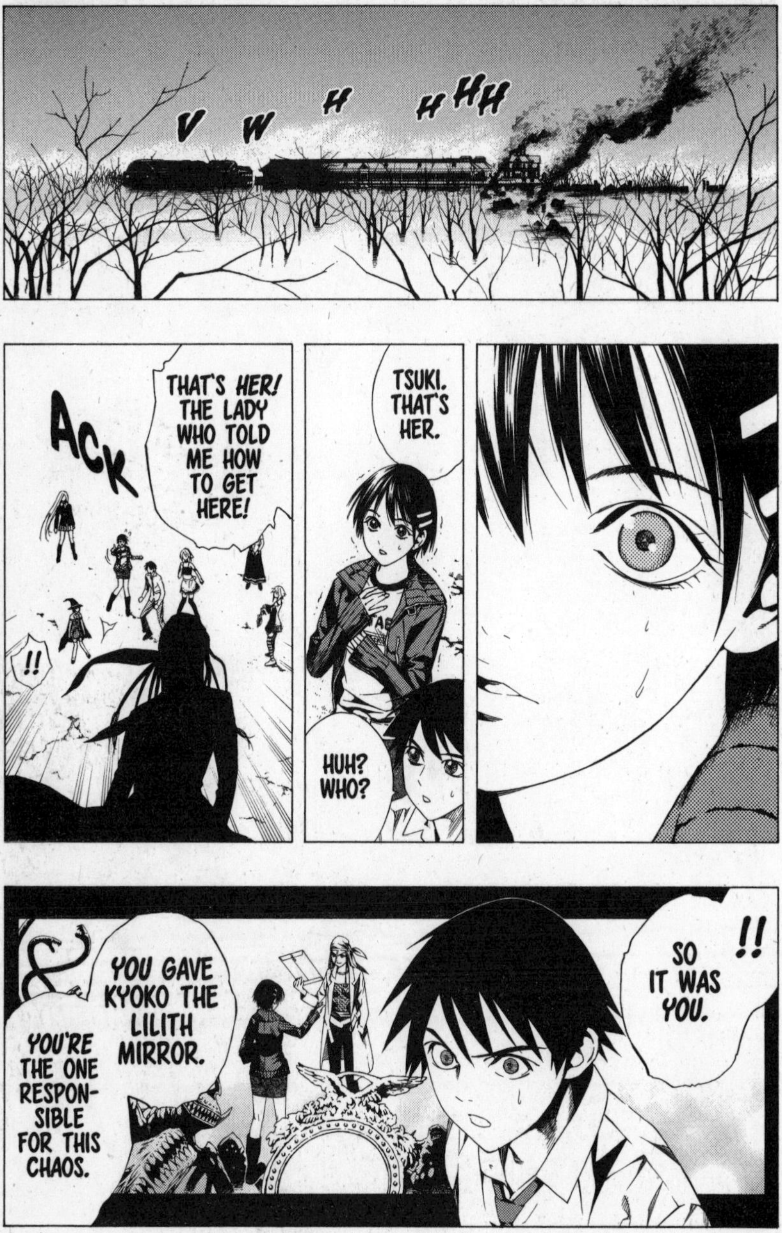
VWHHHHH
TSUKI. THAT'S HER.
HUH? WHO?
THAT'S HER! THE LADY WHO TOLD ME HOW TO GET HERE!
ACK
!!
!!
SO IT WAS YOU.
YOU GAVE KYOKO THE LILITH MIRROR.
YOU'RE THE ONE RESPON-SIBLE FOR THIS CHAOS.

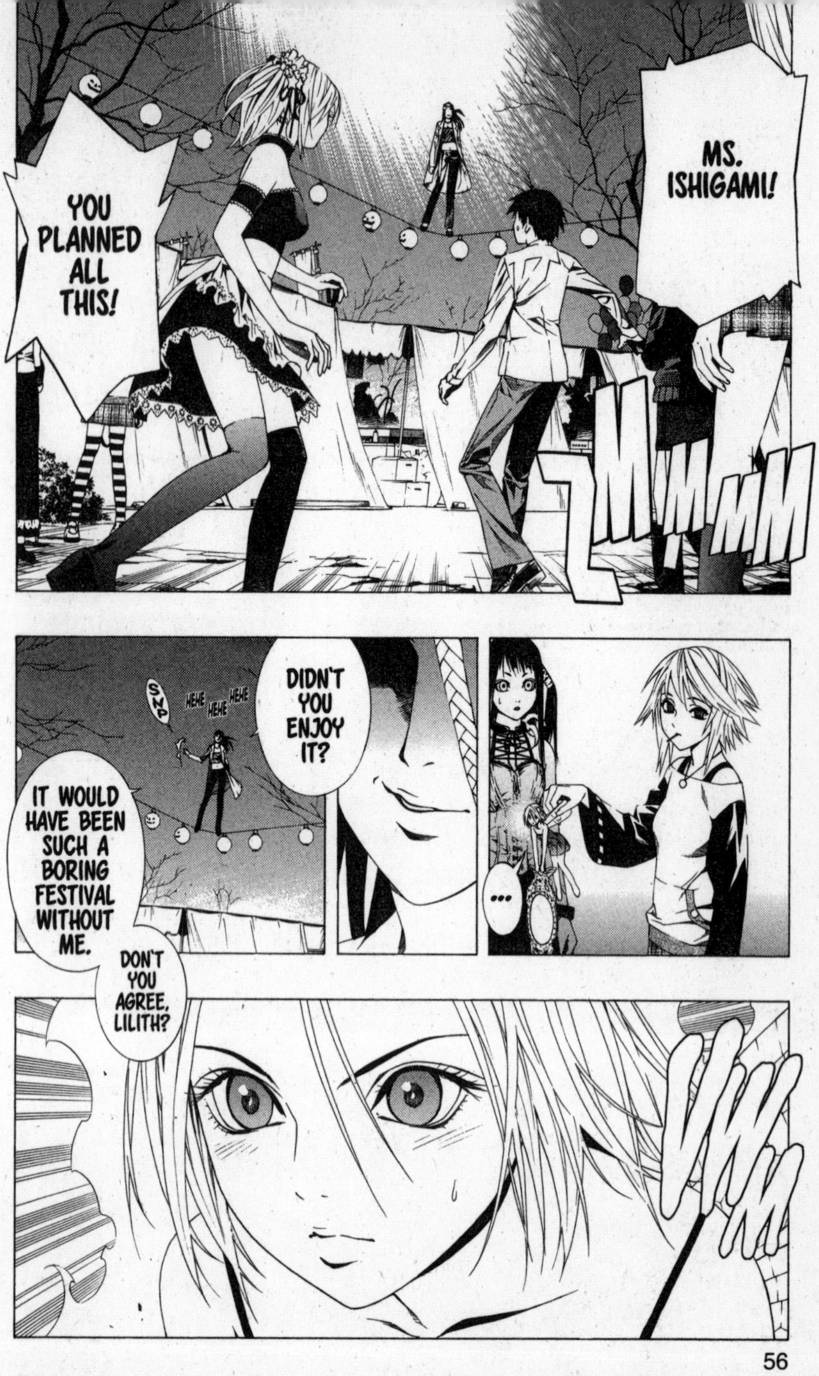
MS. ISHIGAMI!
ZMMMMM
YOU PLANNED ALL THIS!
...
DIDN'T YOU ENJOY IT?
SNP
HEHE HEHE HEHE
IT WOULD HAVE BEEN SUCH A BORING FESTIVAL WITHOUT ME.
DON'T YOU AGREE, LILITH?
VMMM

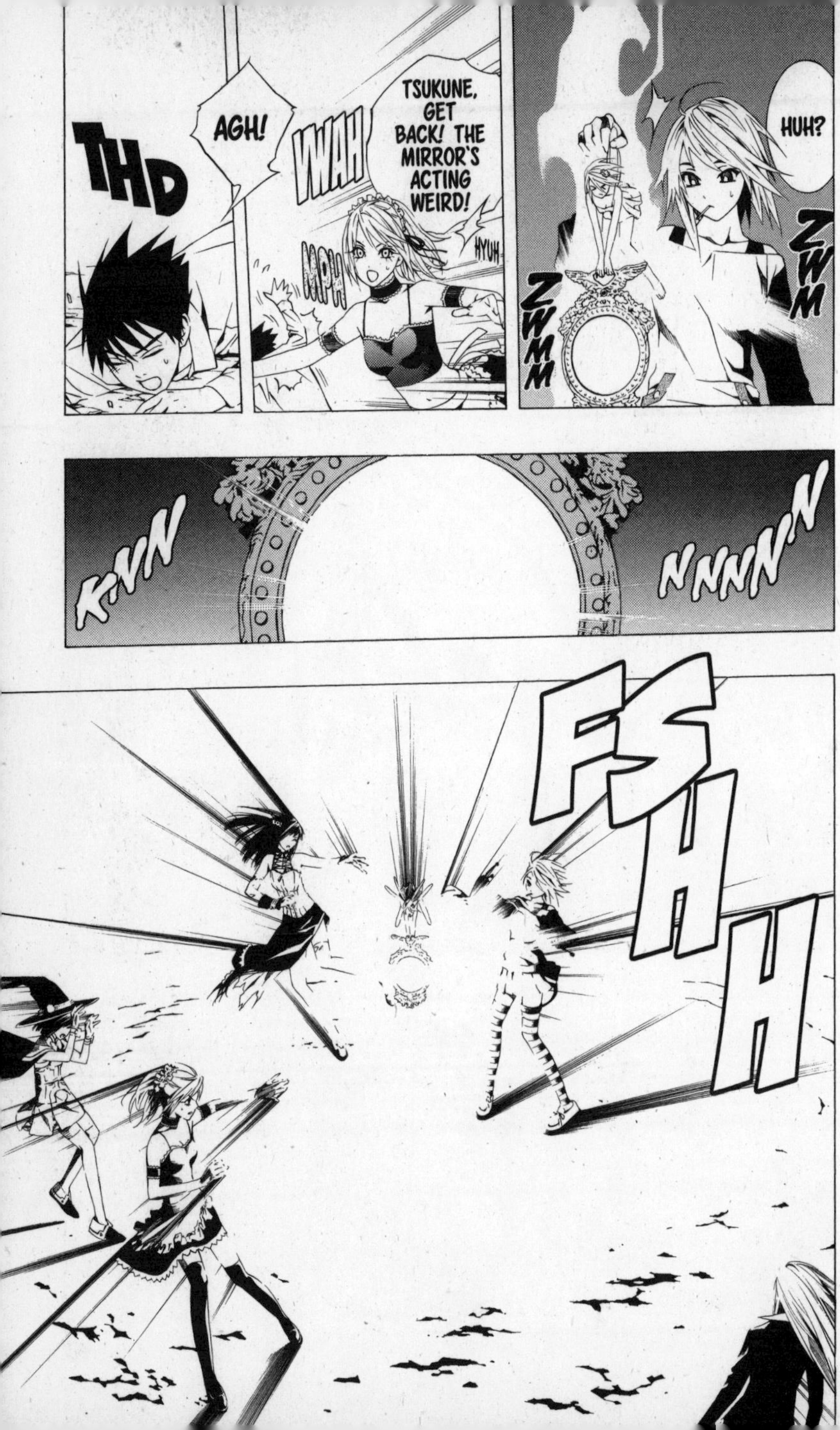
HUH?
ZWM
ZWMM
TSUKUNE, GET BACK! THE MIRROR'S ACTING WEIRD!
VWAH
MPH
HYUH
AGH!
THD
KNN
NNNNN
FSHHH

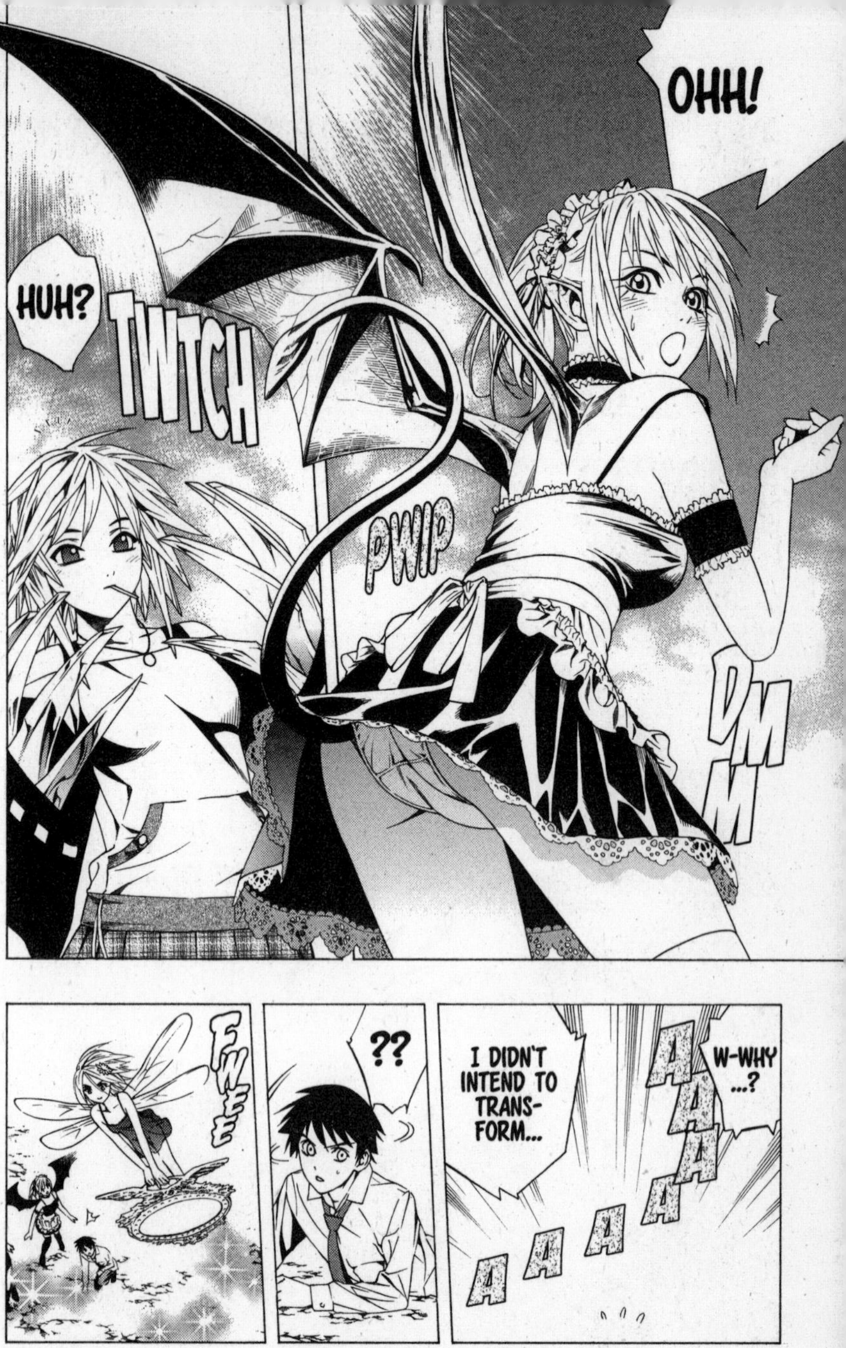
OHH!
HUH?
TWITCH
PWIP
DMMM
W-WHY ...?
I DIDN'T INTEND TO TRANS-FORM...
AAAAAAAAA
??
FWEE

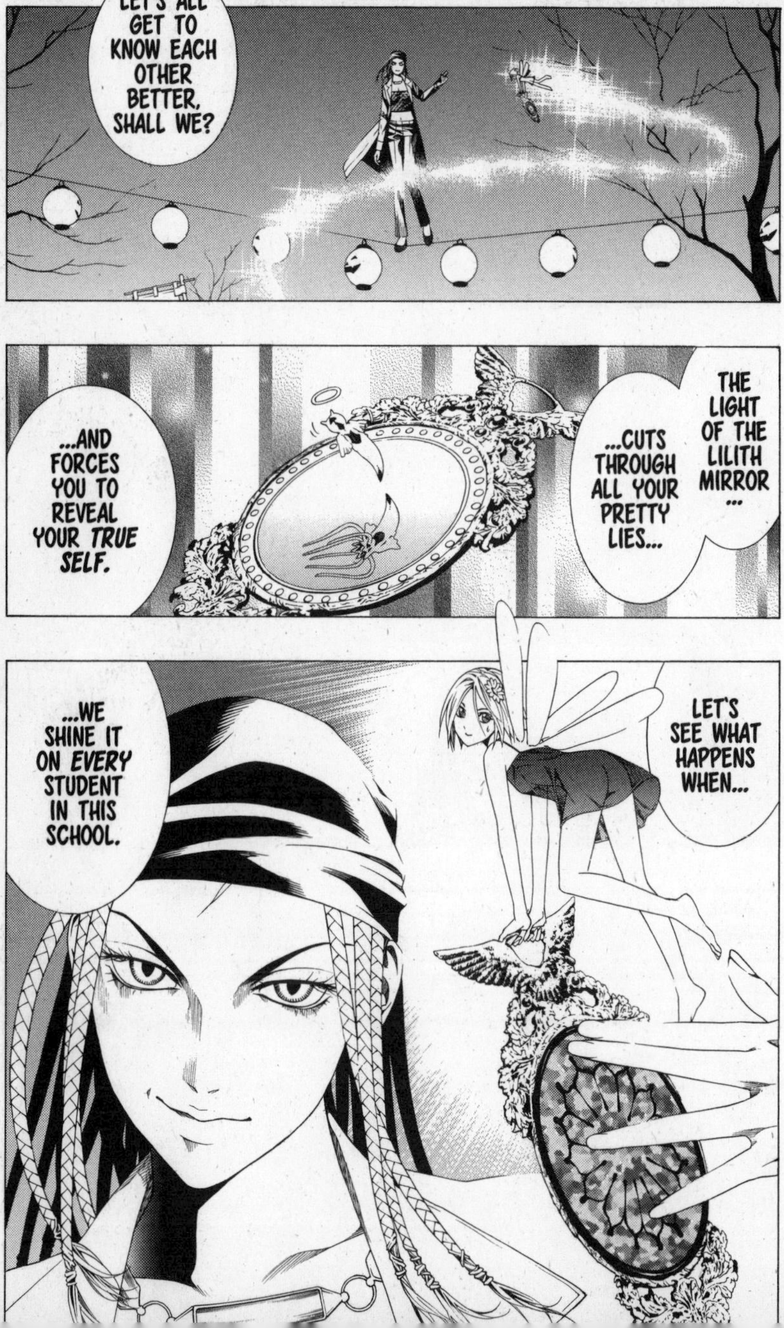
LET'S ALL GET TO KNOW EACH OTHER BETTER, SHALL WE?
THE LIGHT OF THE LILITH MIRROR...
...CUTS THROUGH ALL YOUR PRETTY LIES...
...AND FORCES YOU TO REVEAL YOUR *TRUE SELF*.
LET'S SEE WHAT HAPPENS WHEN...
...WE SHINE IT ON *EVERY* STUDENT IN THIS SCHOOL.

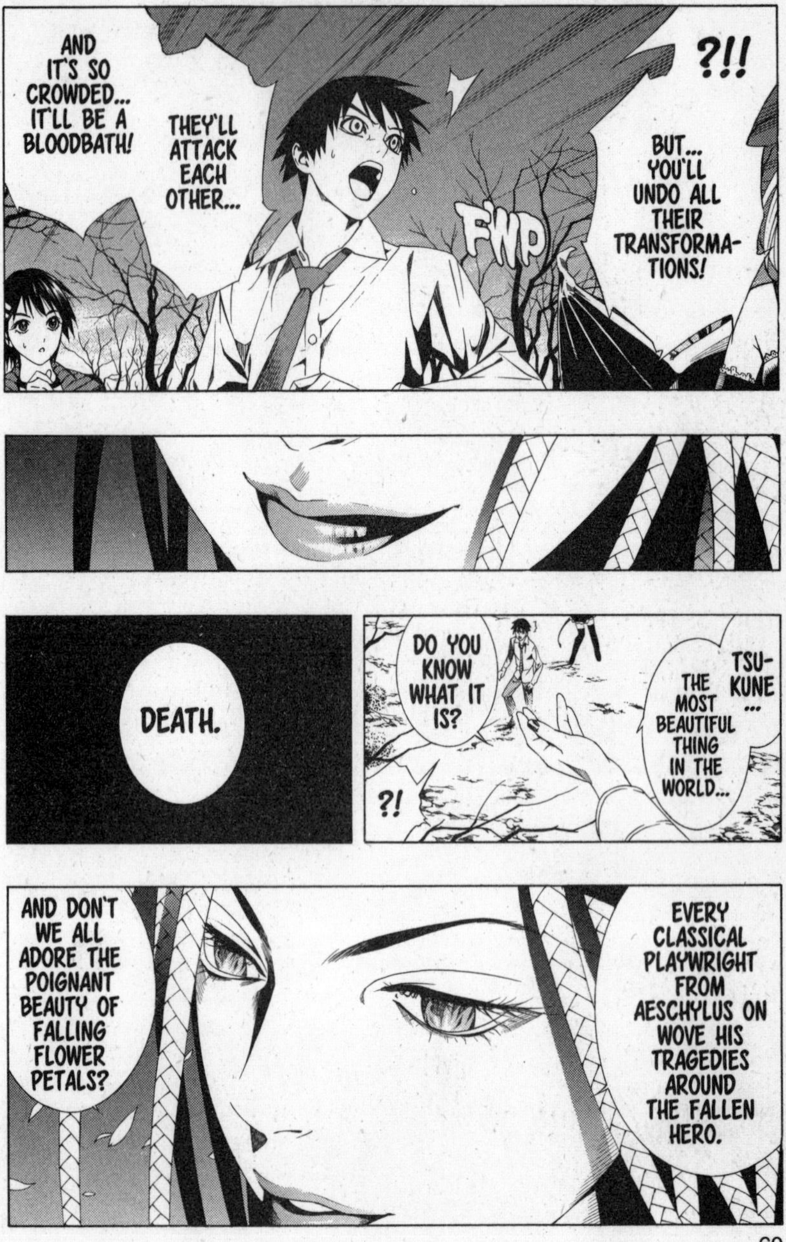
?!!
BUT... YOU'LL UNDO ALL THEIR TRANSFORMATIONS!
FWP
THEY'LL ATTACK EACH OTHER...
AND IT'S SO CROWDED... IT'LL BE A BLOODBATH!
TSUKUNE...
THE MOST BEAUTIFUL THING IN THE WORLD...
DO YOU KNOW WHAT IT IS?
?!
DEATH.
EVERY CLASSICAL PLAYWRIGHT FROM AESCHYLUS ON WOVE HIS TRAGEDIES AROUND THE FALLEN HERO.
AND DON'T WE ALL ADORE THE POIGNANT BEAUTY OF FALLING FLOWER PETALS?

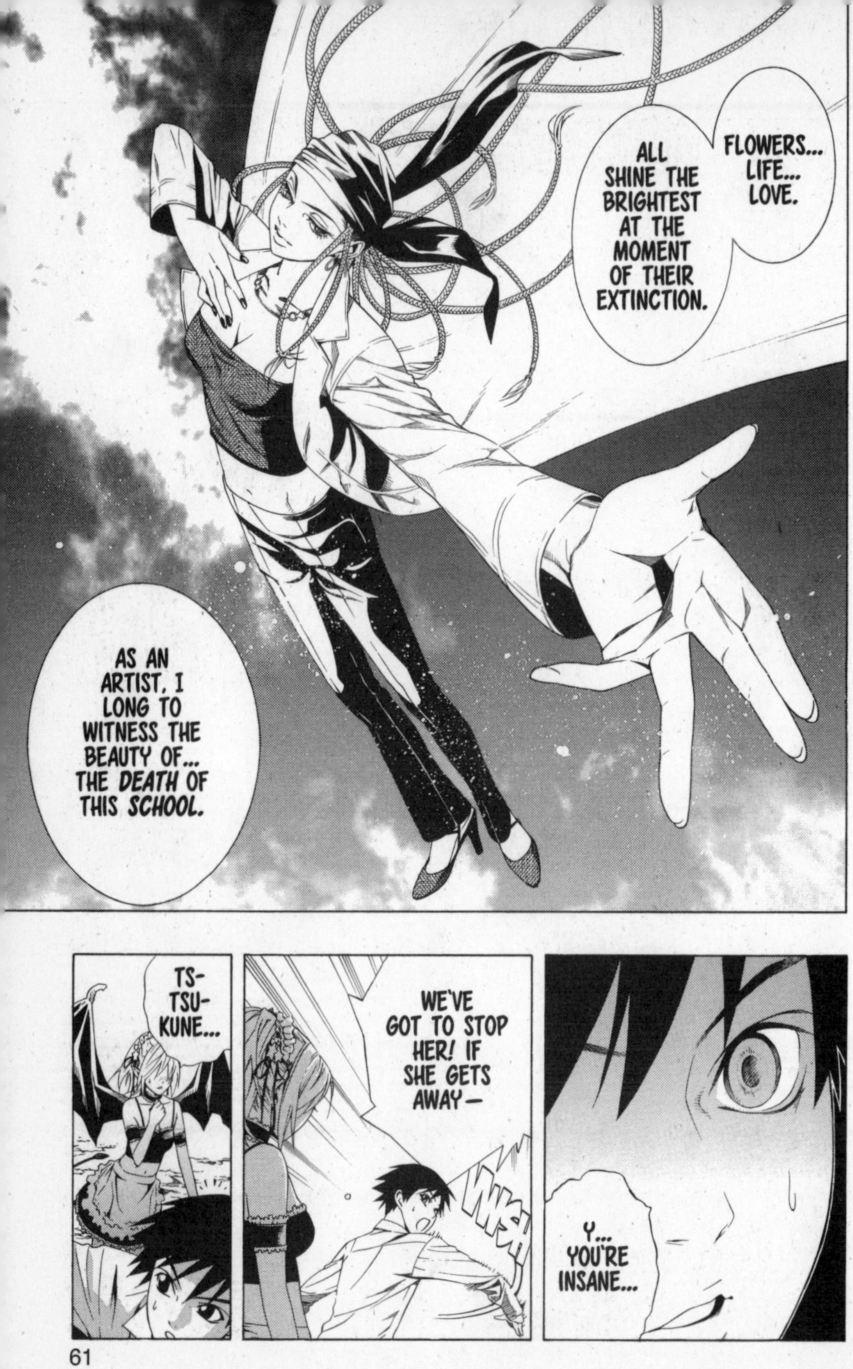
FLOWERS... LIFE... LOVE.
ALL SHINE THE BRIGHTEST AT THE MOMENT OF THEIR EXTINCTION.
AS AN ARTIST, I LONG TO WITNESS THE BEAUTY OF... THE *DEATH* OF THIS *SCHOOL.*
Y... YOU'RE INSANE...
WE'VE GOT TO STOP HER! IF SHE GETS AWAY—
TS-TSUKUNE...

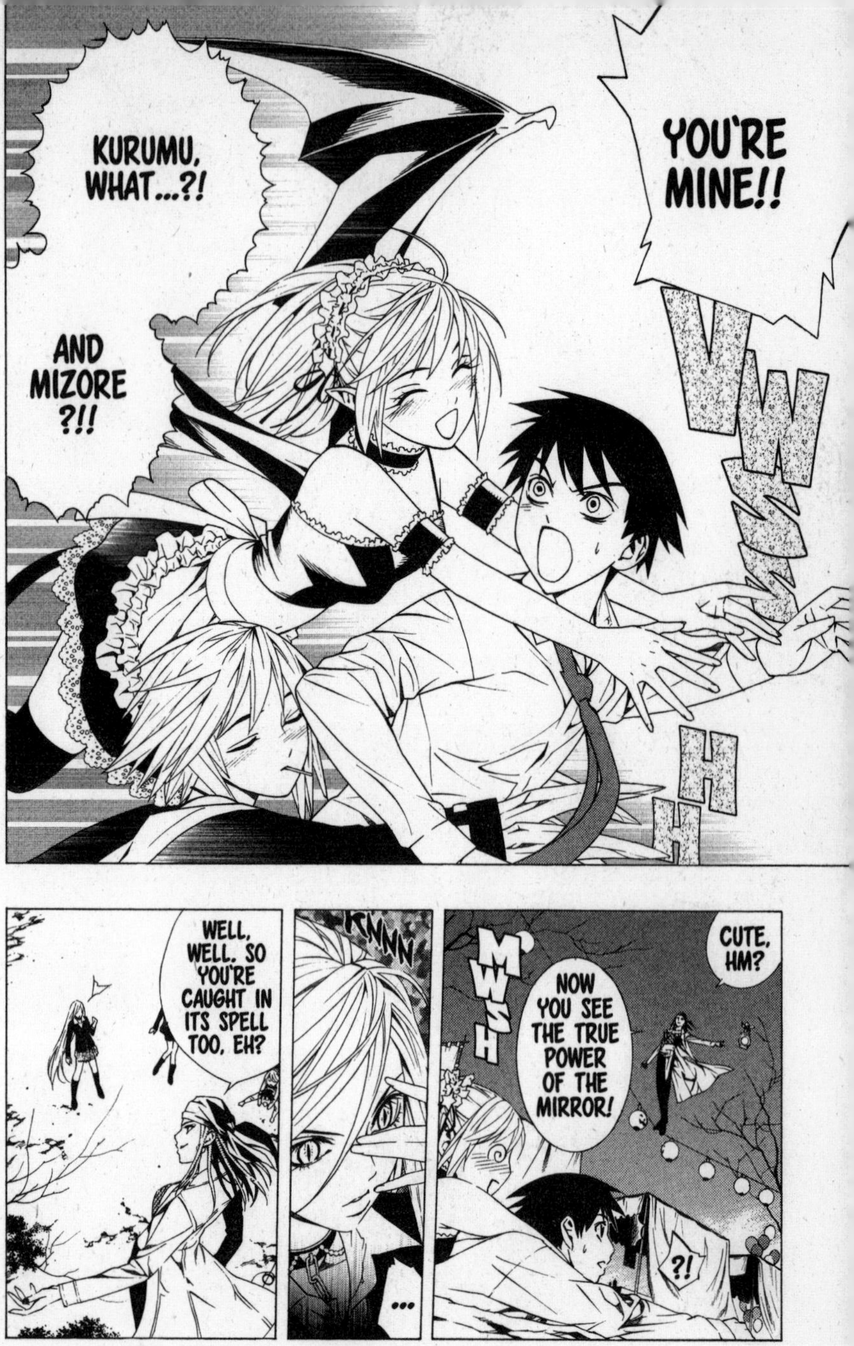
YOU'RE MINE!!
VWSSHHH
KURUMU, WHAT...?!
AND MIZORE ?!!
CUTE, HM?
MWSH
NOW YOU SEE THE TRUE POWER OF THE MIRROR!
?!
...
WELL, WELL. SO YOU'RE CAUGHT IN ITS SPELL TOO, EH?

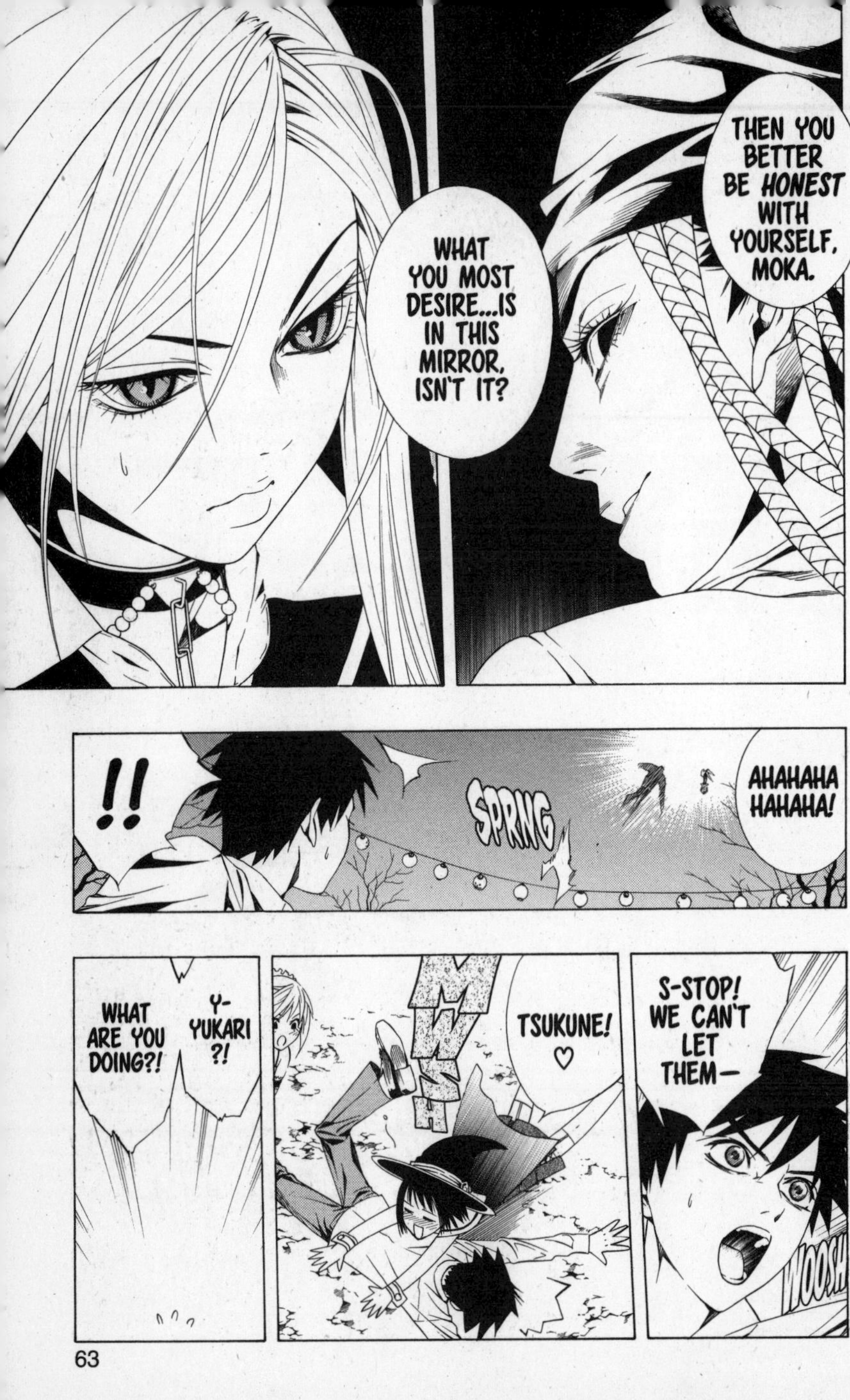
THEN YOU BETTER BE *HONEST* WITH YOURSELF, MOKA.
WHAT YOU MOST DESIRE...IS IN THIS MIRROR, ISN'T IT?
AHAHAHA HAHAHA!
SPRNG
!!
S-STOP! WE CAN'T LET THEM—
WOOSH
TSUKUNE! ♡
MWSH
Y-YUKARI?!
WHAT ARE YOU DOING?!

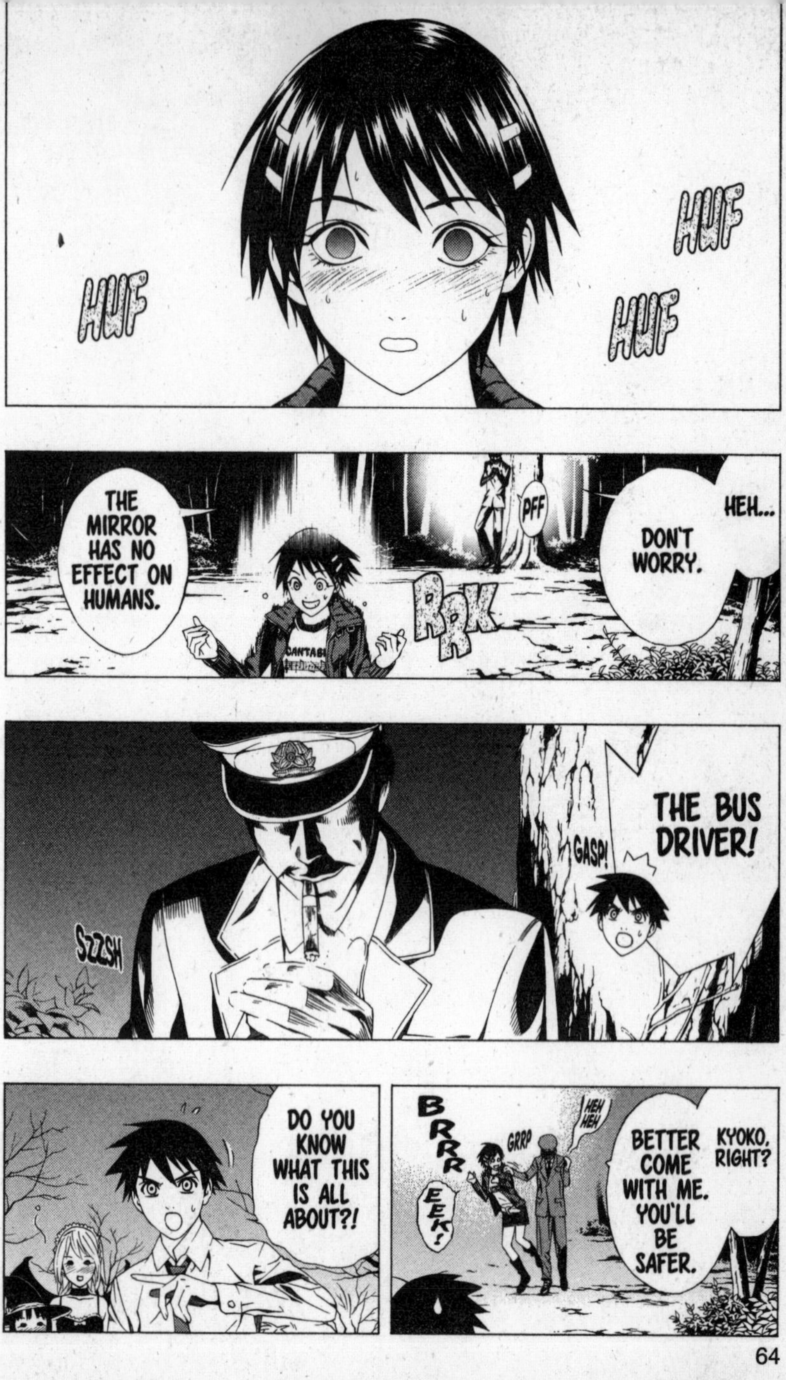
HUF
HUF
HUF
HEH...
DON'T WORRY.
PFF
RRK
THE MIRROR HAS NO EFFECT ON HUMANS.
THE BUS DRIVER!
GASP!
SZZSH
KYOKO, RIGHT?
BETTER COME WITH ME. YOU'LL BE SAFER.
HEH HEH
GRRP
BRRR
EEK!
DO YOU KNOW WHAT THIS IS ALL ABOUT?!

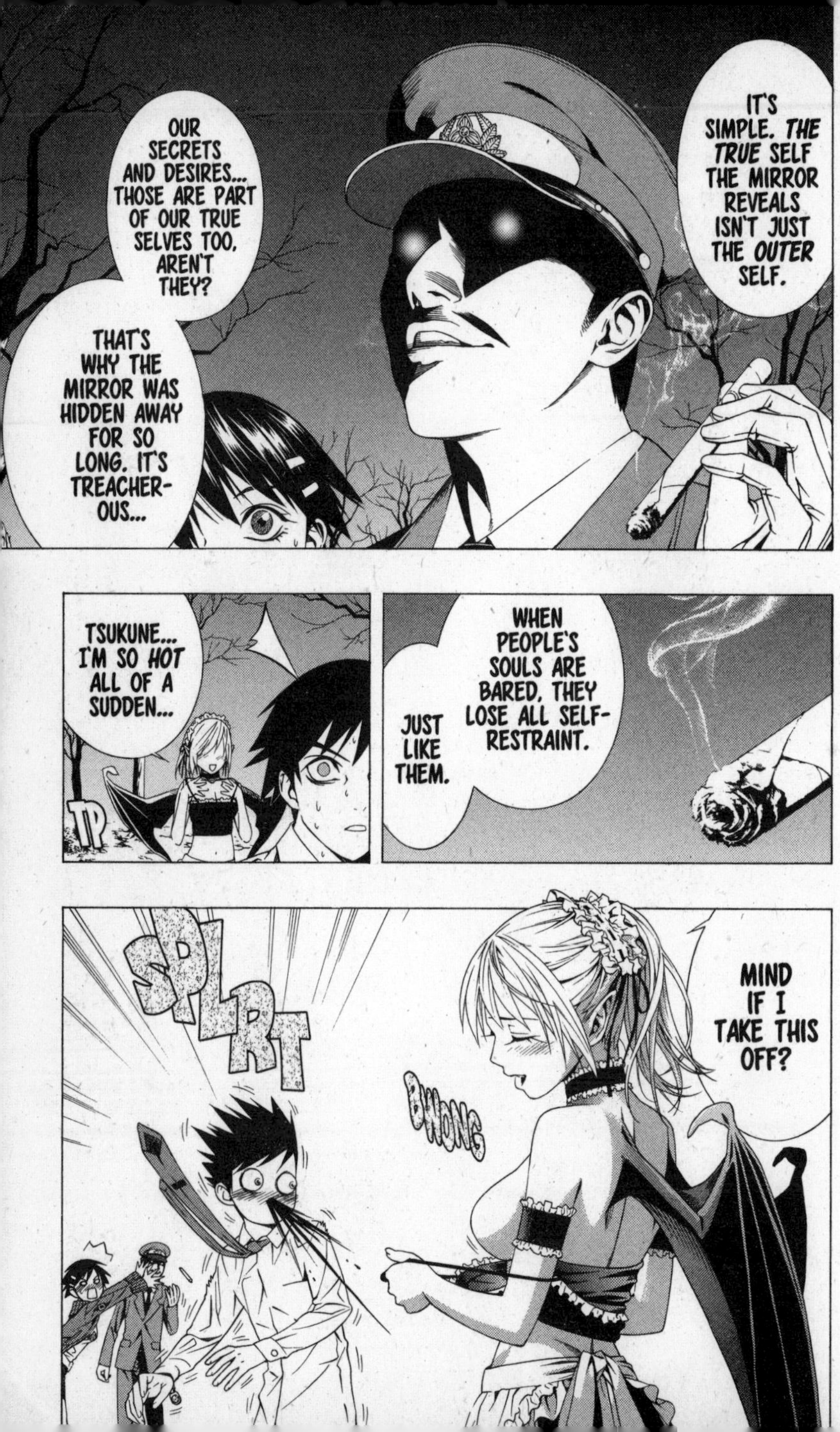
IT'S SIMPLE. *THE TRUE* SELF THE MIRROR REVEALS ISN'T JUST THE *OUTER* SELF.
OUR SECRETS AND DESIRES... THOSE ARE PART OF OUR TRUE SELVES TOO, AREN'T THEY?
THAT'S WHY THE MIRROR WAS HIDDEN AWAY FOR SO LONG. IT'S TREACHER-OUS...
WHEN PEOPLE'S SOULS ARE BARED, THEY LOSE ALL SELF-RESTRAINT.
JUST LIKE THEM.
TSUKUNE... I'M SO *HOT* ALL OF A SUDDEN...
TP
MIND IF I TAKE THIS OFF?
BWONG
SPLRT

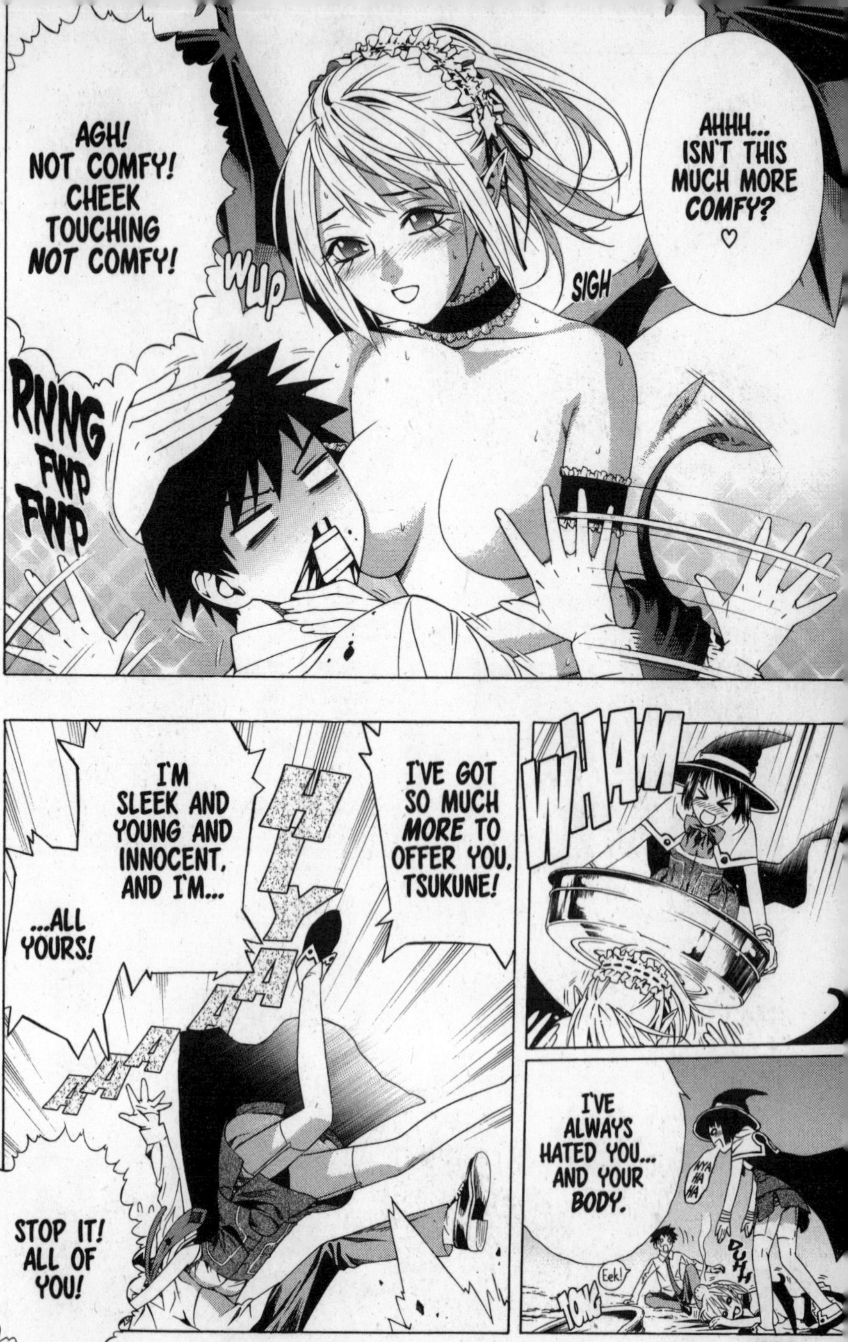
AHHH... ISN'T THIS MUCH MORE COMFY? ♡
SIGH
WUP
AGH! NOT COMFY! CHEEK TOUCHING NOT COMFY!
RNNG
FWP FWP
WHAM
I'VE ALWAYS HATED YOU... AND YOUR BODY.
NYA HA HA
DUHH
Eek!
TONG
I'VE GOT SO MUCH MORE TO OFFER YOU, TSUKUNE!
HIYAAAAAA
I'M SLEEK AND YOUNG AND INNOCENT, AND I'M...
...ALL YOURS!
STOP IT! ALL OF YOU!

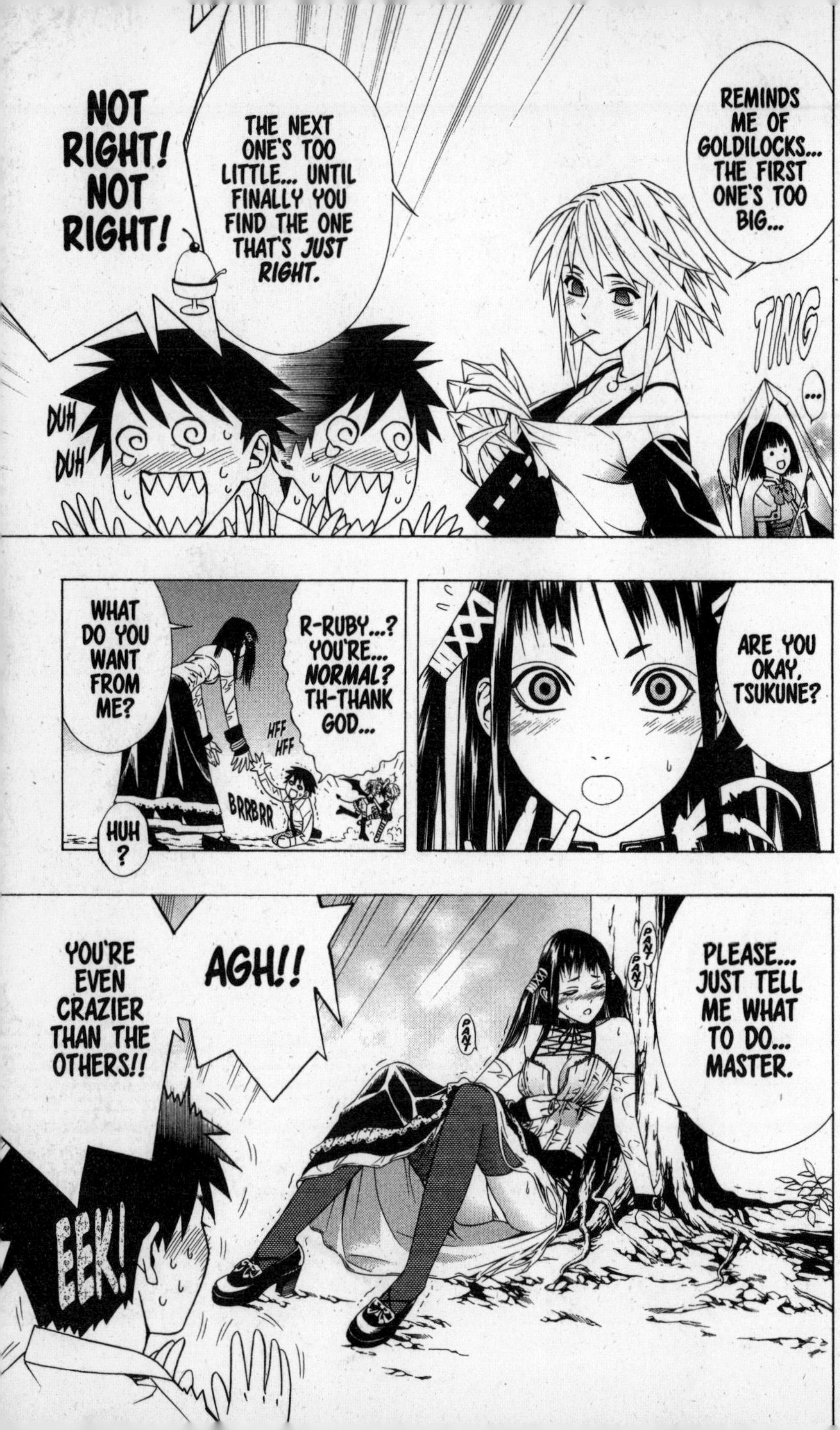
REMINDS ME OF GOLDILOCKS... THE FIRST ONE'S TOO BIG...
TING
...
THE NEXT ONE'S TOO LITTLE... UNTIL FINALLY YOU FIND THE ONE THAT'S *JUST RIGHT.*
NOT RIGHT! NOT RIGHT!
DUH DUH
ARE YOU OKAY, TSUKUNE?
R-RUBY...? YOU'RE... *NORMAL?* TH-THANK GOD...
WHAT DO YOU WANT FROM ME?
HFF HFF
BRRBRR
HUH?
PLEASE... JUST TELL ME WHAT TO DO... MASTER.
PANT PANT
PANT
AGH!!
YOU'RE EVEN CRAZIER THAN THE OTHERS!!
EEK!

?!!

KBMM

WILL YOU ALL GET A GRIP?!

LOOKS LIKE ISHIGAMI'S STARTED HER NEW GAME.

HMPH.

NOW WHAT ?!!

WHA ...?

vwo

TPP

I'M GOING, TSUKUNE. I DON'T NEED TO BABY-SIT YOU ANYMORE!

MOKA!

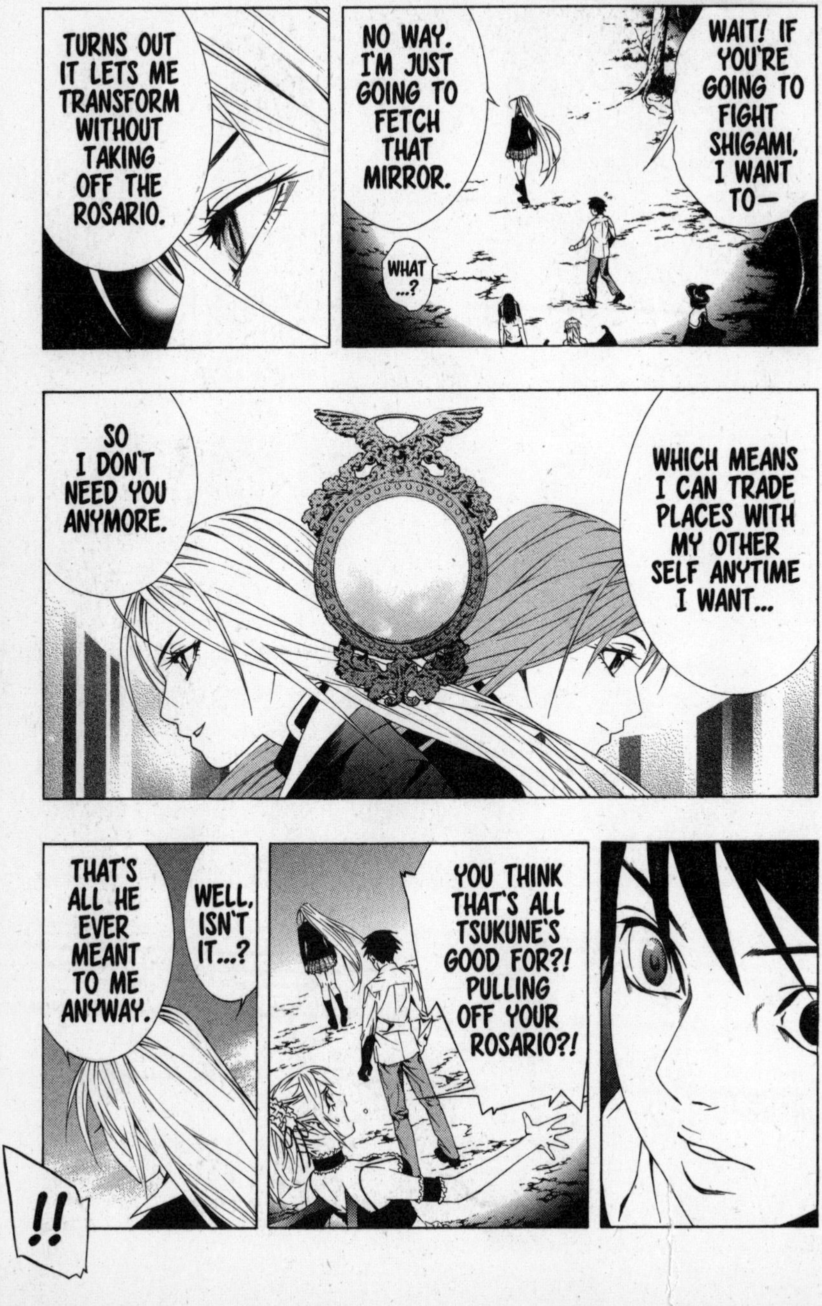
WAIT! IF YOU'RE GOING TO FIGHT SHIGAMI, I WANT TO—
NO WAY. I'M JUST GOING TO FETCH THAT MIRROR.
WHAT ...?
TURNS OUT IT LETS ME TRANSFORM WITHOUT TAKING OFF THE ROSARIO.
WHICH MEANS I CAN TRADE PLACES WITH MY OTHER SELF ANYTIME I WANT...
SO I DON'T NEED YOU ANYMORE.
YOU THINK THAT'S ALL TSUKUNE'S GOOD FOR?! PULLING OFF YOUR ROSARIO?!
WELL, ISN'T IT...?
THAT'S ALL HE EVER MEANT TO ME ANYWAY.
!!

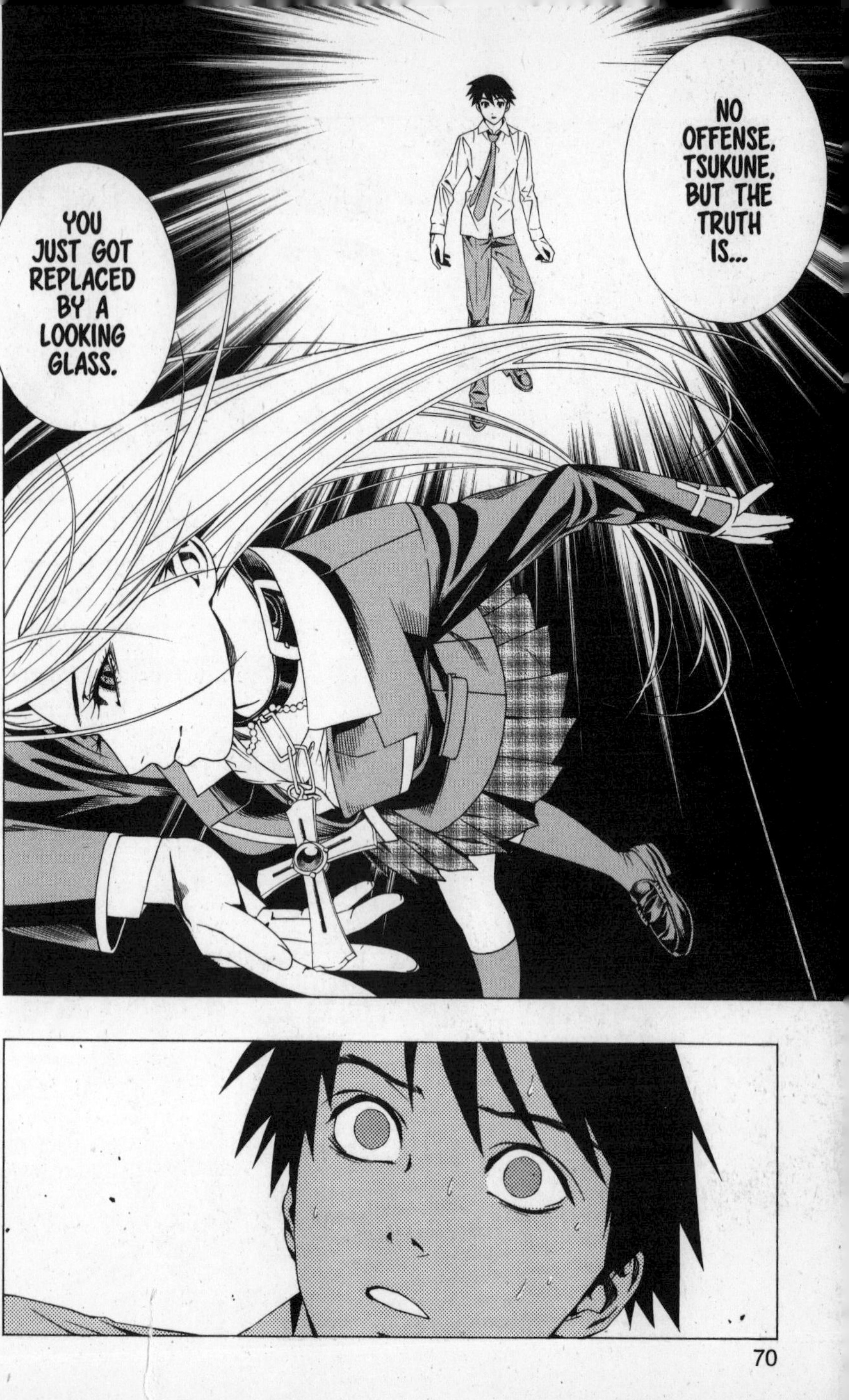
NO OFFENSE, TSUKUNE, BUT THE TRUTH IS...
YOU JUST GOT REPLACED BY A LOOKING GLASS.

READ THIS WAY

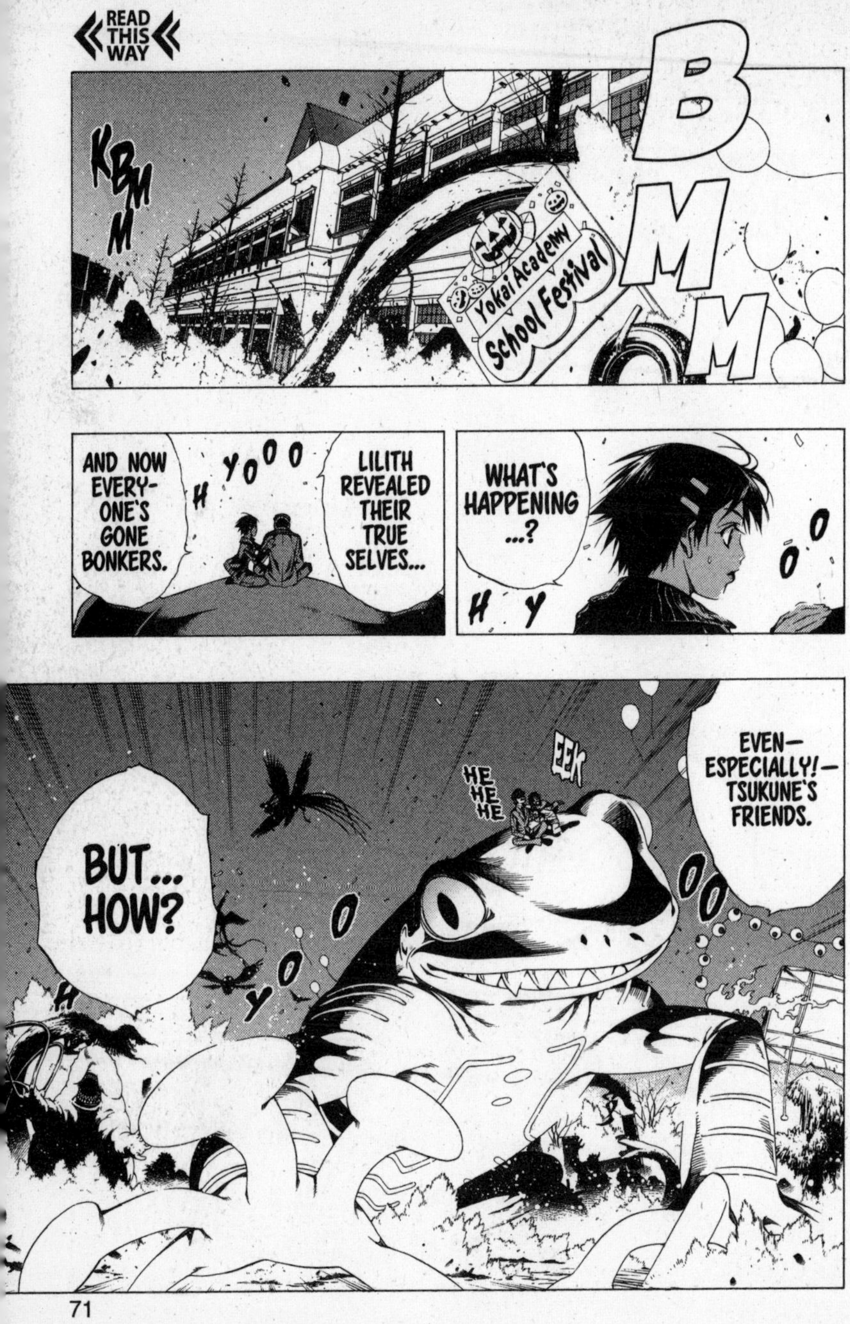
BMMM
Yokai Academy School Festival
KBMM
WHAT'S HAPPENING ...?
HYOOO
LILITH REVEALED THEIR TRUE SELVES...
HYOOO
AND NOW EVERY-ONE'S GONE BONKERS.
EVEN—ESPECIALLY!—TSUKUNE'S FRIENDS.
EEK
HE HE HE
OOO
BUT... HOW?
HYOOO

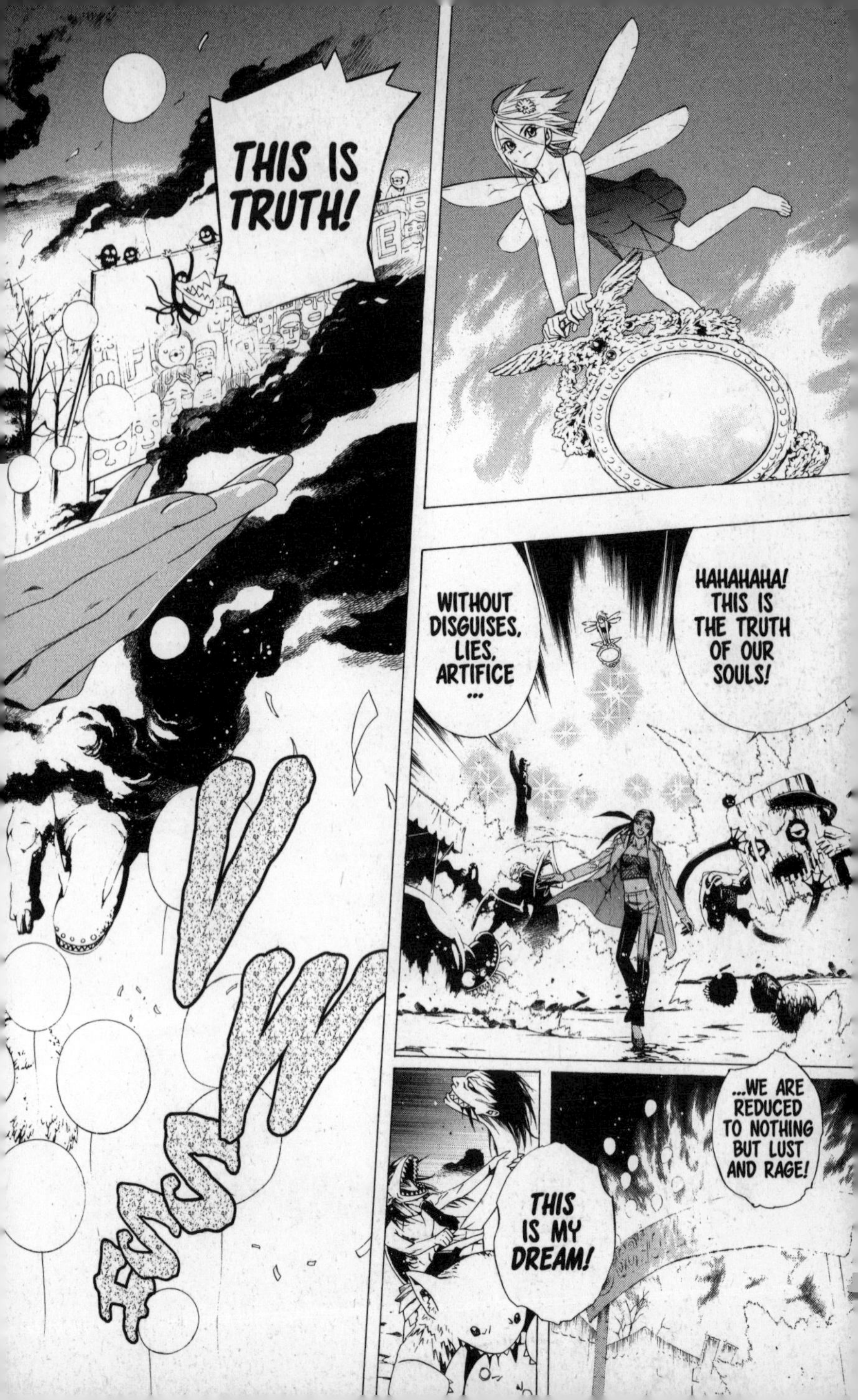
HAHAHAHA! THIS IS THE TRUTH OF OUR SOULS!
WITHOUT DISGUISES, LIES, ARTIFICE...
...WE ARE REDUCED TO NOTHING BUT LUST AND RAGE!
THIS IS MY DREAM!
THIS IS TRUTH!

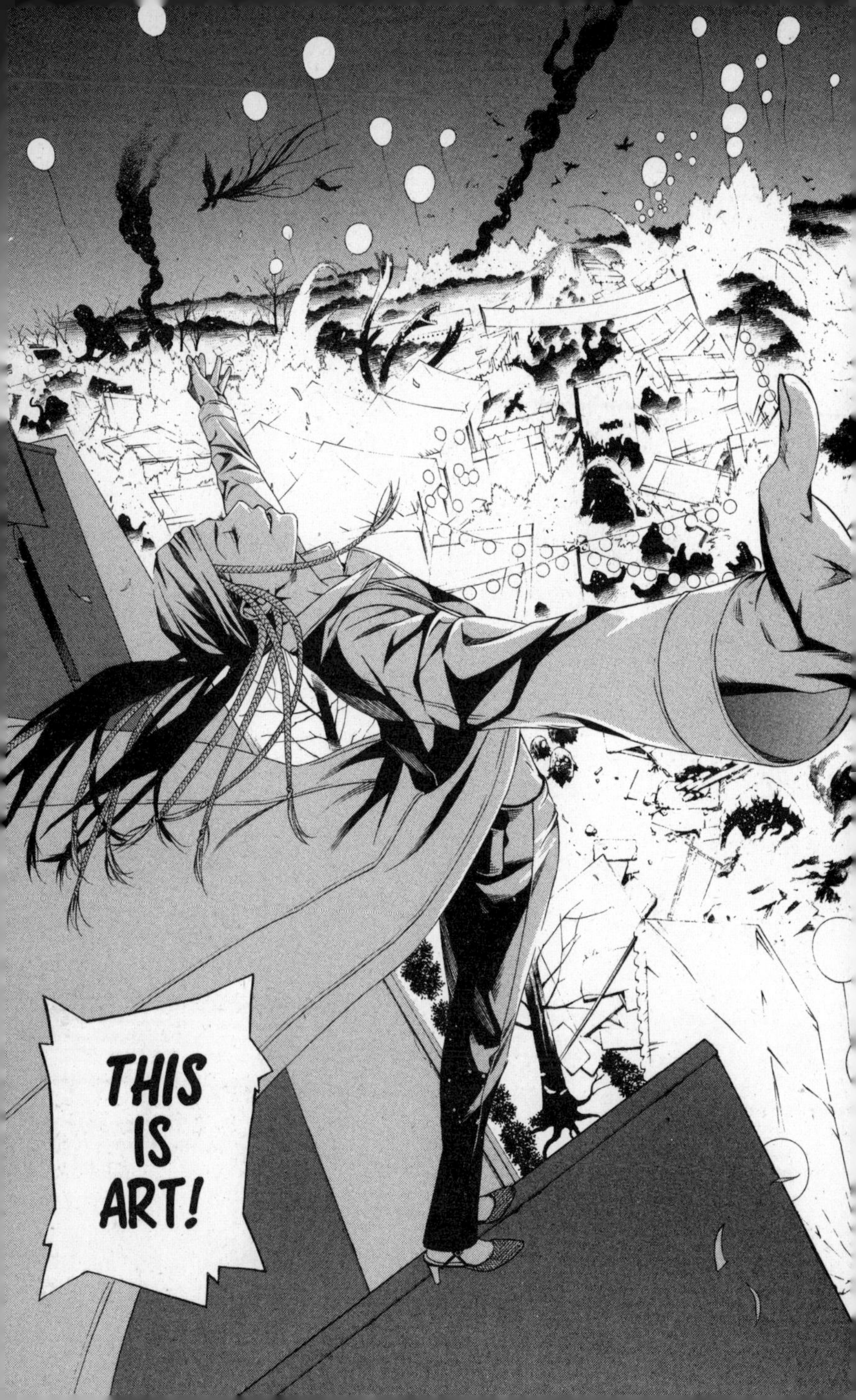
THIS IS ART!

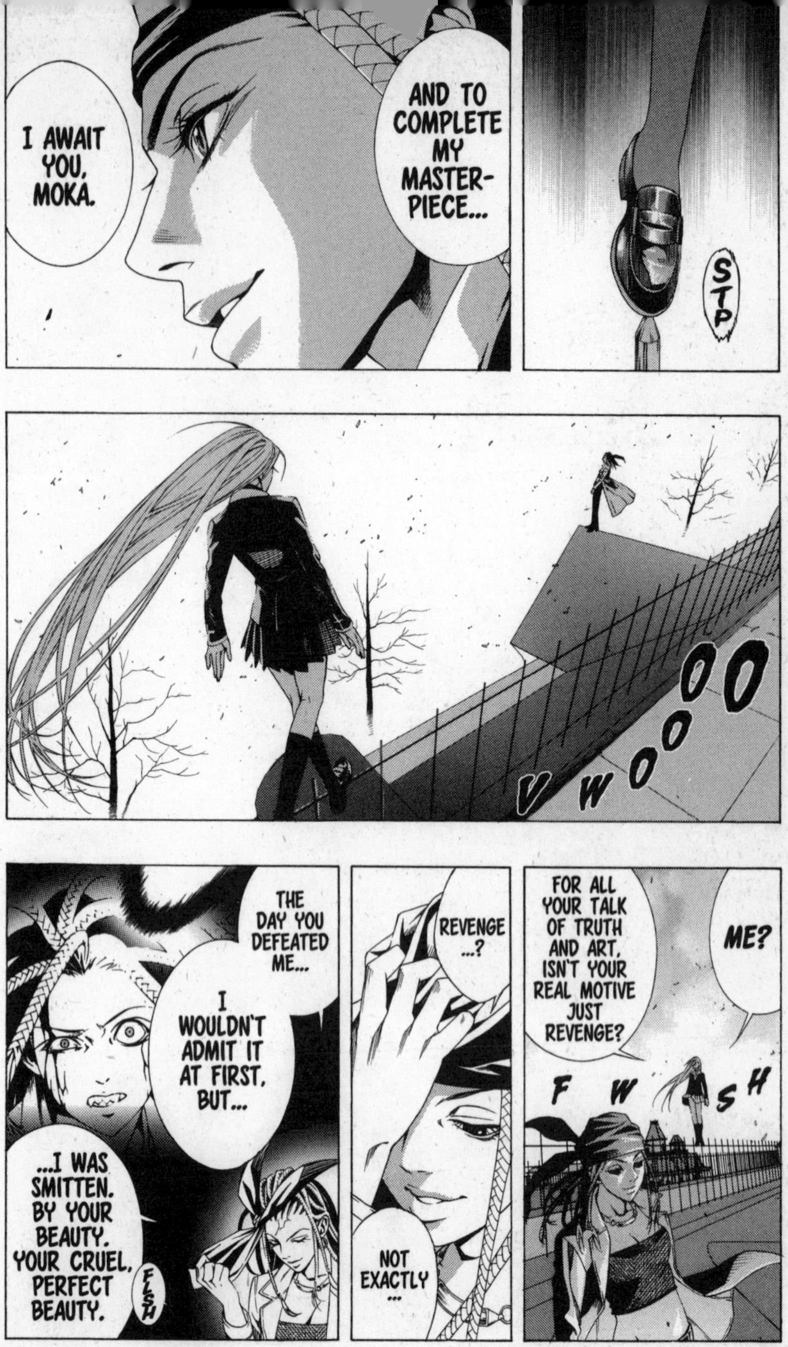
STP
AND TO COMPLETE MY MASTER-PIECE...
I AWAIT YOU, MOKA.
VWOOOOO
ME?
FOR ALL YOUR TALK OF TRUTH AND ART, ISN'T YOUR REAL MOTIVE JUST REVENGE?
FWSH
REVENGE ...?
NOT EXACTLY ...
THE DAY YOU DEFEATED ME...
I WOULDN'T ADMIT IT AT FIRST, BUT...
...I WAS SMITTEN. BY YOUR BEAUTY. YOUR CRUEL, PERFECT BEAUTY.
FLSH

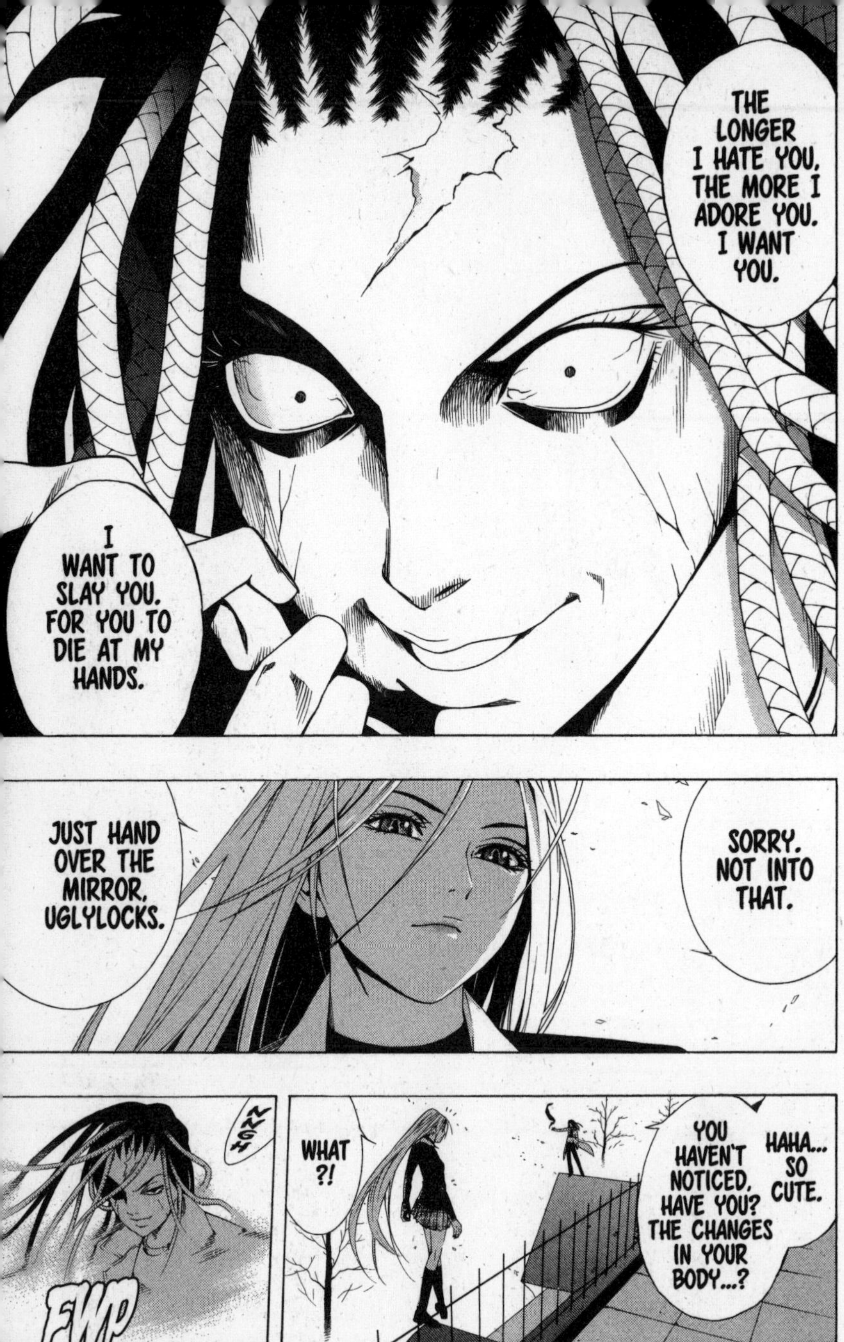
THE LONGER I HATE YOU, THE MORE I ADORE YOU. I WANT YOU.
I WANT TO SLAY YOU. FOR YOU TO DIE AT MY HANDS.
SORRY. NOT INTO THAT.
JUST HAND OVER THE MIRROR, UGLYLOCKS.
HAHA... SO CUTE.
YOU HAVEN'T NOTICED, HAVE YOU? THE CHANGES IN YOUR BODY...?
WHAT?!
NNGH
FWP

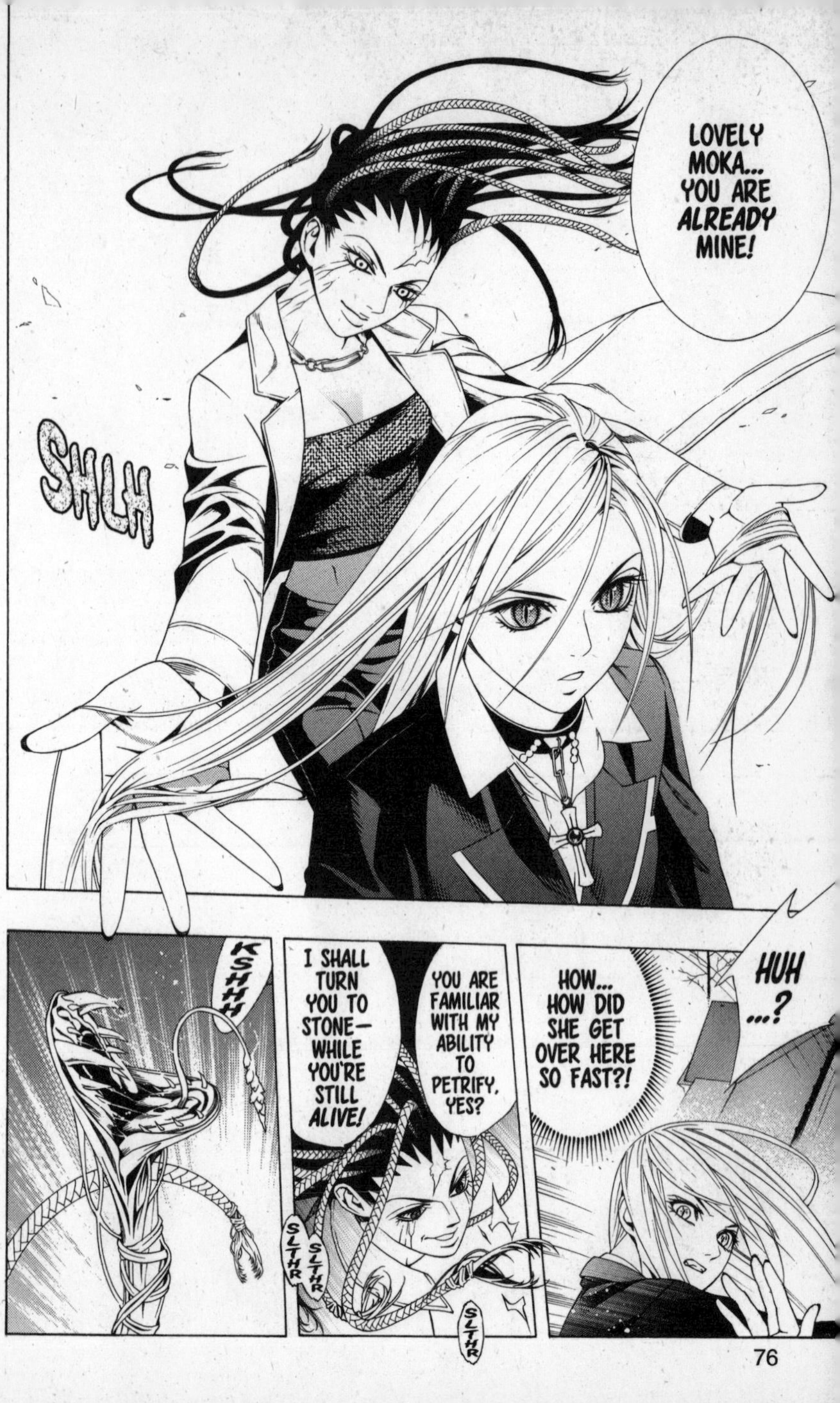
LOVELY MOKA... YOU ARE ALREADY MINE!
SHLH
HUH ...?
HOW... HOW DID SHE GET OVER HERE SO FAST?!
YOU ARE FAMILIAR WITH MY ABILITY TO PETRIFY, YES?
I SHALL TURN YOU TO STONE—WHILE YOU'RE STILL ALIVE!
SLTHR
SLTHR
SLTHR
KSHHHH

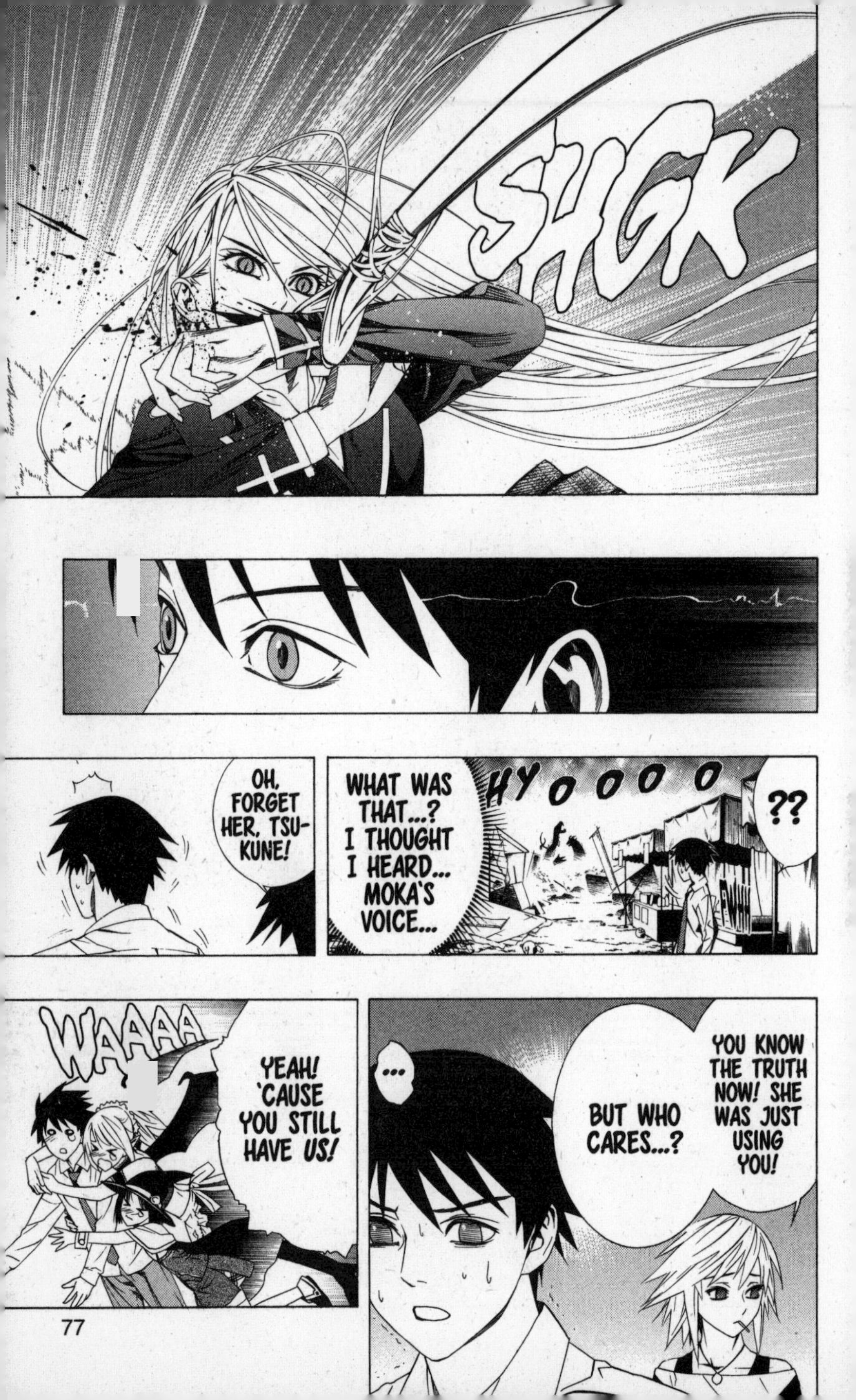
SHGK
??
HYOOOO
WHAT WAS THAT...? I THOUGHT I HEARD... MOKA'S VOICE...
OH, FORGET HER, TSU-KUNE!
YOU KNOW THE TRUTH NOW! SHE WAS JUST USING YOU!
BUT WHO CARES...?
...
WAAAA
YEAH! 'CAUSE YOU STILL HAVE US!

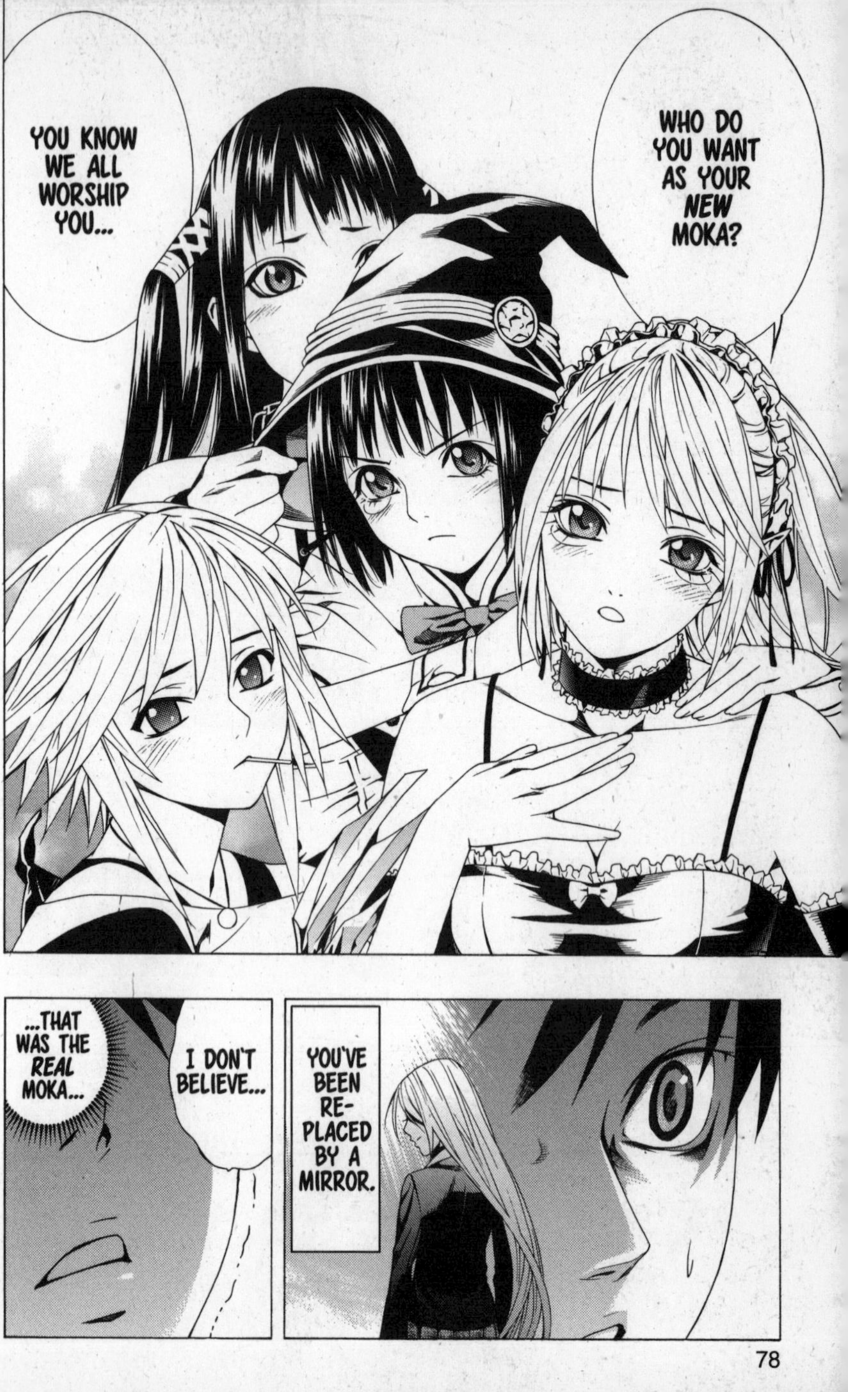
WHO DO YOU WANT AS YOUR NEW MOKA?
YOU KNOW WE ALL WORSHIP YOU...
YOU'VE BEEN RE-PLACED BY A MIRROR.
I DON'T BELIEVE...
...THAT WAS THE REAL MOKA...

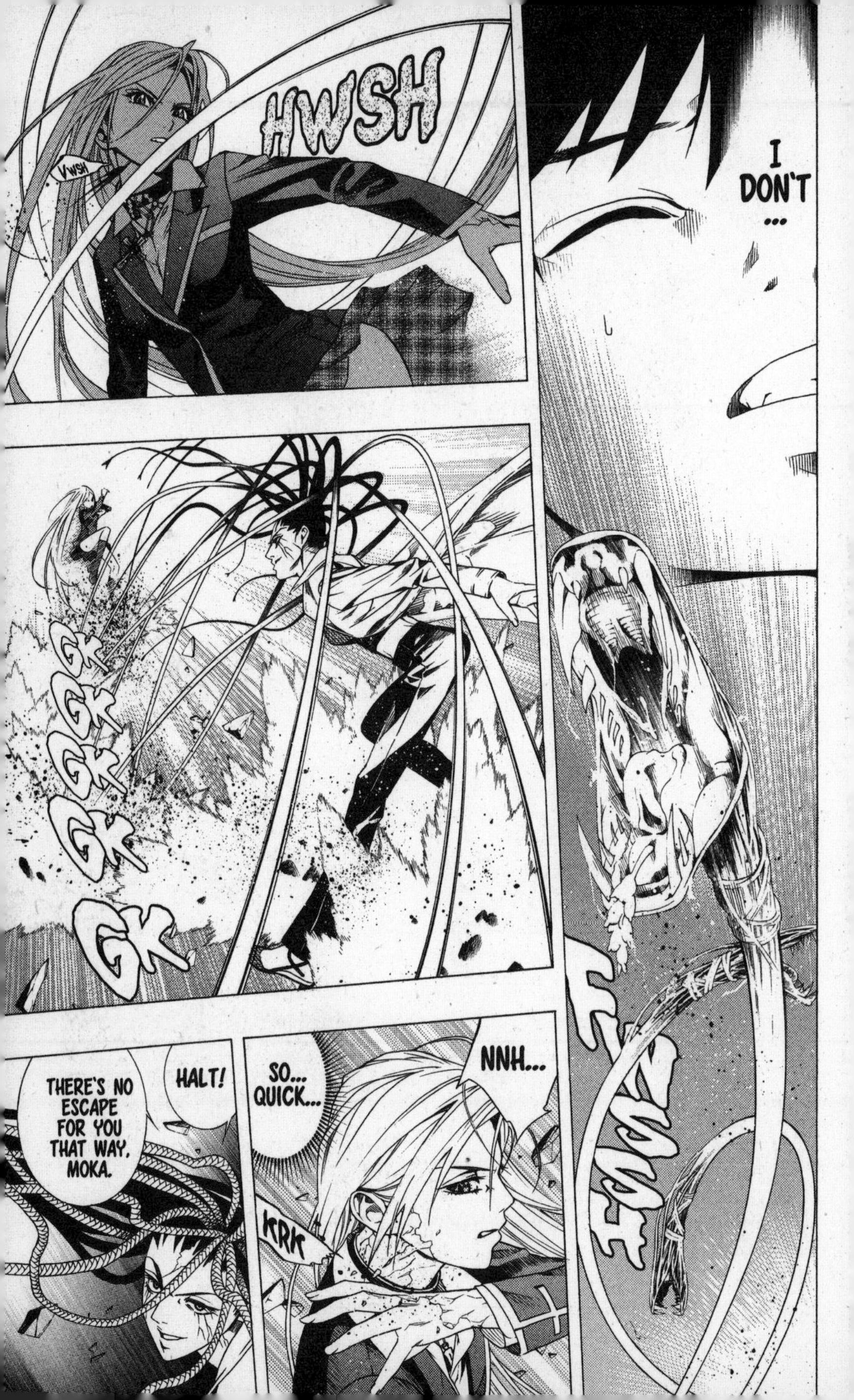
I DON'T...
HWSH
VWSH
GK GK GK GK GK
NNH...
SO... QUICK...
KRK
HALT!
THERE'S NO ESCAPE FOR YOU THAT WAY, MOKA.

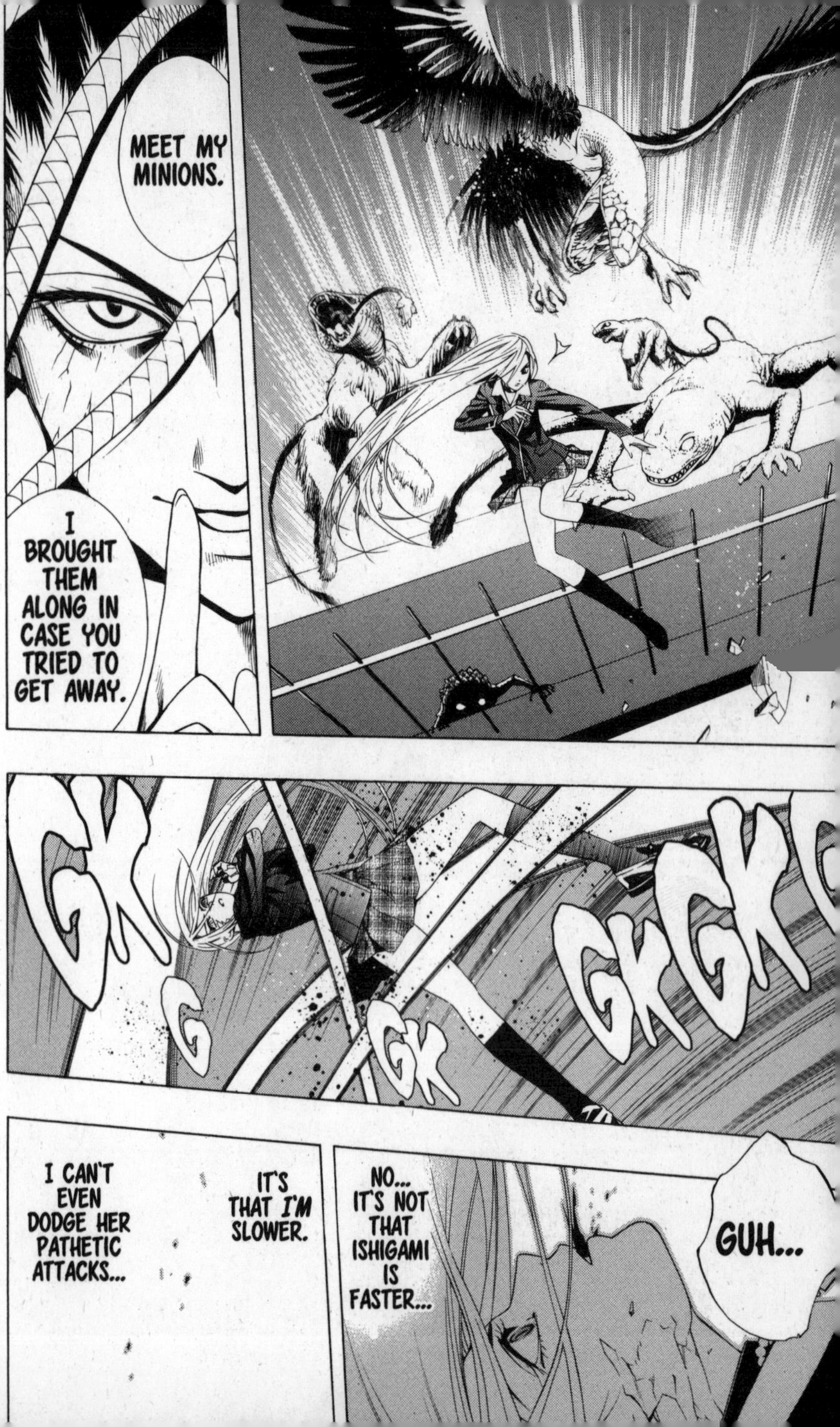
MEET MY MINIONS.
I BROUGHT THEM ALONG IN CASE YOU TRIED TO GET AWAY.
GKGK
GK
G
GK
GUH...
NO... IT'S NOT THAT ISHIGAMI IS FASTER...
IT'S THAT *I'M* SLOWER.
I CAN'T EVEN DODGE HER PATHETIC ATTACKS...

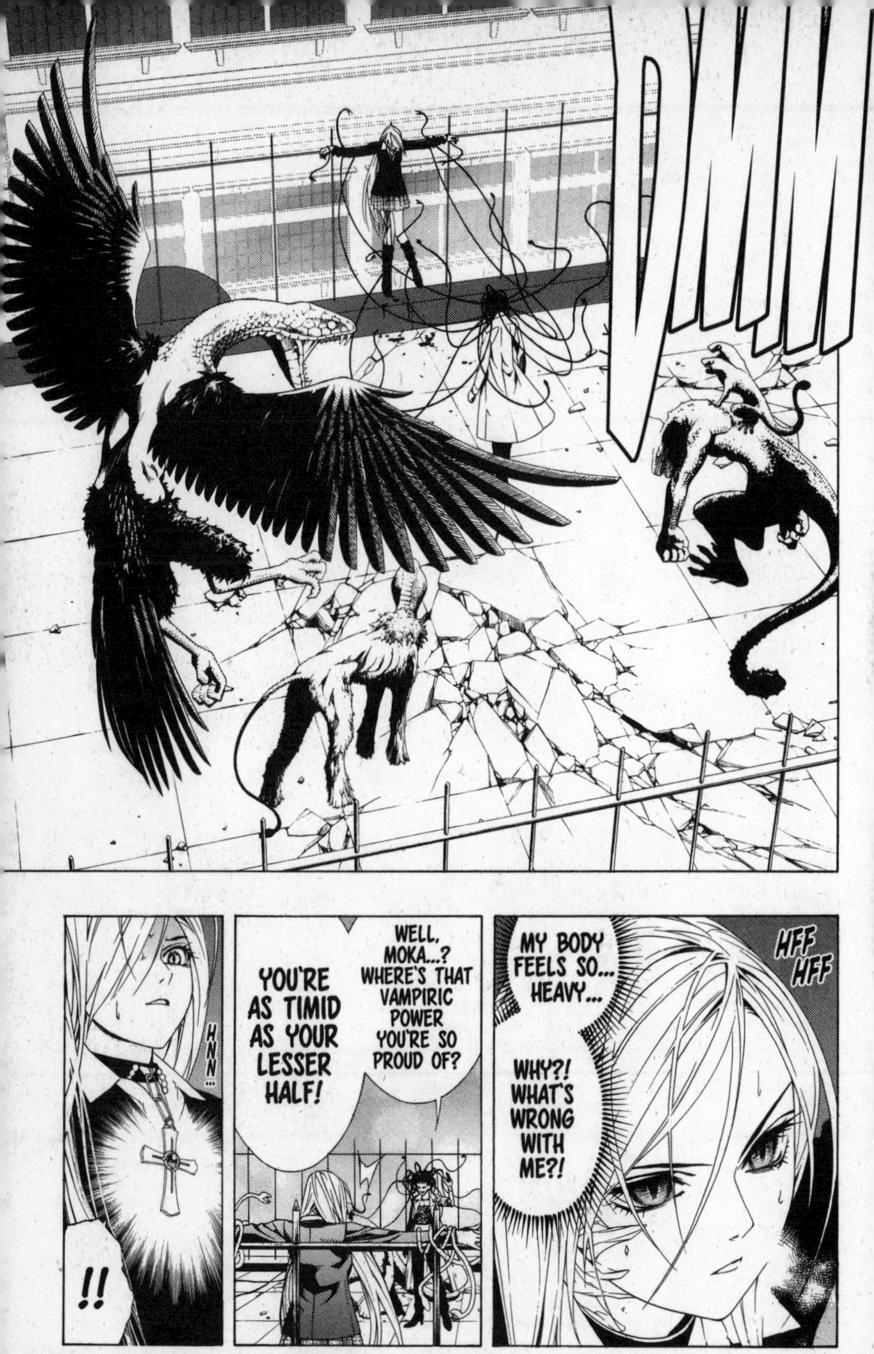
HFF HFF
MY BODY FEELS SO... HEAVY...
WHY?! WHAT'S WRONG WITH ME?!
WELL, MOKA...? WHERE'S THAT VAMPIRIC POWER YOU'RE SO PROUD OF?
YOU'RE AS TIMID AS YOUR LESSER HALF!
HNN...
!!

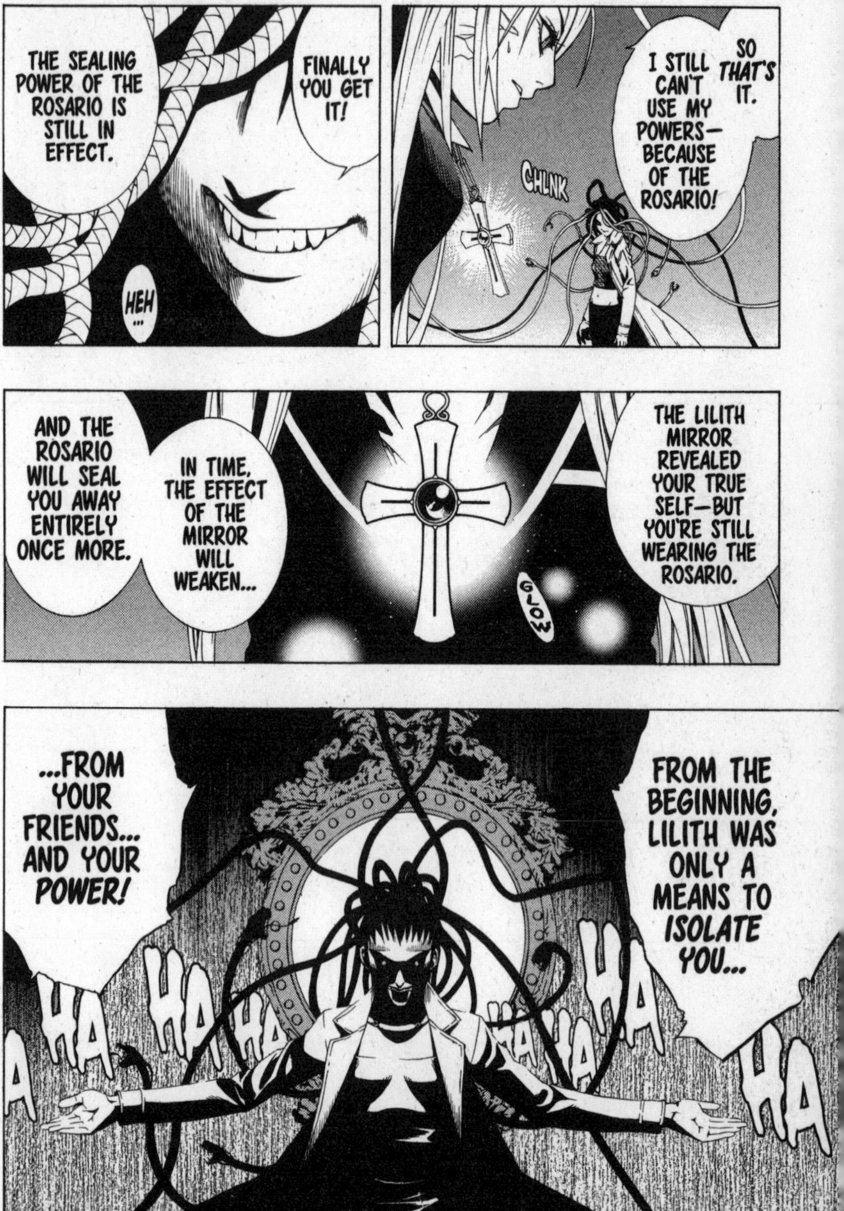

SO THAT'S IT.
I STILL CAN'T USE MY POWERS—BECAUSE OF THE ROSARIO!
CHLNK
FINALLY YOU GET IT!
THE SEALING POWER OF THE ROSARIO IS STILL IN EFFECT.
HEH...
THE LILITH MIRROR REVEALED YOUR TRUE SELF—BUT YOU'RE STILL WEARING THE ROSARIO.
GLOW
IN TIME, THE EFFECT OF THE MIRROR WILL WEAKEN...
AND THE ROSARIO WILL SEAL YOU AWAY ENTIRELY ONCE MORE.
FROM THE BEGINNING, LILITH WAS ONLY A MEANS TO ISOLATE YOU...
...FROM YOUR FRIENDS... AND YOUR POWER!
HA HA HA HA HA HA HA HA HA HA

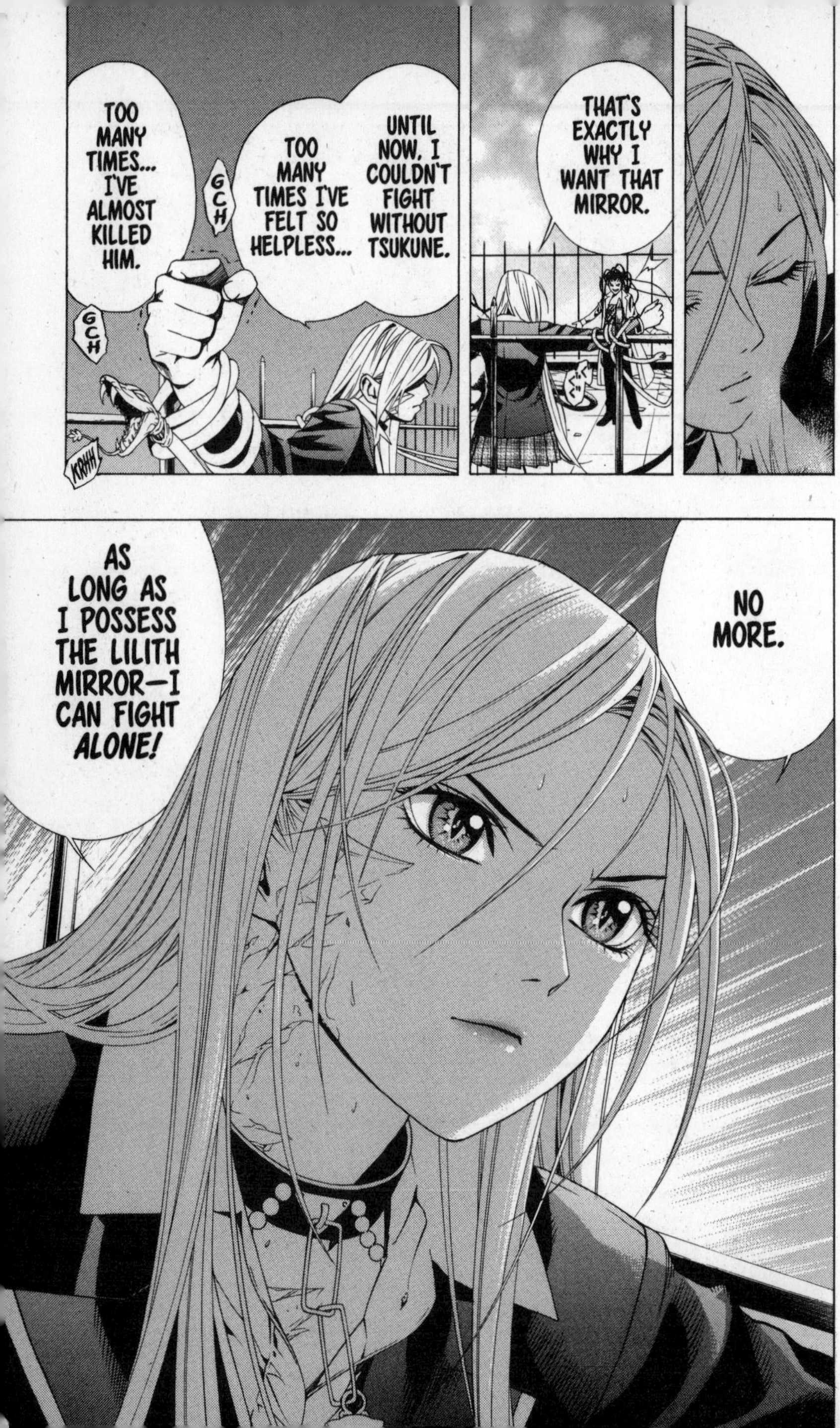
THAT'S EXACTLY WHY I WANT THAT MIRROR.
UNTIL NOW, I COULDN'T FIGHT WITHOUT TSUKUNE.
TOO MANY TIMES I'VE FELT SO HELPLESS...
TOO MANY TIMES... I'VE ALMOST KILLED HIM.
GCH
GCH
KRHH
NO MORE.
AS LONG AS I POSSESS THE LILITH MIRROR—I CAN FIGHT ALONE!

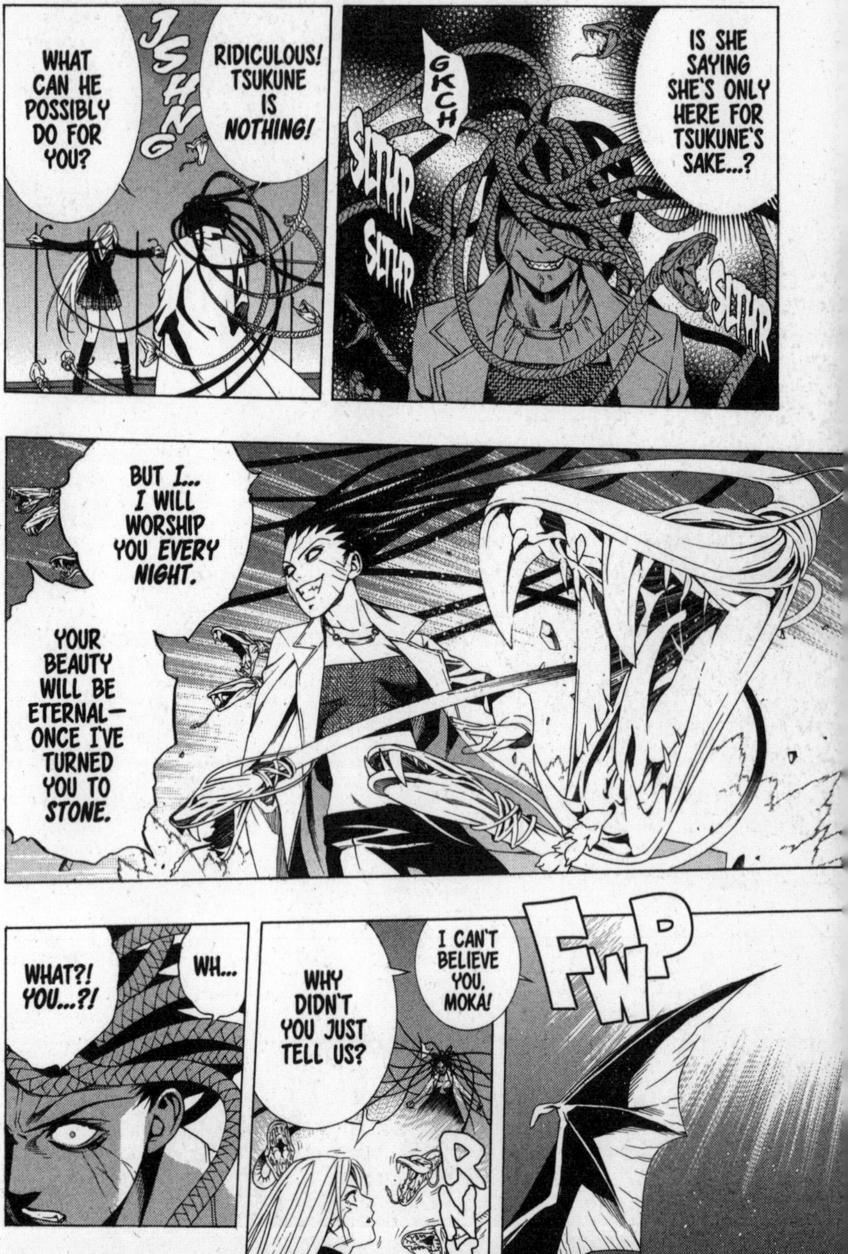
IS SHE SAYING SHE'S ONLY HERE FOR TSUKUNE'S SAKE...?
GKCH
SLITHR
SLITHR
SLITHR
RIDICULOUS! TSUKUNE IS NOTHING!
JSHNG
WHAT CAN HE POSSIBLY DO FOR YOU?
BUT I... I WILL WORSHIP YOU EVERY NIGHT.
YOUR BEAUTY WILL BE ETERNAL—ONCE I'VE TURNED YOU TO STONE.
FWP
I CAN'T BELIEVE YOU, MOKA!
WHY DIDN'T YOU JUST TELL US?
RRNK
WH...
WHAT?! YOU...?!

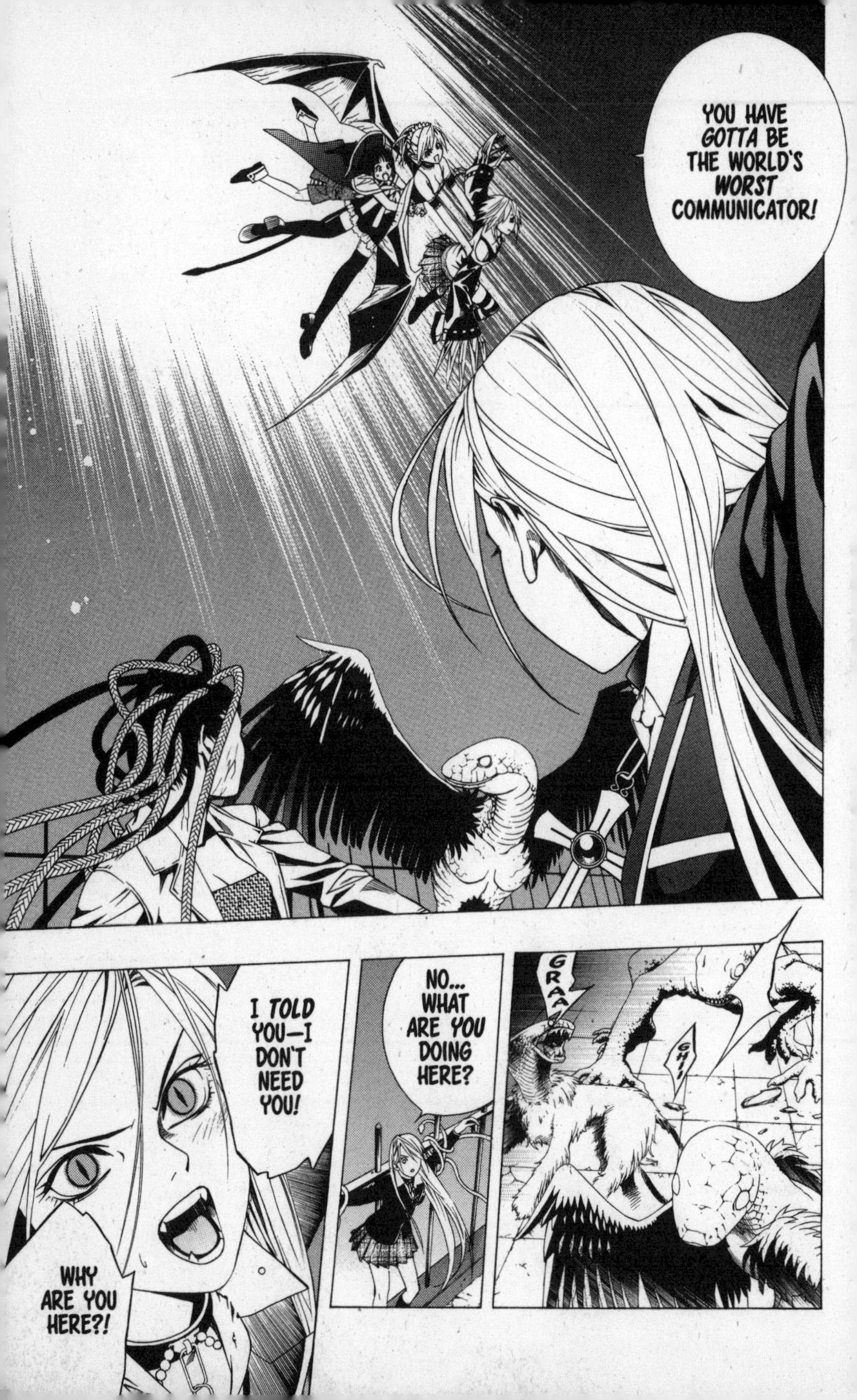
YOU HAVE GOTTA BE THE WORLD'S WORST COMMUNICATOR!
GRAA
GHI
NO... WHAT ARE YOU DOING HERE?
I TOLD YOU—I DON'T NEED YOU!
WHY ARE YOU HERE?!

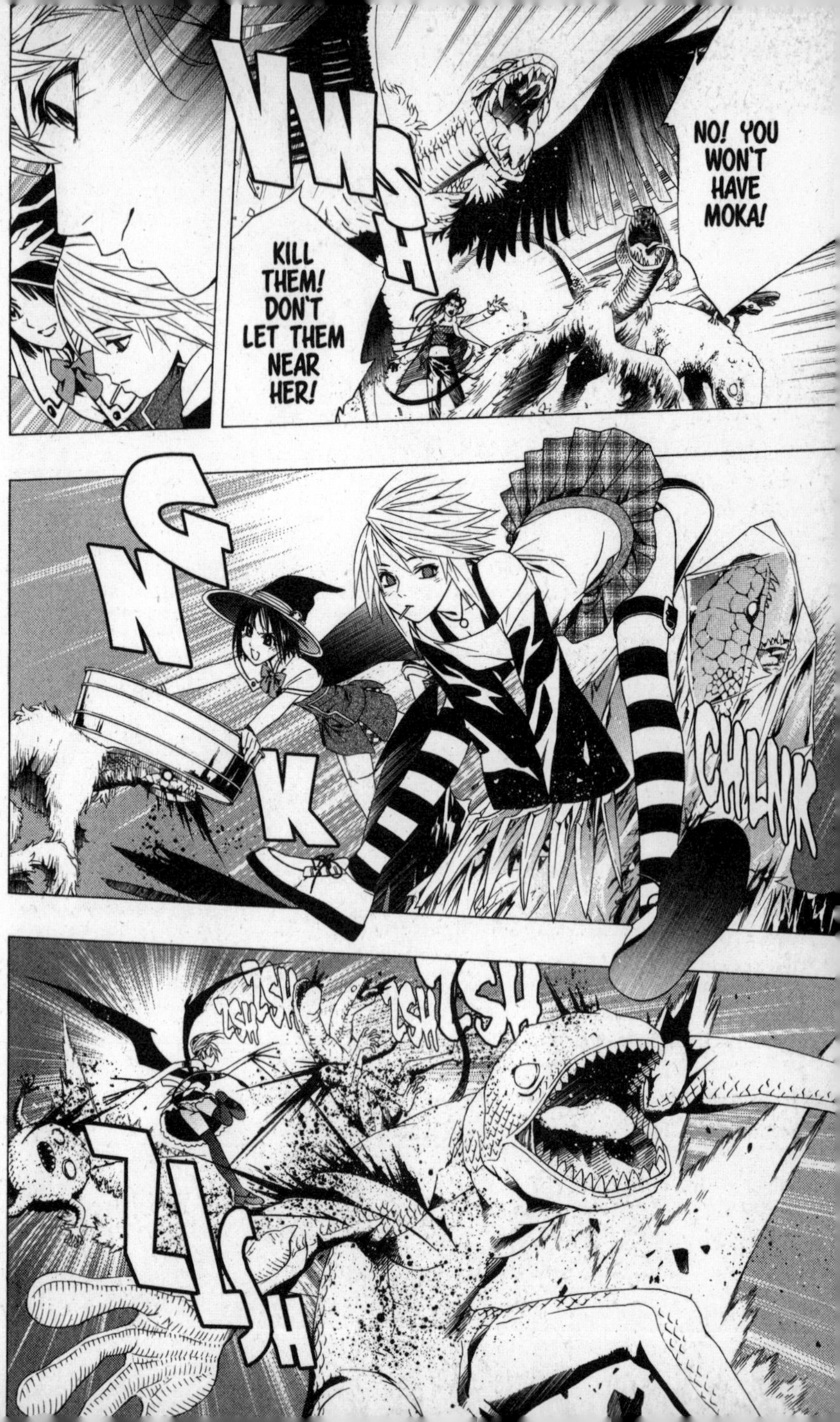
NO! YOU WON'T HAVE MOKA!
VWSH
KILL THEM! DON'T LET THEM NEAR HER!
CHUNK
GNK
ZSH
ZSH
ZSH
ZISH

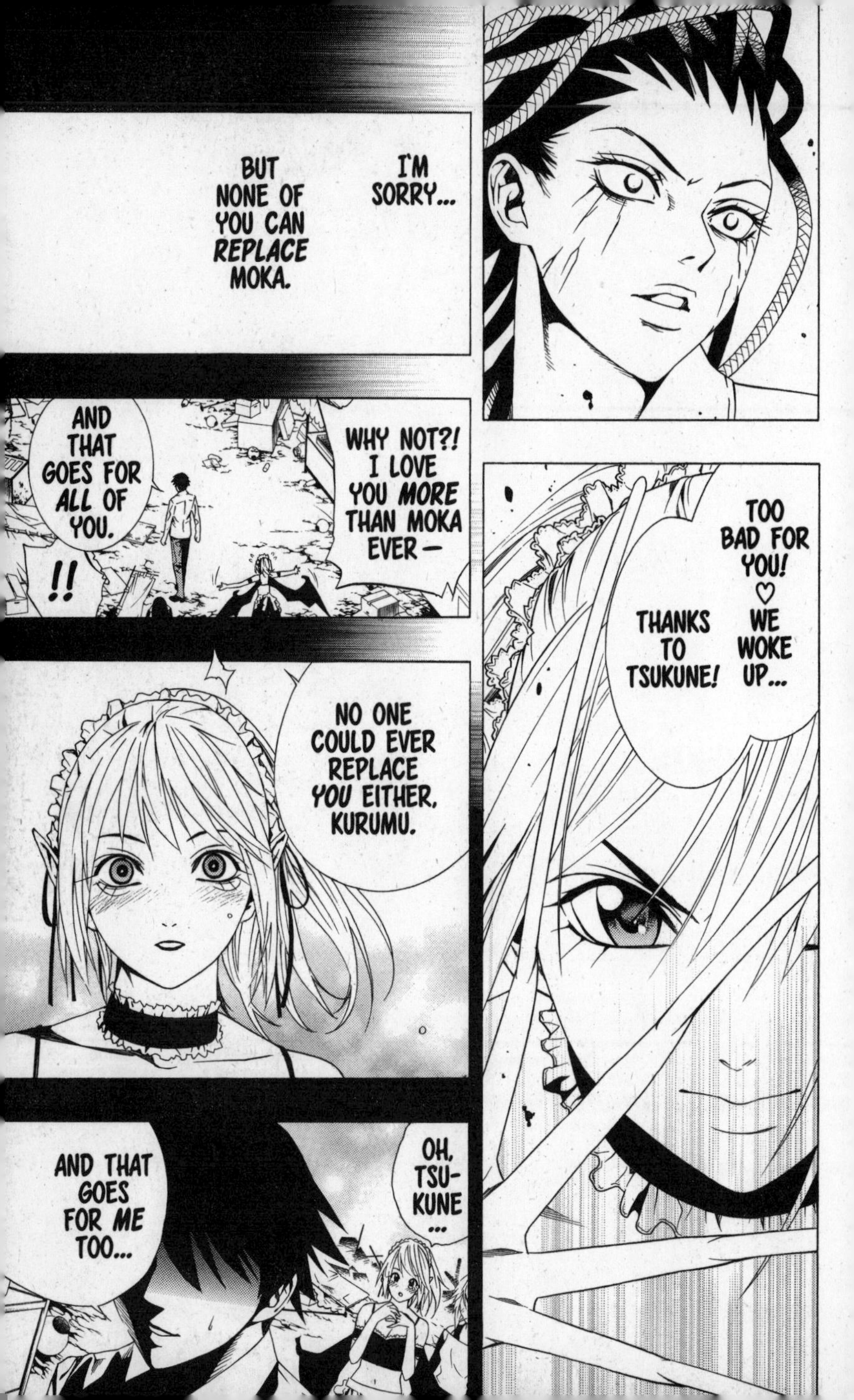
I'M SORRY...
BUT NONE OF YOU CAN REPLACE MOKA.
WHY NOT?! I LOVE YOU MORE THAN MOKA EVER—
AND THAT GOES FOR ALL OF YOU.
!!
NO ONE COULD EVER REPLACE YOU EITHER, KURUMU.
OH, TSU-KUNE...
AND THAT GOES FOR ME TOO...
TOO BAD FOR YOU! ♡ WE WOKE UP...
THANKS TO TSUKUNE!

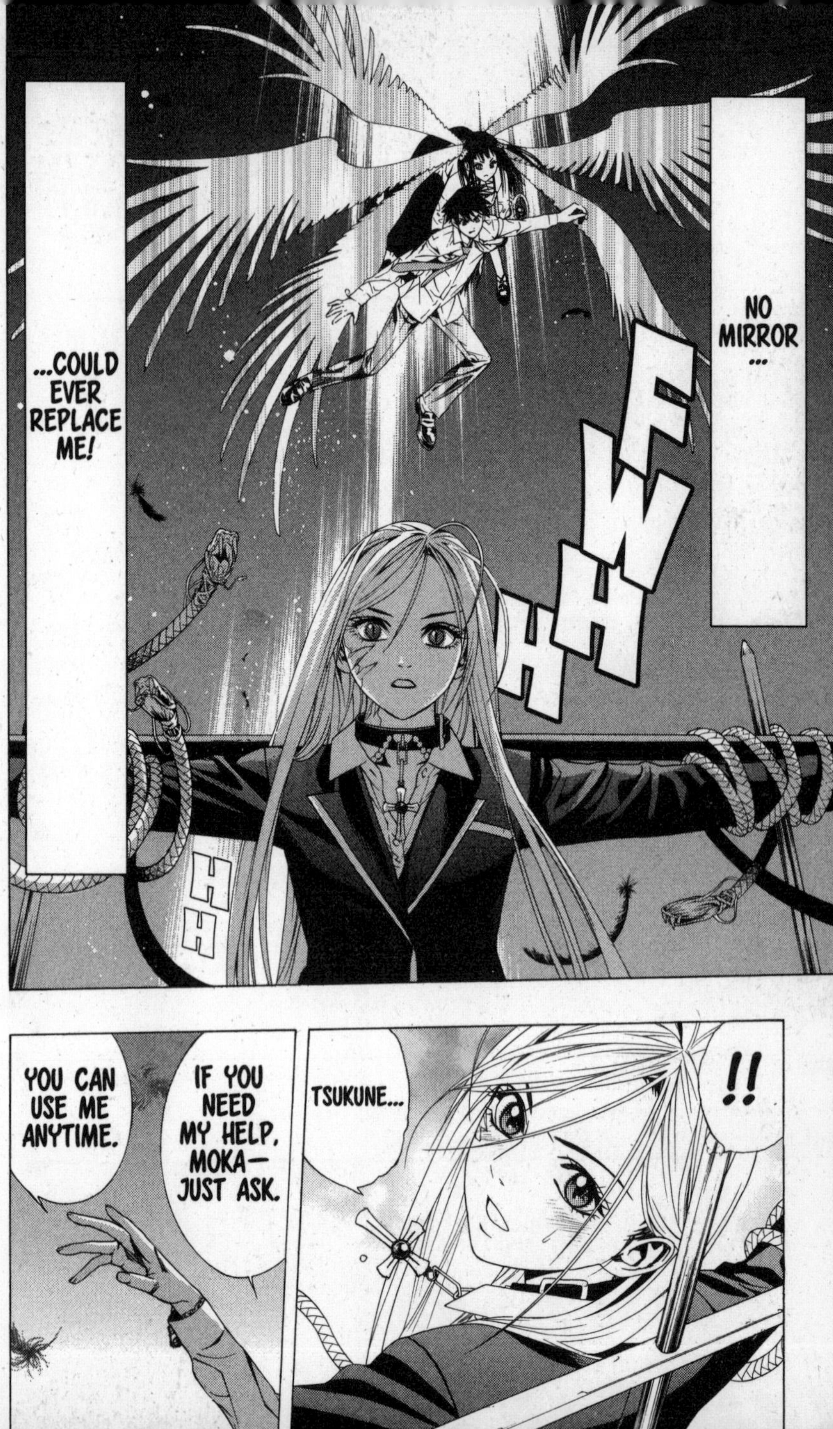
NO MIRROR ...
FWHHH
...COULD EVER REPLACE ME!
HH
!!
TSUKUNE...
IF YOU NEED MY HELP, MOKA— JUST ASK.
YOU CAN USE ME ANYTIME.

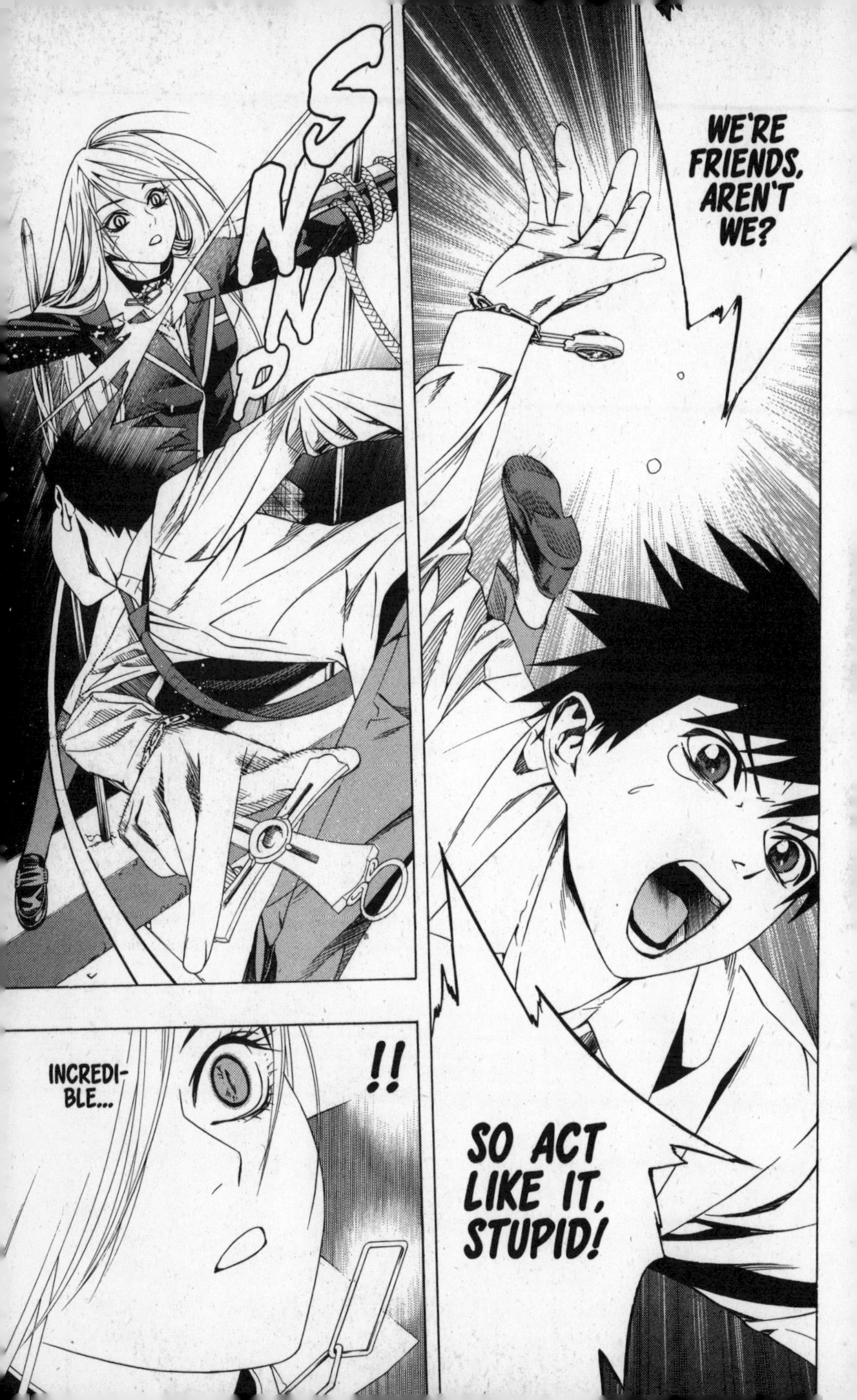
WE'RE FRIENDS, AREN'T WE?
SO ACT LIKE IT, STUPID!
SNAP
!!
INCREDIBLE...

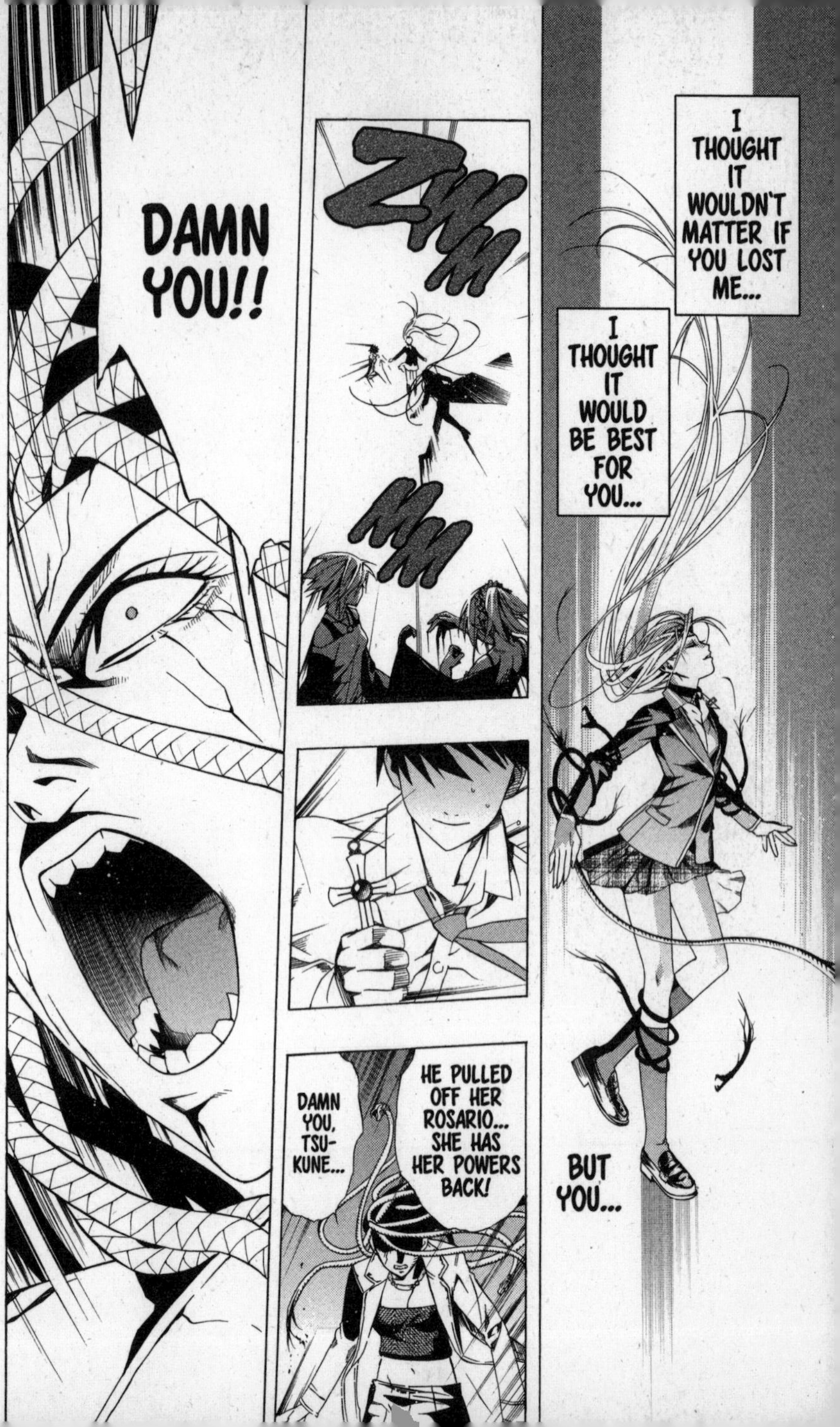
I THOUGHT IT WOULDN'T MATTER IF YOU LOST ME...
I THOUGHT IT WOULD BE BEST FOR YOU...
BUT YOU...
ZWMM
MMM
HE PULLED OFF HER ROSARIO... SHE HAS HER POWERS BACK!
DAMN YOU, TSU-KUNE...
DAMN YOU!!

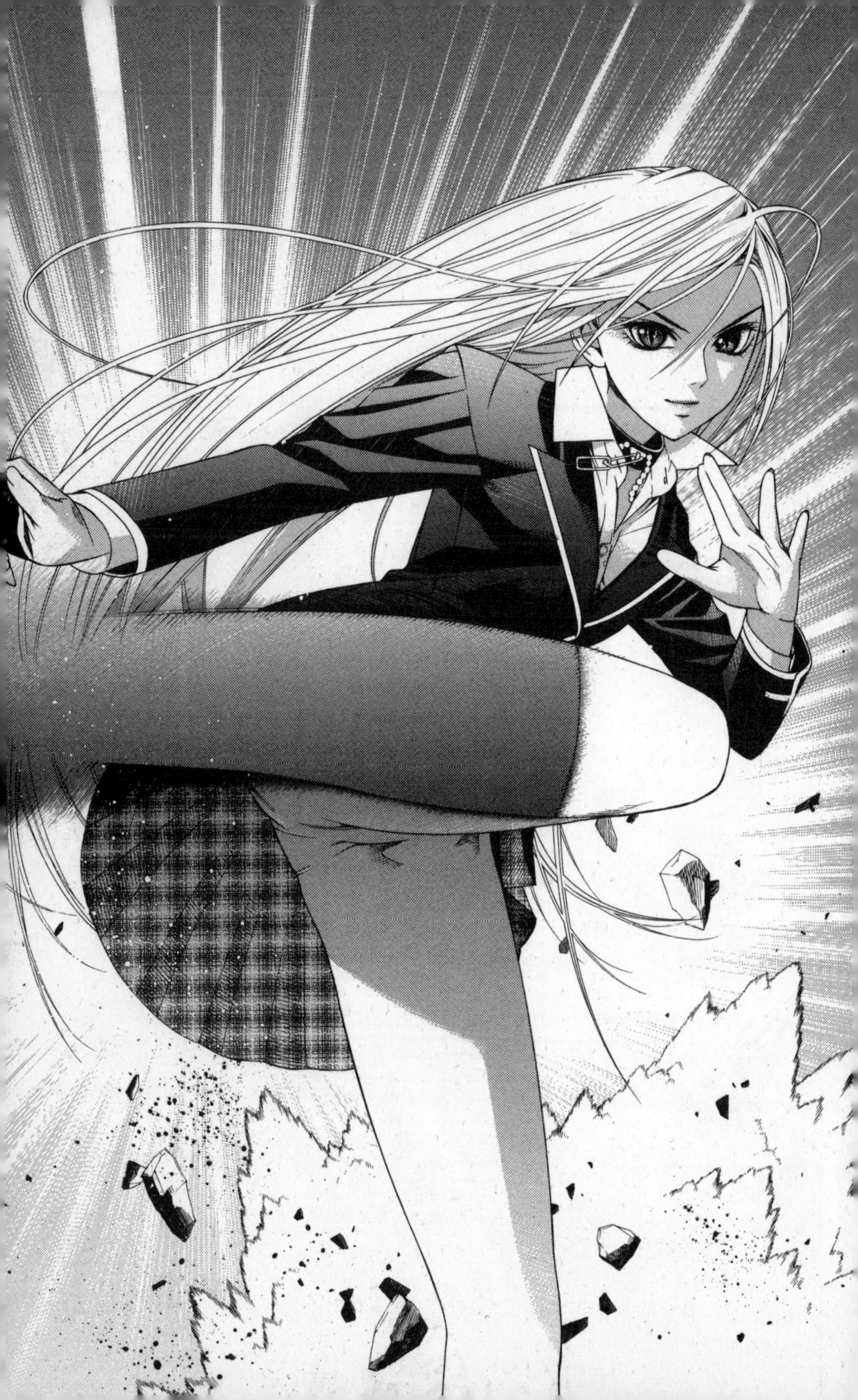

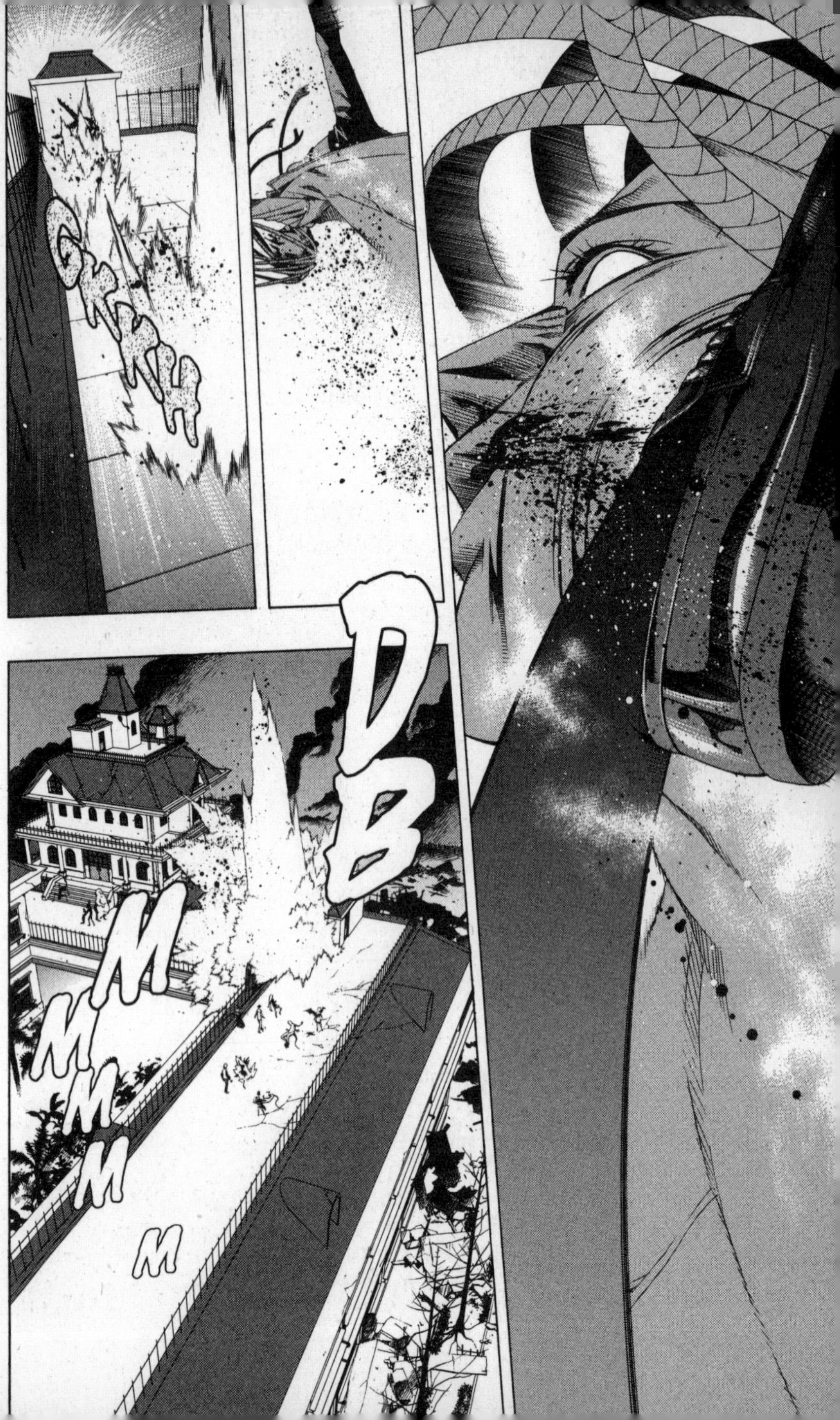
GKKKH
DB
MMMMM

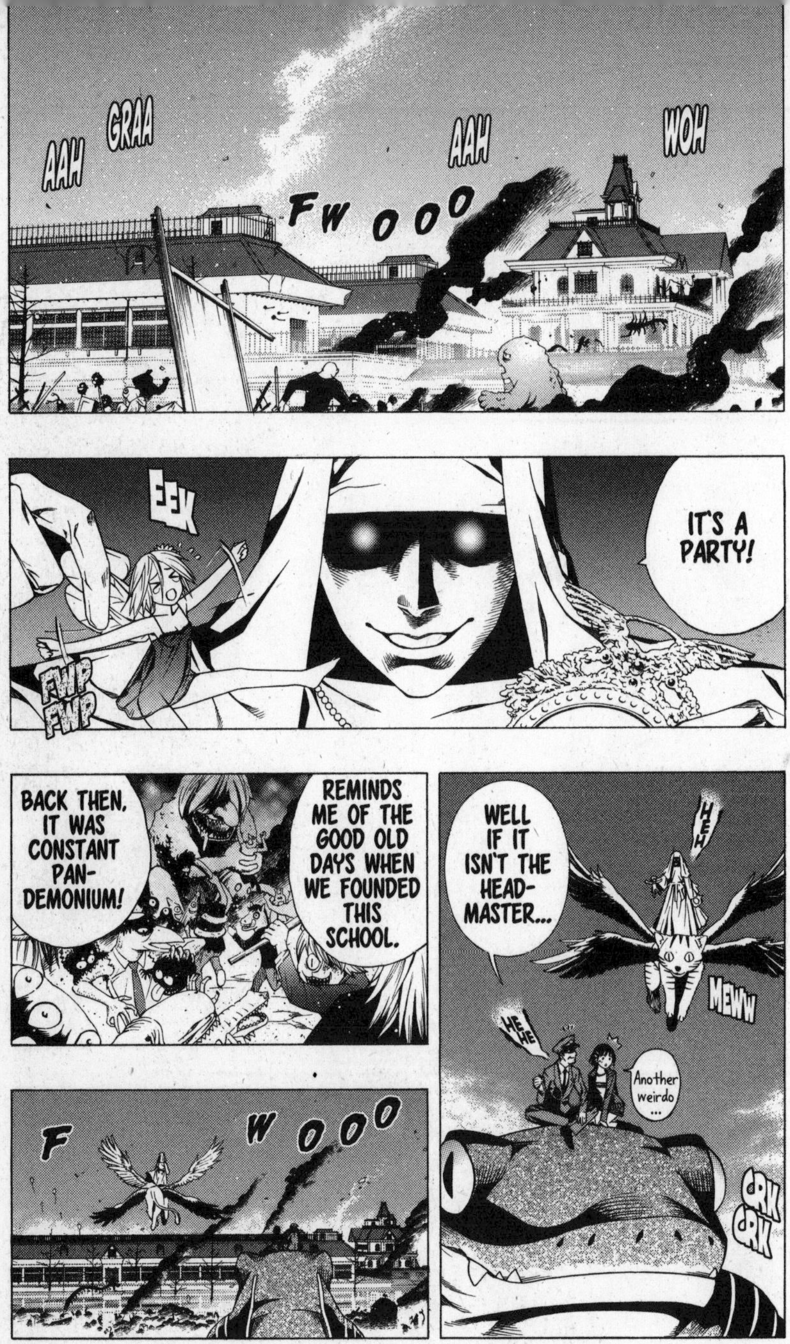
WOH
AAH
FW OOO
GRAA
AAH
IT'S A PARTY!
EEK
FWP FWP
HEH
WELL IF IT ISN'T THE HEAD-MASTER...
MEWW
HEHE
Another weirdo ...
CRK CRK
REMINDS ME OF THE GOOD OLD DAYS WHEN WE FOUNDED THIS SCHOOL.
BACK THEN, IT WAS CONSTANT PAN-DEMONIUM!
F W OOO

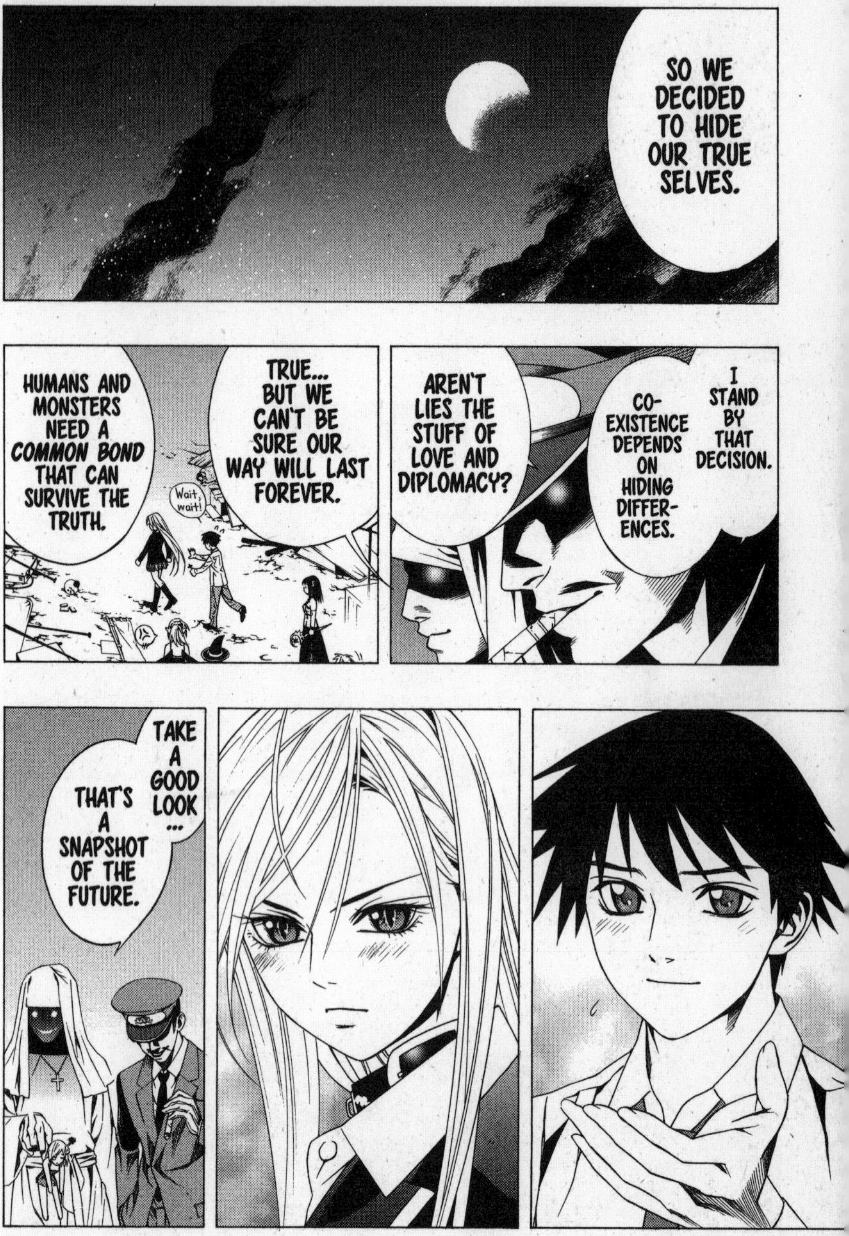
SO WE DECIDED TO HIDE OUR TRUE SELVES.
I STAND BY THAT DECISION.
CO-EXISTENCE DEPENDS ON HIDING DIFFERENCES.
AREN'T LIES THE STUFF OF LOVE AND DIPLOMACY?
TRUE... BUT WE CAN'T BE SURE OUR WAY WILL LAST FOREVER.
HUMANS AND MONSTERS NEED A *COMMON BOND* THAT CAN SURVIVE THE TRUTH.
Wait, wait!
TAKE A GOOD LOOK...
THAT'S A SNAPSHOT OF THE FUTURE.

READ THIS WAY

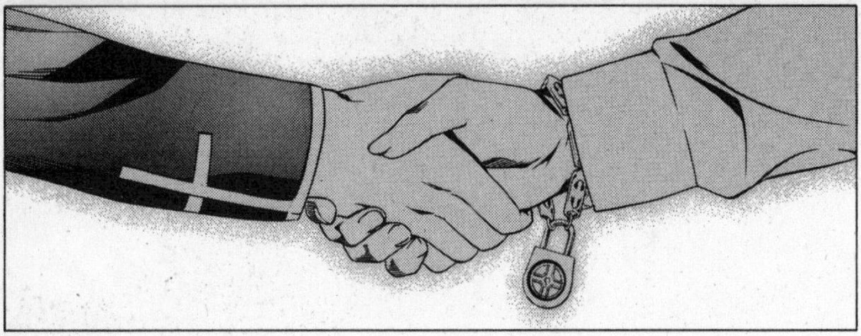

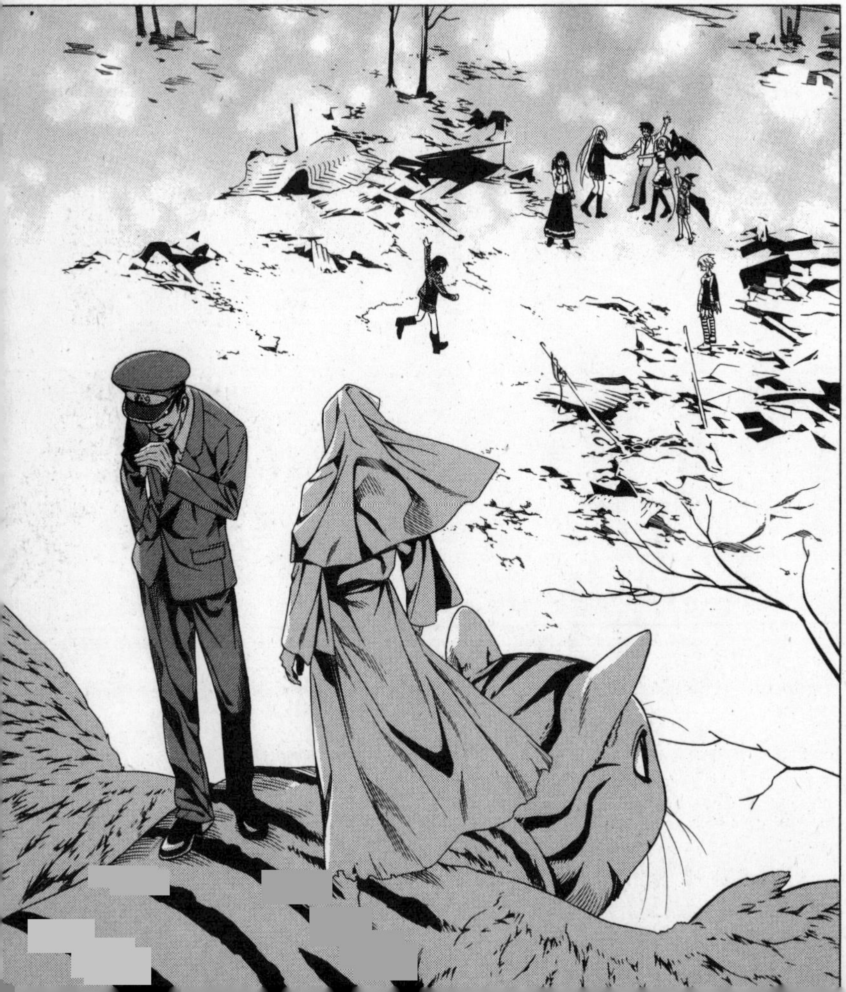

ROSARIO+VAMPIRE

39: The Promise of a Reunion

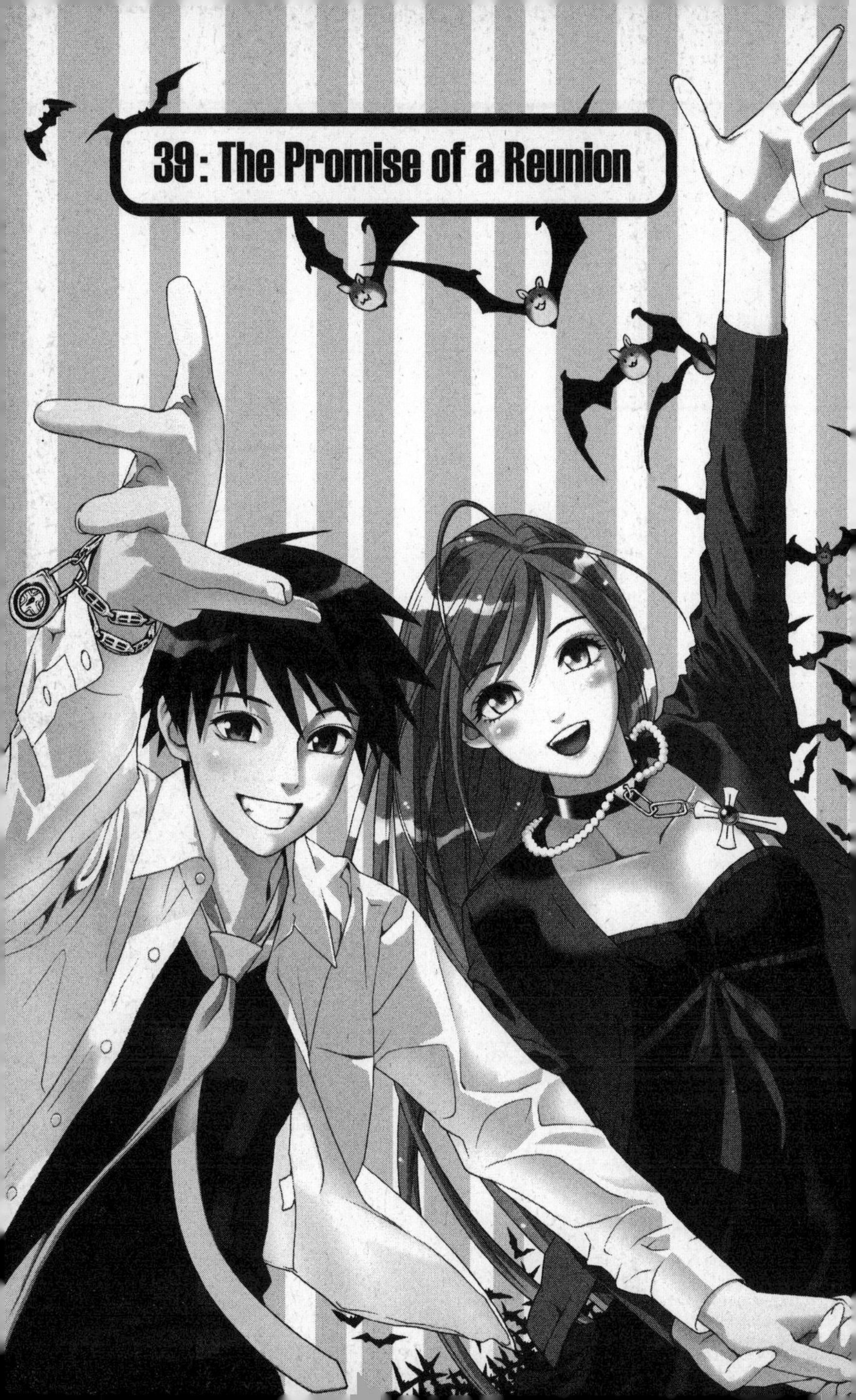

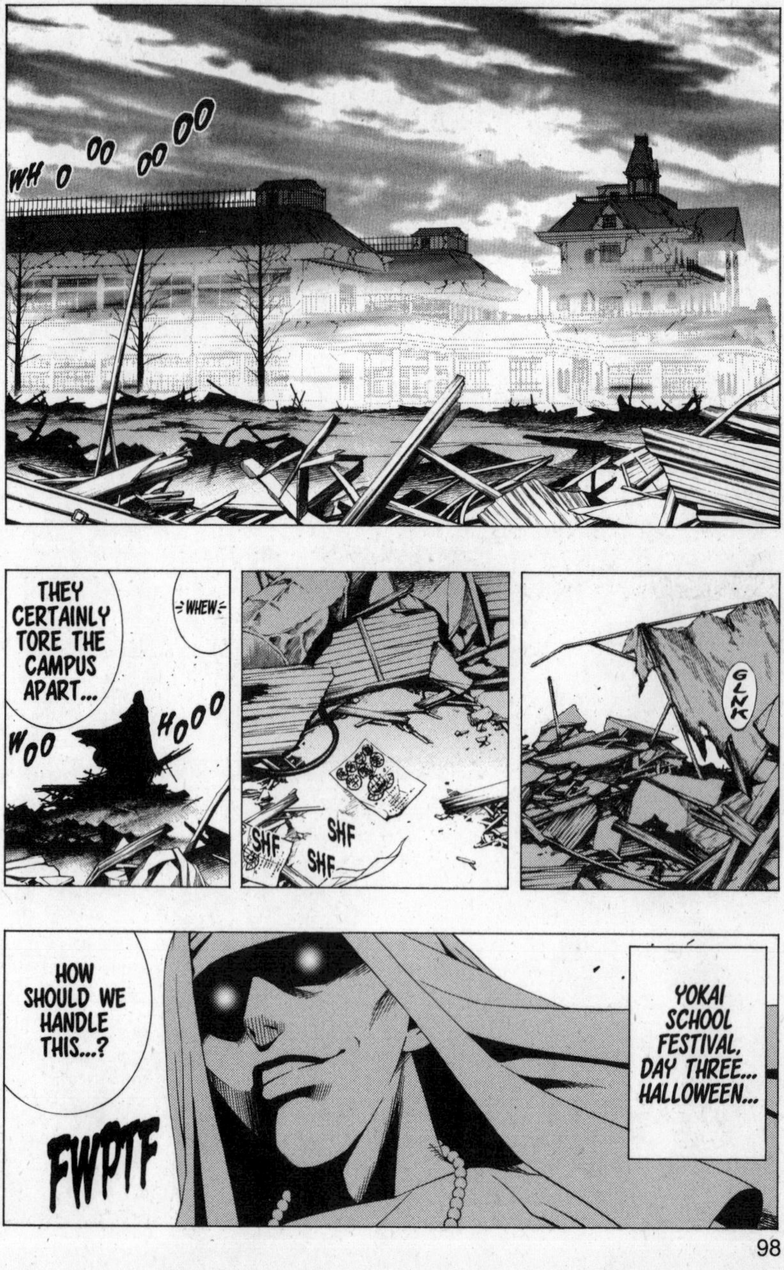
WH O OO OO OO
GLNK
SHF SHF SHF
WHEW
THEY CERTAINLY TORE THE CAMPUS APART...
WOO HOOO
YOKAI SCHOOL FESTIVAL, DAY THREE... HALLOWEEN...
HOW SHOULD WE HANDLE THIS...?
FWPTF

READ THIS WAY

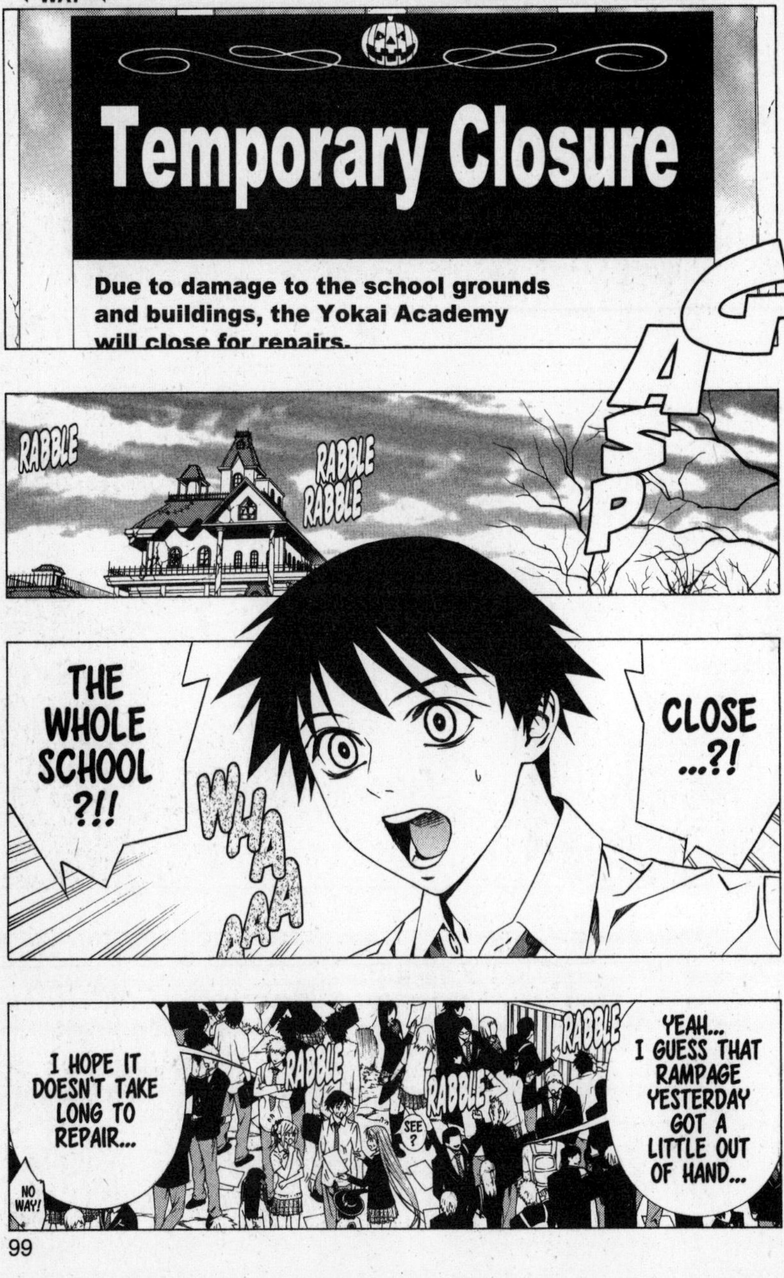
Temporary Closure
Due to damage to the school grounds and buildings, the Yokai Academy will close for repairs.
GASP
RABBLE RABBLE
RABBLE
CLOSE ...?!
WHAAAA
THE WHOLE SCHOOL ?!!
YEAH... I GUESS THAT RAMPAGE YESTERDAY GOT A LITTLE OUT OF HAND...
RABBLE
RABBLE
SEE?
RABBLE
I HOPE IT DOESN'T TAKE LONG TO REPAIR...
NO WAY!

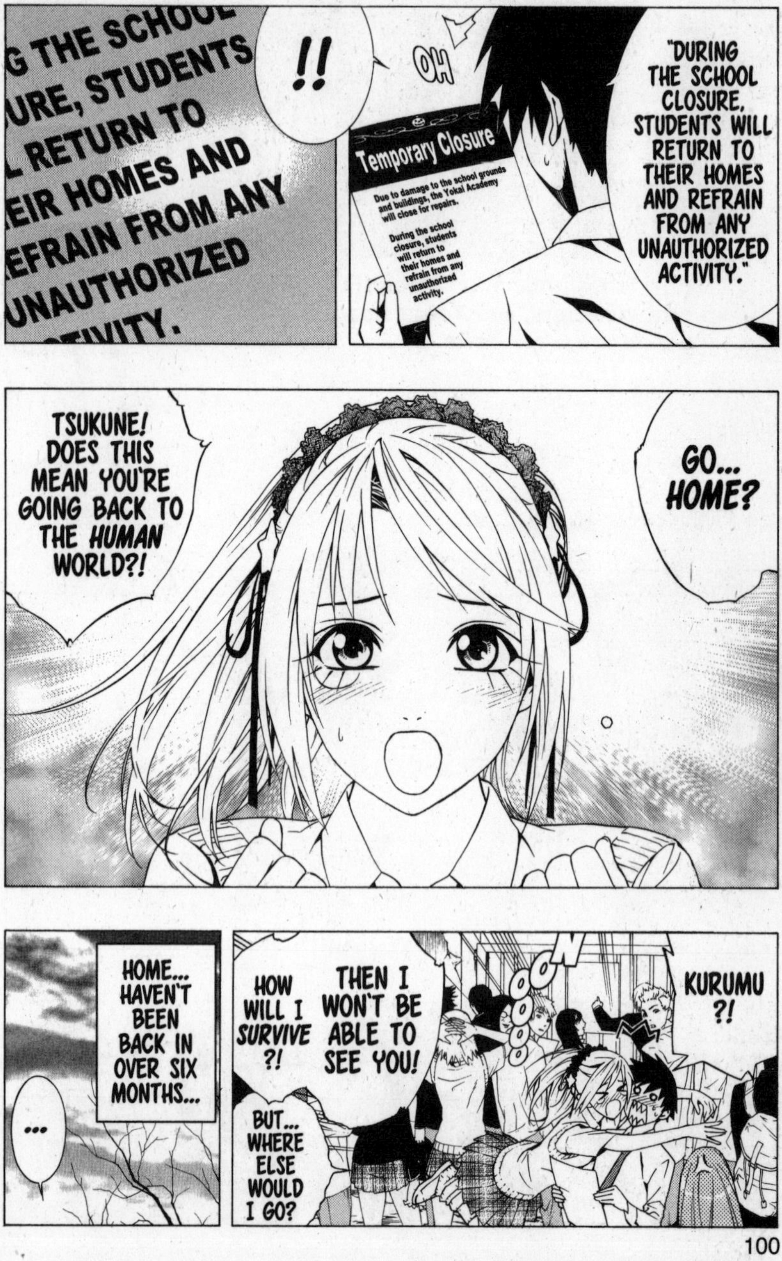

"DURING THE SCHOOL CLOSURE, STUDENTS WILL RETURN TO THEIR HOMES AND REFRAIN FROM ANY UNAUTHORIZED ACTIVITY."
OH
Temporary Closure
Due to damage to the school grounds and buildings, the Yokai Academy will close for repairs.
During the school closure, students will return to their homes and refrain from any unauthorized activity.
!!
G THE SCHOOL
URE, STUDENTS
L RETURN TO
EIR HOMES AND
EFRAIN FROM ANY
UNAUTHORIZED
TIVITY.
GO... HOME?
TSUKUNE! DOES THIS MEAN YOU'RE GOING BACK TO THE HUMAN WORLD?!
KURUMU ?!
NOOOOOOO
THEN I WON'T BE ABLE TO SEE YOU!
HOW WILL I SURVIVE ?!
BUT... WHERE ELSE WOULD I GO?
HOME... HAVEN'T BEEN BACK IN OVER SIX MONTHS...
...

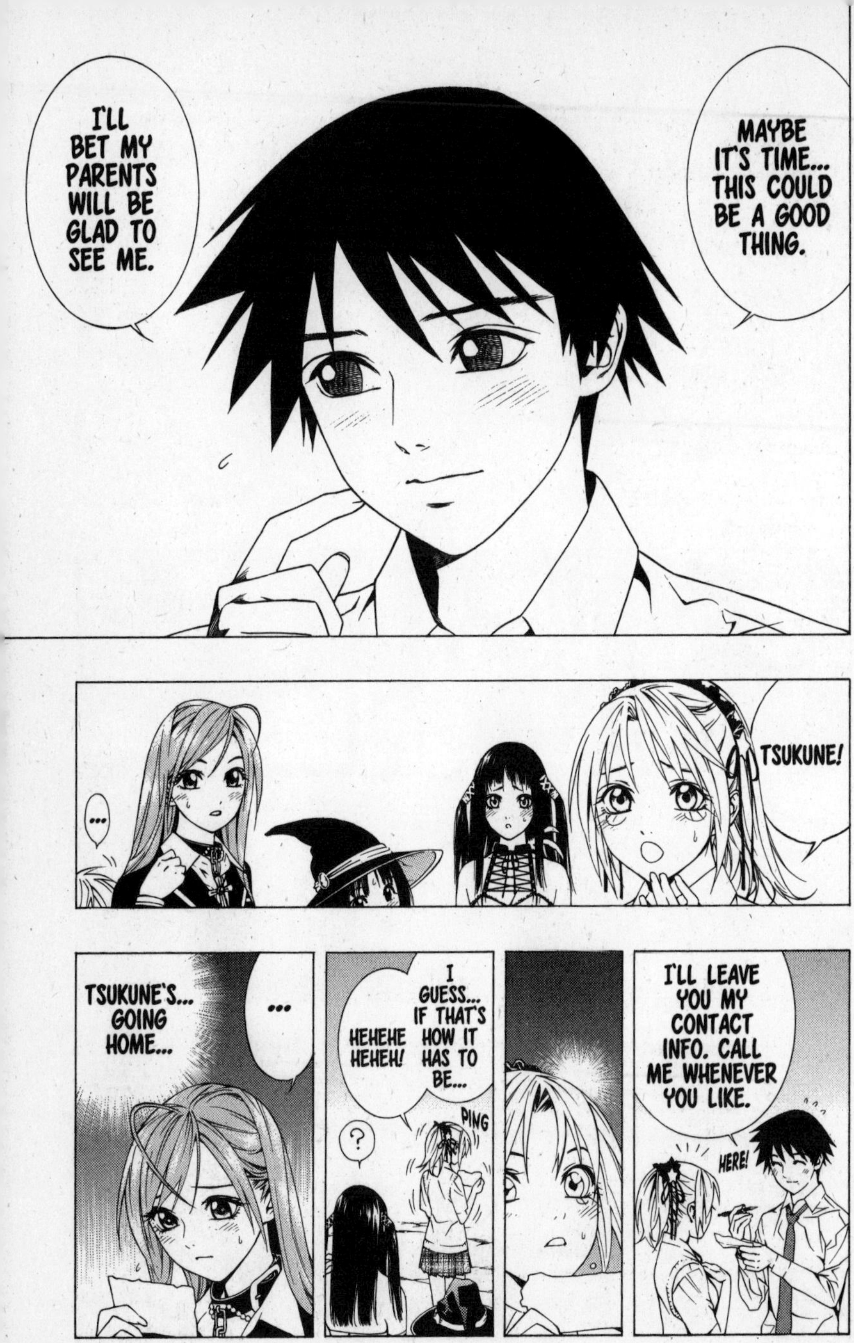
MAYBE IT'S TIME... THIS COULD BE A GOOD THING.
I'LL BET MY PARENTS WILL BE GLAD TO SEE ME.
TSUKUNE!
...
I'LL LEAVE YOU MY CONTACT INFO. CALL ME WHENEVER YOU LIKE.
HERE!
I GUESS... IF THAT'S HOW IT HAS TO BE...
HEHEHE HEHEH!
PING
?
...
TSUKUNE'S... GOING HOME...

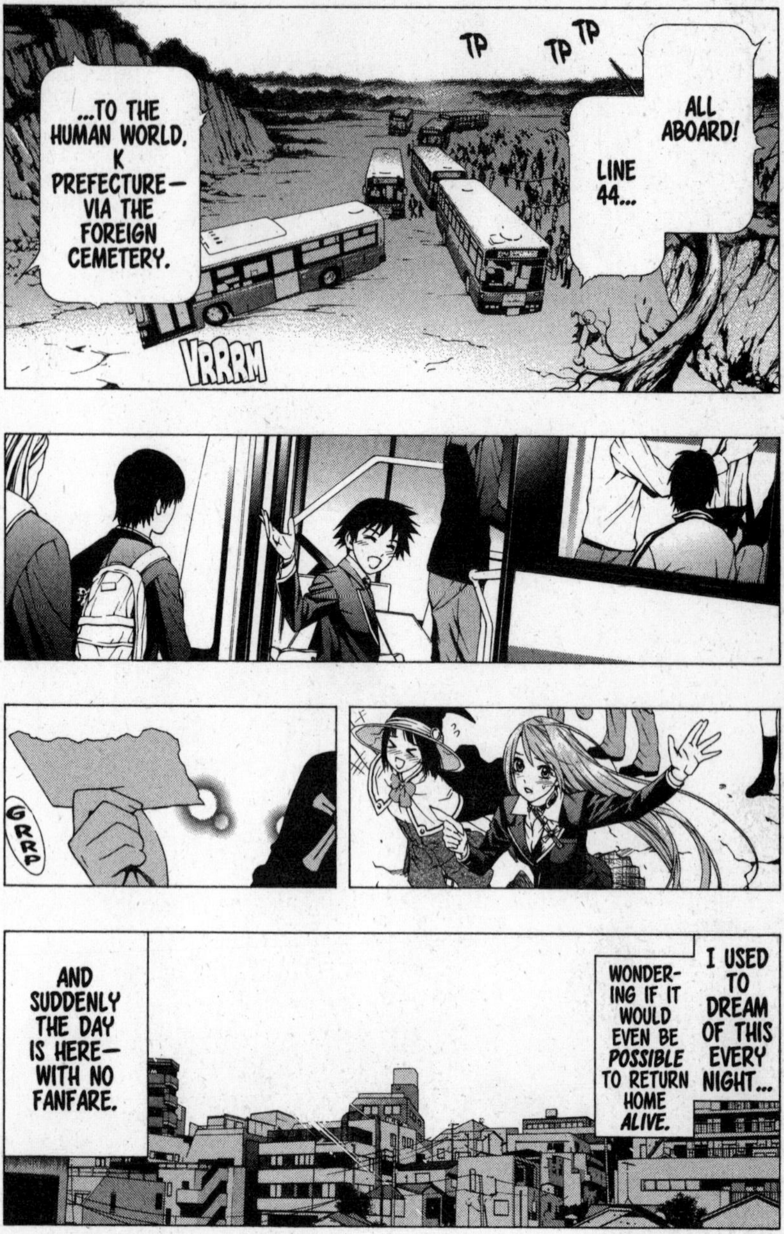
TP TP TP
ALL ABOARD!
LINE 44...
...TO THE HUMAN WORLD, K PREFECTURE—VIA THE FOREIGN CEMETERY.
VRRRM
GRRP
I USED TO DREAM OF THIS EVERY NIGHT...
WONDERING IF IT WOULD EVEN BE *POSSIBLE* TO RETURN HOME *ALIVE*.
AND SUDDENLY THE DAY IS HERE—WITH NO FANFARE.

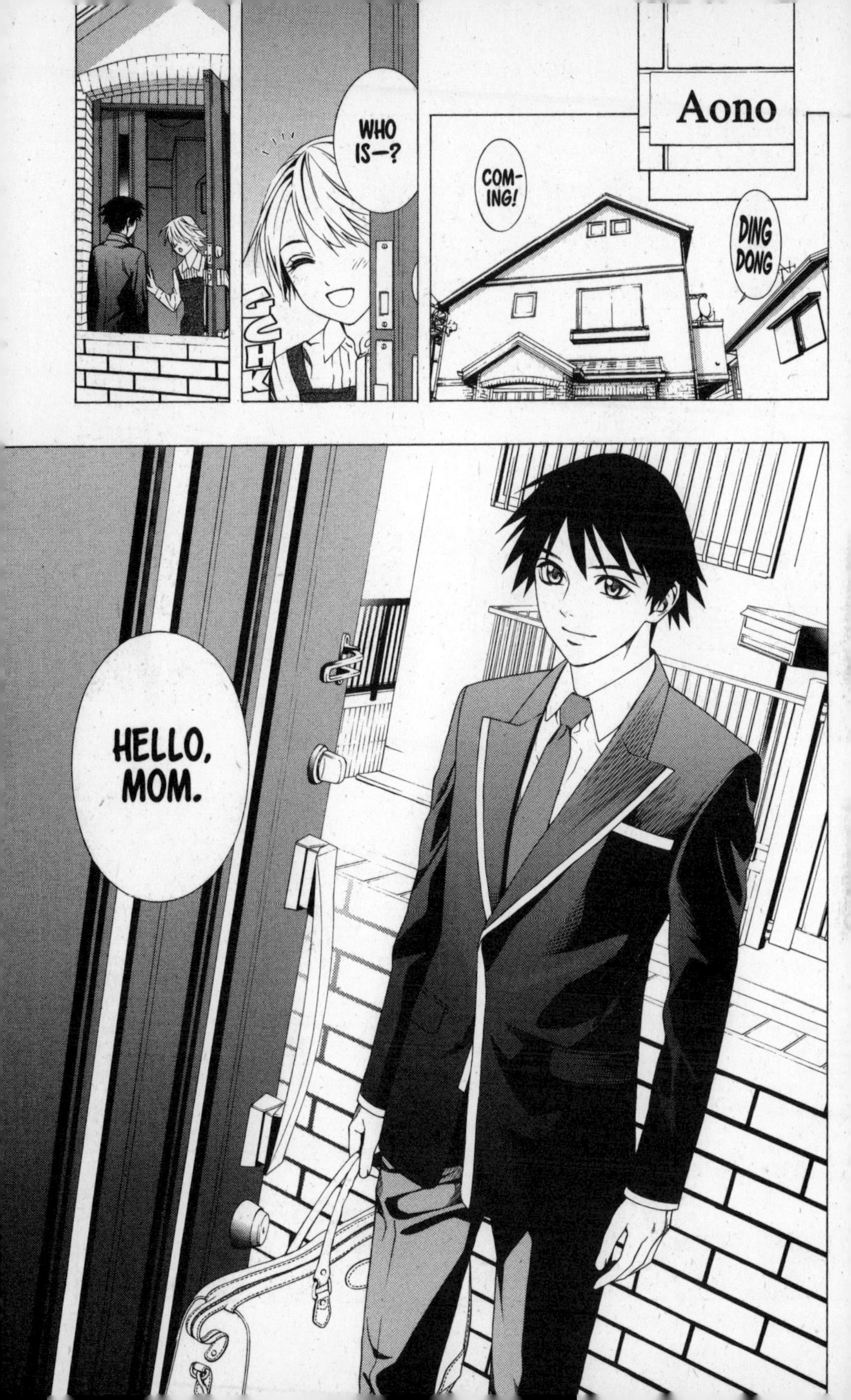

Aono
DING DONG
COM-ING!
WHO IS—?
HELLO, MOM.

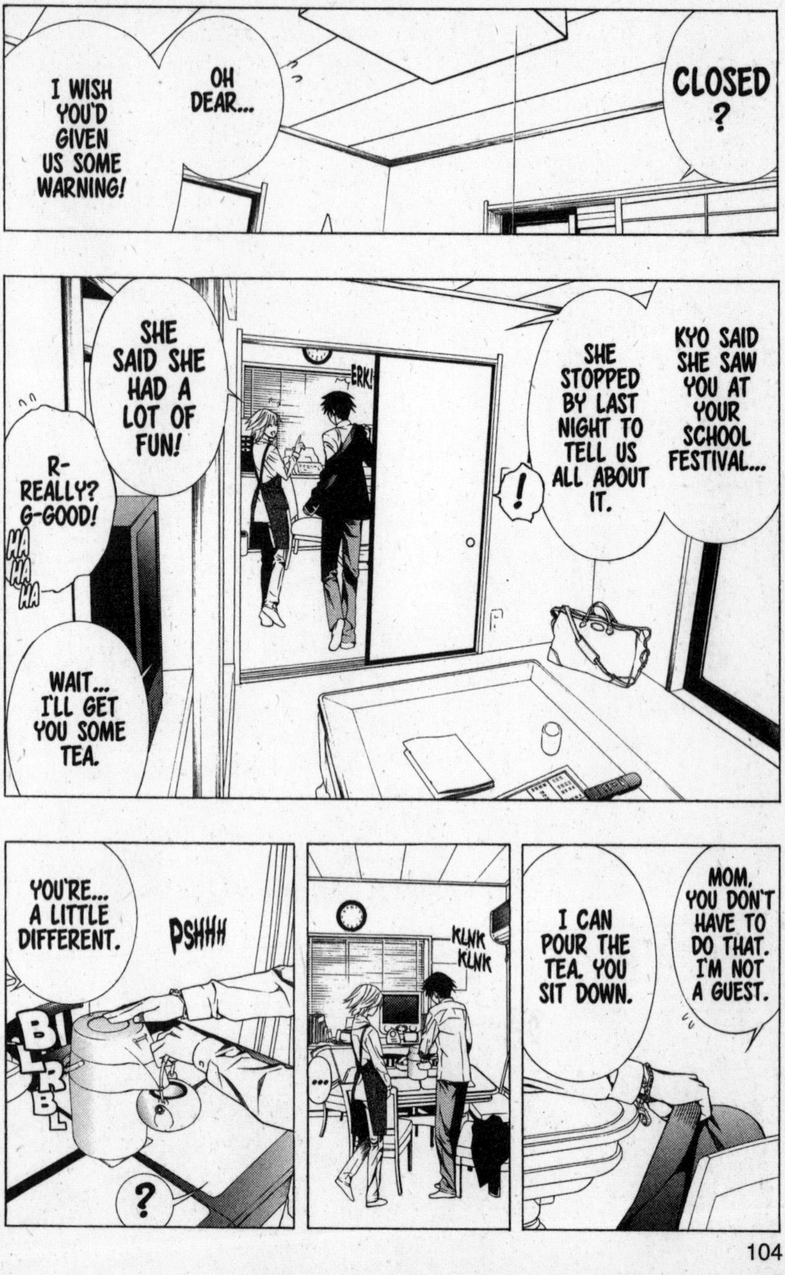
CLOSED?
OH DEAR...
I WISH YOU'D GIVEN US SOME WARNING!
KYO SAID SHE SAW YOU AT YOUR SCHOOL FESTIVAL...
SHE STOPPED BY LAST NIGHT TO TELL US ALL ABOUT IT.
!
ERK!
SHE SAID SHE HAD A LOT OF FUN!
R-REALLY? G-GOOD!
HA HA HA
WAIT... I'LL GET YOU SOME TEA.
MOM, YOU DON'T HAVE TO DO THAT. I'M NOT A GUEST.
I CAN POUR THE TEA. YOU SIT DOWN.
KLNK KLNK
...
PSHHH
YOU'RE... A LITTLE DIFFERENT.
BLRBL
?

READ THIS WAY

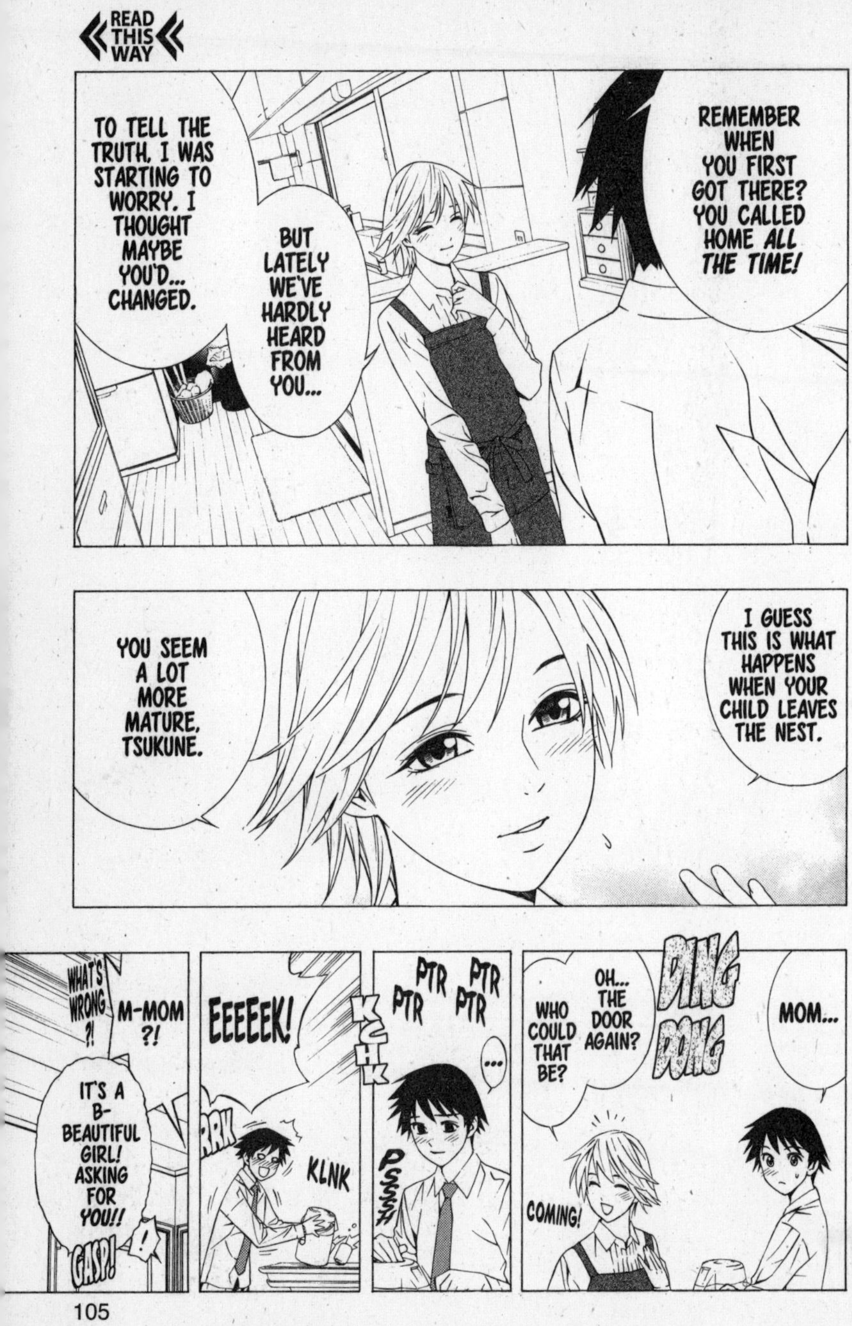
REMEMBER WHEN YOU FIRST GOT THERE? YOU CALLED HOME *ALL THE TIME!*
BUT LATELY WE'VE HARDLY HEARD FROM YOU...
TO TELL THE TRUTH, I WAS STARTING TO WORRY. I THOUGHT MAYBE YOU'D... CHANGED.
I GUESS THIS IS WHAT HAPPENS WHEN YOUR CHILD LEAVES THE NEST.
YOU SEEM A LOT MORE MATURE, TSUKUNE.
MOM...
DING DONG
OH... THE DOOR AGAIN?
WHO COULD THAT BE?
COMING!
PTR PTR PTR PTR
...
KCHK
PSSSH
EEEEEK!
RRK
KLNK
M-MOM ?!
WHAT'S WRONG ?!
IT'S A B-BEAUTIFUL GIRL! ASKING FOR *YOU!!*
!
GASP!

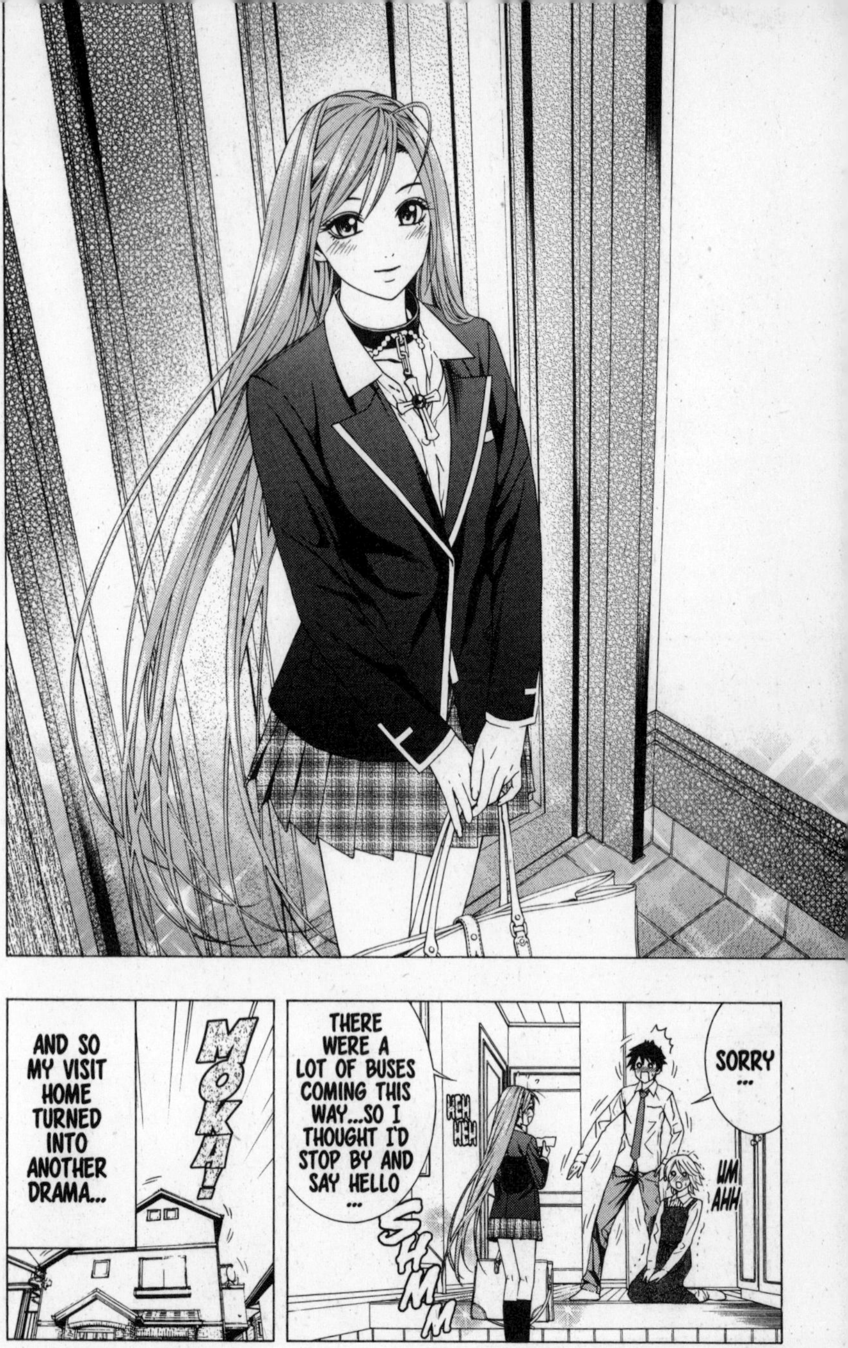
SORRY ...
UM AHH
HEH HEH
THERE WERE A LOT OF BUSES COMING THIS WAY...SO I THOUGHT I'D STOP BY AND SAY HELLO ...
SHMM
MOKA!
AND SO MY VISIT HOME TURNED INTO ANOTHER DRAMA...

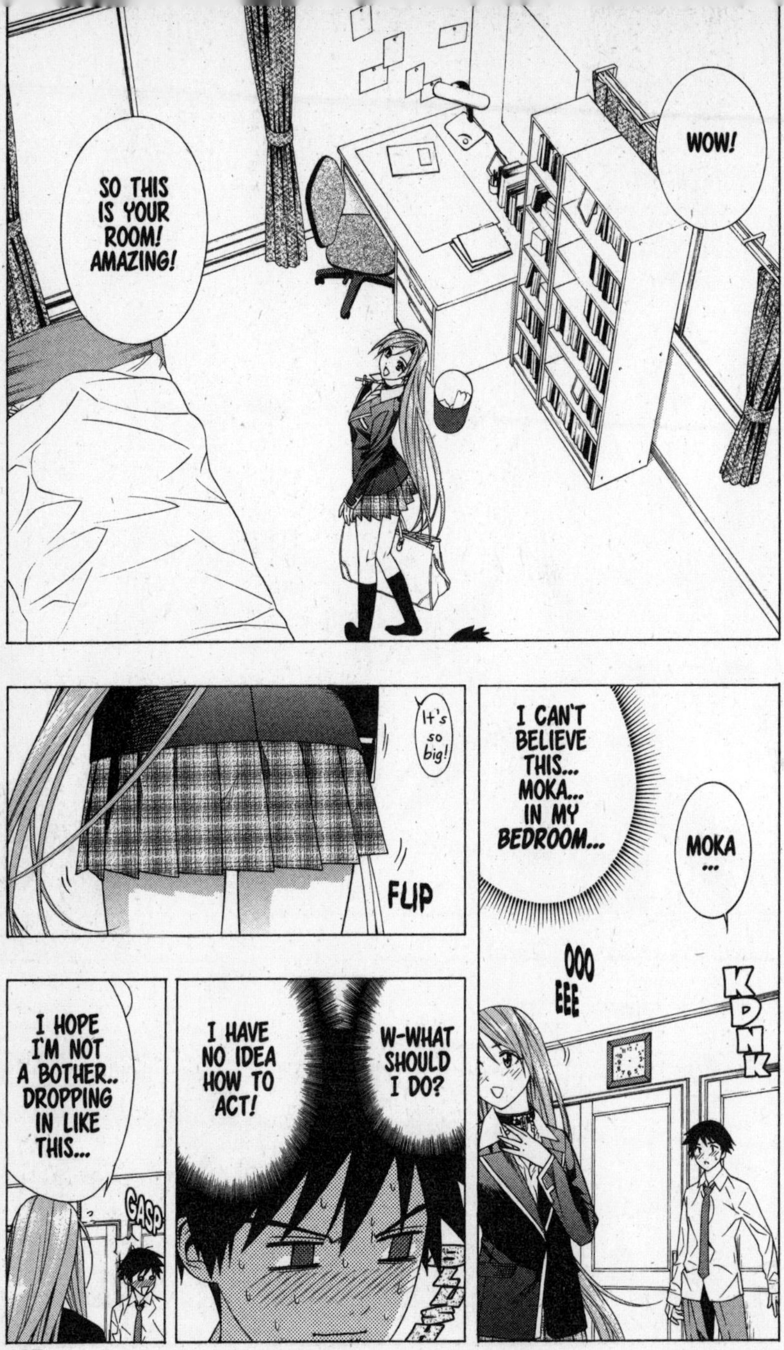
WOW!
SO THIS IS YOUR ROOM! AMAZING!
MOKA...
I CAN'T BELIEVE THIS... MOKA... IN MY BEDROOM...
KDNK
OOO EEE
It's so big!
FLIP
W-WHAT SHOULD I DO?
I HAVE NO IDEA HOW TO ACT!
I HOPE I'M NOT A BOTHER.. DROPPING IN LIKE THIS...
GASP

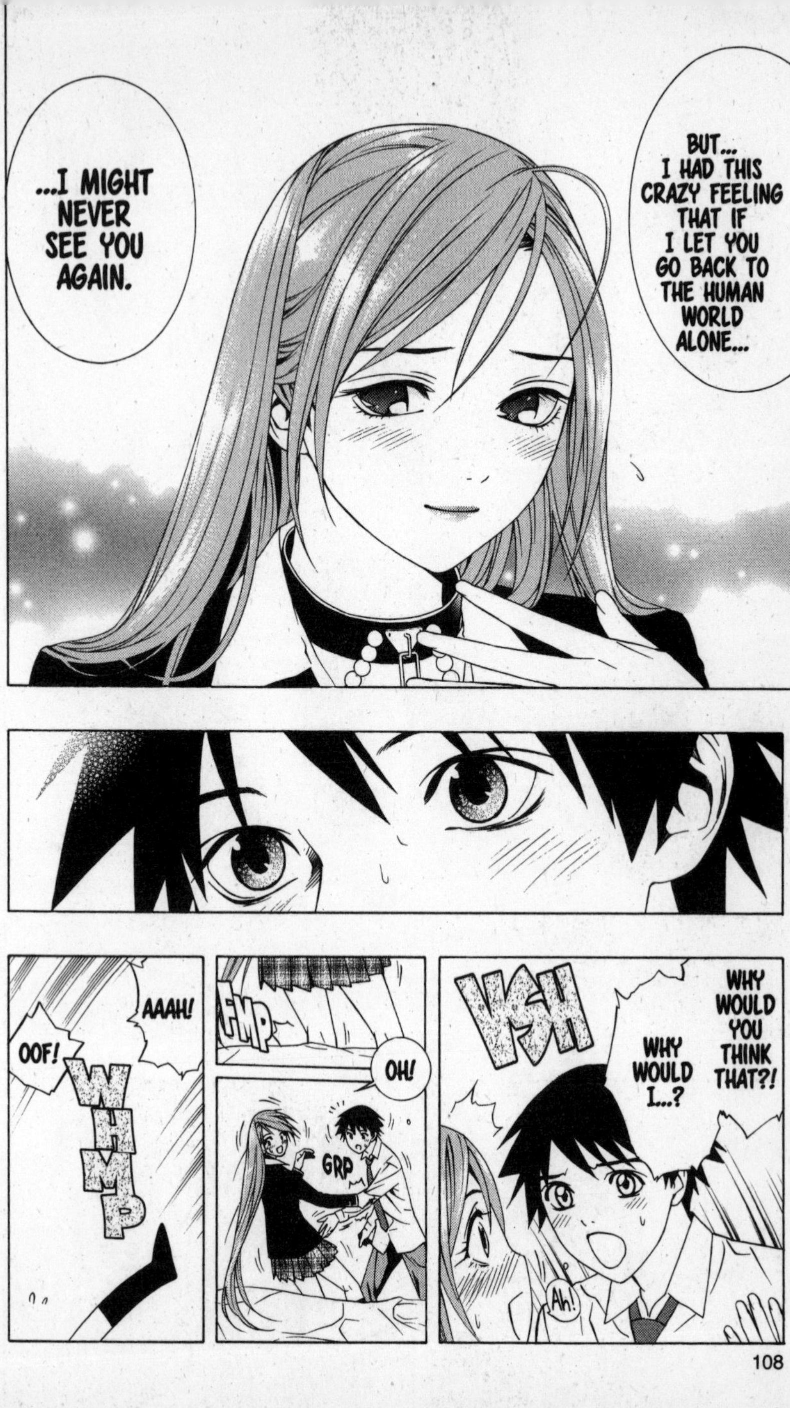
BUT... I HAD THIS CRAZY FEELING THAT IF I LET YOU GO BACK TO THE HUMAN WORLD ALONE...
...I MIGHT NEVER SEE YOU AGAIN.
VSH
WHY WOULD YOU THINK THAT?!
WHY WOULD I...?
Ah!
FMP
OH!
GRP
AAAH!
OOF!
WHMP

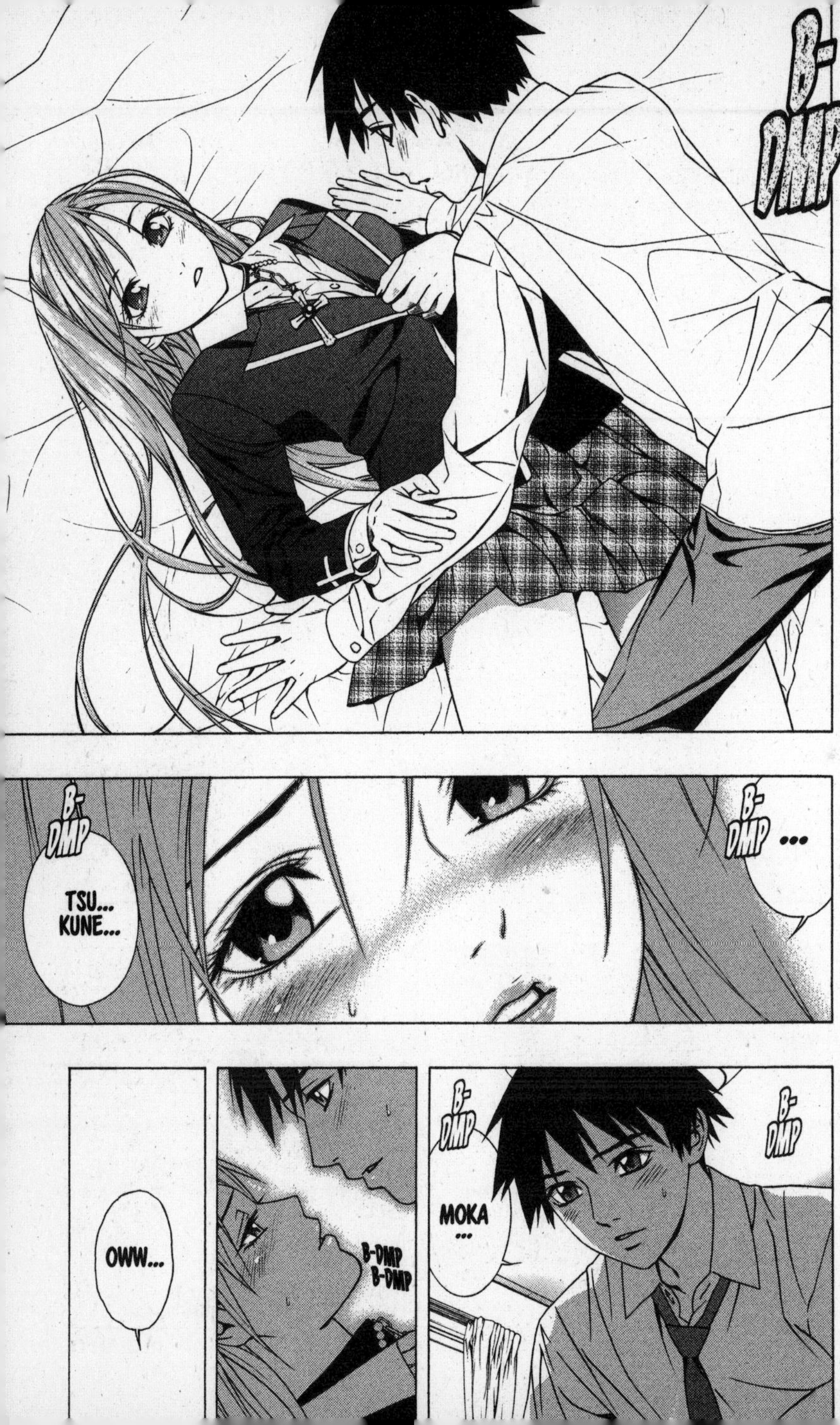
B-DMP
B-DMP ...
B-DMP
TSU... KUNE...
B-DMP
B-DMP
MOKA ...
B-DMP B-DMP
OWW...

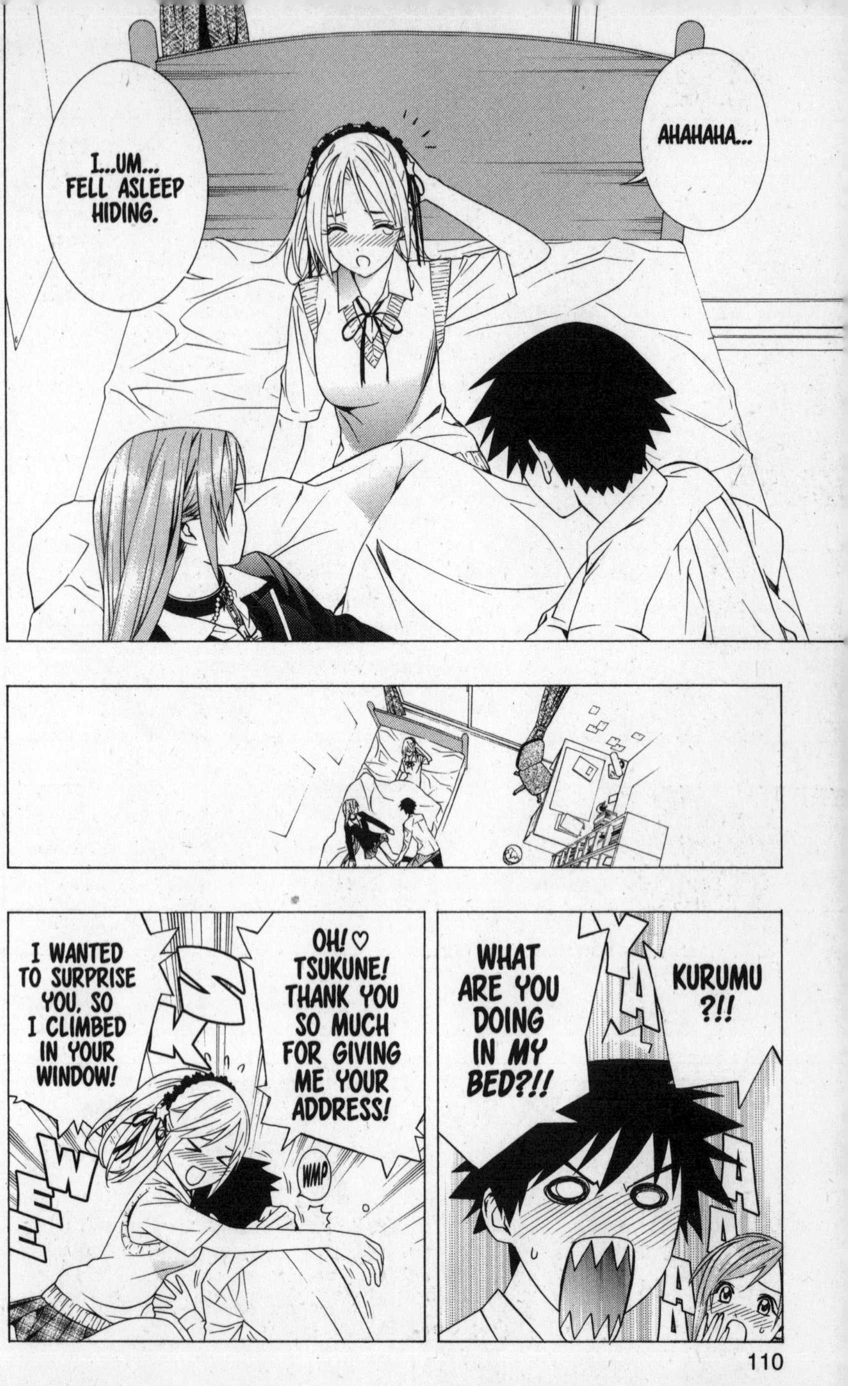
AHAHAHA...
I...UM... FELL ASLEEP HIDING.
KURUMU?!!
WHAT ARE YOU DOING IN MY BED?!!
OH! ♡ TSUKUNE! THANK YOU SO MUCH FOR GIVING ME YOUR ADDRESS!
I WANTED TO SURPRISE YOU, SO I CLIMBED IN YOUR WINDOW!
WMP

READ THIS WAY

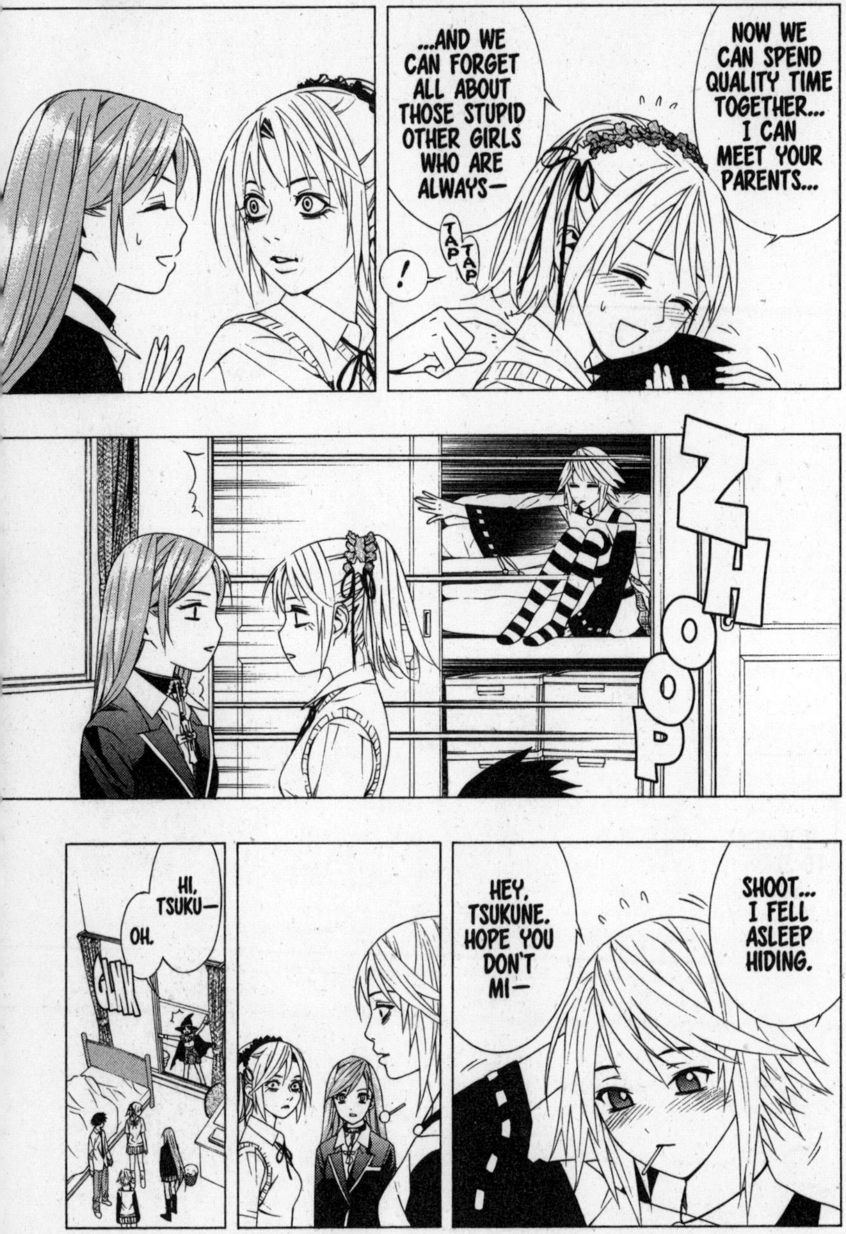
NOW WE CAN SPEND QUALITY TIME TOGETHER... I CAN MEET YOUR PARENTS...
...AND WE CAN FORGET ALL ABOUT THOSE STUPID OTHER GIRLS WHO ARE ALWAYS—
TAP TAP
!
ZHOOOP
SHOOT... I FELL ASLEEP HIDING.
HEY, TSUKUNE. HOPE YOU DON'T MI—
HI, TSUKU—
OH.

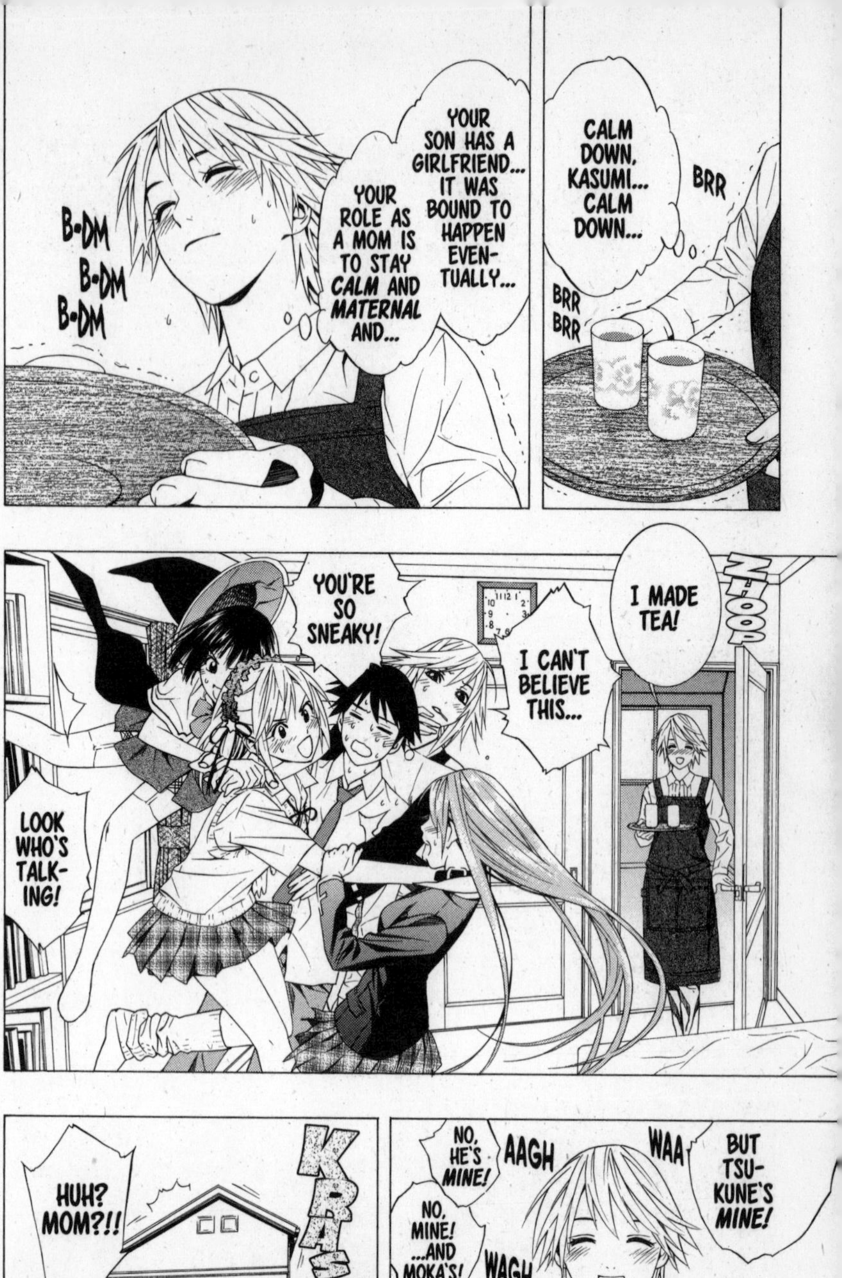
CALM DOWN, KASUMI... CALM DOWN...
BRR
BRR BRR
YOUR SON HAS A GIRLFRIEND... IT WAS BOUND TO HAPPEN EVEN-TUALLY...
YOUR ROLE AS A MOM IS TO STAY CALM AND MATERNAL AND...
B-DM B-DM B-DM
ZHOOP
I MADE TEA!
I CAN'T BELIEVE THIS...
YOU'RE SO SNEAKY!
LOOK WHO'S TALK-ING!
BUT TSU-KUNE'S MINE!
WAA
AAGH
NO, HE'S MINE!
NO, MINE! ...AND MOKA'S!
WAGH
...
KRASH
HUH? MOM?!!

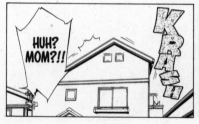

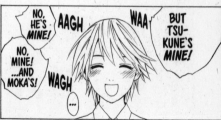

READ THIS WAY

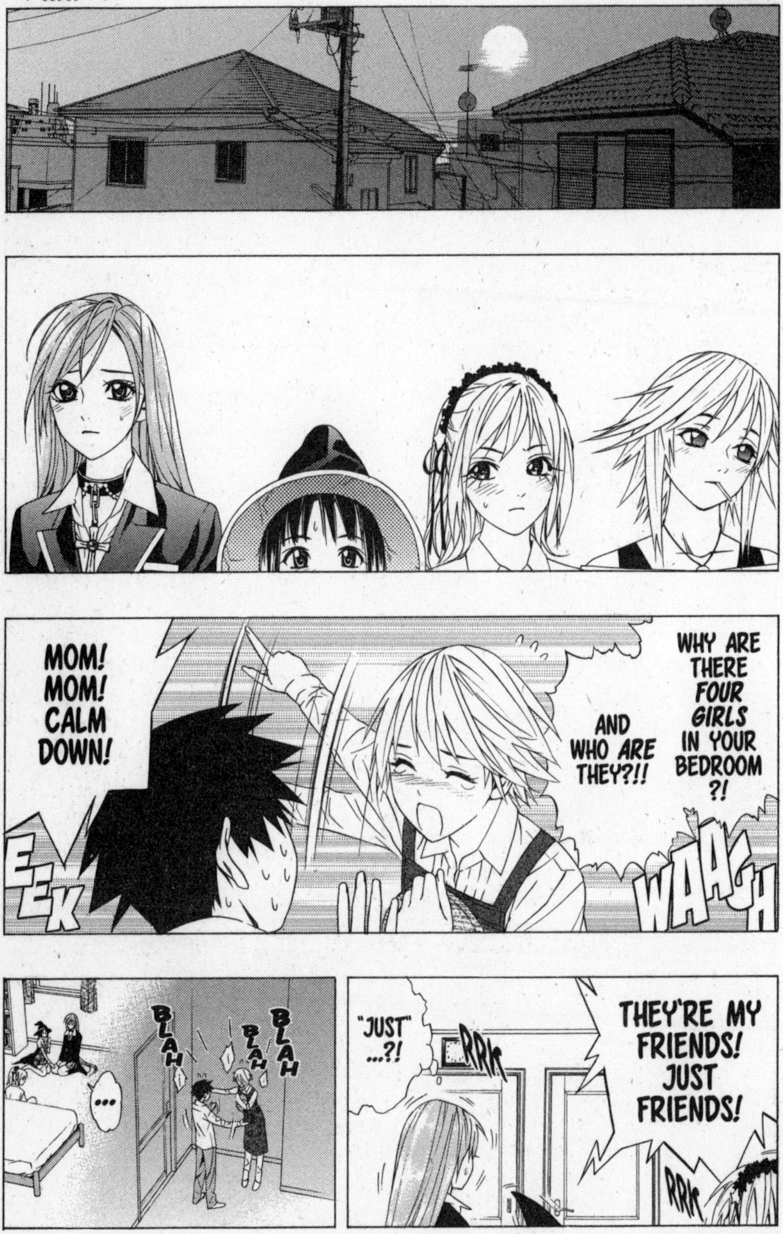

WHY ARE THERE FOUR GIRLS IN YOUR BEDROOM ?!
AND WHO ARE THEY?!!
WAAGH
MOM! MOM! CALM DOWN!
EEEK
THEY'RE MY FRIENDS! JUST FRIENDS!
"JUST" ...?!
RRK
RRK
BLAH
BLAH
BLAH
...

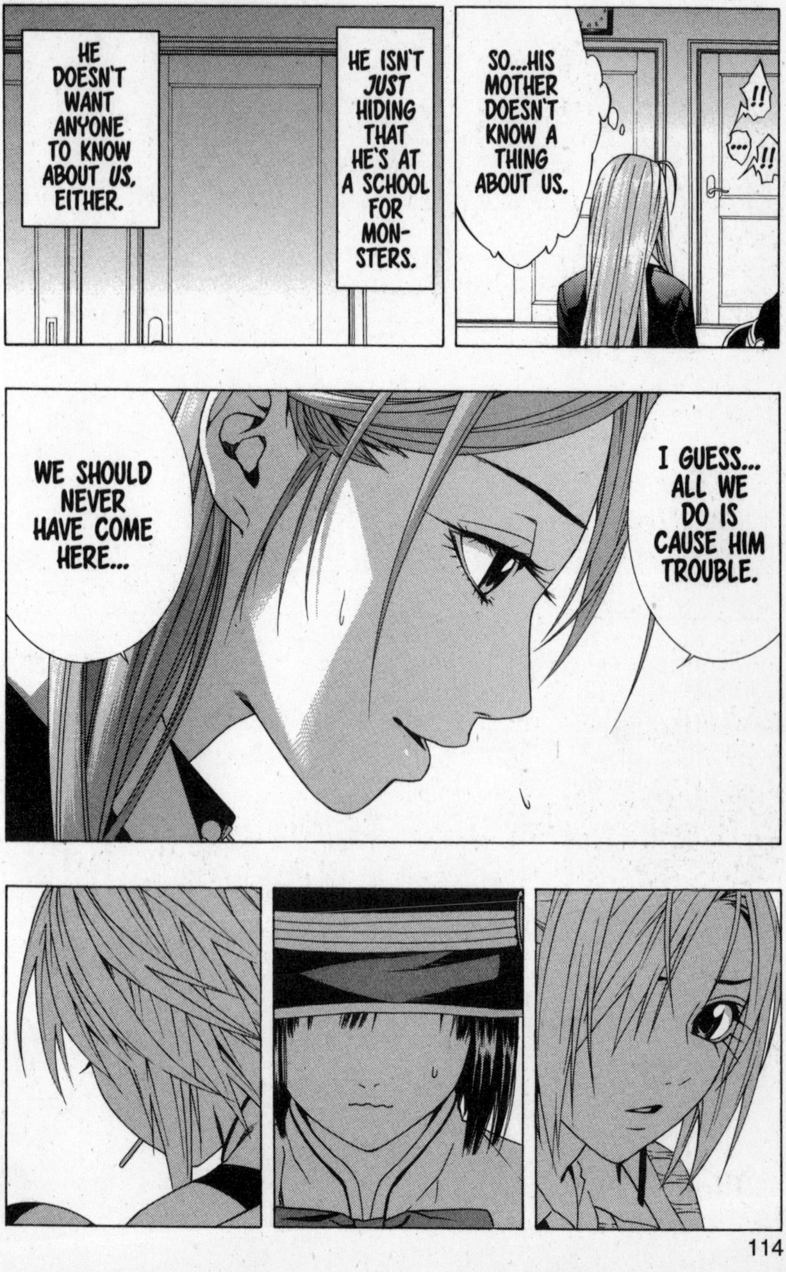
SO...HIS MOTHER DOESN'T KNOW A THING ABOUT US.
!!
...
!!
HE ISN'T *JUST* HIDING THAT HE'S AT A SCHOOL FOR MON-STERS.
HE DOESN'T WANT ANYONE TO KNOW ABOUT *US*, EITHER.
I GUESS... ALL WE DO IS CAUSE HIM TROUBLE.
WE SHOULD NEVER HAVE COME HERE...

READ THIS WAY

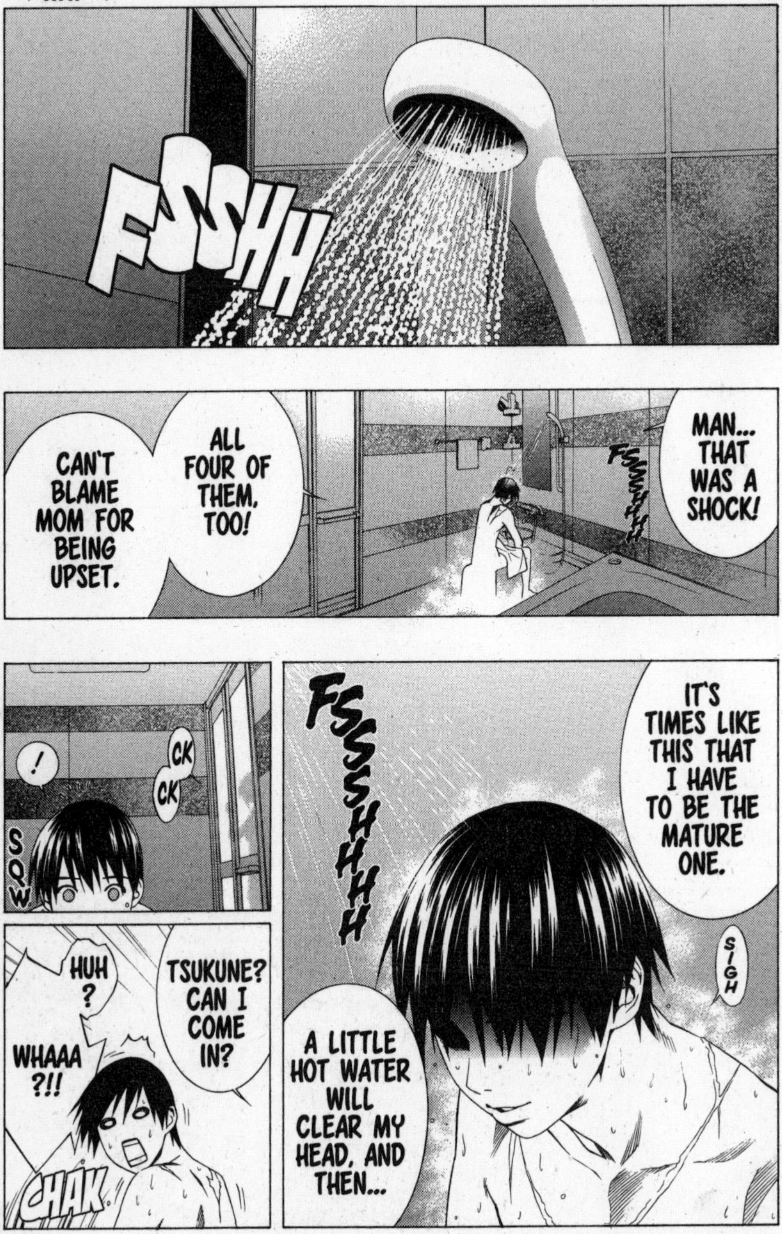

FSSHH
MAN... THAT WAS A SHOCK!
FSSSHHH
ALL FOUR OF THEM, TOO!
CAN'T BLAME MOM FOR BEING UPSET.
IT'S TIMES LIKE THIS THAT I HAVE TO BE THE MATURE ONE.
SIGH
FSSSHHHHH
A LITTLE HOT WATER WILL CLEAR MY HEAD, AND THEN...
CK
CK
!
SQW
TSUKUNE? CAN I COME IN?
HUH?
WHAAA?!!
CHAK

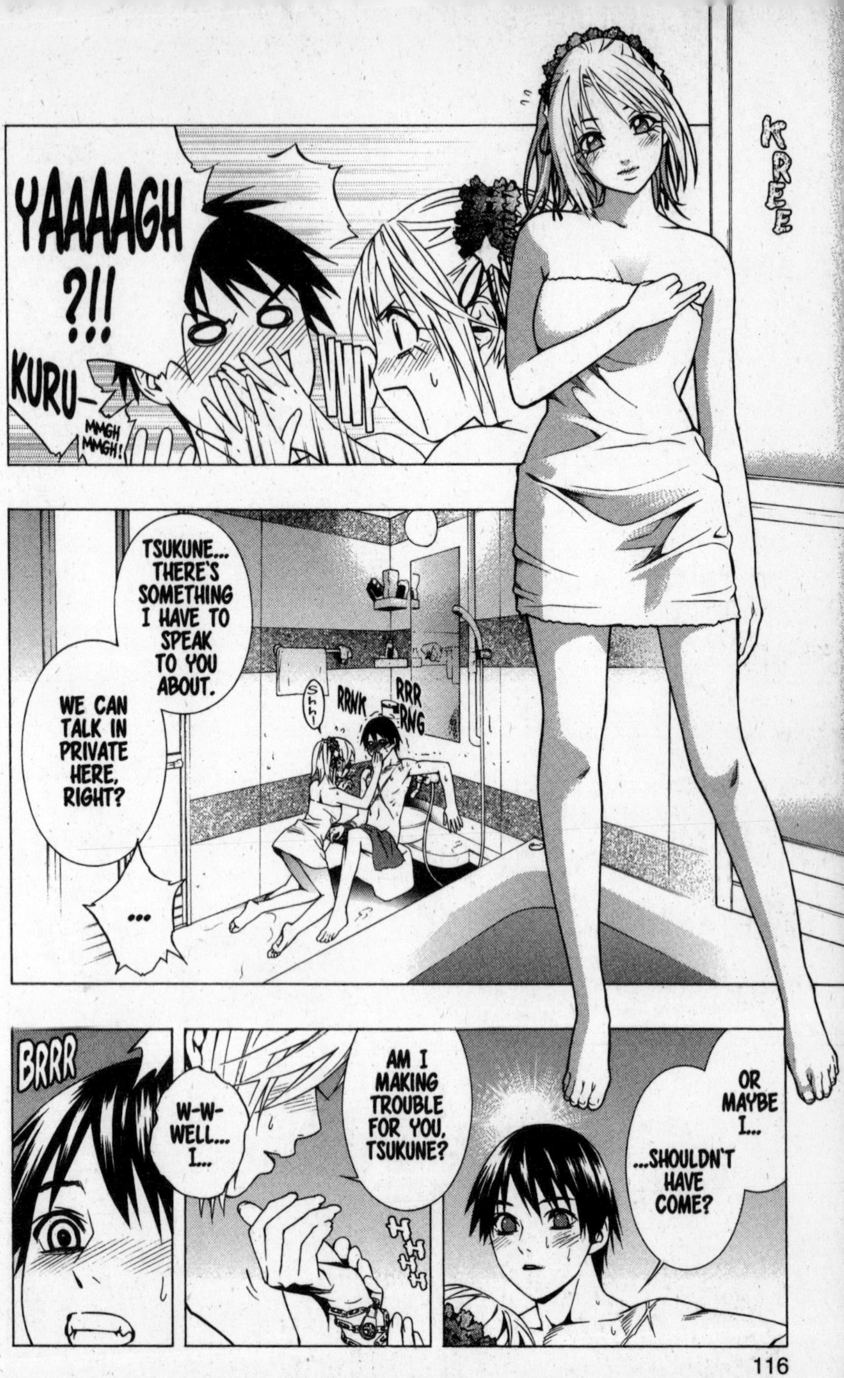
KREE
YAAAAGH ?!!
KURU–
MMGH MMGH!
RRR RNG
RRNK
Shh!
TSUKUNE... THERE'S SOMETHING I HAVE TO SPEAK TO YOU ABOUT.
WE CAN TALK IN PRIVATE HERE, RIGHT?
...
OR MAYBE I...
...SHOULDN'T HAVE COME?
AM I MAKING TROUBLE FOR YOU, TSUKUNE?
W-W-WELL... I...
BRRR

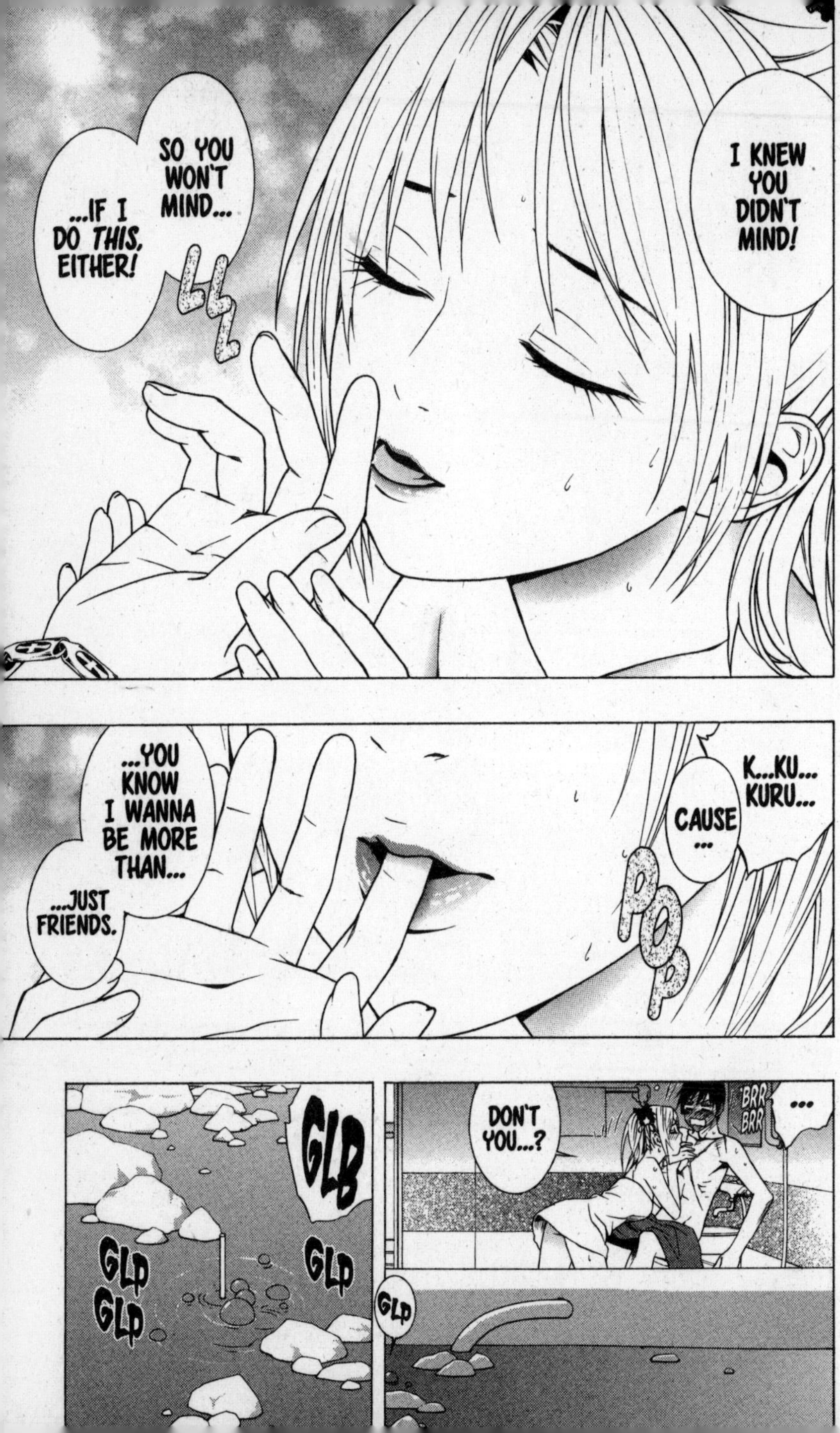
I KNEW YOU DIDN'T MIND!
SO YOU WON'T MIND...
...IF I DO *THIS*, EITHER!
LL
K...KU... KURU...
CAUSE ...
...YOU KNOW I WANNA BE MORE THAN...
...JUST FRIENDS.
POP
...
BRR BRR
DON'T YOU...?
GLP
GLB
GLP
GLP GLP

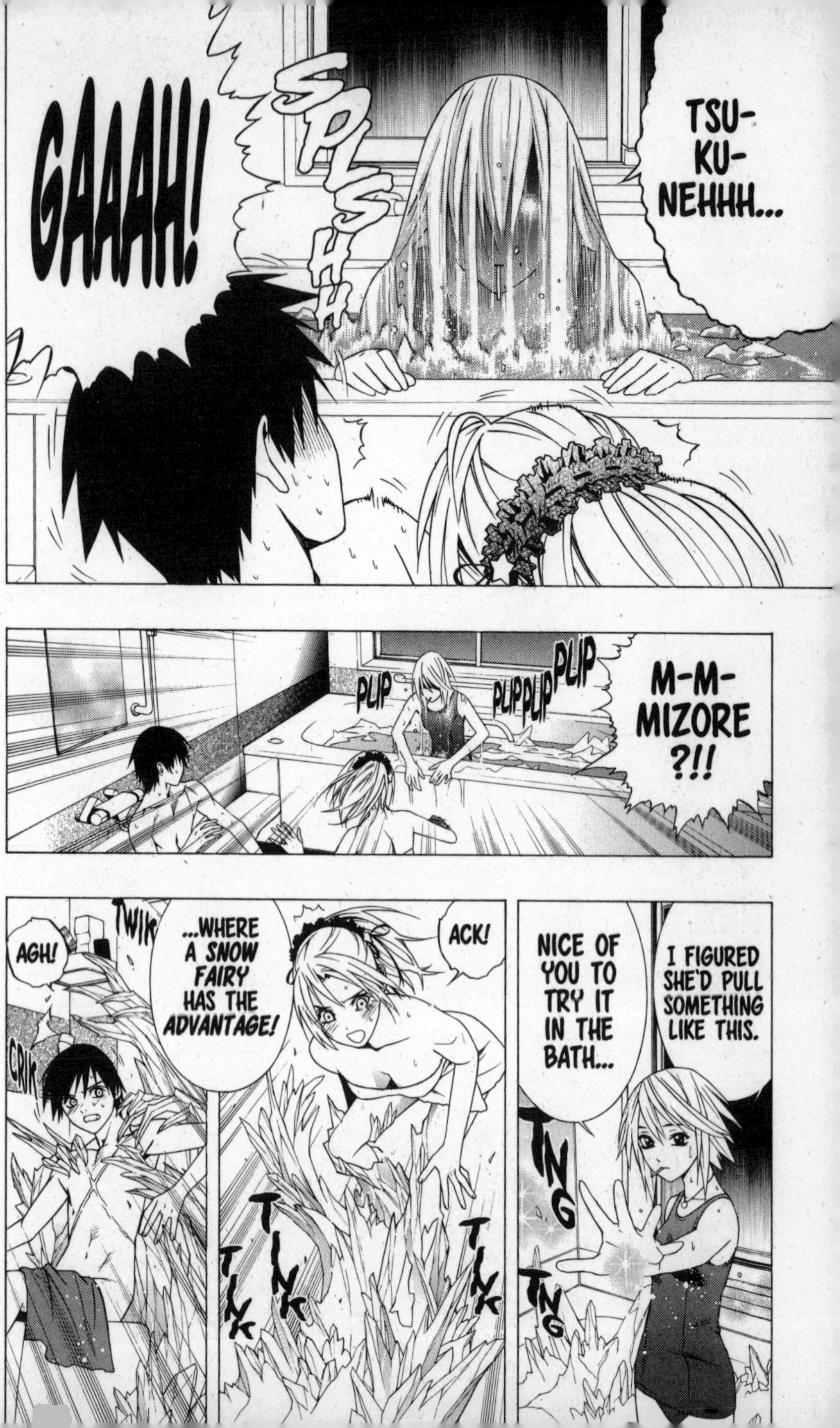
TSU-KU-NEHHH...
SPLSHH
GAAAH!
M-M-MIZORE?!!
PLIP
PLIPPLIP
PLIP
I FIGURED SHE'D PULL SOMETHING LIKE THIS.
NICE OF YOU TO TRY IT IN THE BATH...
TNG
TNG
ACK!
...WHERE A SNOW FAIRY HAS THE ADVANTAGE!
TINK
TINK
TINK
TWIK
AGH!
CRIK

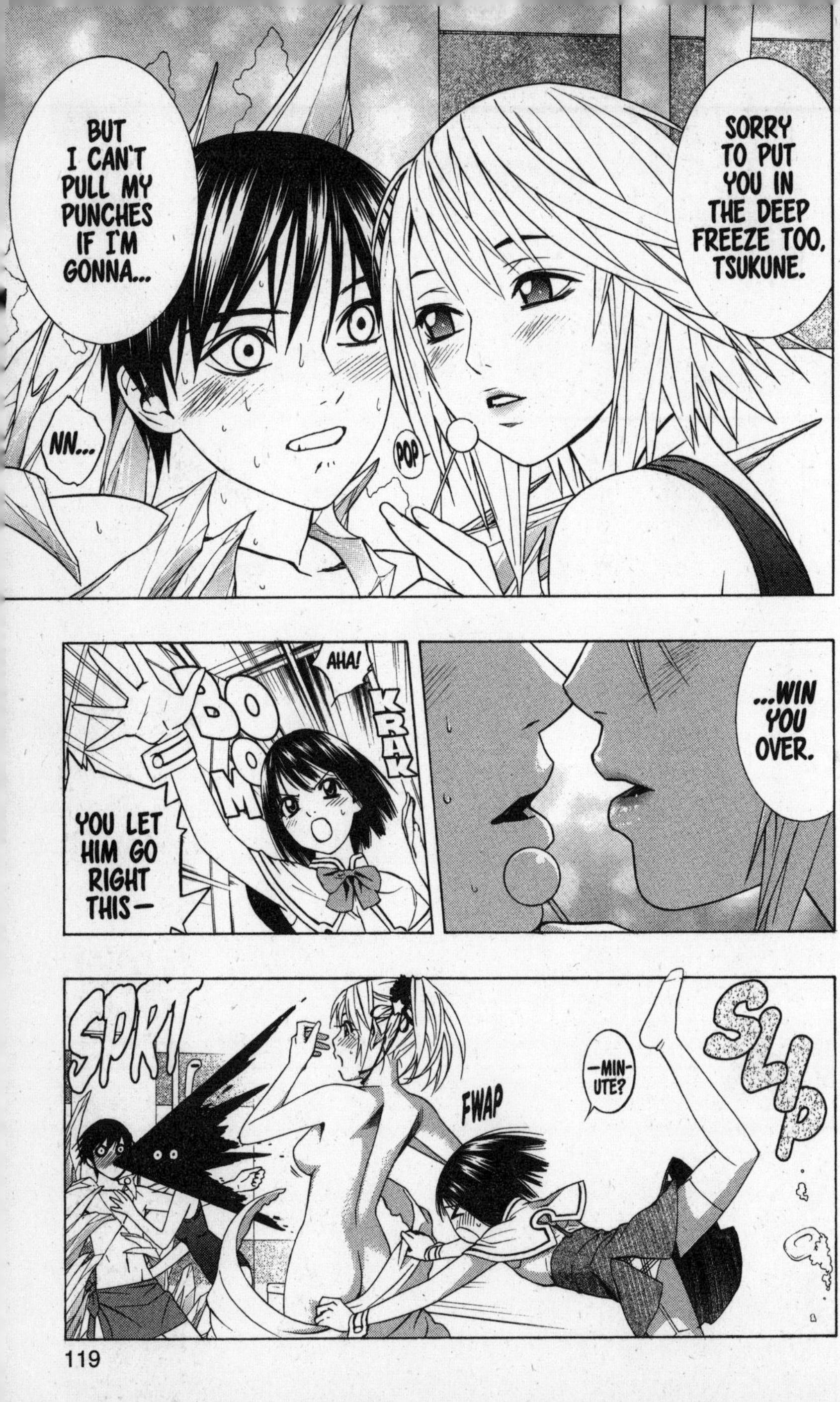
SORRY TO PUT YOU IN THE DEEP FREEZE TOO, TSUKUNE.
POP
BUT I CAN'T PULL MY PUNCHES IF I'M GONNA...
NN...
...WIN YOU OVER.
AHA!
KRAK
BOOM
YOU LET HIM GO RIGHT THIS—
SLIP
—MIN-UTE?
FWAP
SPRT

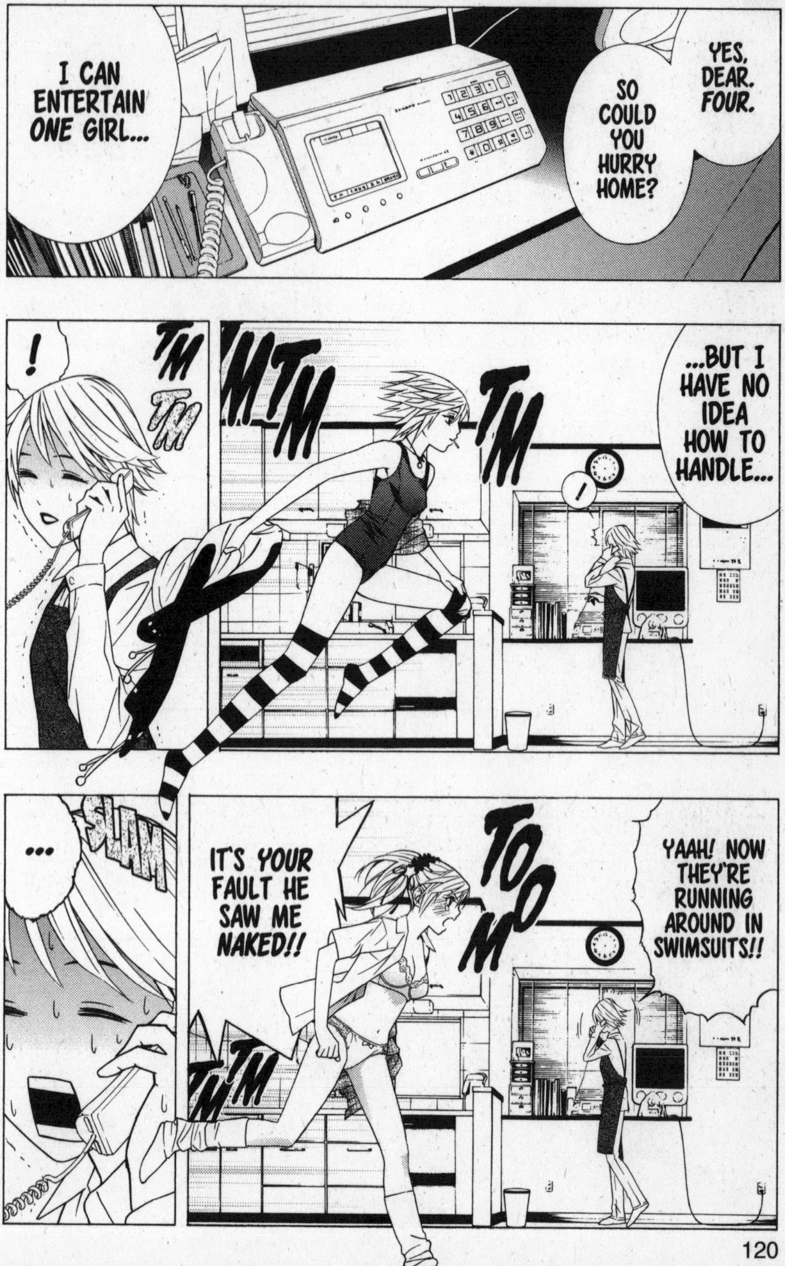
YES, DEAR. FOUR.
SO COULD YOU HURRY HOME?
I CAN ENTERTAIN ONE GIRL...
...BUT I HAVE NO IDEA HOW TO HANDLE...
TM
!
TM TM TM
!
TM
TM
YAAH! NOW THEY'RE RUNNING AROUND IN SWIMSUITS!!
TOOM
IT'S YOUR FAULT HE SAW ME NAKED!!
TM TM
SLAM
...

READ THIS WAY

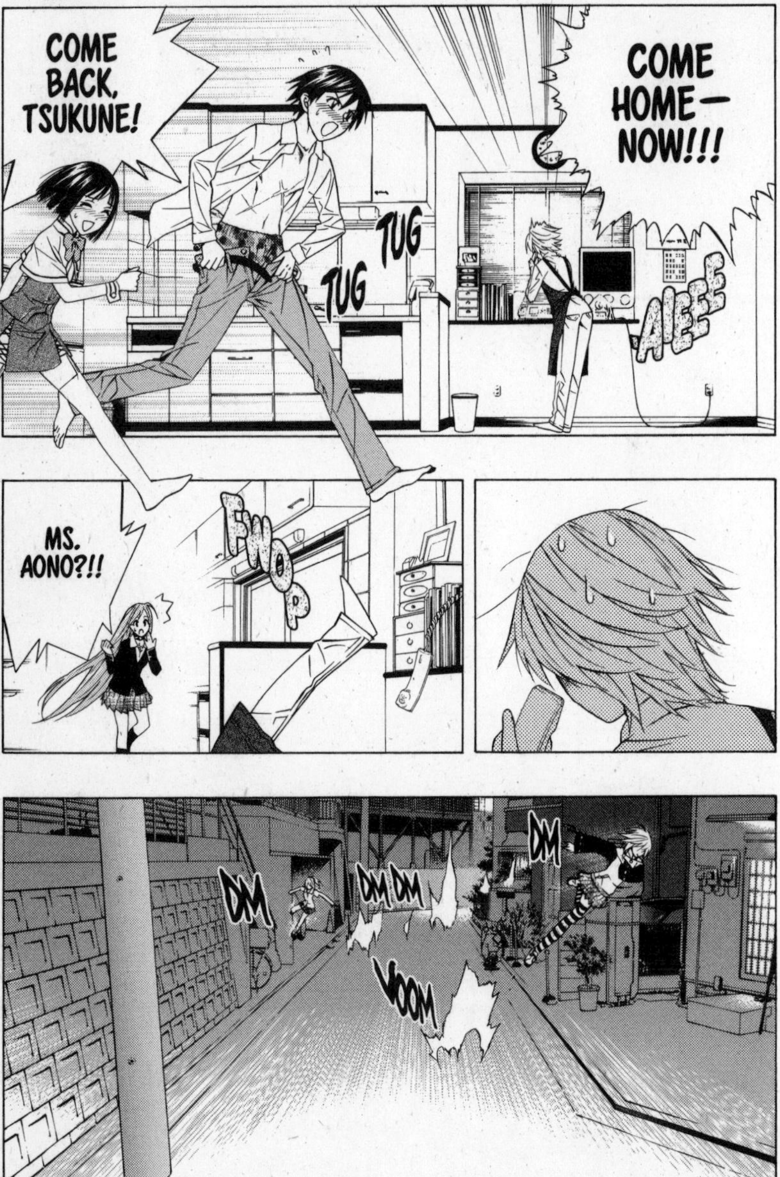
COME HOME—NOW!!!
AIEEE
TUG
TUG
COME BACK, TSUKUNE!
FWOP
MS. AONO?!!
DM
DM DM
DM
VOOM

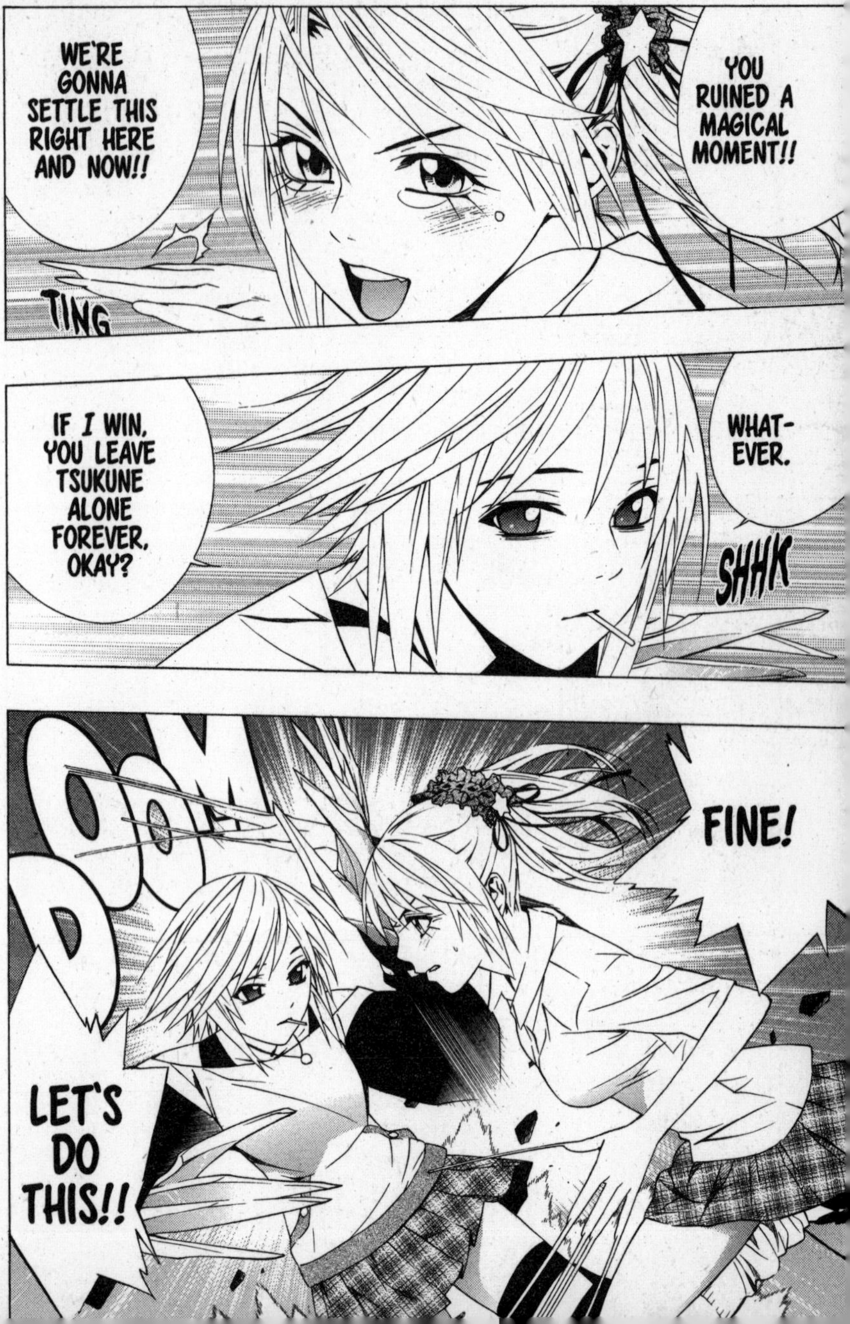
YOU RUINED A MAGICAL MOMENT!!
WE'RE GONNA SETTLE THIS RIGHT HERE AND NOW!!
TING
WHAT-EVER.
SHHK
IF I WIN, YOU LEAVE TSUKUNE ALONE FOREVER, OKAY?
FINE!
DOOM
LET'S DO THIS!!

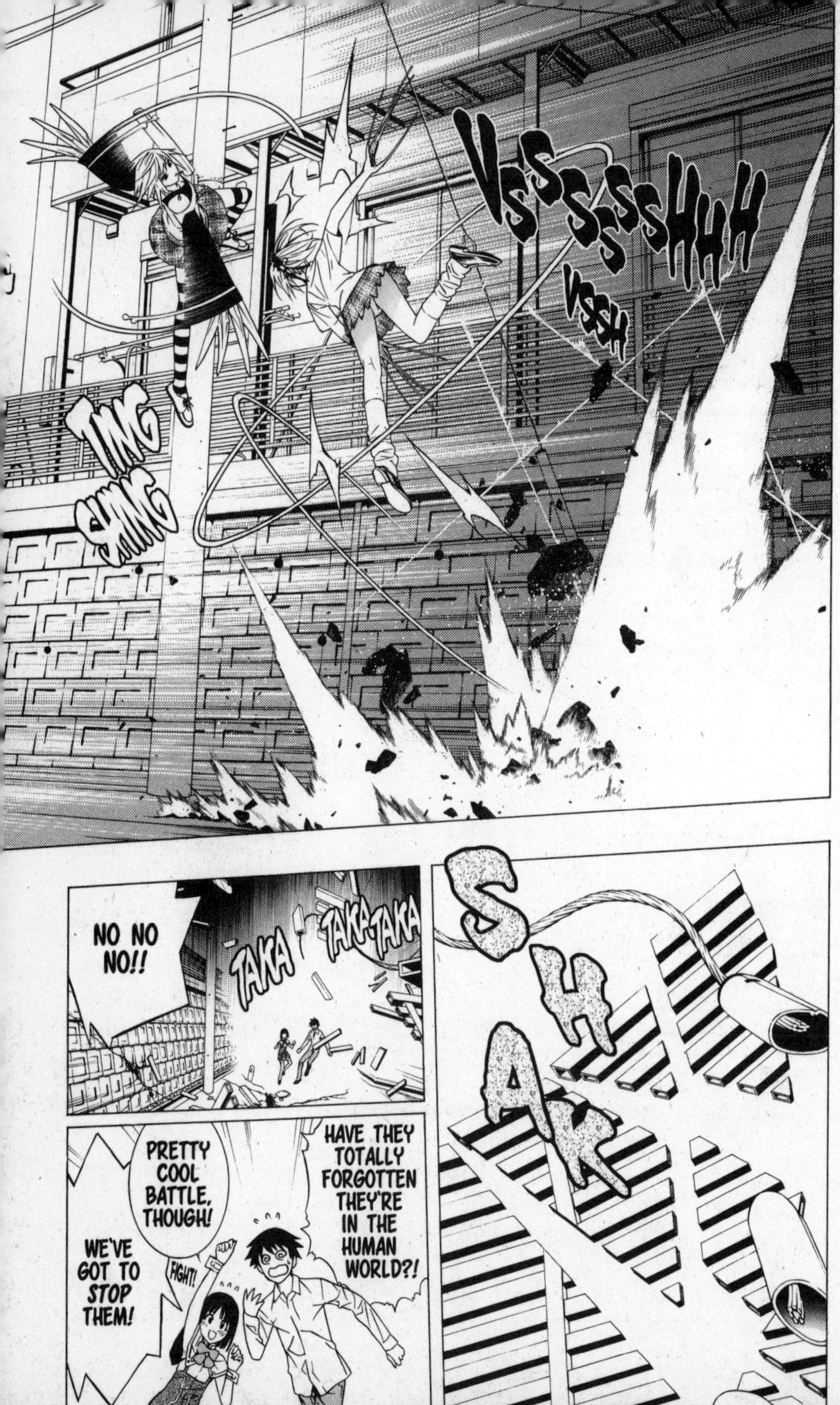
VSSSSSHHH
VSSH
TING
SHING
SHAAK
TAKATAKA
TAKA
NO NO NO!!
HAVE THEY TOTALLY FORGOTTEN THEY'RE IN THE HUMAN WORLD?!
PRETTY COOL BATTLE, THOUGH!
FIGHT!
WE'VE GOT TO STOP THEM!

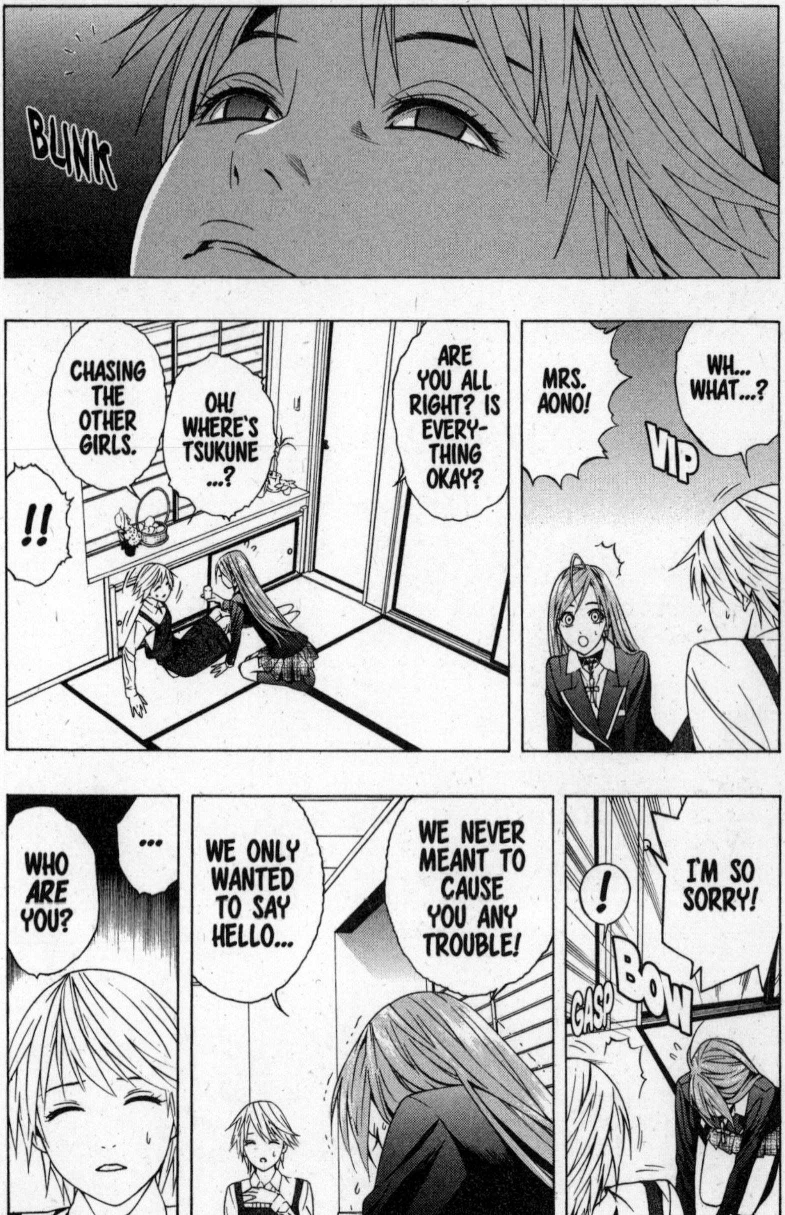
BLINK
WH... WHAT...?
VIP
MRS. AONO!
ARE YOU ALL RIGHT? IS EVERY-THING OKAY?
OH! WHERE'S TSUKUNE ...?
CHASING THE OTHER GIRLS.
!!
I'M SO SORRY!
!
BOW
GASP
WE NEVER MEANT TO CAUSE YOU ANY TROUBLE!
WE ONLY WANTED TO SAY HELLO...
...
WHO ARE YOU?

READ THIS WAY

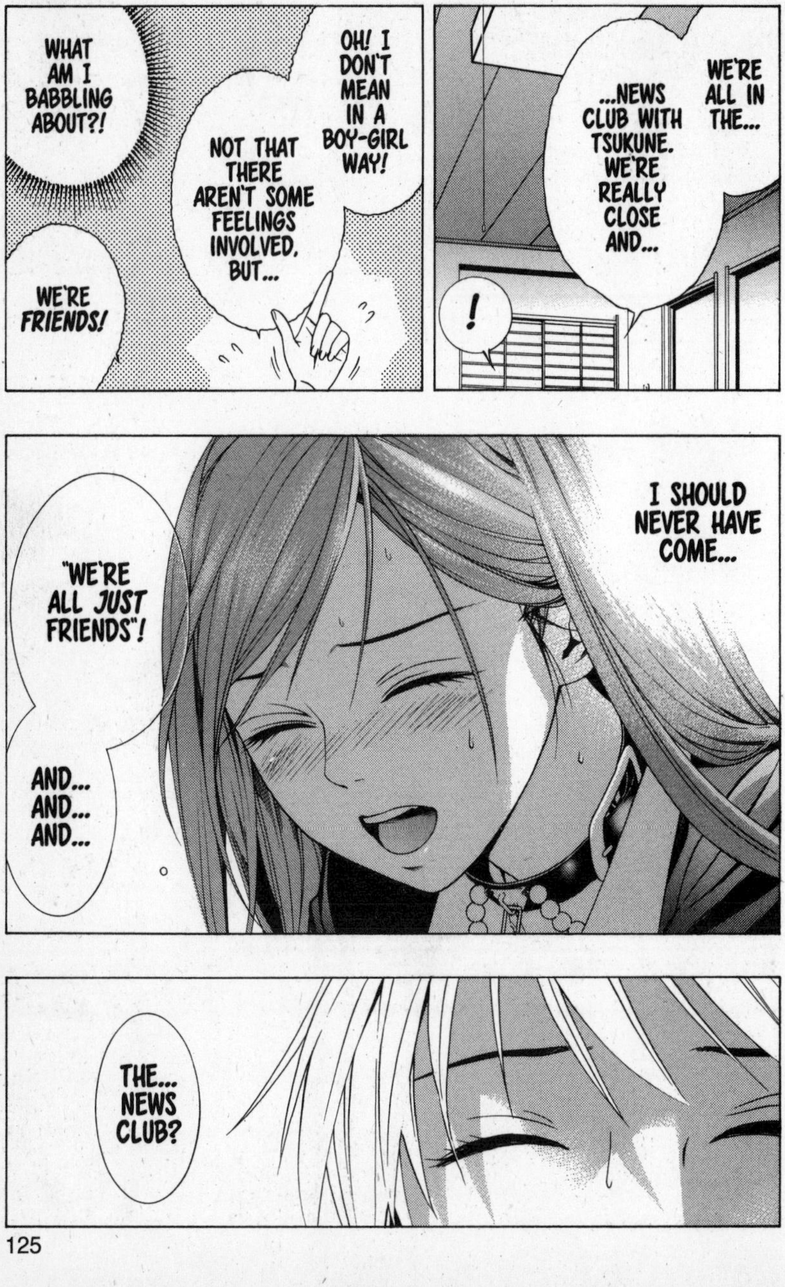
WE'RE ALL IN THE...
...NEWS CLUB WITH TSUKUNE. WE'RE REALLY CLOSE AND...
!
OH! I DON'T MEAN IN A BOY-GIRL WAY!
NOT THAT THERE AREN'T SOME FEELINGS INVOLVED, BUT...
WHAT AM I BABBLING ABOUT?!
WE'RE FRIENDS!
I SHOULD NEVER HAVE COME...
"WE'RE ALL *JUST* FRIENDS"!
AND... AND... AND...
THE... NEWS CLUB?

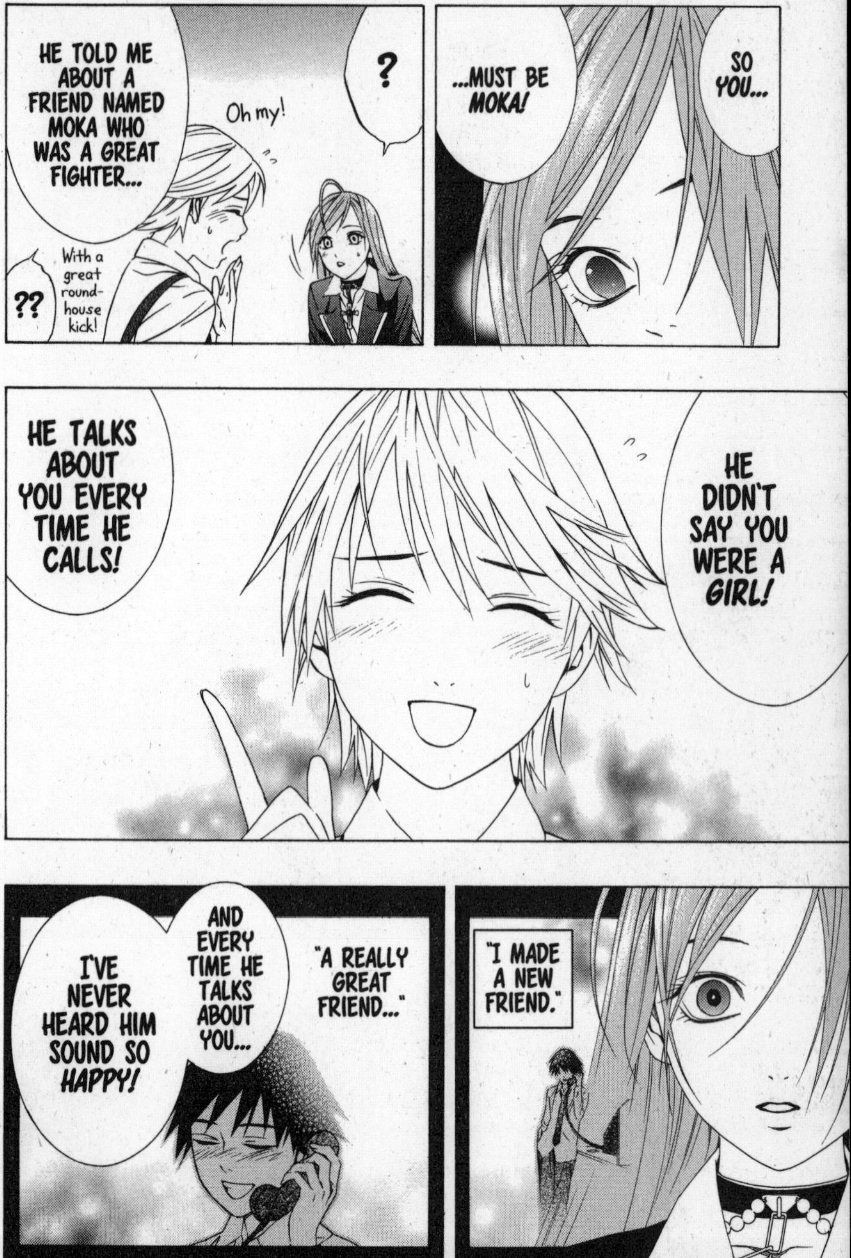
SO YOU...
...MUST BE MOKA!
?
HE TOLD ME ABOUT A FRIEND NAMED MOKA WHO WAS A GREAT FIGHTER...
Oh my!
With a great round-house kick!
??
HE DIDN'T SAY YOU WERE A GIRL!
HE TALKS ABOUT YOU EVERY TIME HE CALLS!
"I MADE A NEW FRIEND."
"A REALLY GREAT FRIEND..."
AND EVERY TIME HE TALKS ABOUT YOU...
I'VE NEVER HEARD HIM SOUND SO HAPPY!

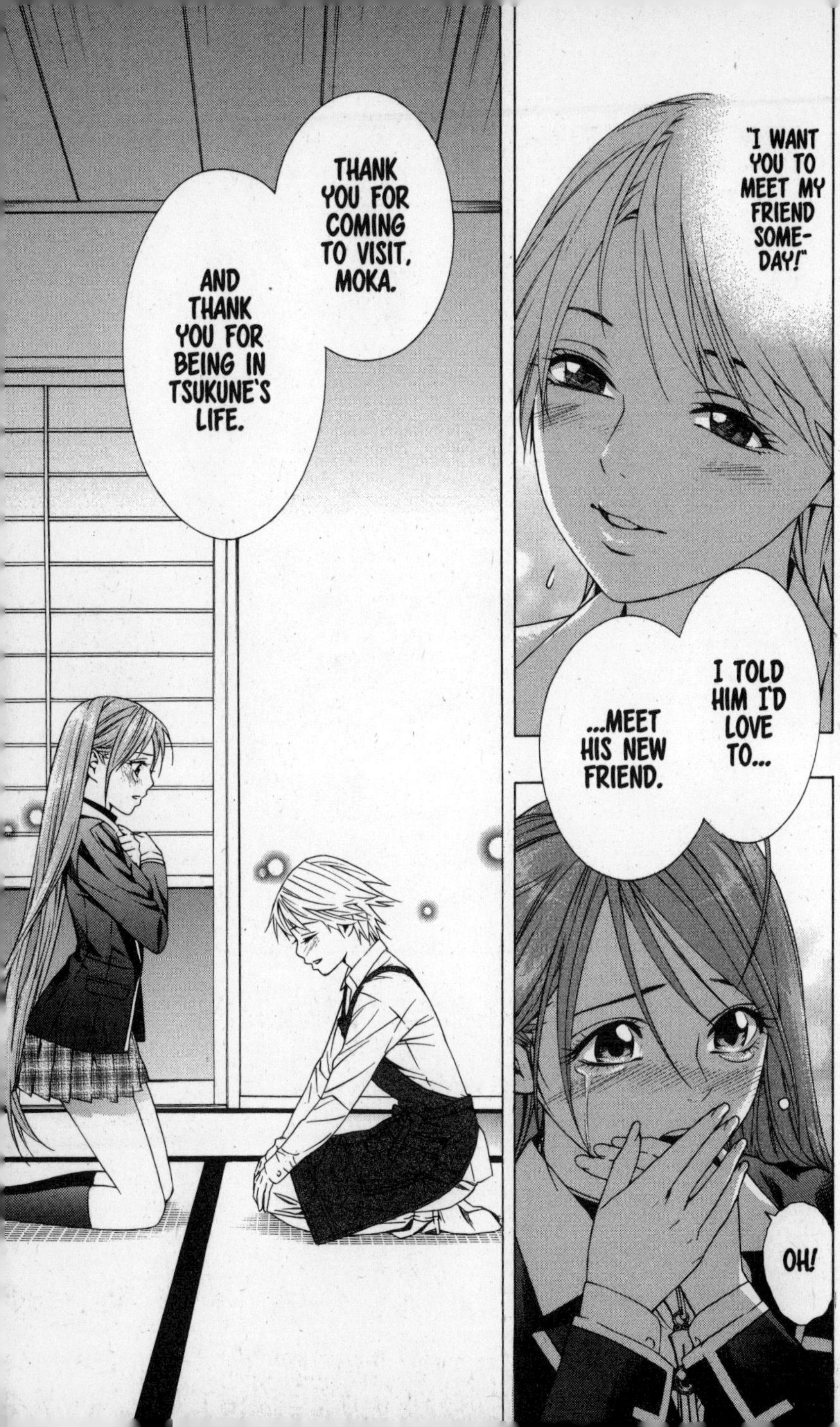
"I WANT YOU TO MEET MY FRIEND SOME-DAY!"
I TOLD HIM I'D LOVE TO...
...MEET HIS NEW FRIEND.
OH!
THANK YOU FOR COMING TO VISIT, MOKA.
AND THANK YOU FOR BEING IN TSUKUNE'S LIFE.

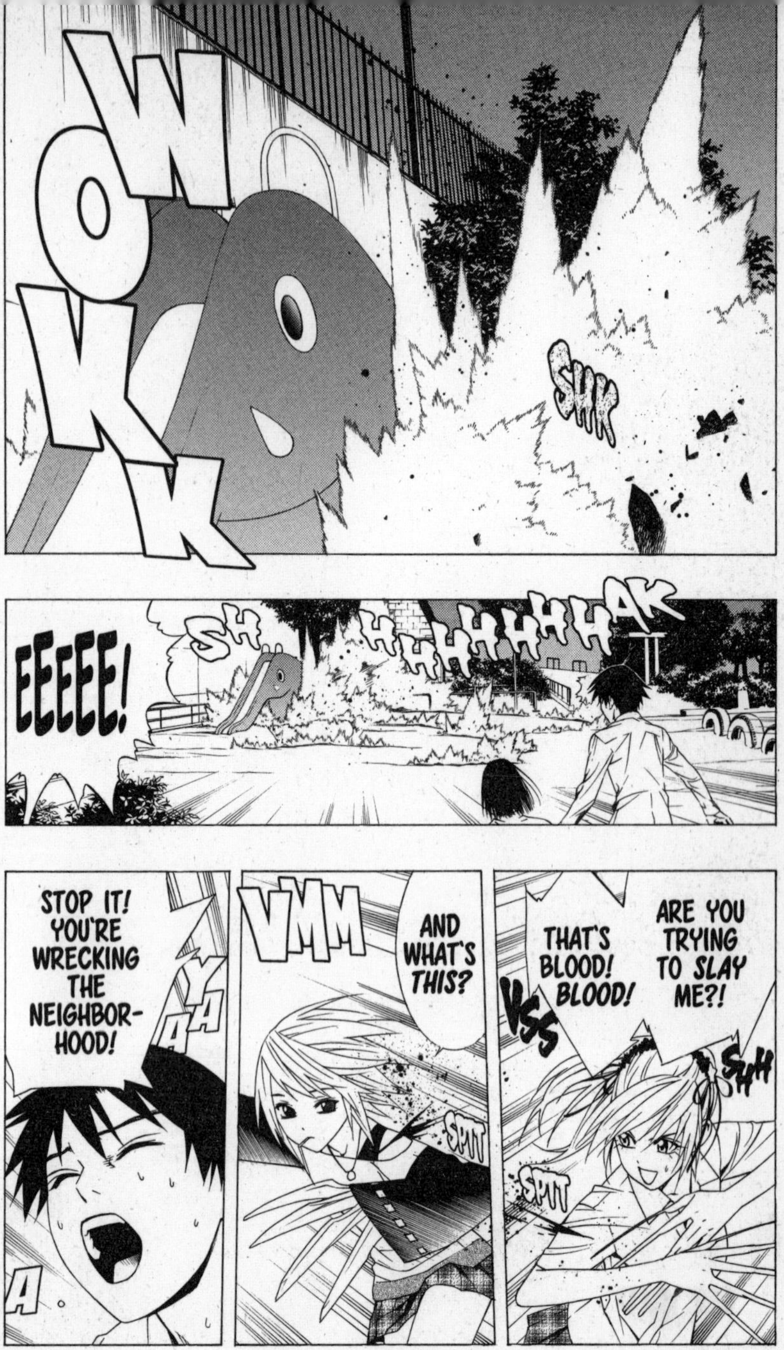
WOKK
SHK
SHHHHHHHHAK
EEEEE!
ARE YOU TRYING TO SLAY ME?!
THAT'S BLOOD! BLOOD!
VSS
SHH
SPIT
AND WHAT'S THIS?
VMM
SPIT
STOP IT! YOU'RE WRECKING THE NEIGHBOR-HOOD!
YAA
A

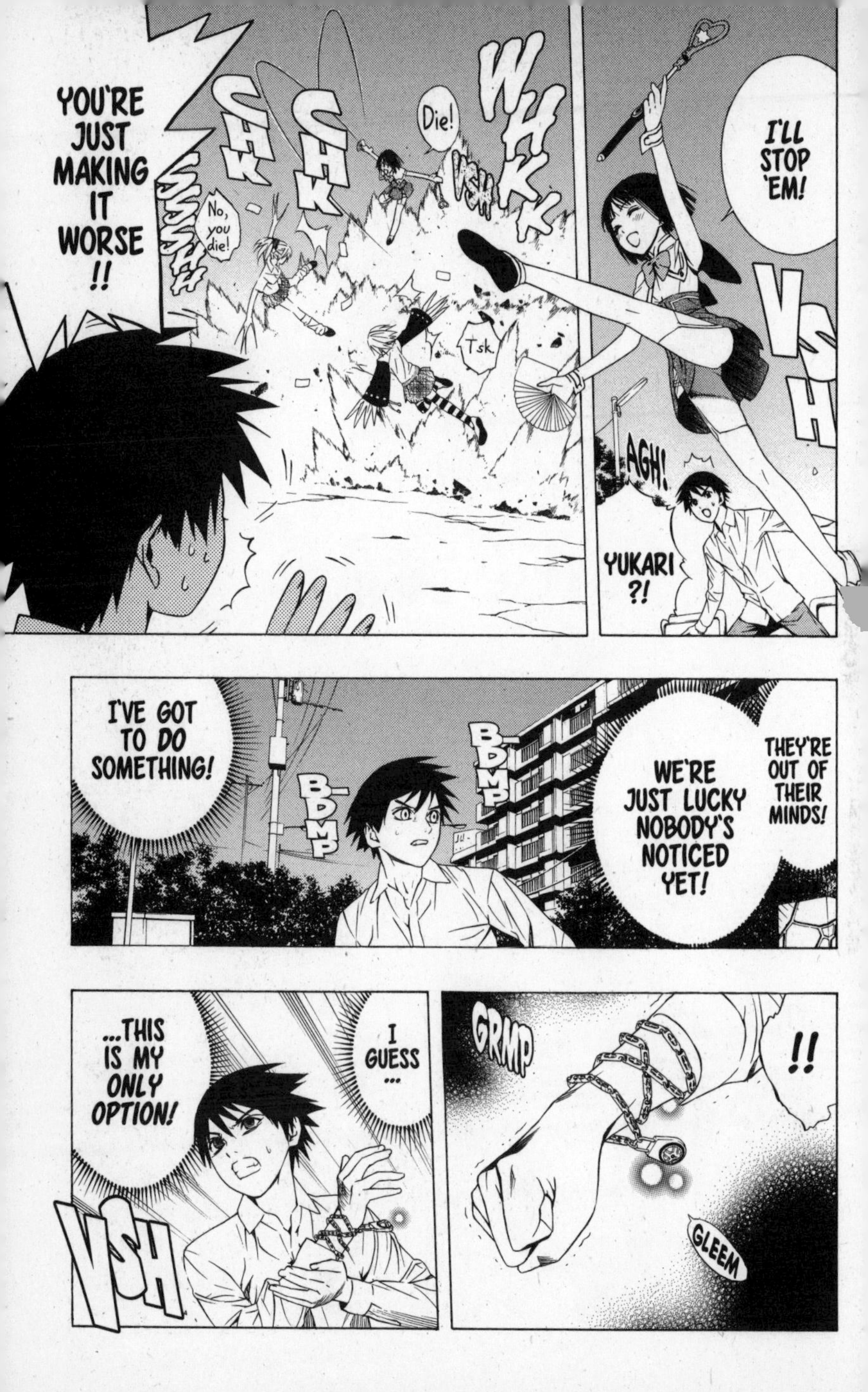
I'LL STOP 'EM!
VSH
AGH!
YUKARI ?!
WHKK
VSH
Die!
CHK
CHK
No, you die!
Tsk.
YOU'RE JUST MAKING IT WORSE !!
THEY'RE OUT OF THEIR MINDS!
WE'RE JUST LUCKY NOBODY'S NOTICED YET!
B-DMP
B-DMP
I'VE GOT TO DO SOMETHING!
!!
GRMP
GLEEM
I GUESS ...
...THIS IS MY ONLY OPTION!
VSH

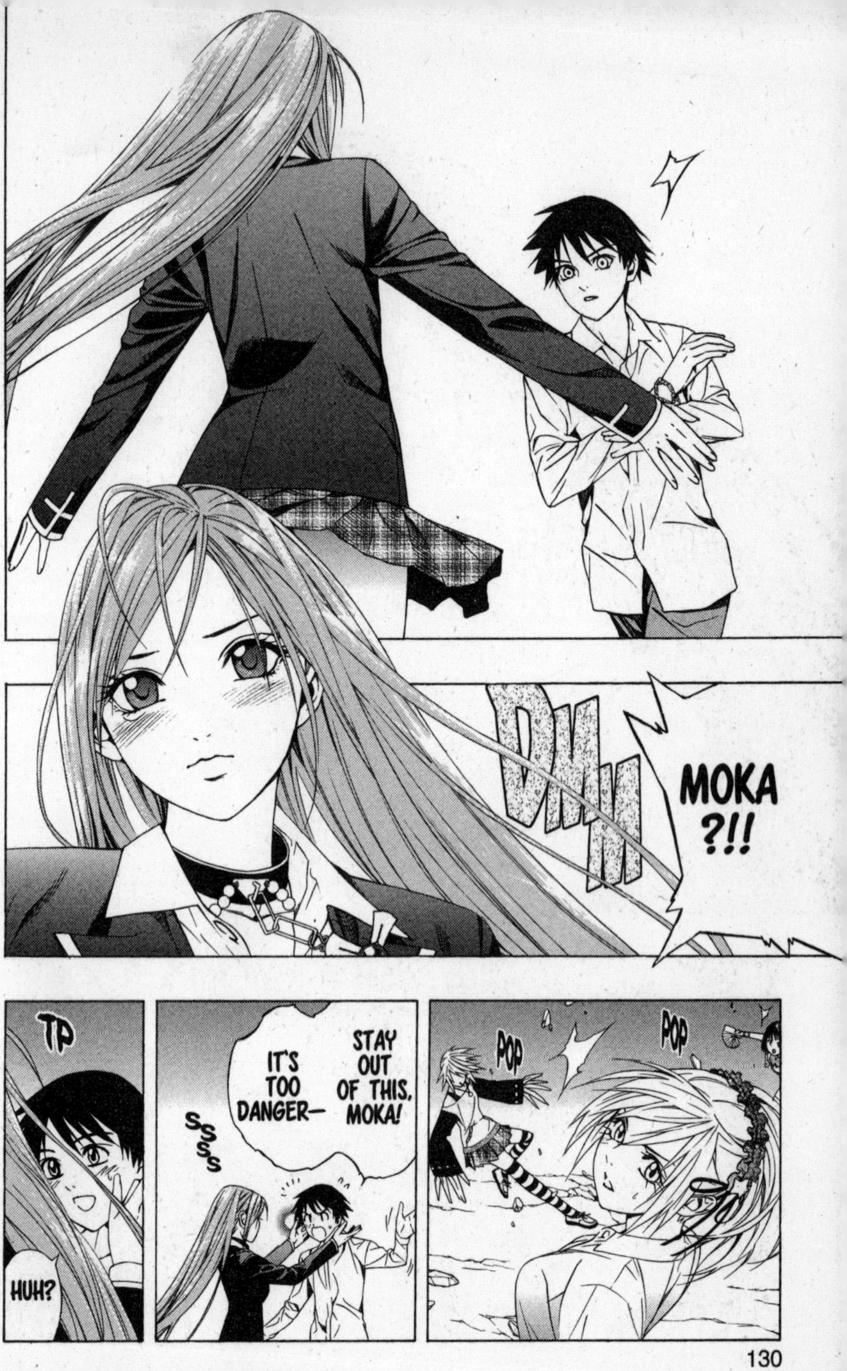
MOKA ?!!
DMM
POP
POP
STAY OUT OF THIS, MOKA!
IT'S TOO DANGER—
SSS
TP
HUH?

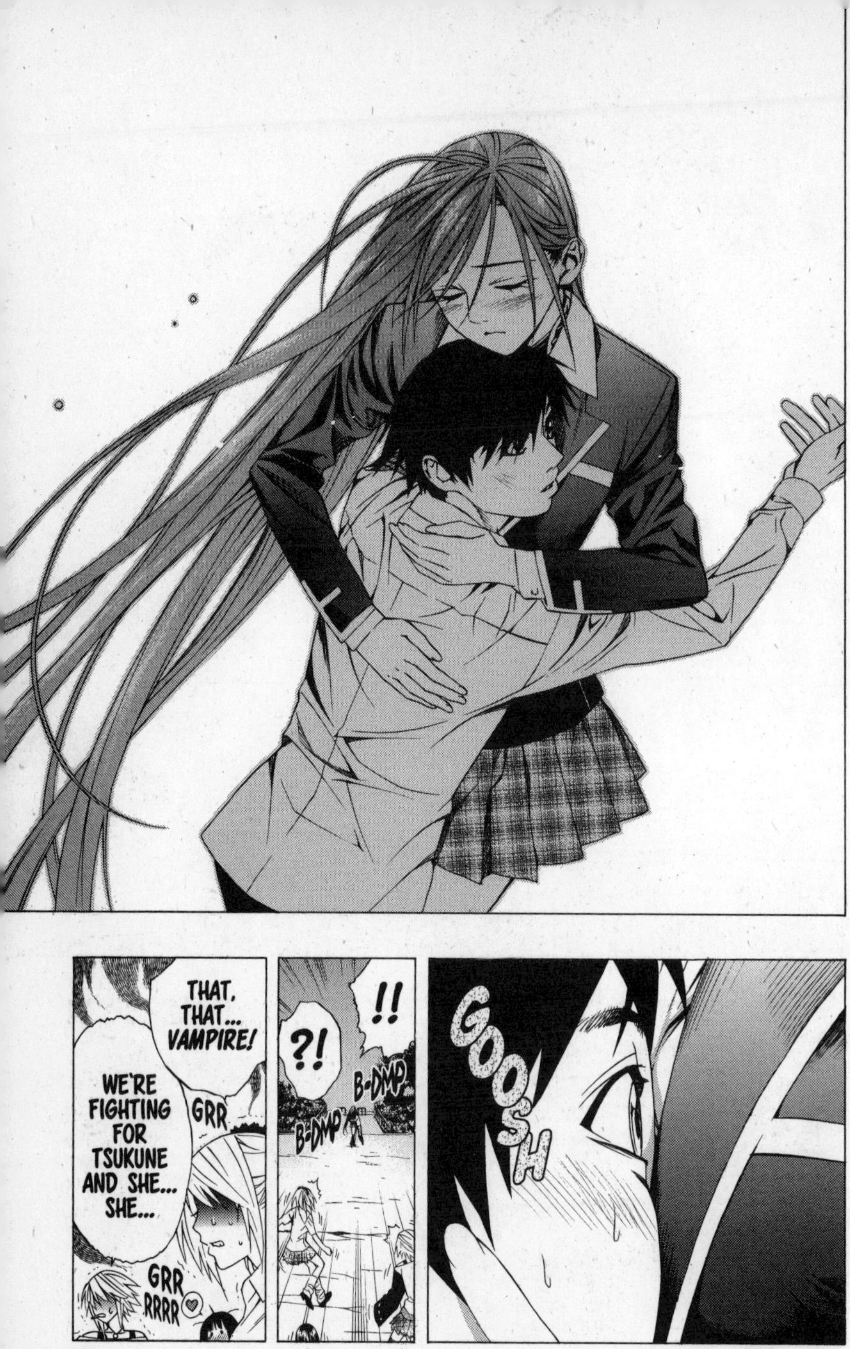
GOOSH
!!
?!
B-DMP
B-DMP
THAT, THAT... VAMPIRE!
WE'RE FIGHTING FOR TSUKUNE AND SHE... SHE...
GRR
GRR RRRR

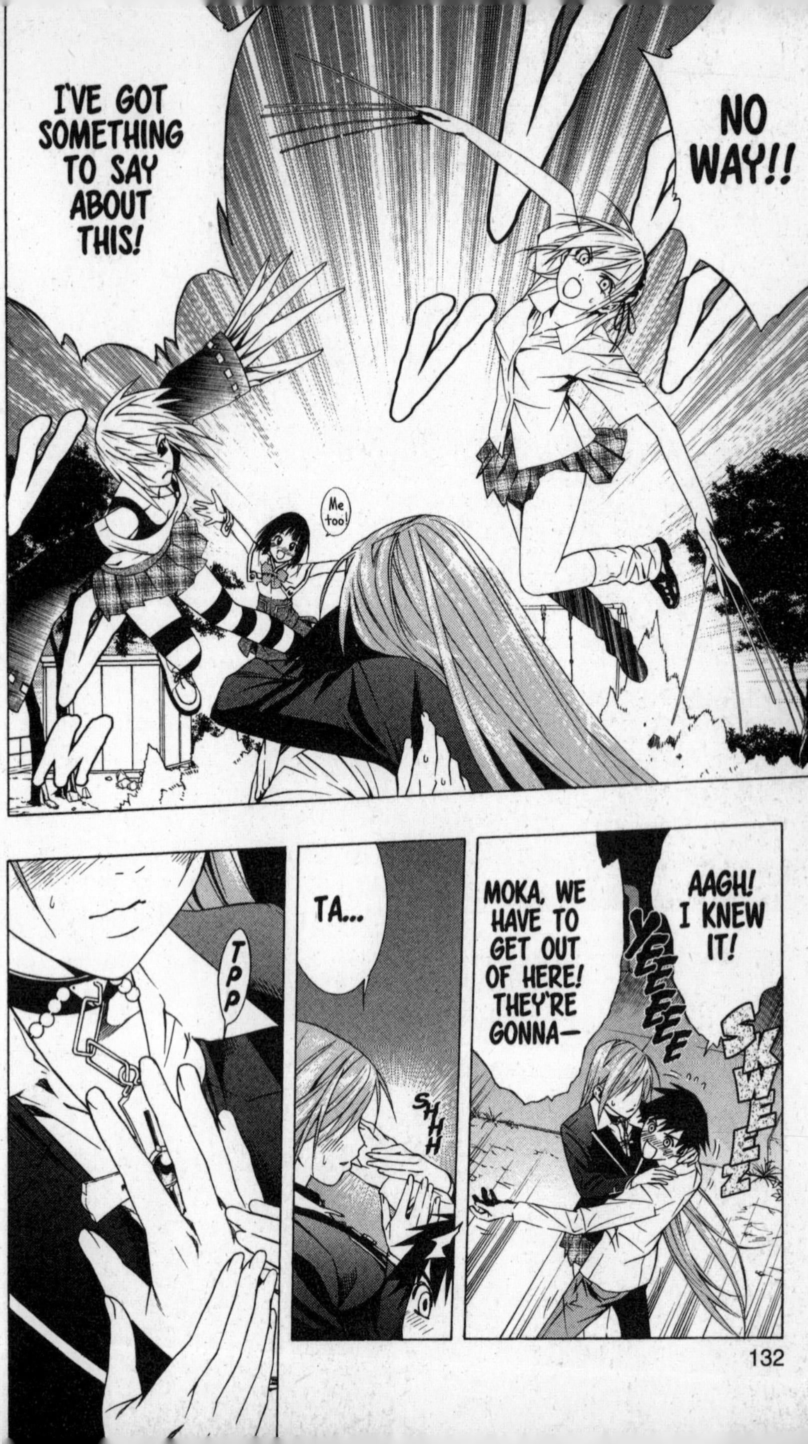
NO WAY!!
I'VE GOT SOMETHING TO SAY ABOUT THIS!
Me too!
AAGH! I KNEW IT!
YEEEEE
MOKA, WE HAVE TO GET OUT OF HERE! THEY'RE GONNA—
SKWEEZ
TA...
SHHH
TPP

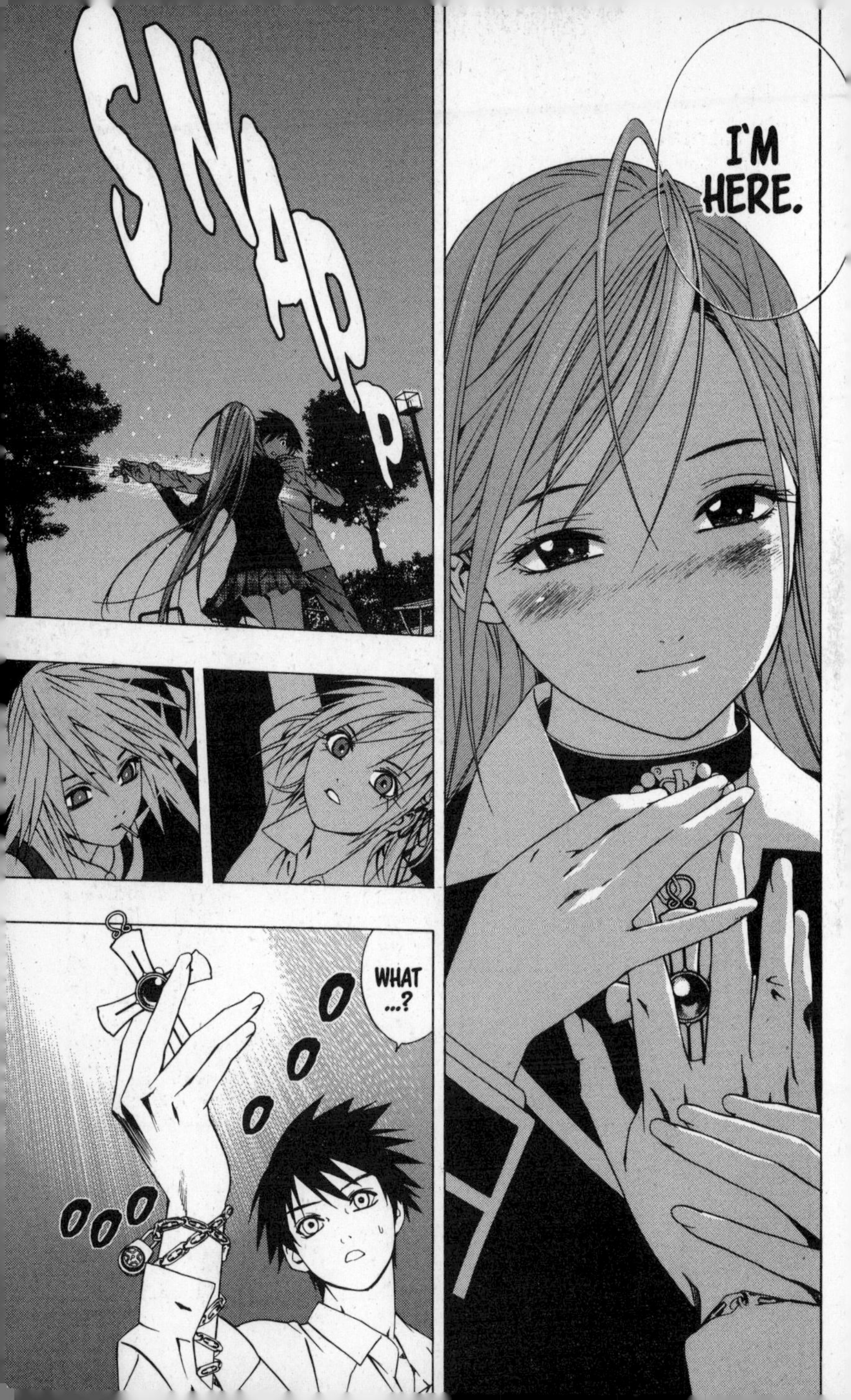
I'M HERE.
SNAP
WHAT ...?

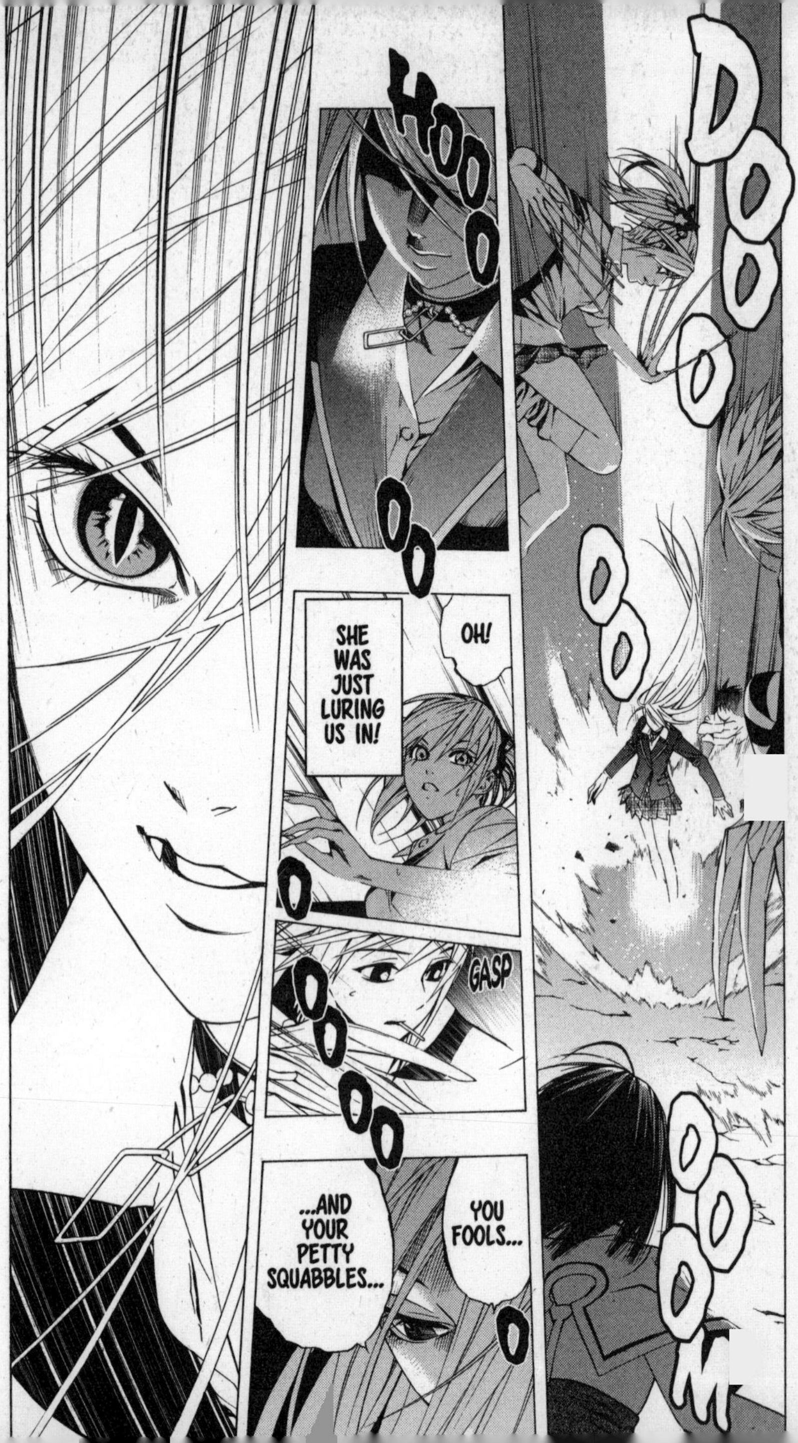
DOOOOOOOOOOOM
HOOOOOOOOOOOOOOO
OH!
SHE WAS JUST LURING US IN!
GASP
YOU FOOLS...
...AND YOUR PETTY SQUABBLES...

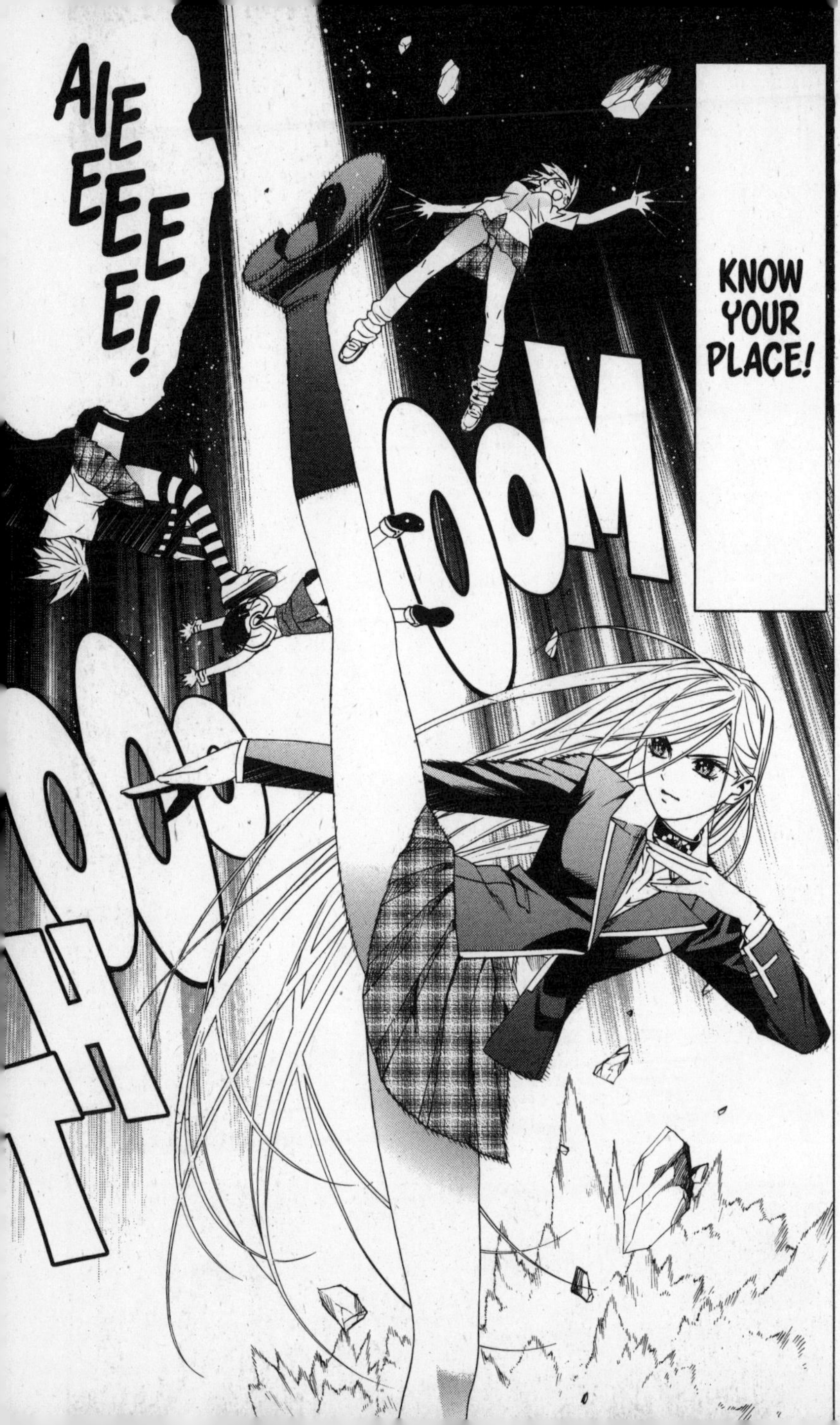
KNOW YOUR PLACE!
WHOOOOOM
AIEEEEE!

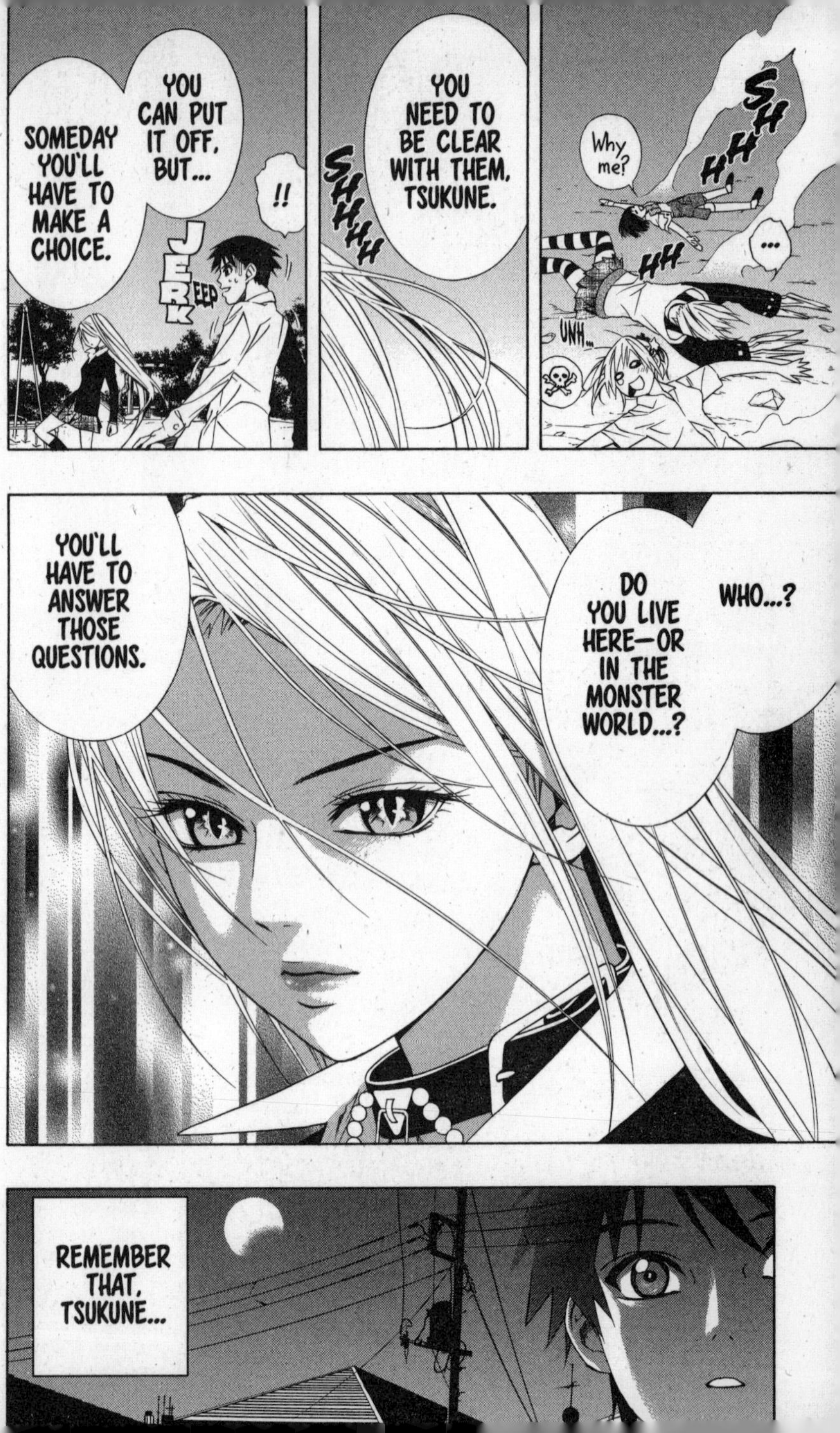
SHHHH
Why me?
...
HH
UNH...
YOU NEED TO BE CLEAR WITH THEM, TSUKUNE.
SHHHH
YOU CAN PUT IT OFF, BUT...
SOMEDAY YOU'LL HAVE TO MAKE A CHOICE.
!!
JERK
EEP
WHO...?
DO YOU LIVE HERE—OR IN THE MONSTER WORLD...?
YOU'LL HAVE TO ANSWER THOSE QUESTIONS.
REMEMBER THAT, TSUKUNE...

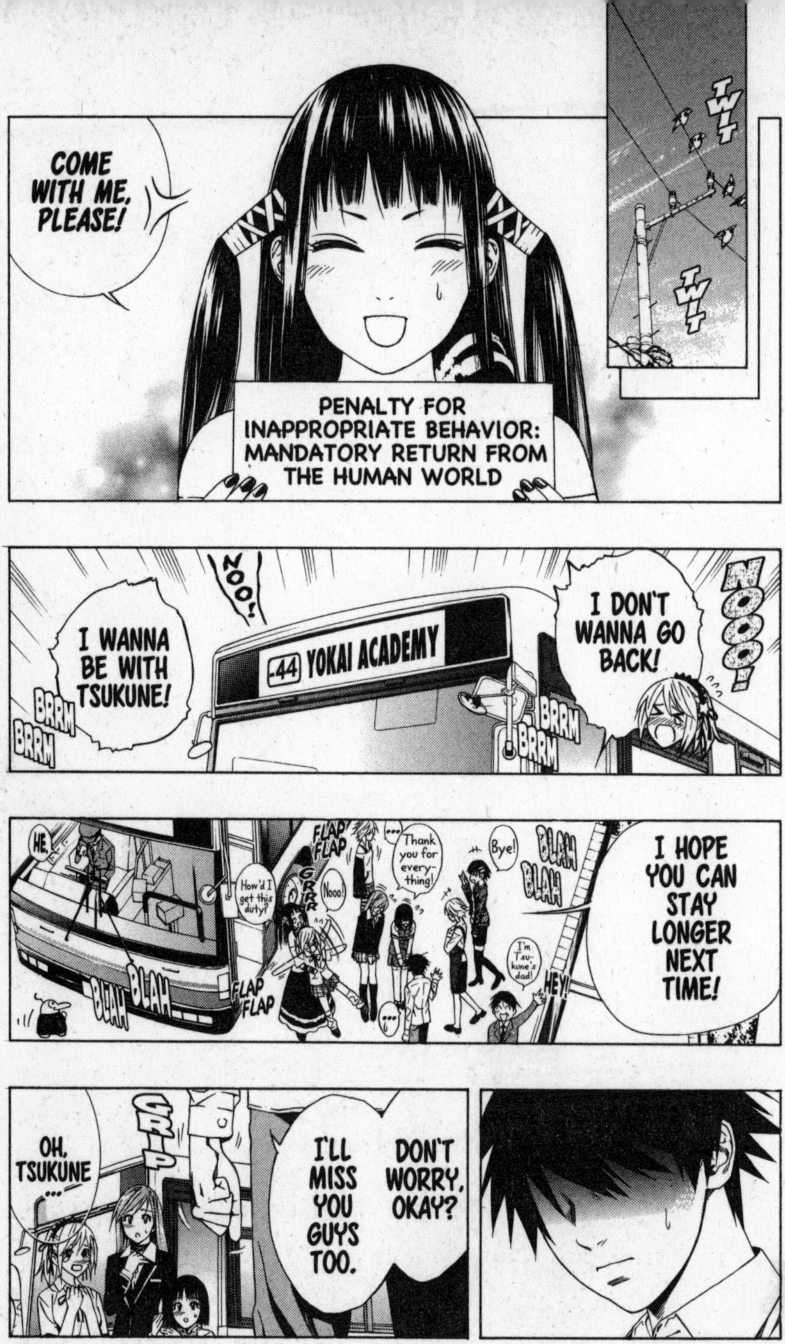
TWIT
TWIT
COME WITH ME, PLEASE!
PENALTY FOR INAPPROPRIATE BEHAVIOR: MANDATORY RETURN FROM THE HUMAN WORLD
NOOOO!
I DON'T WANNA GO BACK!
BRRM BRRM
-44 YOKAI ACADEMY
NOO!
I WANNA BE WITH TSUKUNE!
BRRM BRRM
I HOPE YOU CAN STAY LONGER NEXT TIME!
BLAH BLAH
Bye!
HEY!
I'm Tsukune's dad!
Thank you for everything!
...
FLAP FLAP
GRRR
Nooo
How'd I get this duty?
HE
FLAP FLAP
...
BLAH BLAH
DON'T WORRY, OKAY?
I'LL MISS YOU GUYS TOO.
GRIP
OH, TSUKUNE...

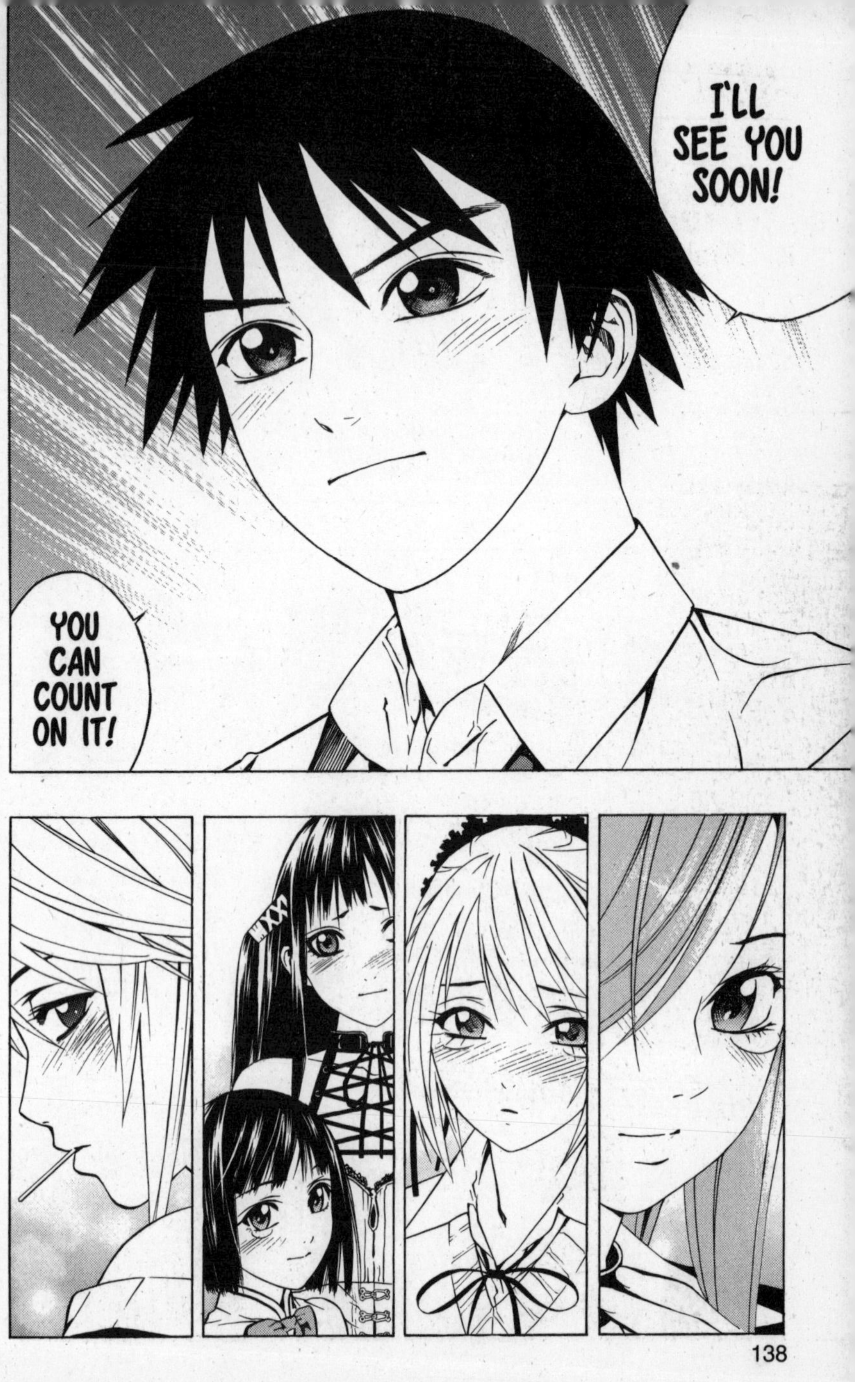
I'LL SEE YOU SOON!
YOU CAN COUNT ON IT!

READ THIS WAY

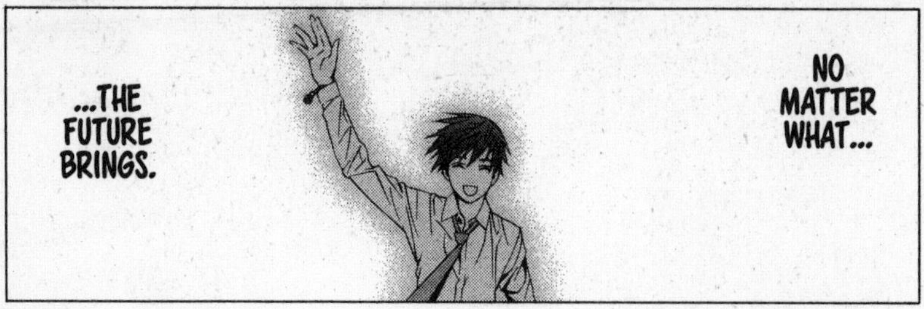
NO MATTER WHAT...
...THE FUTURE BRINGS.

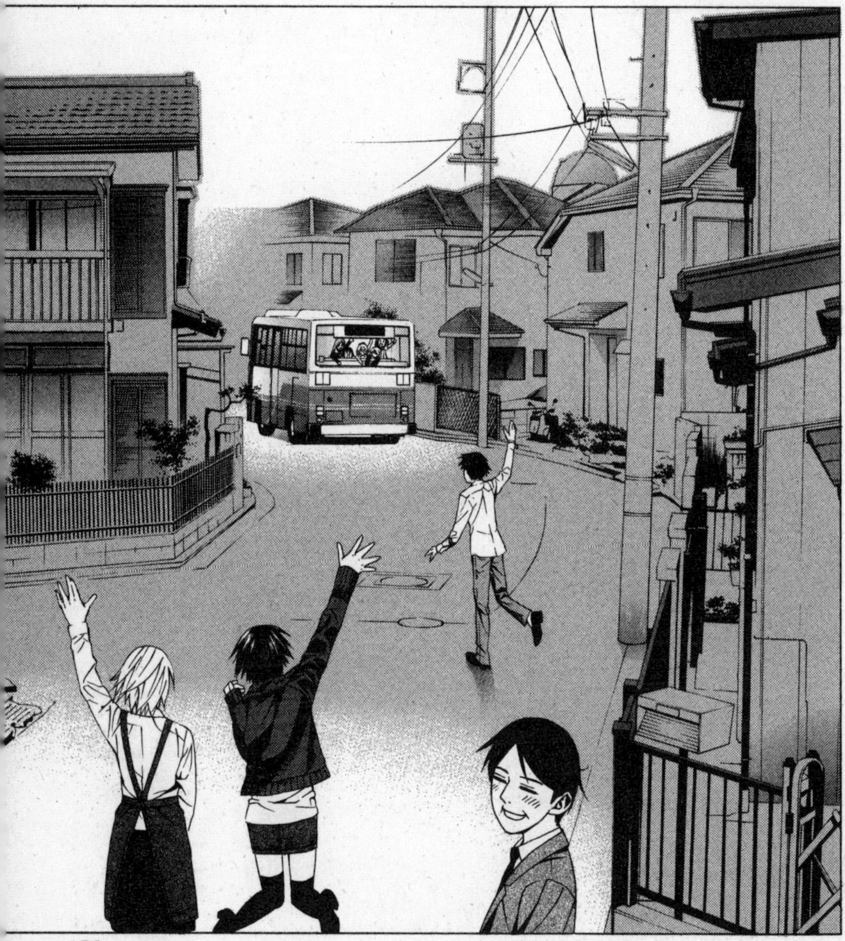

ROSARIO+VAMPIRE

40: Forecast of Happiness
(Bonus Story)

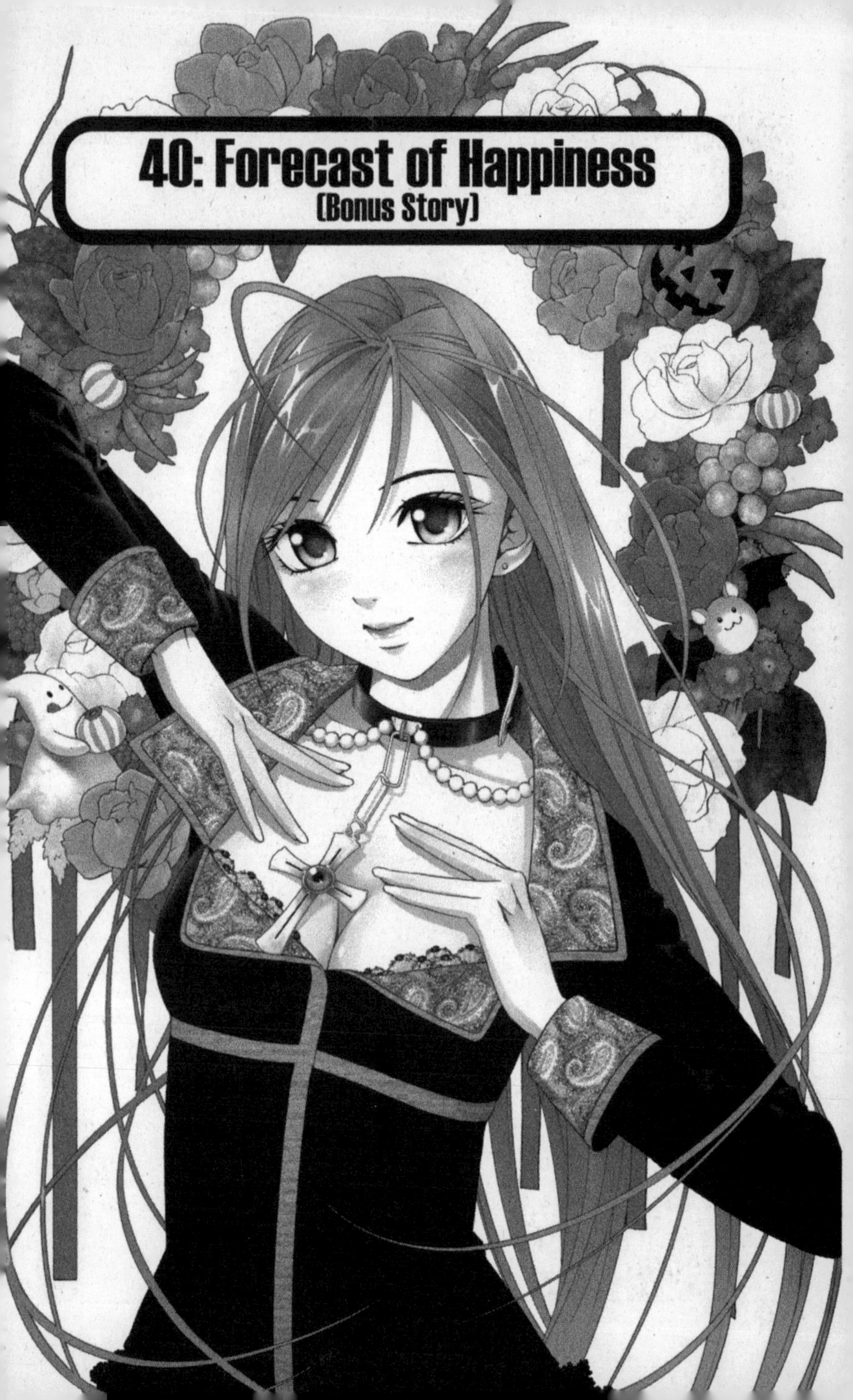

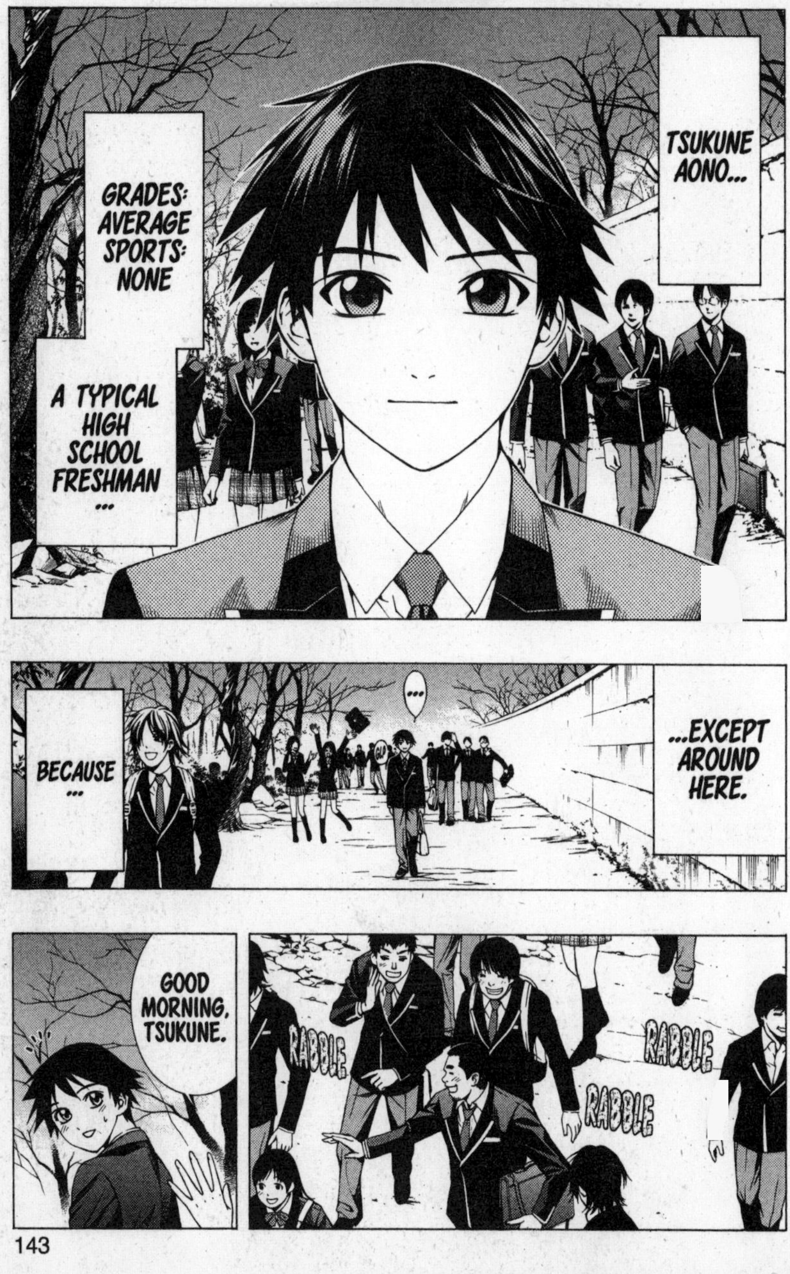
TSUKUNE AONO...
GRADES: AVERAGE SPORTS: NONE
A TYPICAL HIGH SCHOOL FRESHMAN ...
...EXCEPT AROUND HERE.
...
BECAUSE ...
RABBLE
RABBLE
RABBLE
GOOD MORNING, TSUKUNE.

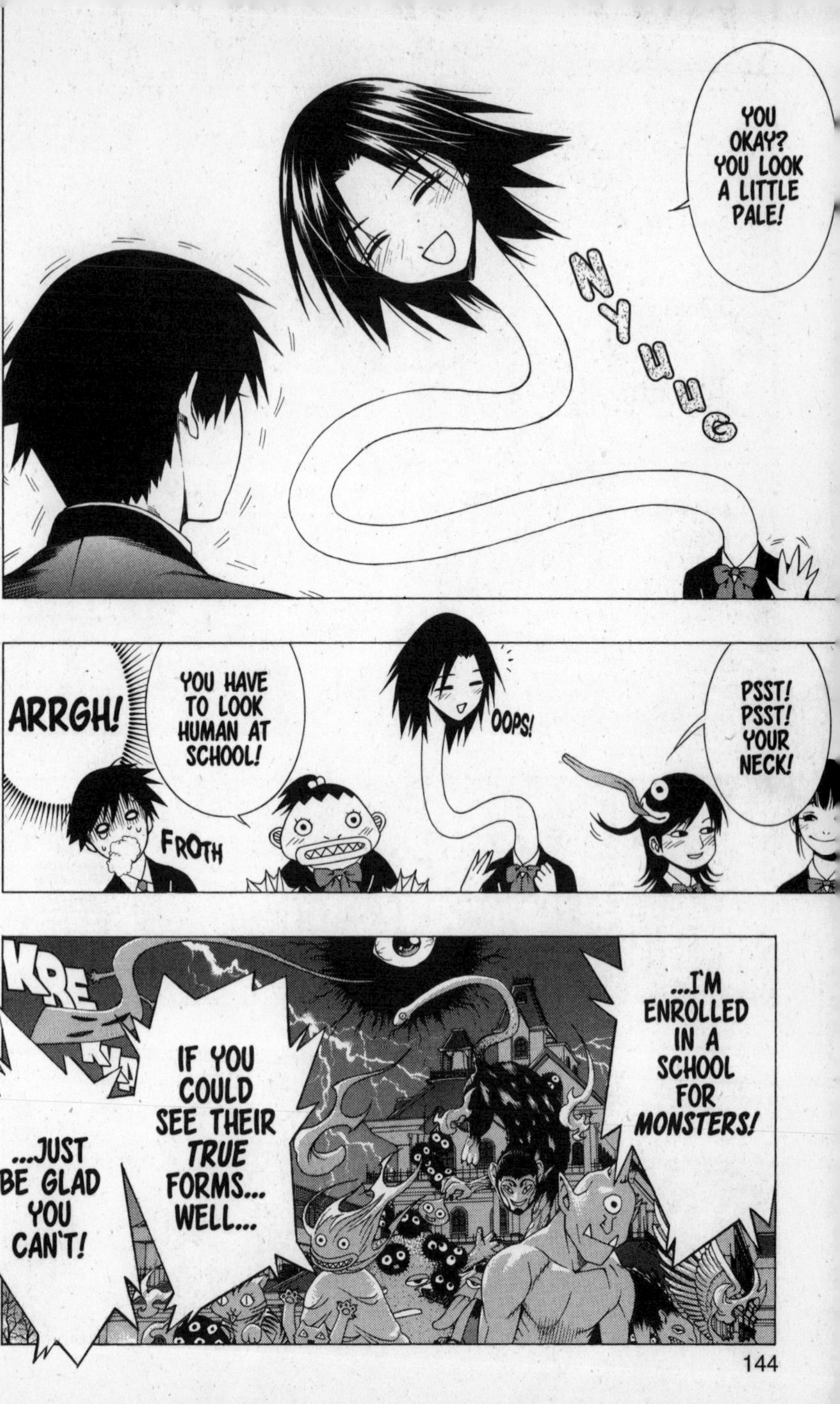
YOU OKAY? YOU LOOK A LITTLE PALE!
NYUUG
PSST! PSST! YOUR NECK!
OOPS!
YOU HAVE TO LOOK HUMAN AT SCHOOL!
FROTH
ARRGH!
...I'M ENROLLED IN A SCHOOL FOR MONSTERS!
IF YOU COULD SEE THEIR TRUE FORMS... WELL...
...JUST BE GLAD YOU CAN'T!

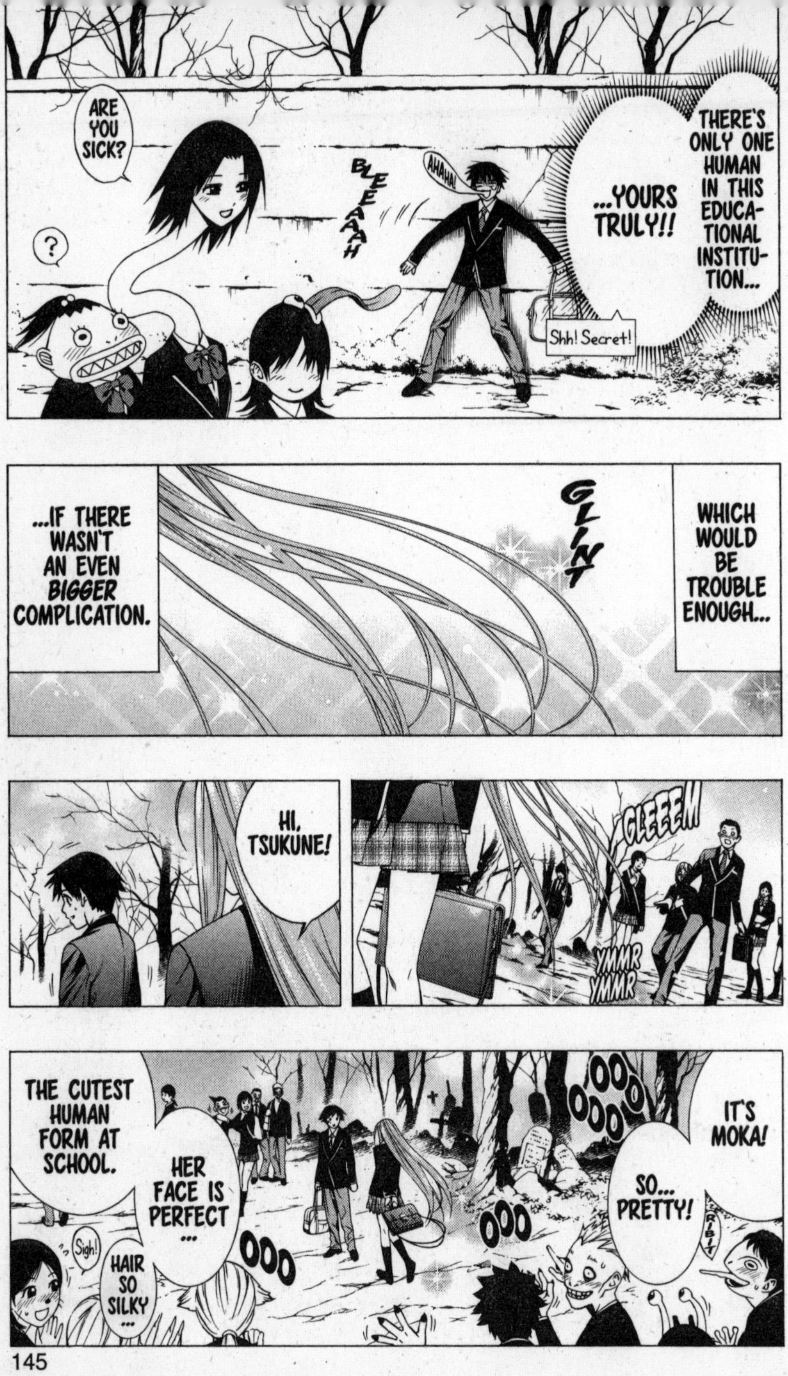
THERE'S ONLY ONE HUMAN IN THIS EDUCATIONAL INSTITUTION...
...YOURS TRULY!!
AHAHA!
BLEEAAAH
Shh! Secret!
ARE YOU SICK?
?
WHICH WOULD BE TROUBLE ENOUGH...
GLINT
...IF THERE WASN'T AN EVEN BIGGER COMPLICATION.
GLEEEM
YMMR YMMR
HI, TSUKUNE!
IT'S MOKA!
OOOO OOOO
SO... PRETTY!
RIBIT
OOO
HER FACE IS PERFECT...
THE CUTEST HUMAN FORM AT SCHOOL.
OOO
Sigh!
HAIR SO SILKY...

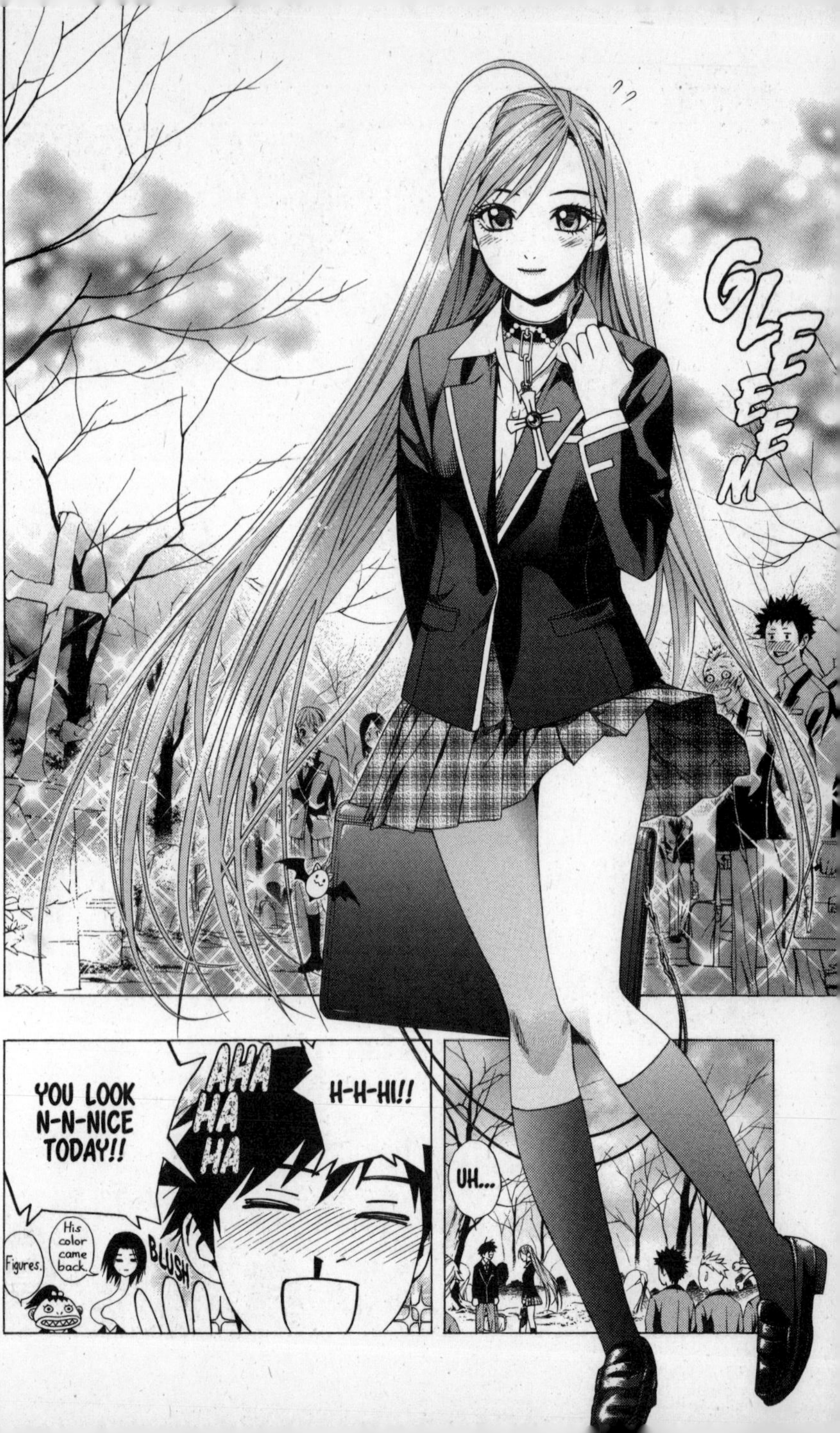
GLEEEM
UH...
H-H-HI!!
AHA HA HA
YOU LOOK N-N-NICE TODAY!!
BLUSH
His color came back.
Figures.

READ THIS WAY

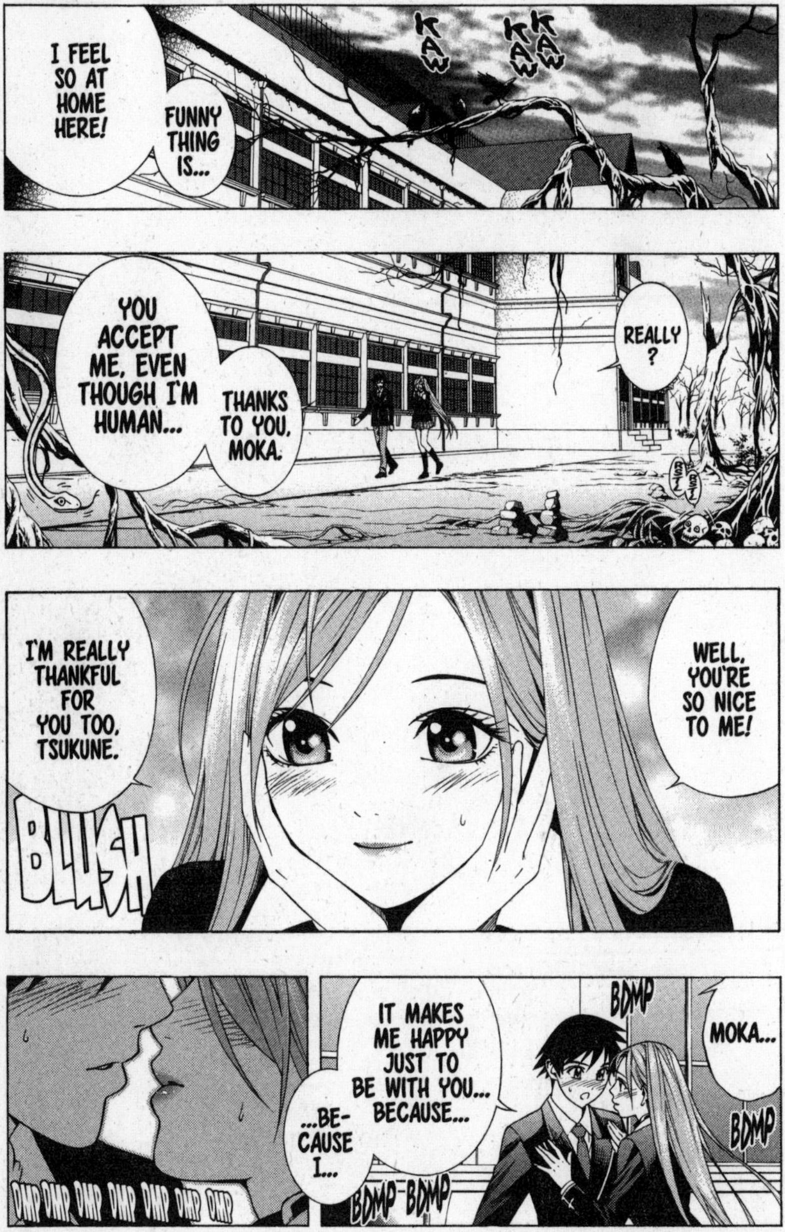
KAW
KKAW KAW
FUNNY THING IS...
I FEEL SO AT HOME HERE!
REALLY?
THANKS TO YOU, MOKA.
YOU ACCEPT ME, EVEN THOUGH I'M HUMAN...
RSL RSL
WELL, YOU'RE SO NICE TO ME!
I'M REALLY THANKFUL FOR YOU TOO, TSUKUNE.
BLUSH
MOKA...
BDMP
BDMP
IT MAKES ME HAPPY JUST TO BE WITH YOU... BECAUSE...
...BE-CAUSE I...
BDMP BDMP
DMP DMP DMP DMP DMP DMP DMP

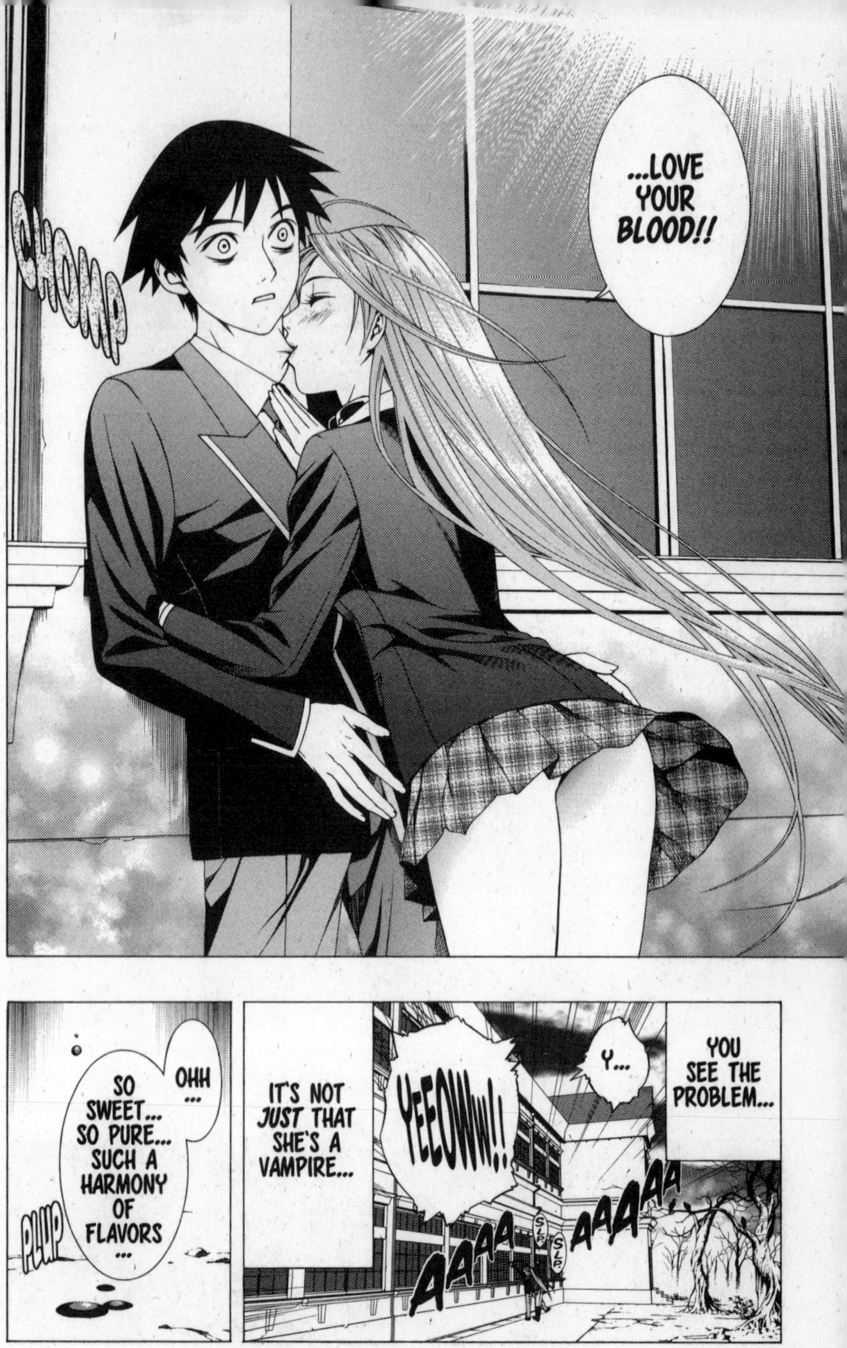
...LOVE YOUR BLOOD!!
CHOMP
YOU SEE THE PROBLEM...
Y...
YEEOWW!!
IT'S NOT *JUST* THAT SHE'S A VAMPIRE...
AAAAAAAAAA
SLP
SLP
OHH ...
SO SWEET... SO PURE... SUCH A HARMONY OF FLAVORS ...
PLUP

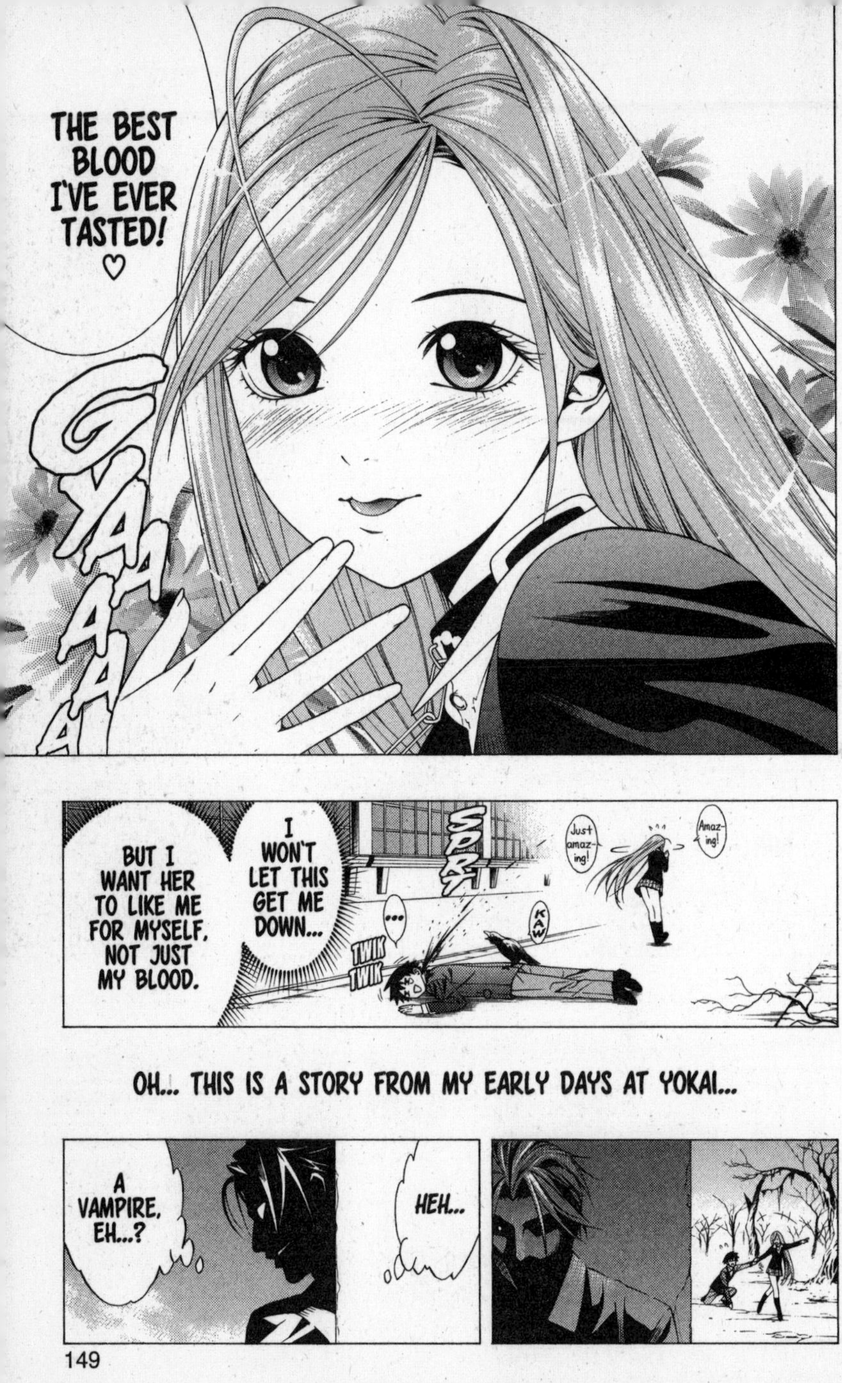
THE BEST BLOOD I'VE EVER TASTED! ♡
GYAAAAAA
Amaz-ing!
Just amaz-ing!
KAW
...
TWIK TWIK
I WON'T LET THIS GET ME DOWN...
BUT I WANT HER TO LIKE ME FOR MYSELF, NOT JUST MY BLOOD.
OH... THIS IS A STORY FROM MY EARLY DAYS AT YOKAI...
HEH...
A VAMPIRE, EH...?

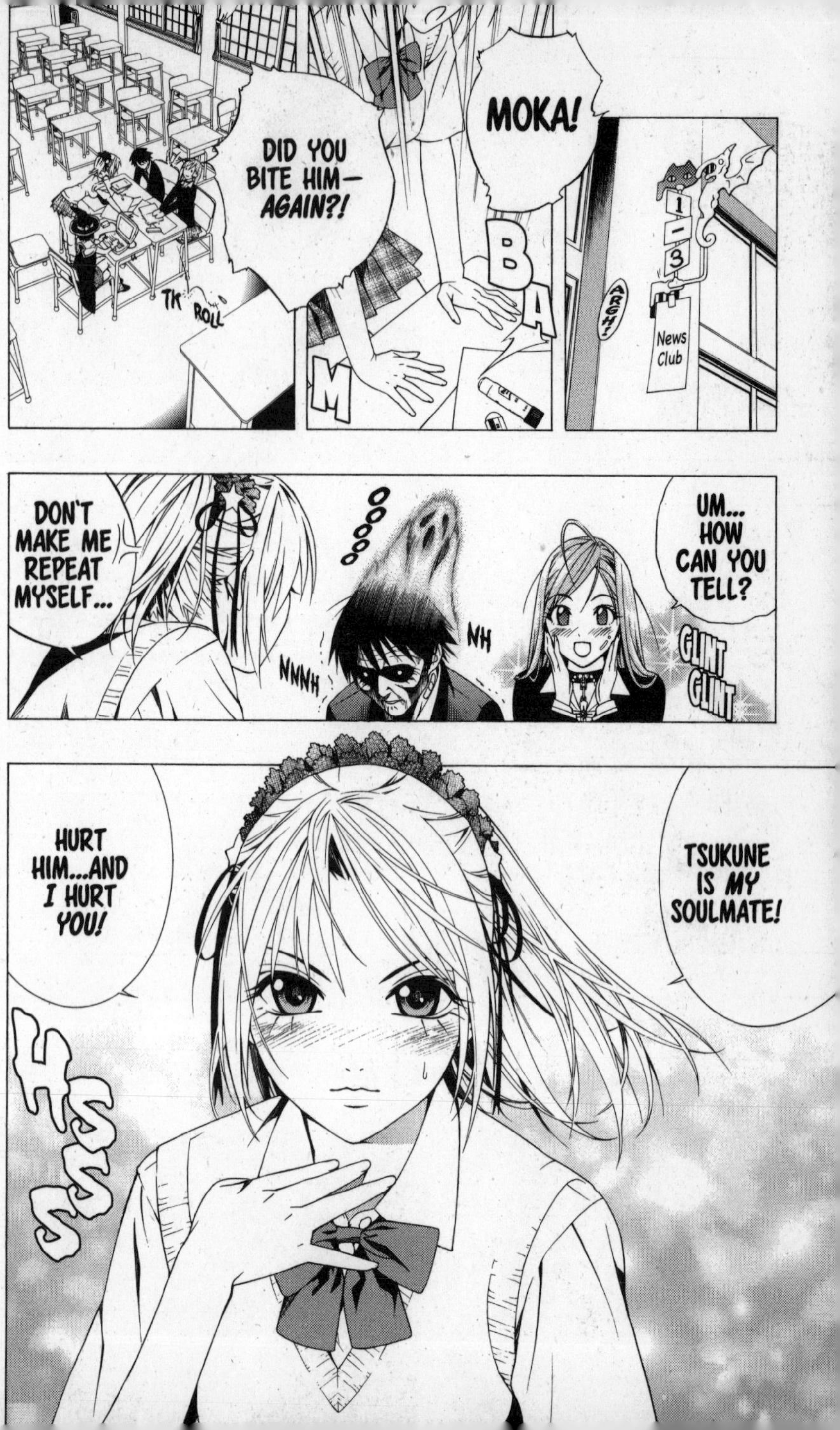
1
-
3
News Club
ARGH!
MOKA!
BAM
DID YOU BITE HIM—AGAIN?!
TK
ROLL
UM... HOW CAN YOU TELL?
GLINT GLINT
NH
NNNH
DON'T MAKE ME REPEAT MYSELF...
TSUKUNE IS MY SOULMATE!
HURT HIM...AND I HURT YOU!
HSSSS

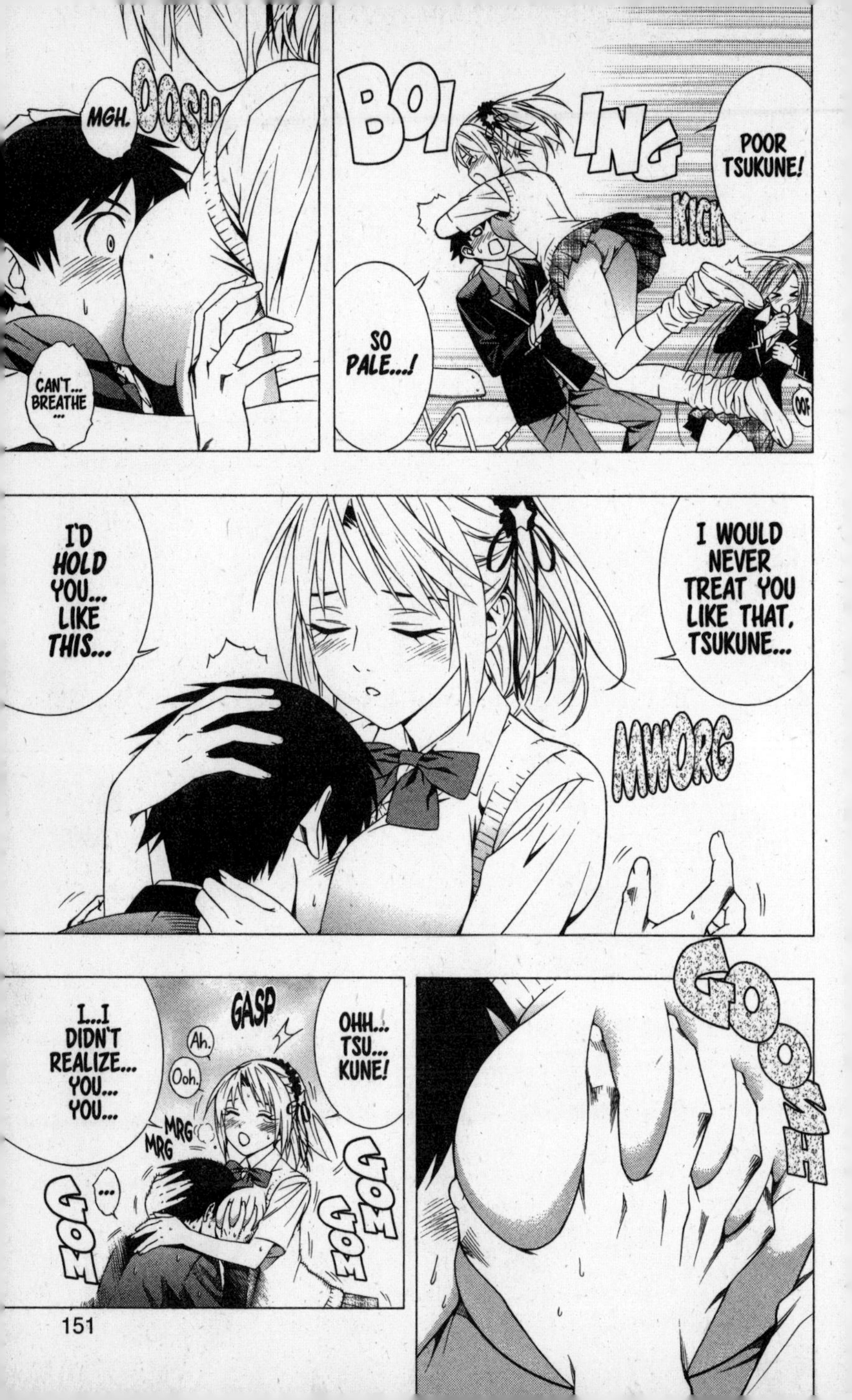
POOR TSUKUNE!
BOI
ING
KICK
SO PALE...!
OOF
OOSH
MGH.
CAN'T... BREATHE ...
I WOULD NEVER TREAT YOU LIKE THAT, TSUKUNE...
I'D HOLD YOU... LIKE THIS...
MWORG
GOOOSH
OHH... TSU... KUNE!
GASP
Ah.
Ooh.
I...I DIDN'T REALIZE... YOU... YOU...
MRG
MRG
GOM GOM
...
GOM

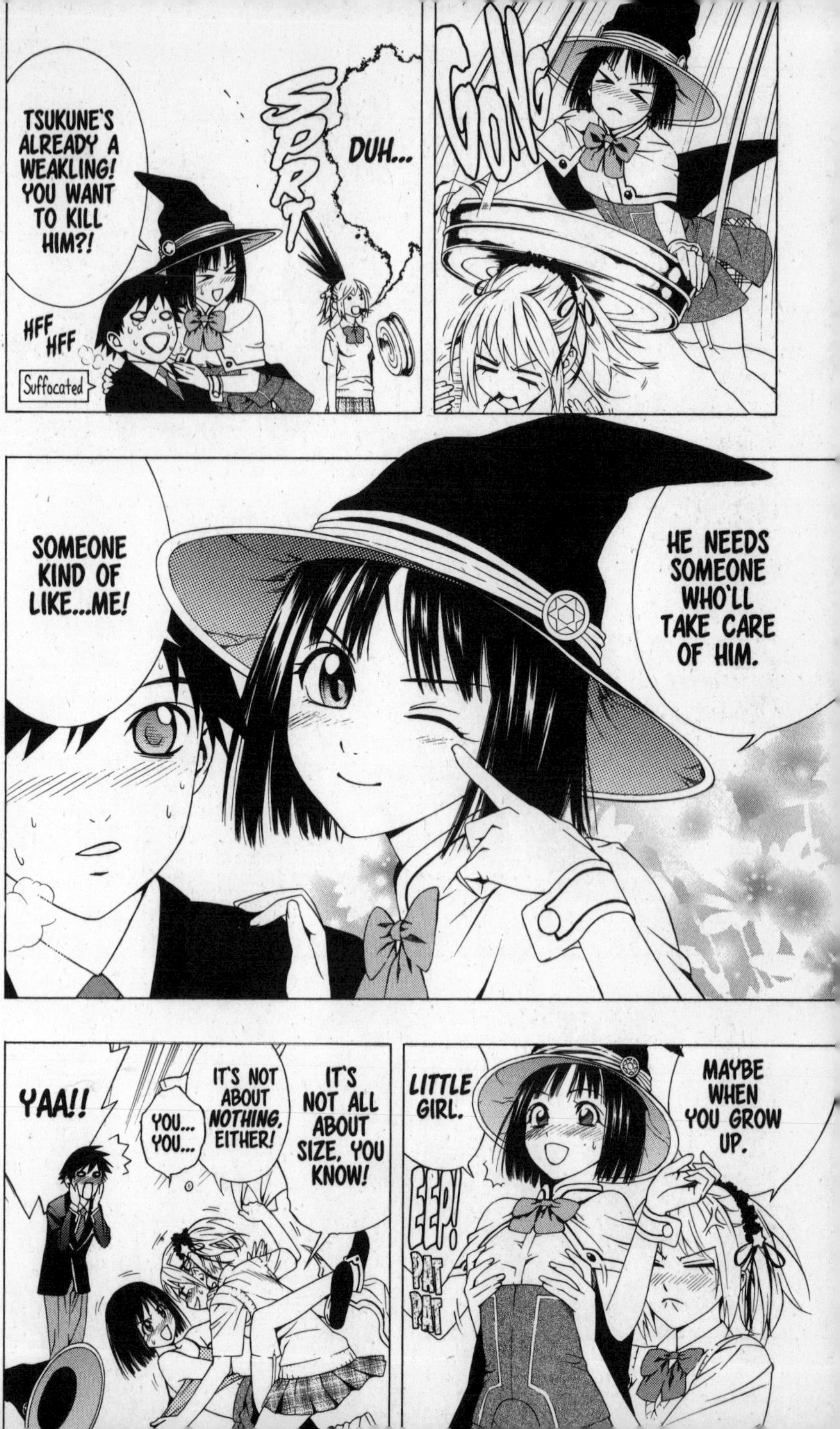
GONG
DUH...
SPRT
TSUKUNE'S ALREADY A WEAKLING! YOU WANT TO KILL HIM?!
HFF HFF
Suffocated
HE NEEDS SOMEONE WHO'LL TAKE CARE OF HIM.
SOMEONE KIND OF LIKE...ME!
MAYBE WHEN YOU GROW UP.
LITTLE GIRL.
EEP!
PAT PAT
IT'S NOT ALL ABOUT SIZE, YOU KNOW!
IT'S NOT ABOUT NOTHING, EITHER!
YOU... YOU...
YAA!!

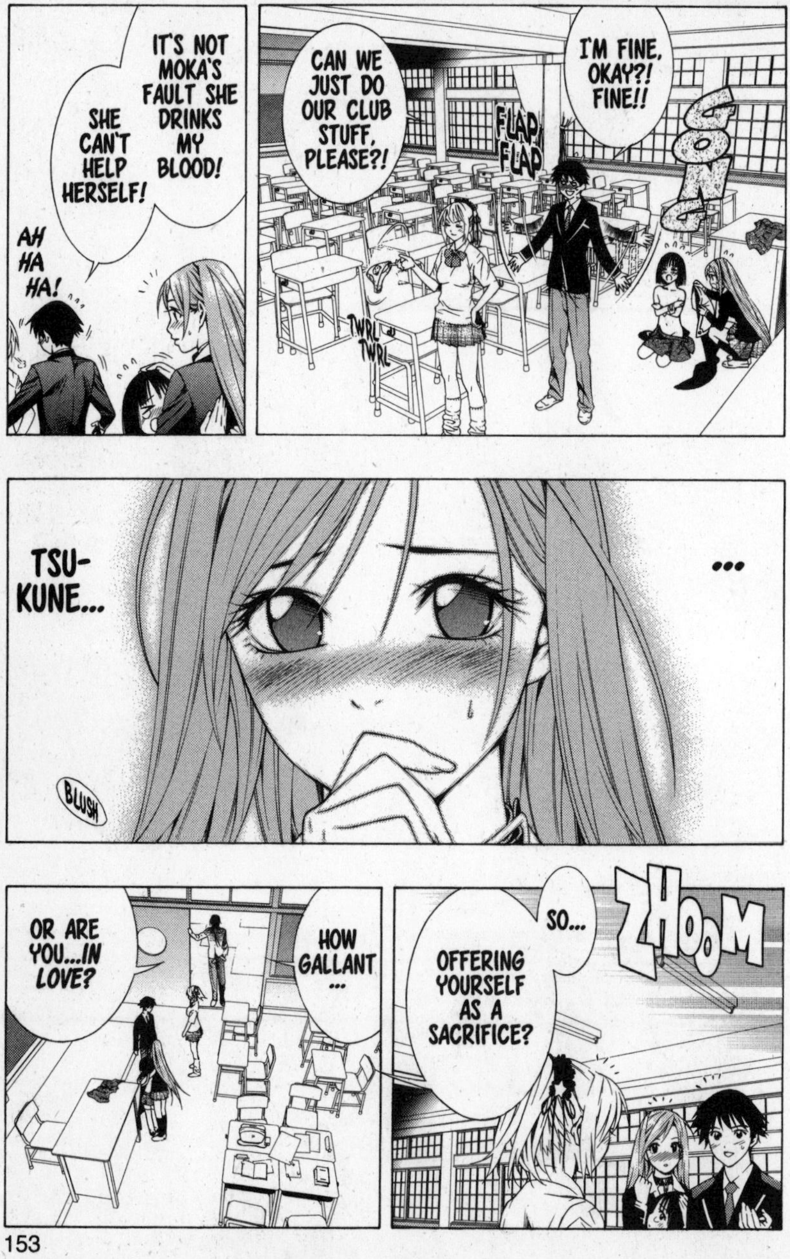
I'M FINE, OKAY?! FINE!!
GONG
FLAP FLAP
CAN WE JUST DO OUR CLUB STUFF, PLEASE?!
TWRL TWRL
IT'S NOT MOKA'S FAULT SHE DRINKS MY BLOOD!
SHE CAN'T HELP HERSELF!
AH HA HA!
...
TSU-KUNE...
BLUSH
ZHOOM
SO...
OFFERING YOURSELF AS A SACRIFICE?
HOW GALLANT ...
OR ARE YOU...IN LOVE?

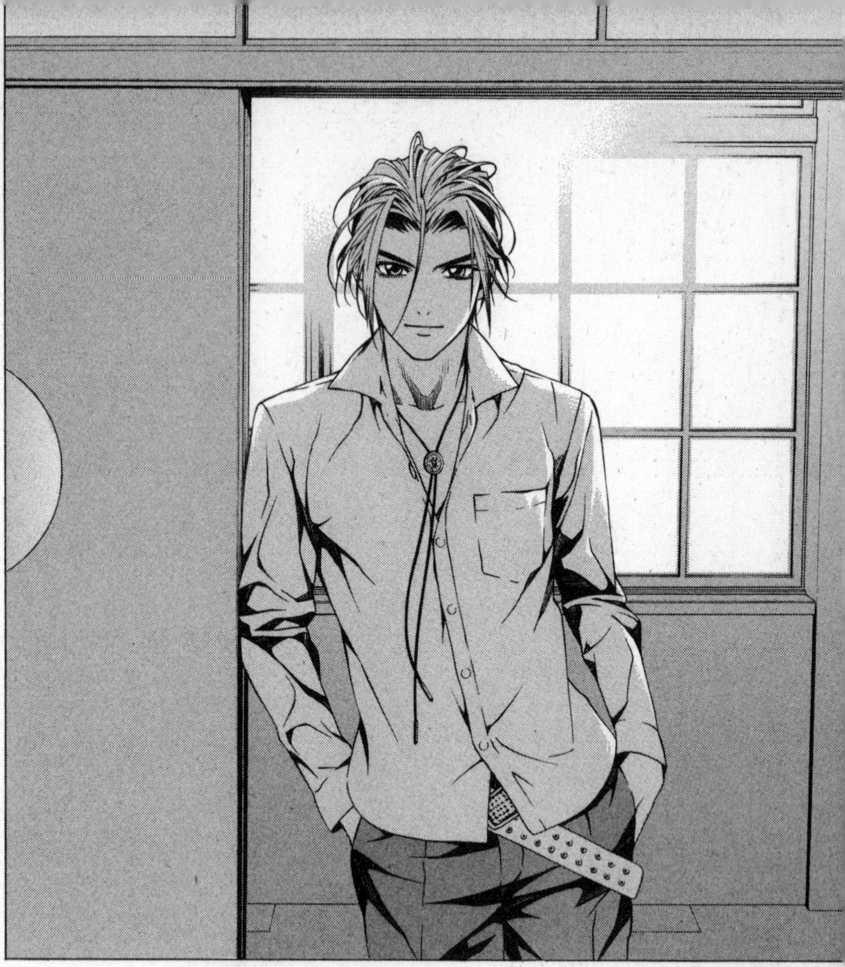

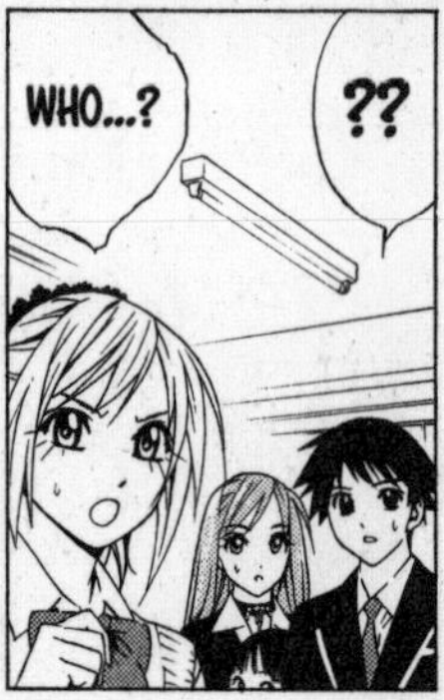
??
WHO...?

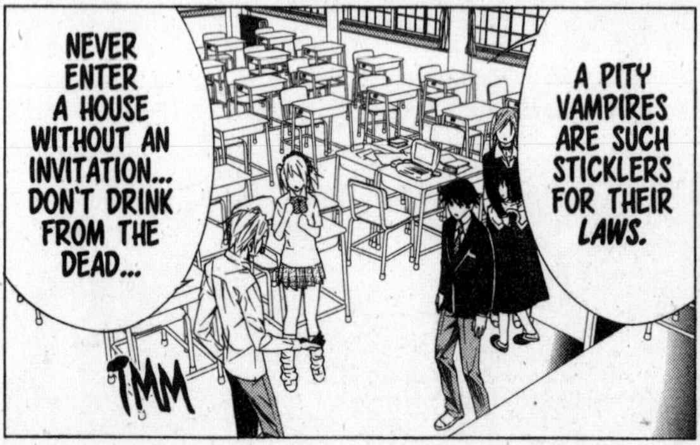
A PITY VAMPIRES ARE SUCH STICKLERS FOR THEIR *LAWS.*
NEVER ENTER A HOUSE WITHOUT AN INVITATION... DON'T DRINK FROM THE DEAD...
TMM

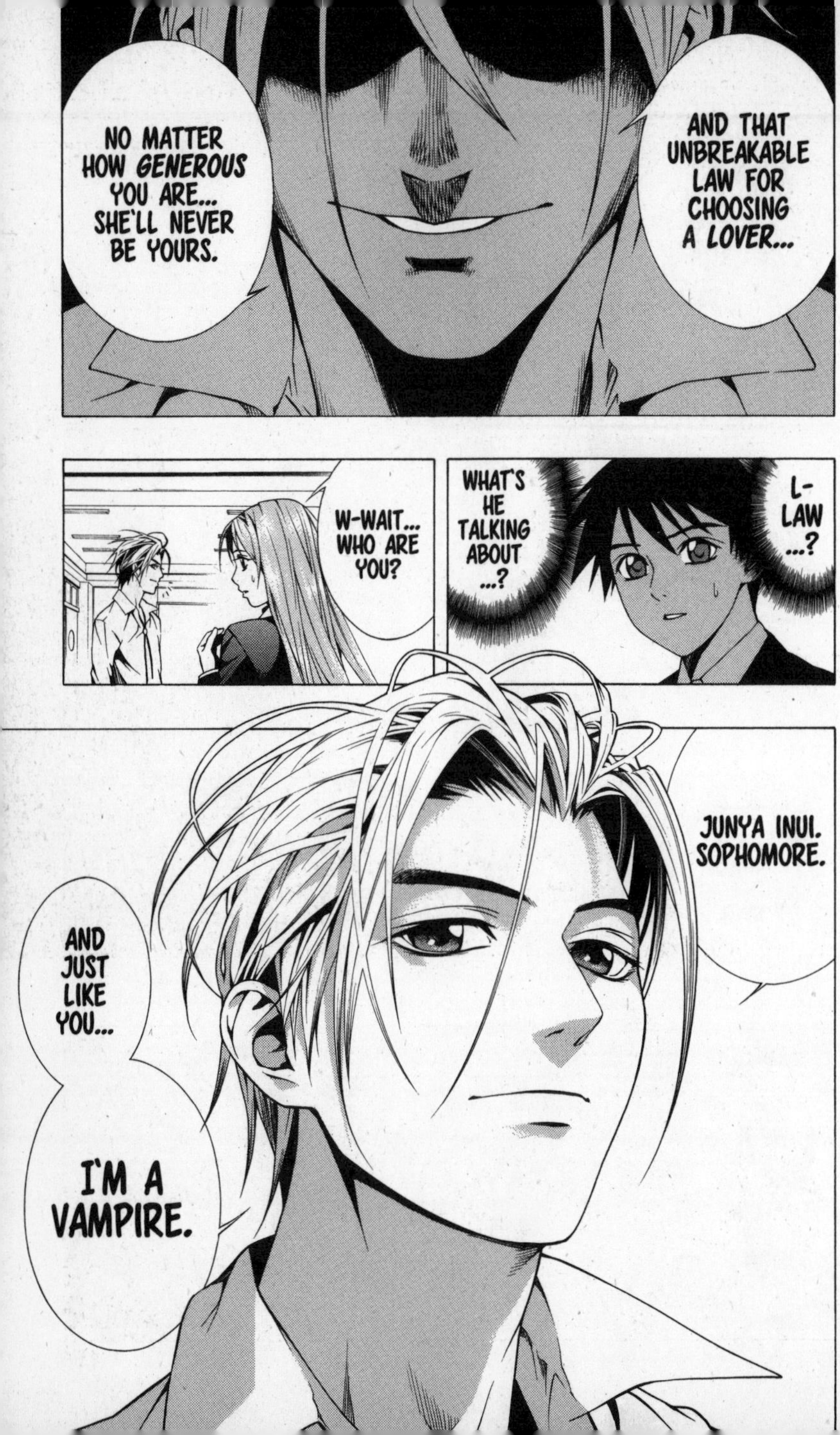
AND THAT UNBREAKABLE LAW FOR CHOOSING A *LOVER*...
NO MATTER HOW *GENEROUS* YOU ARE... SHE'LL NEVER BE YOURS.
L-LAW ...?
WHAT'S HE TALKING ABOUT ...?
W-WAIT... WHO ARE YOU?
JUNYA INUI. SOPHOMORE.
AND JUST LIKE YOU...
I'M A VAMPIRE.

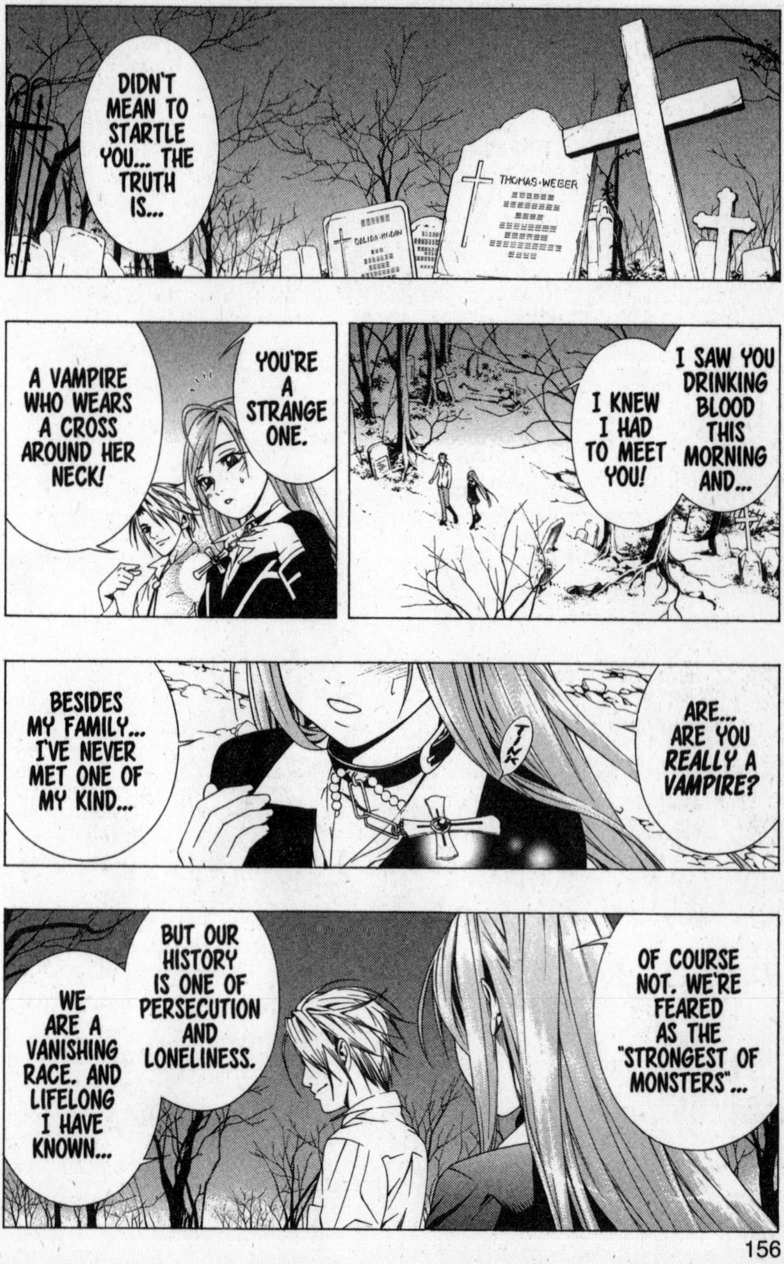
DIDN'T MEAN TO STARTLE YOU... THE TRUTH IS...
THOMAS·WEBER
DALIDA·RODIN
I SAW YOU DRINKING BLOOD THIS MORNING AND...
I KNEW I HAD TO MEET YOU!
YOU'RE A STRANGE ONE.
A VAMPIRE WHO WEARS A CROSS AROUND HER NECK!
ARE... ARE YOU *REALLY* A VAMPIRE?
TINK
BESIDES MY FAMILY... I'VE NEVER MET ONE OF MY KIND...
OF COURSE NOT. WE'RE FEARED AS THE "STRONGEST OF MONSTERS"...
BUT OUR HISTORY IS ONE OF PERSECUTION AND LONELINESS.
WE ARE A VANISHING RACE. AND LIFELONG I HAVE KNOWN...

READ THIS WAY

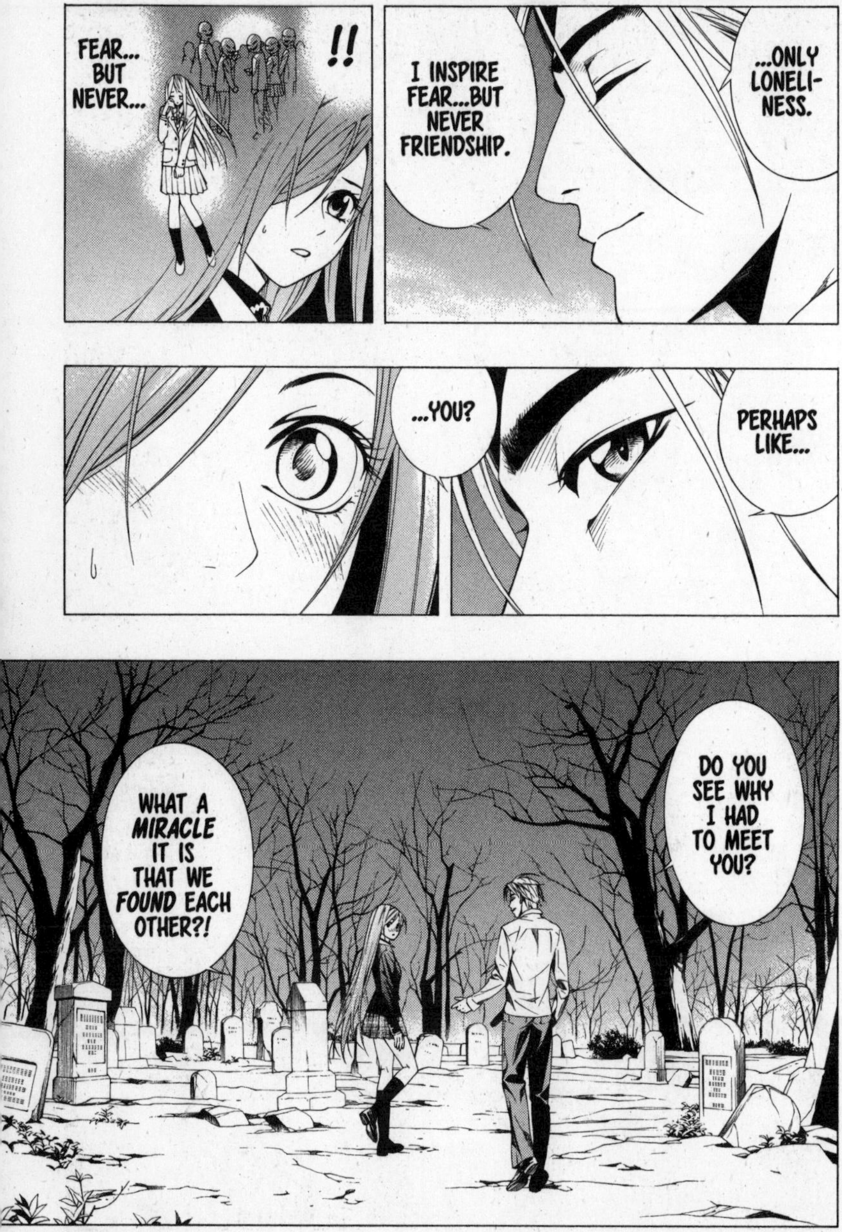
I INSPIRE FEAR...BUT NEVER FRIENDSHIP.
...ONLY LONELI-NESS.
FEAR... BUT NEVER...
!!
PERHAPS LIKE...
...YOU?
DO YOU SEE WHY I HAD TO MEET YOU?
WHAT A MIRACLE IT IS THAT WE FOUND EACH OTHER?!

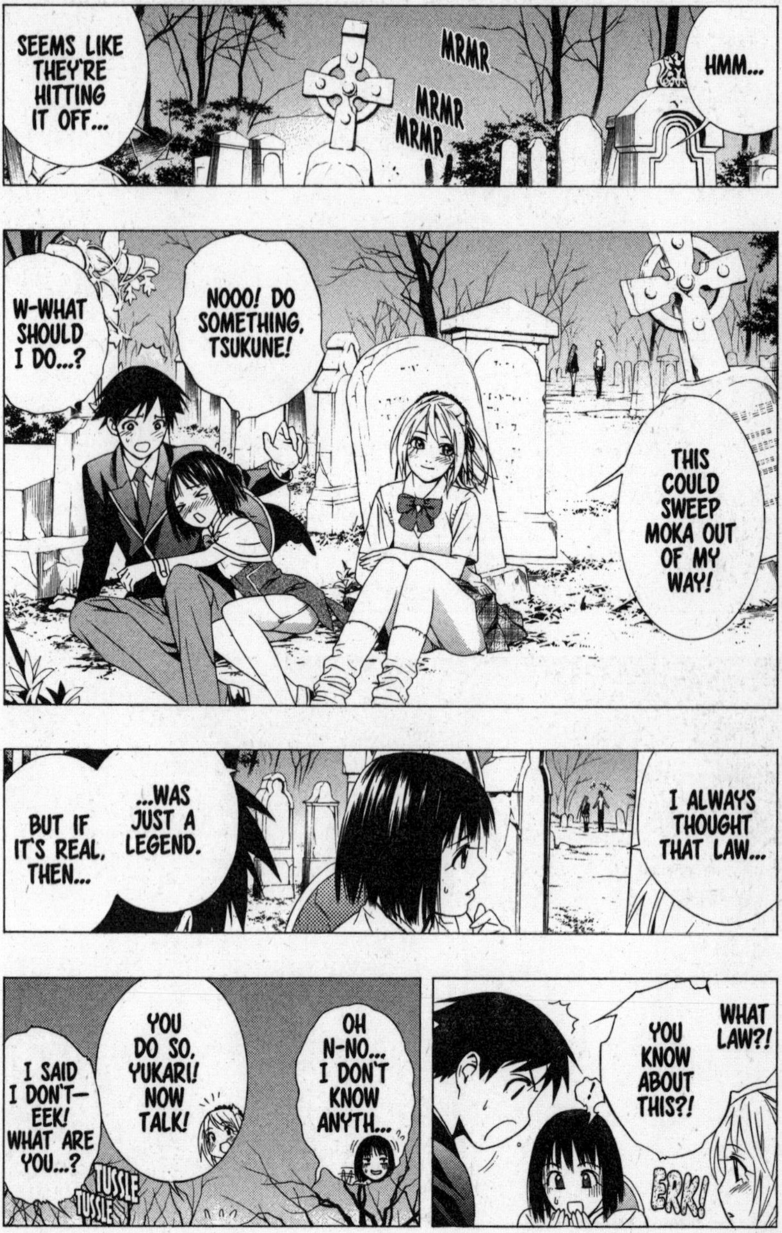
HMM...
MRMR
MRMR MRMR
SEEMS LIKE THEY'RE HITTING IT OFF...
THIS COULD SWEEP MOKA OUT OF MY WAY!
NOOO! DO SOMETHING, TSUKUNE!
W-WHAT SHOULD I DO...?
I ALWAYS THOUGHT THAT LAW...
...WAS JUST A LEGEND.
BUT IF IT'S REAL, THEN...
WHAT LAW?!
YOU KNOW ABOUT THIS?!
ERK!
OH N-NO... I DON'T KNOW ANYTH...
YOU DO SO, YUKARI! NOW TALK!
I SAID I DON'T— EEK! WHAT ARE YOU...?
TUSSLE TUSSLE

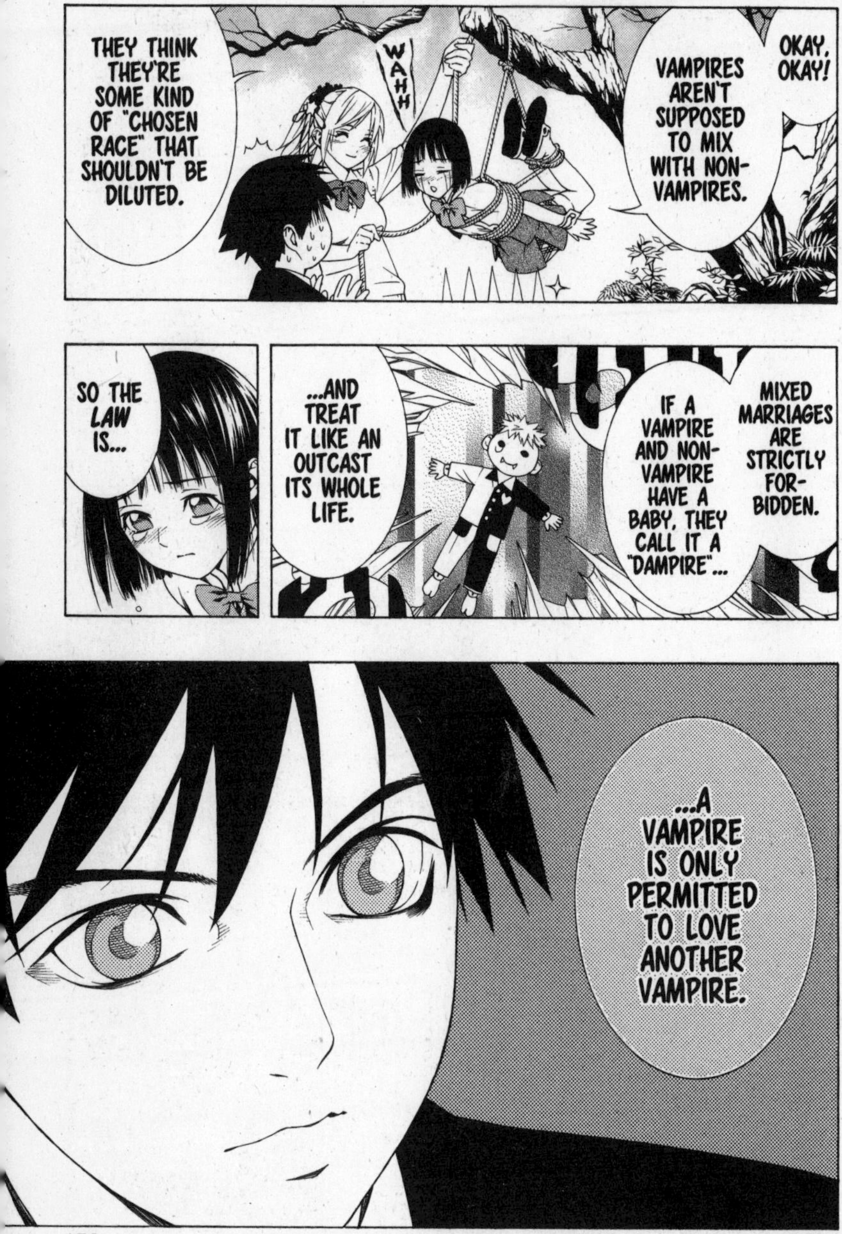
OKAY, OKAY!
VAMPIRES AREN'T SUPPOSED TO MIX WITH NON-VAMPIRES.
WAHH
THEY THINK THEY'RE SOME KIND OF "CHOSEN RACE" THAT SHOULDN'T BE DILUTED.
MIXED MARRIAGES ARE STRICTLY FOR-BIDDEN.
IF A VAMPIRE AND NON-VAMPIRE HAVE A BABY, THEY CALL IT A "DAMPIRE"...
...AND TREAT IT LIKE AN OUTCAST ITS WHOLE LIFE.
SO THE *LAW* IS...
...A VAMPIRE IS ONLY PERMITTED TO LOVE ANOTHER VAMPIRE.

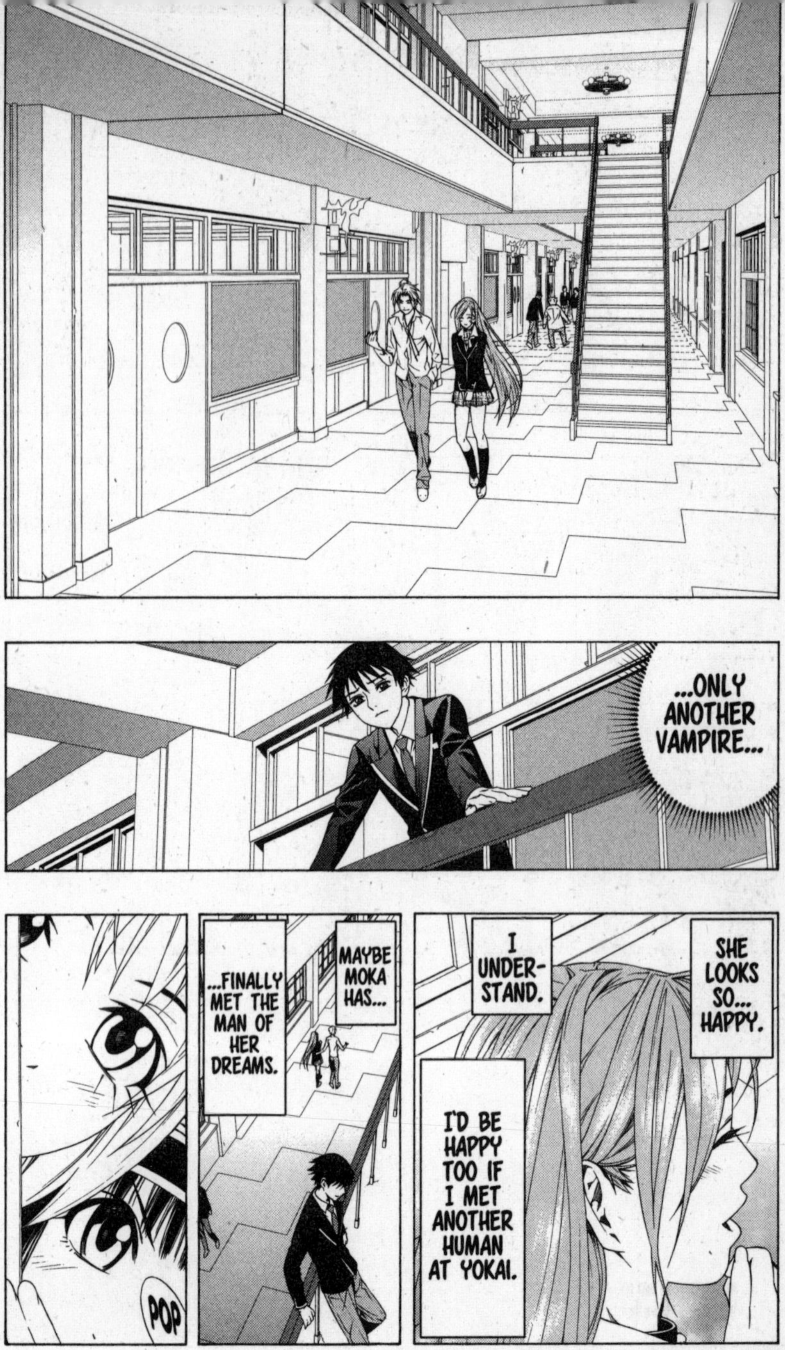
...ONLY ANOTHER VAMPIRE...
SHE LOOKS SO... HAPPY.
I UNDER-STAND.
I'D BE HAPPY TOO IF I MET ANOTHER HUMAN AT YOKAI.
MAYBE MOKA HAS...
...FINALLY MET THE MAN OF HER DREAMS.
POP

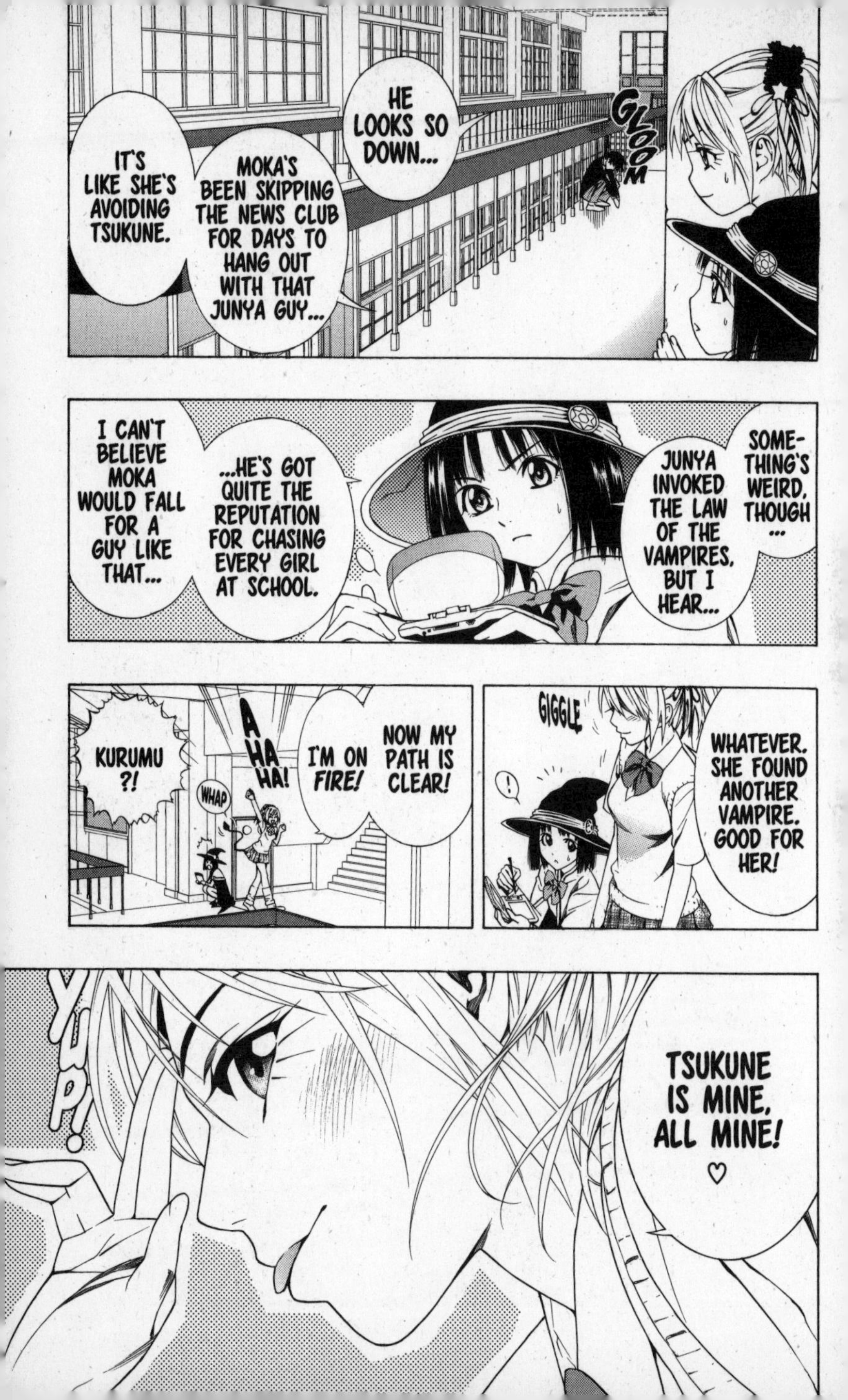
GLOOM
HE LOOKS SO DOWN...
MOKA'S BEEN SKIPPING THE NEWS CLUB FOR DAYS TO HANG OUT WITH THAT JUNYA GUY...
IT'S LIKE SHE'S AVOIDING TSUKUNE.
SOMETHING'S WEIRD, THOUGH...
JUNYA INVOKED THE LAW OF THE VAMPIRES, BUT I HEAR...
...HE'S GOT QUITE THE REPUTATION FOR CHASING EVERY GIRL AT SCHOOL.
I CAN'T BELIEVE MOKA WOULD FALL FOR A GUY LIKE THAT...
GIGGLE
WHATEVER. SHE FOUND ANOTHER VAMPIRE. GOOD FOR HER!
!
NOW MY PATH IS CLEAR!
I'M ON FIRE!
AHAHA!
WHAP
KURUMU?!
TSUKUNE IS MINE, ALL MINE! ♡
YUP!

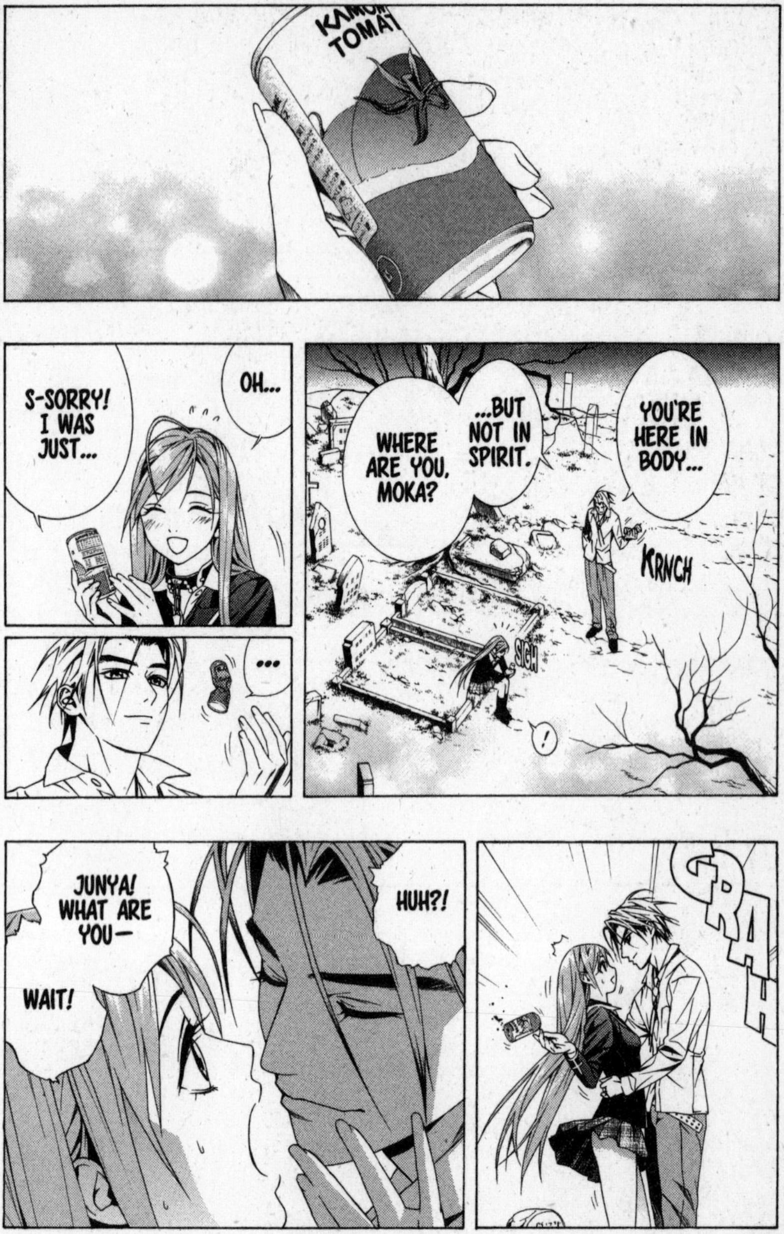
KAMOM
TOMAT
YOU'RE HERE IN BODY...
...BUT NOT IN SPIRIT.
WHERE ARE YOU, MOKA?
KRNCH
SIGH
!
OH...
S-SORRY! I WAS JUST...
...
GRAH
HUH?!
JUNYA! WHAT ARE YOU—
WAIT!

READ THIS WAY

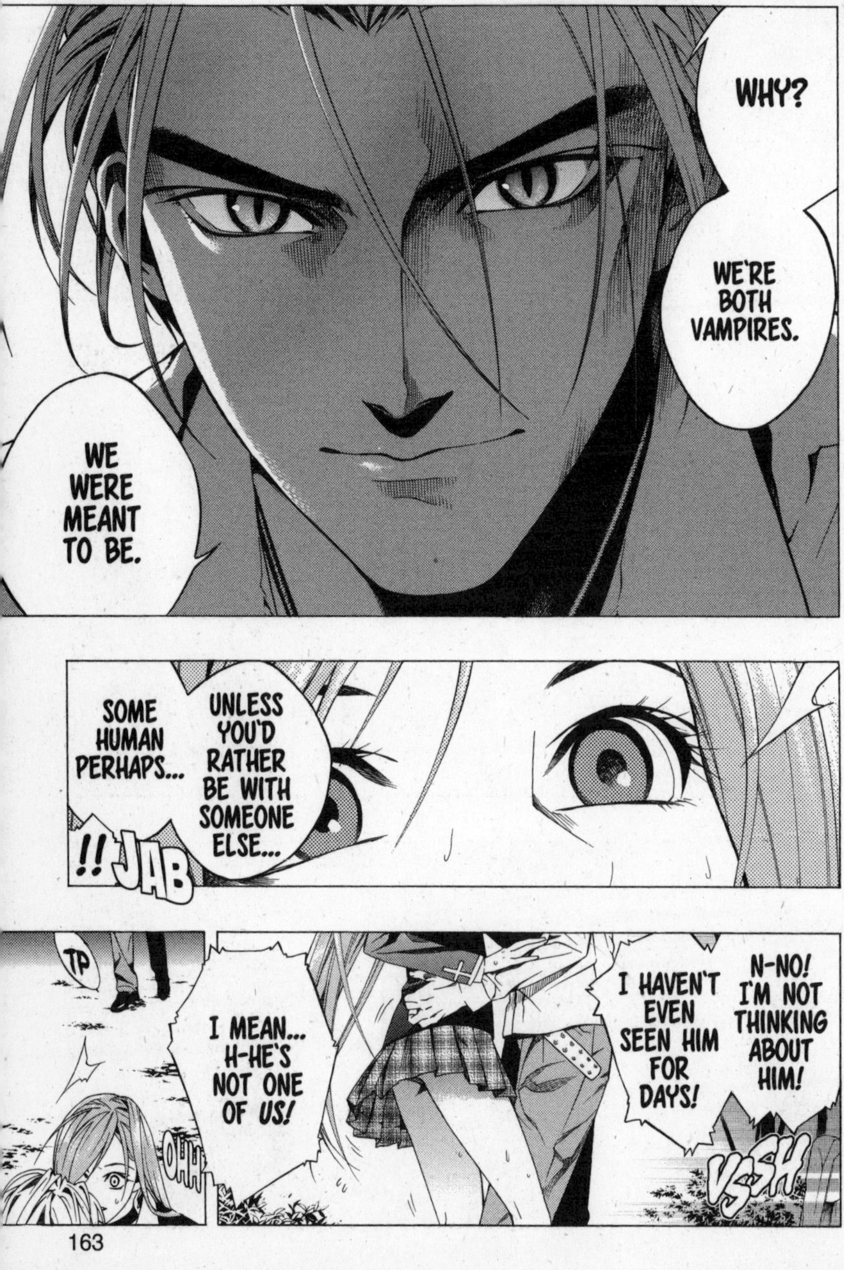

WHY?
WE'RE BOTH VAMPIRES.
WE WERE MEANT TO BE.
UNLESS YOU'D RATHER BE WITH SOMEONE ELSE...
SOME HUMAN PERHAPS...
!!
JAB
N-NO! I'M NOT THINKING ABOUT HIM!
I HAVEN'T EVEN SEEN HIM FOR DAYS!
VSSH
I MEAN... H-HE'S NOT ONE OF US!
TP
OHH

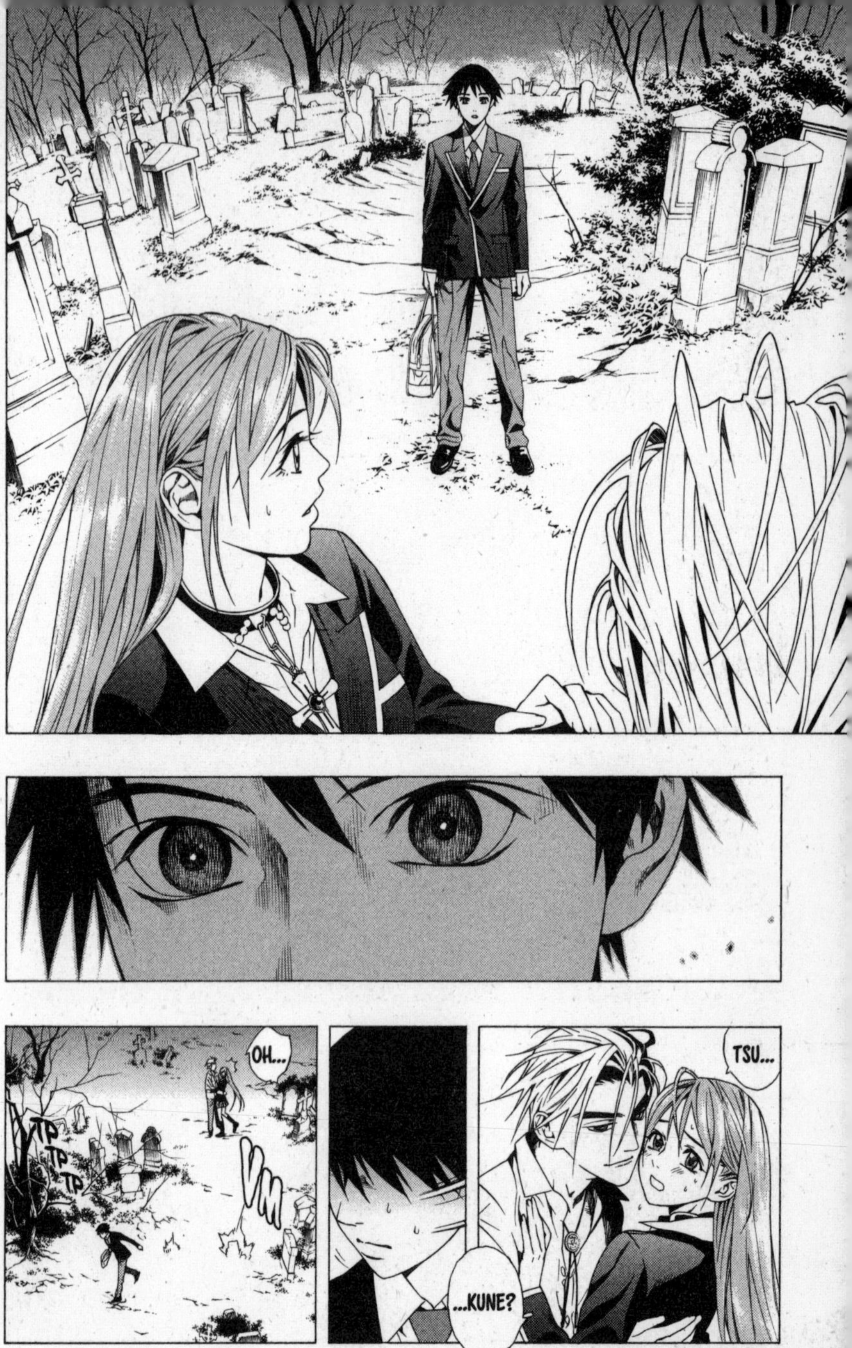
TSU...
...KUNE?
OH...
VM
TP TP TP

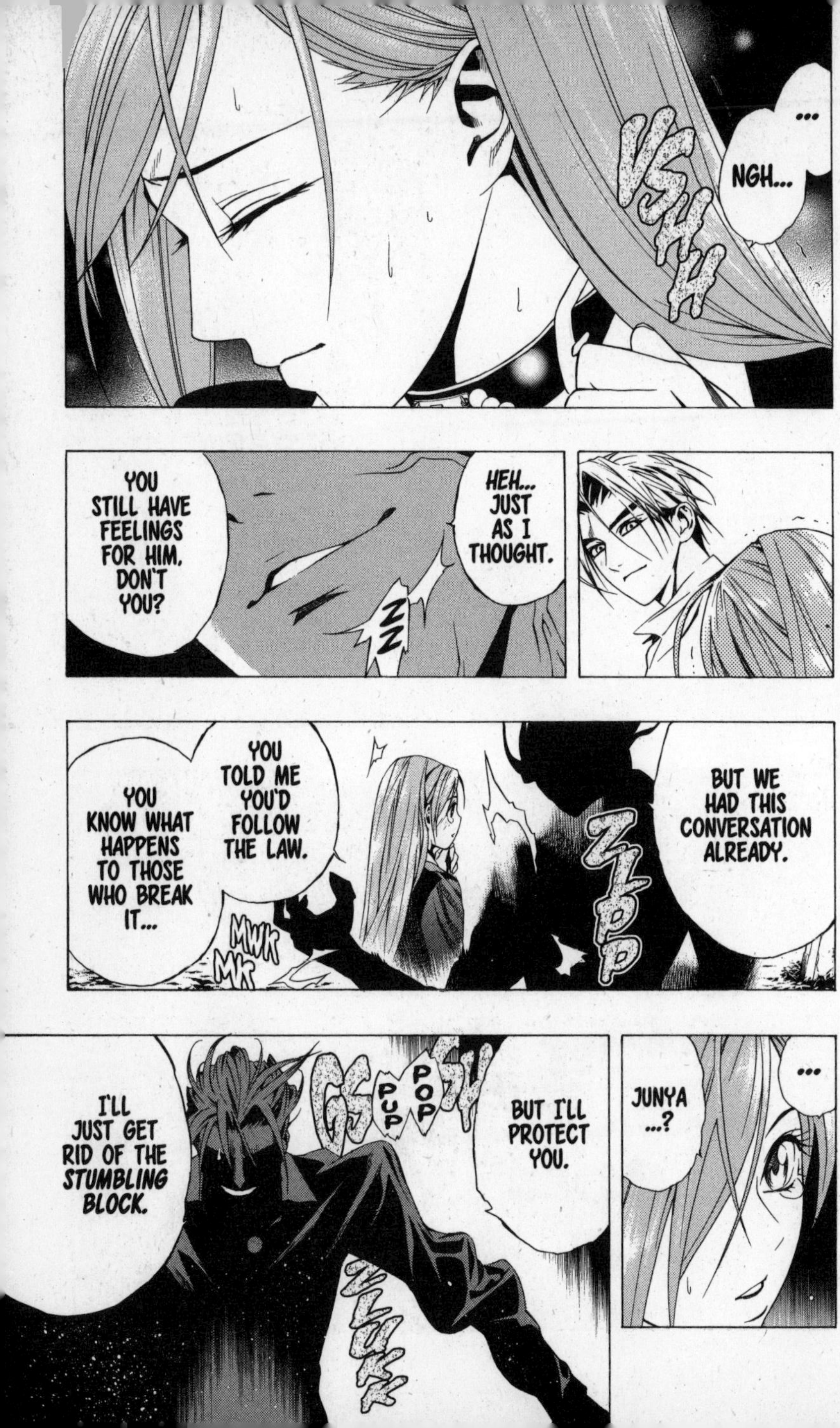
...
NGH...
HEH... JUST AS I THOUGHT.
YOU STILL HAVE FEELINGS FOR HIM, DON'T YOU?
ZZ
BUT WE HAD THIS CONVERSATION ALREADY.
YOU TOLD ME YOU'D FOLLOW THE LAW.
YOU KNOW WHAT HAPPENS TO THOSE WHO BREAK IT...
MWK MK
...
JUNYA ...?
BUT I'LL PROTECT YOU.
POP
PUP
I'LL JUST GET RID OF THE STUMBLING BLOCK.

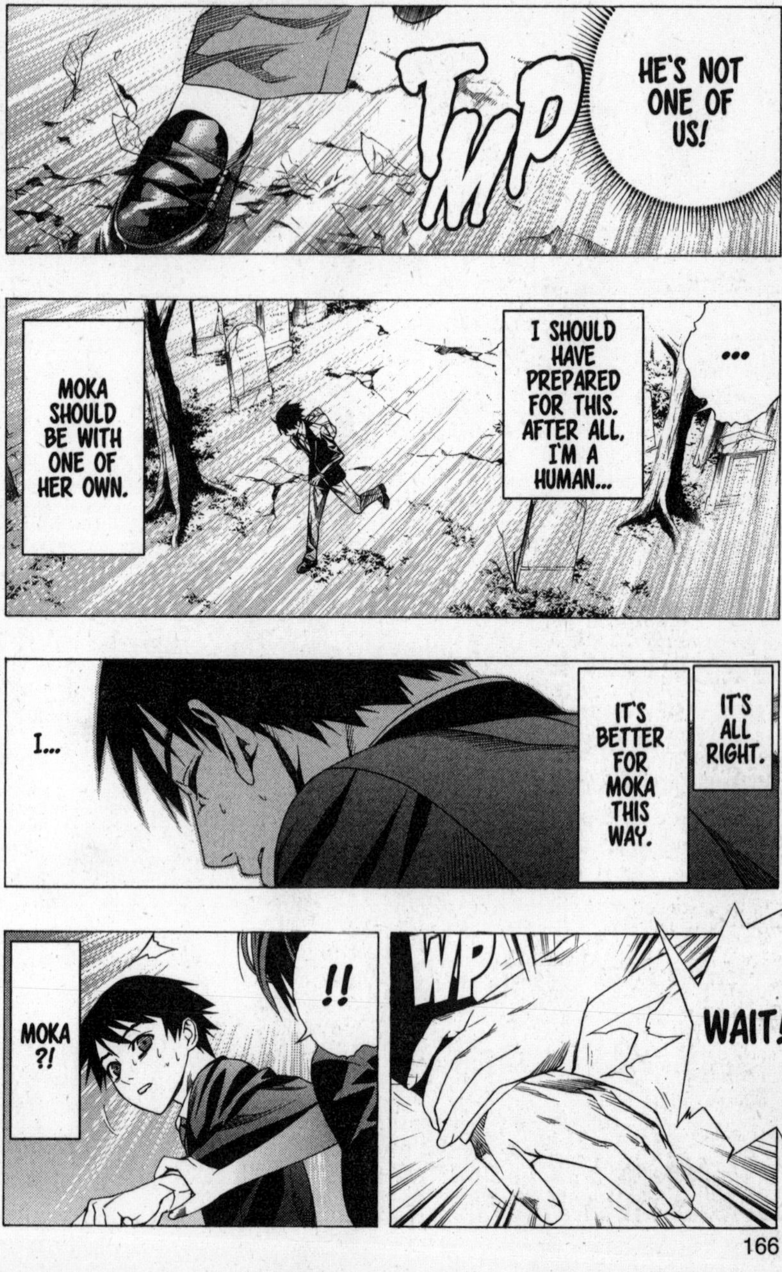
HE'S NOT ONE OF US!
TMP
...
I SHOULD HAVE PREPARED FOR THIS. AFTER ALL, I'M A HUMAN...
MOKA SHOULD BE WITH ONE OF HER OWN.
IT'S ALL RIGHT.
IT'S BETTER FOR MOKA THIS WAY.
I...
WAIT!
WP
!!
MOKA ?!

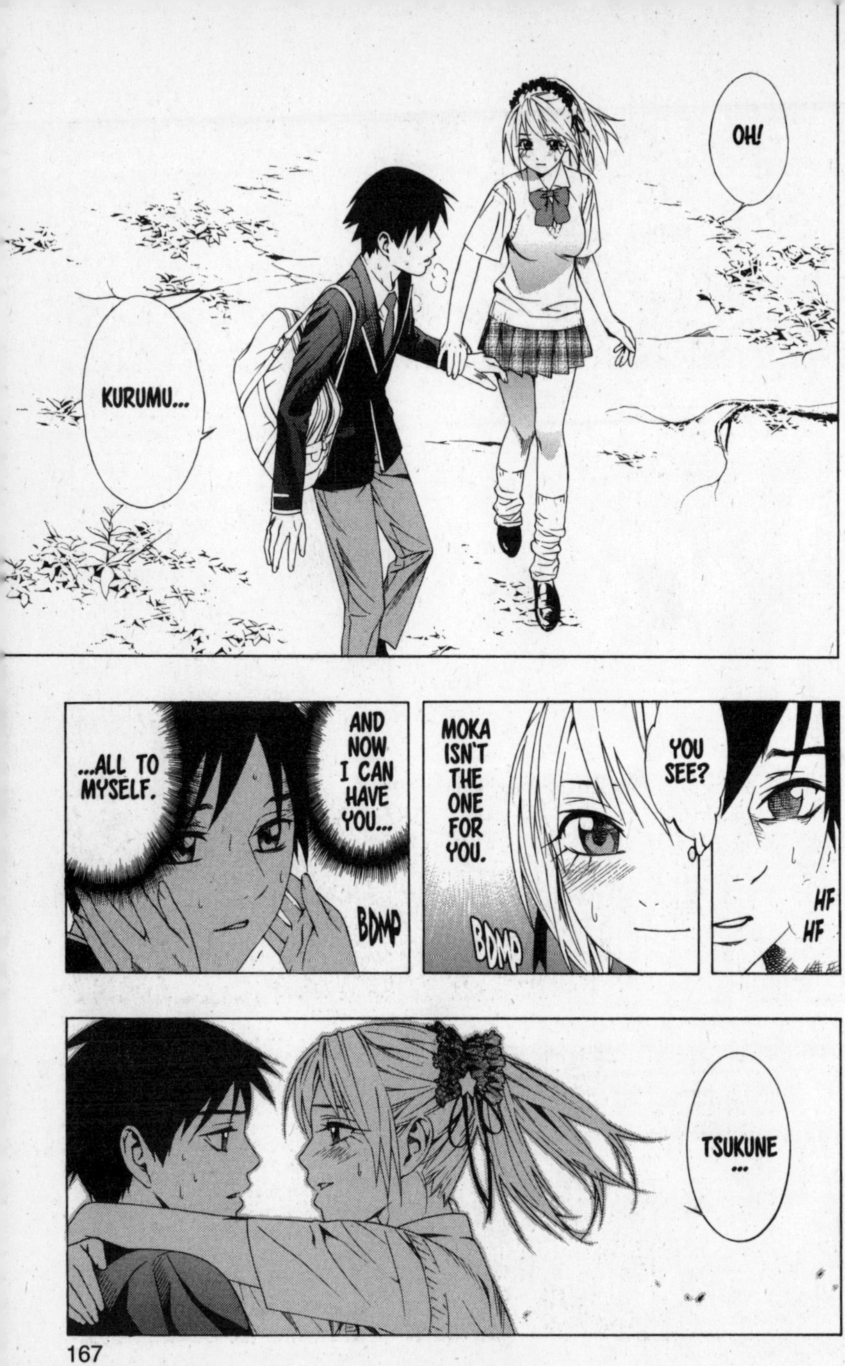

OH!
KURUMU...
YOU SEE?
HF HF
MOKA ISN'T THE ONE FOR YOU.
BDMP
AND NOW I CAN HAVE YOU...
...ALL TO MYSELF.
BDMP
TSUKUNE...

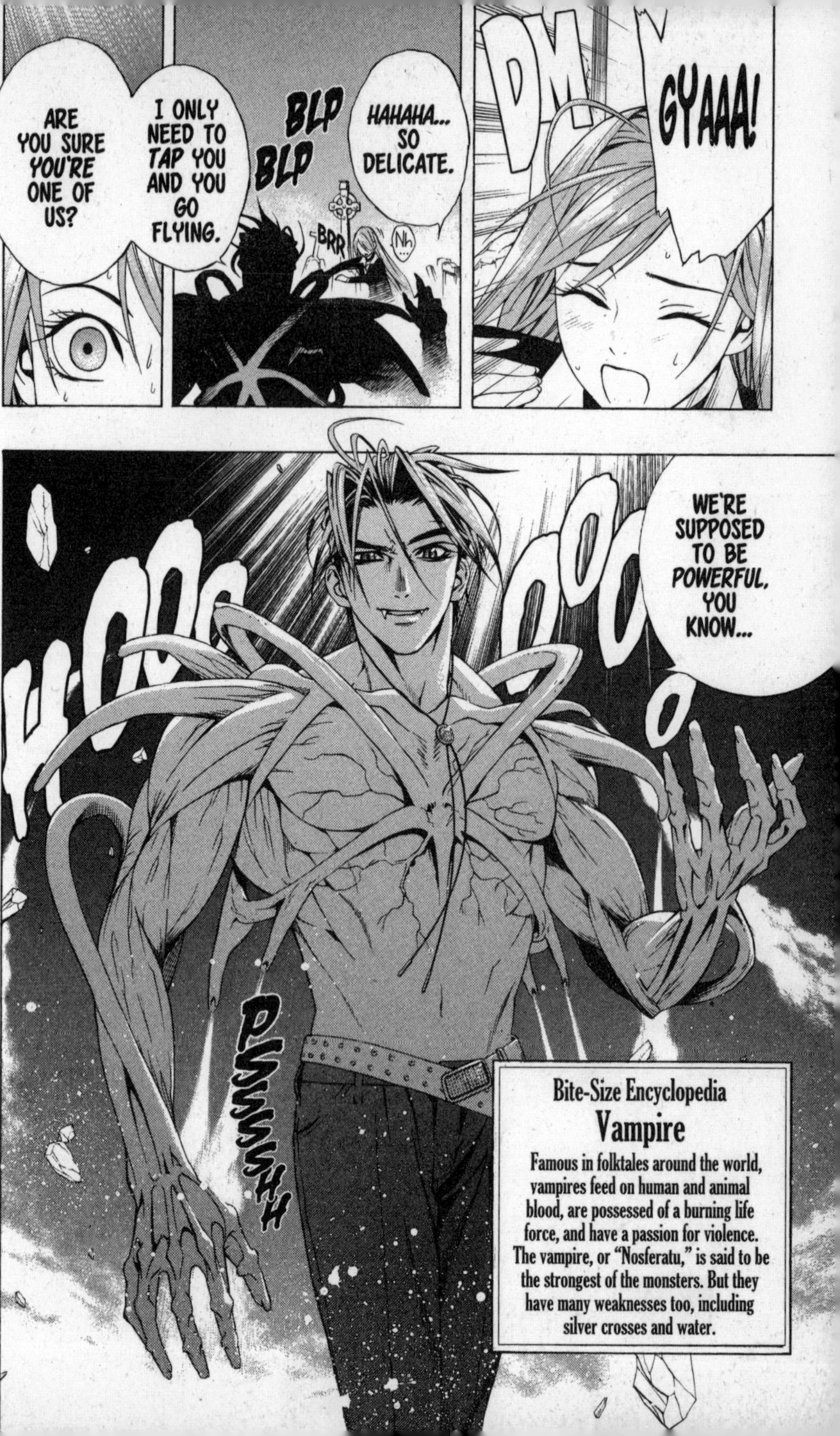
DM
GYAAA!
HAHAHA... SO DELICATE.
BLP BLP
BRR
Nh...
I ONLY NEED TO TAP YOU AND YOU GO FLYING.
ARE YOU SURE YOU'RE ONE OF US?
WE'RE SUPPOSED TO BE POWERFUL, YOU KNOW...
PSSSSHH
Bite-Size Encyclopedia
Vampire
Famous in folktales around the world, vampires feed on human and animal blood, are possessed of a burning life force, and have a passion for violence. The vampire, or "Nosferatu," is said to be the strongest of the monsters. But they have many weaknesses too, including silver crosses and water.

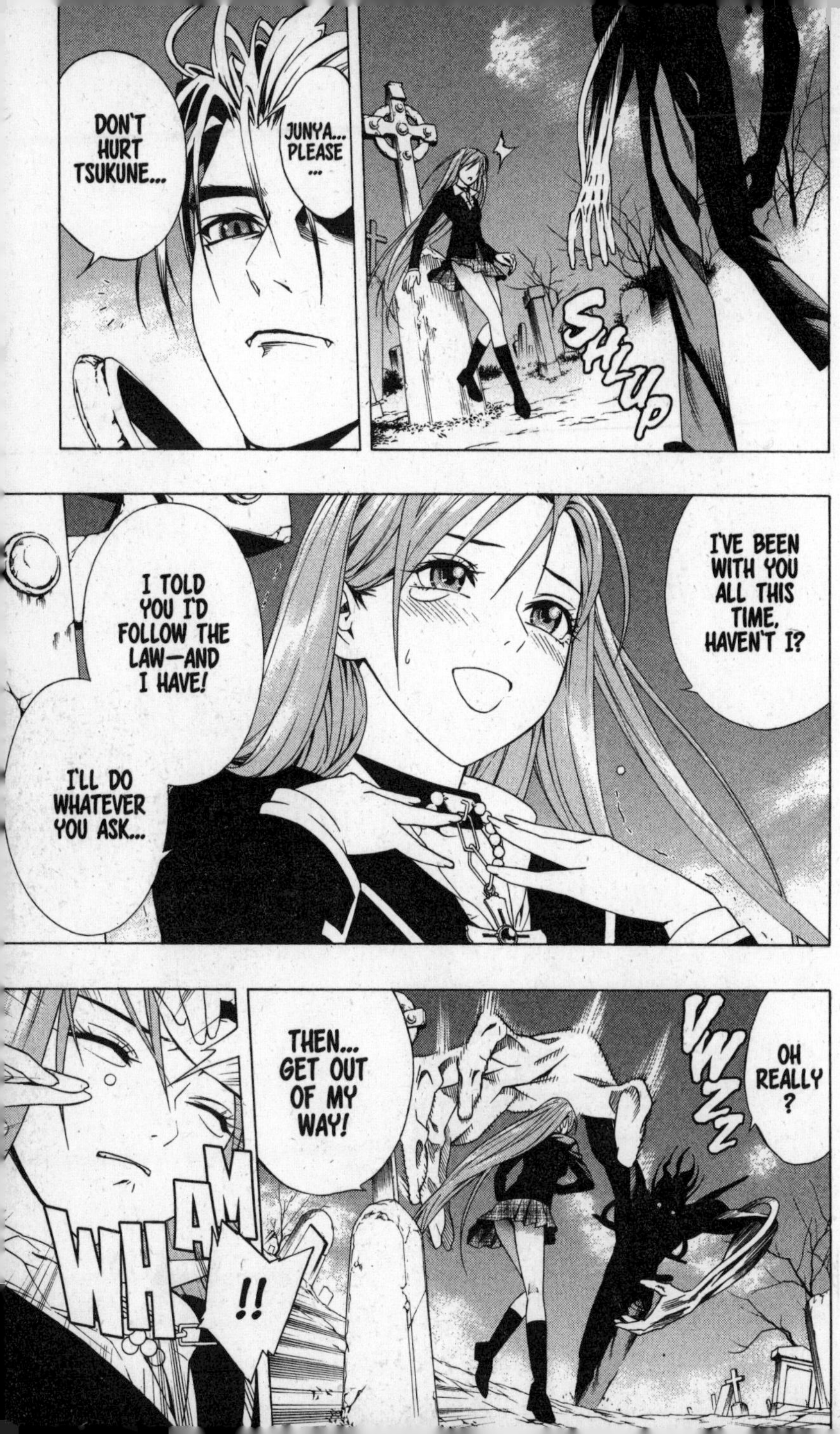
SHLUP
JUNYA... PLEASE ...
DON'T HURT TSUKUNE...
I'VE BEEN WITH YOU ALL THIS TIME, HAVEN'T I?
I TOLD YOU I'D FOLLOW THE LAW—AND I HAVE!
I'LL DO WHATEVER YOU ASK...
OH REALLY ?
VWZZ
THEN... GET OUT OF MY WAY!
WHAM
!!

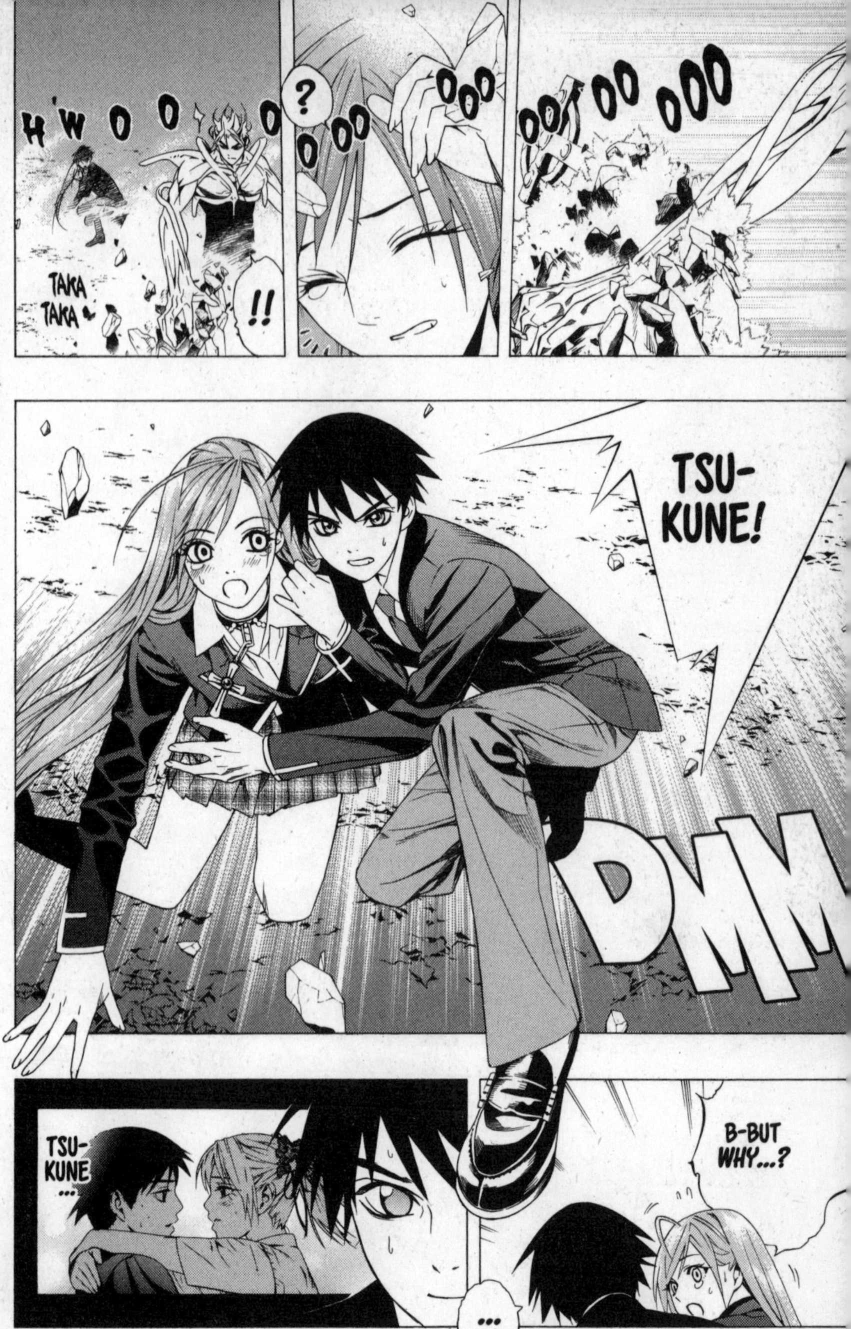
OOO OO OOO
OOOO
?
HWOOO
TAKA TAKA
!!
TSU-KUNE!
DMM
B-BUT WHY...?
...
TSU-KUNE...

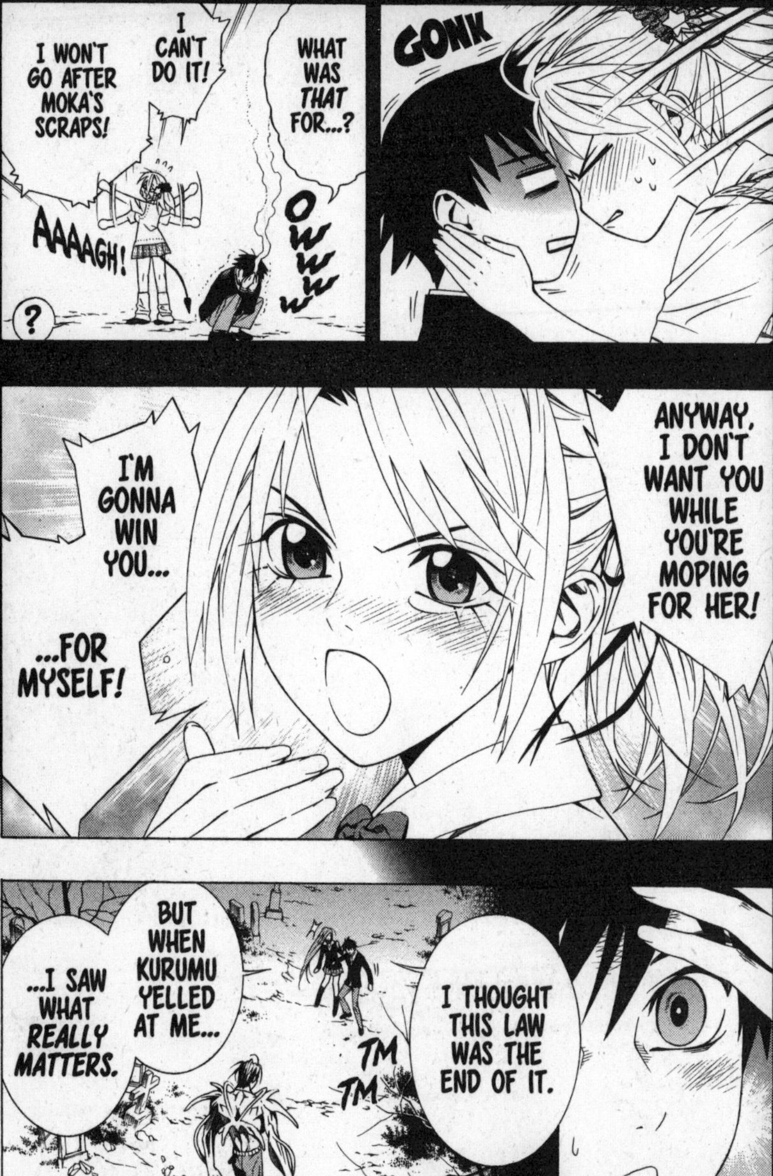
GONK
WHAT WAS THAT FOR...?
OWWWW
I CAN'T DO IT!
I WON'T GO AFTER MOKA'S SCRAPS!
AAAAGH!
?
ANYWAY, I DON'T WANT YOU WHILE YOU'RE MOPING FOR HER!
I'M GONNA WIN YOU...
...FOR MYSELF!
I THOUGHT THIS LAW WAS THE END OF IT.
TM TM
BUT WHEN KURUMU YELLED AT ME...
...I SAW WHAT *REALLY* MATTERS.

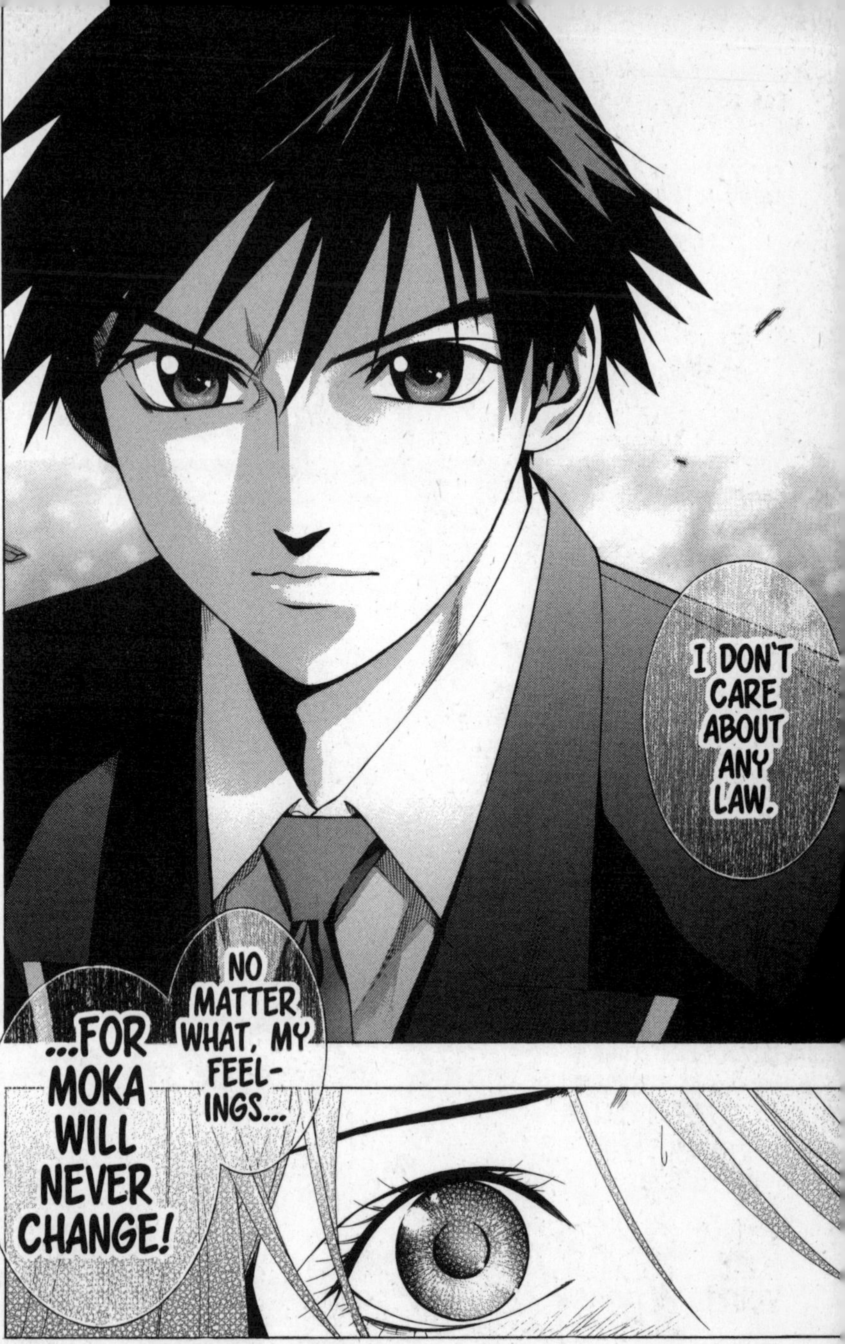
I DON'T CARE ABOUT ANY LAW.
NO MATTER WHAT, MY FEEL- INGS...
...FOR MOKA WILL NEVER CHANGE!

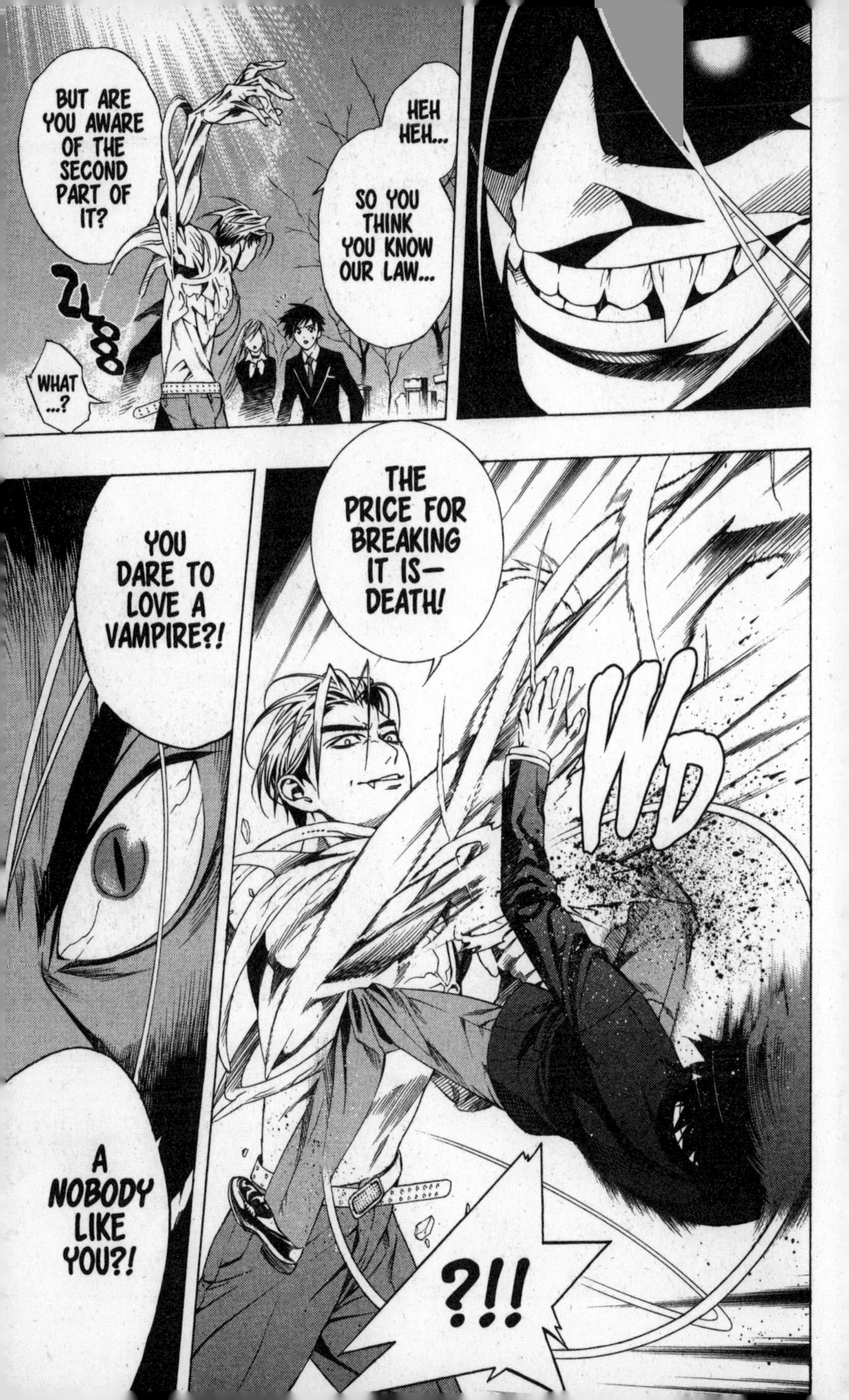

HEH HEH...
SO YOU THINK YOU KNOW OUR LAW...
BUT ARE YOU AWARE OF THE SECOND PART OF IT?
WHAT ...?
THE PRICE FOR BREAKING IT IS— DEATH!
?!!
YOU DARE TO LOVE A VAMPIRE?!
A NOBODY LIKE YOU?!

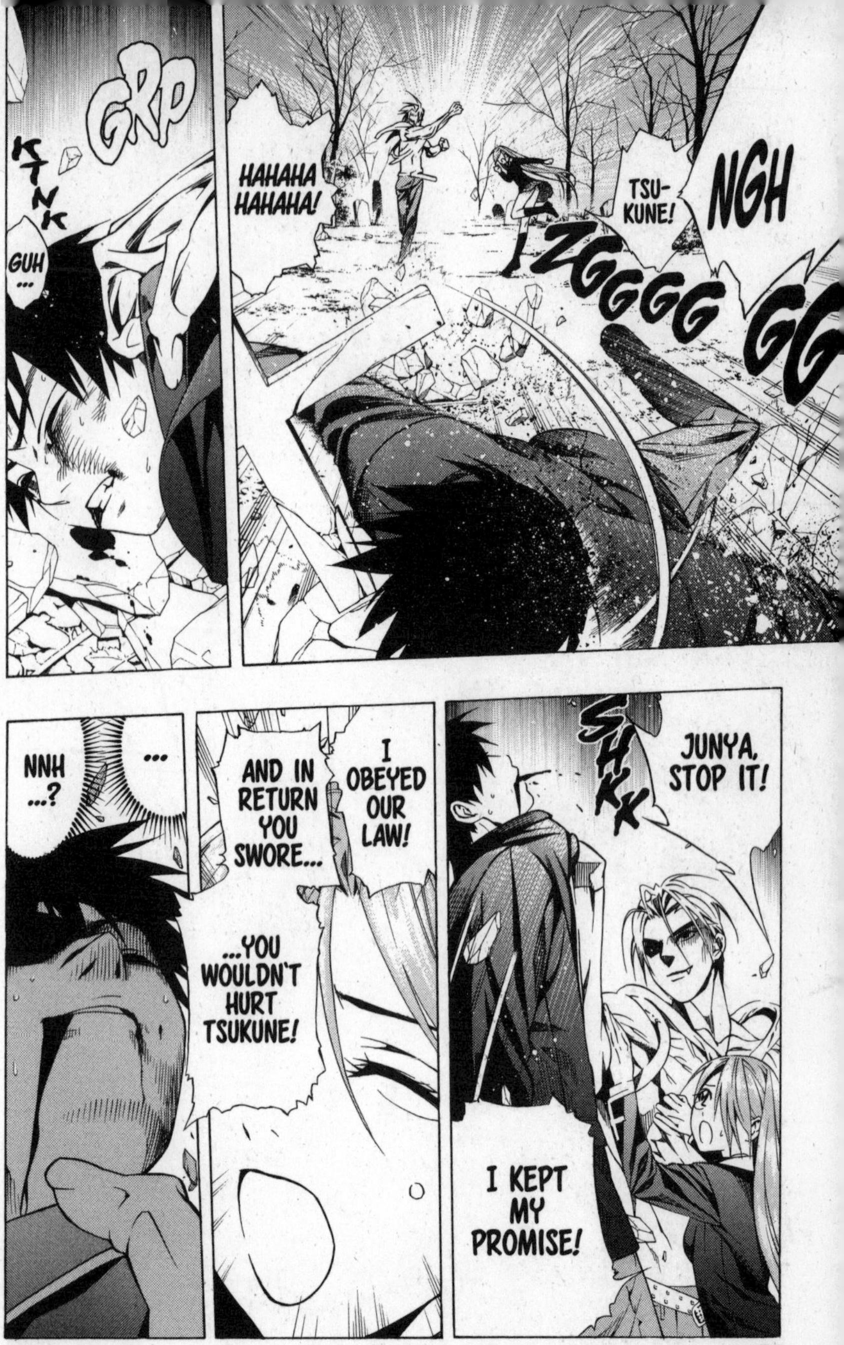
NGH
TSU-KUNE!
HAHAHA HAHAHA!
ZGGGG GG
GRP
KTNK
GUH ...
SHKK
JUNYA, STOP IT!
I KEPT MY PROMISE!
I OBEYED OUR LAW!
AND IN RETURN YOU SWORE...
...YOU WOULDN'T HURT TSUKUNE!
...
NNH ...?

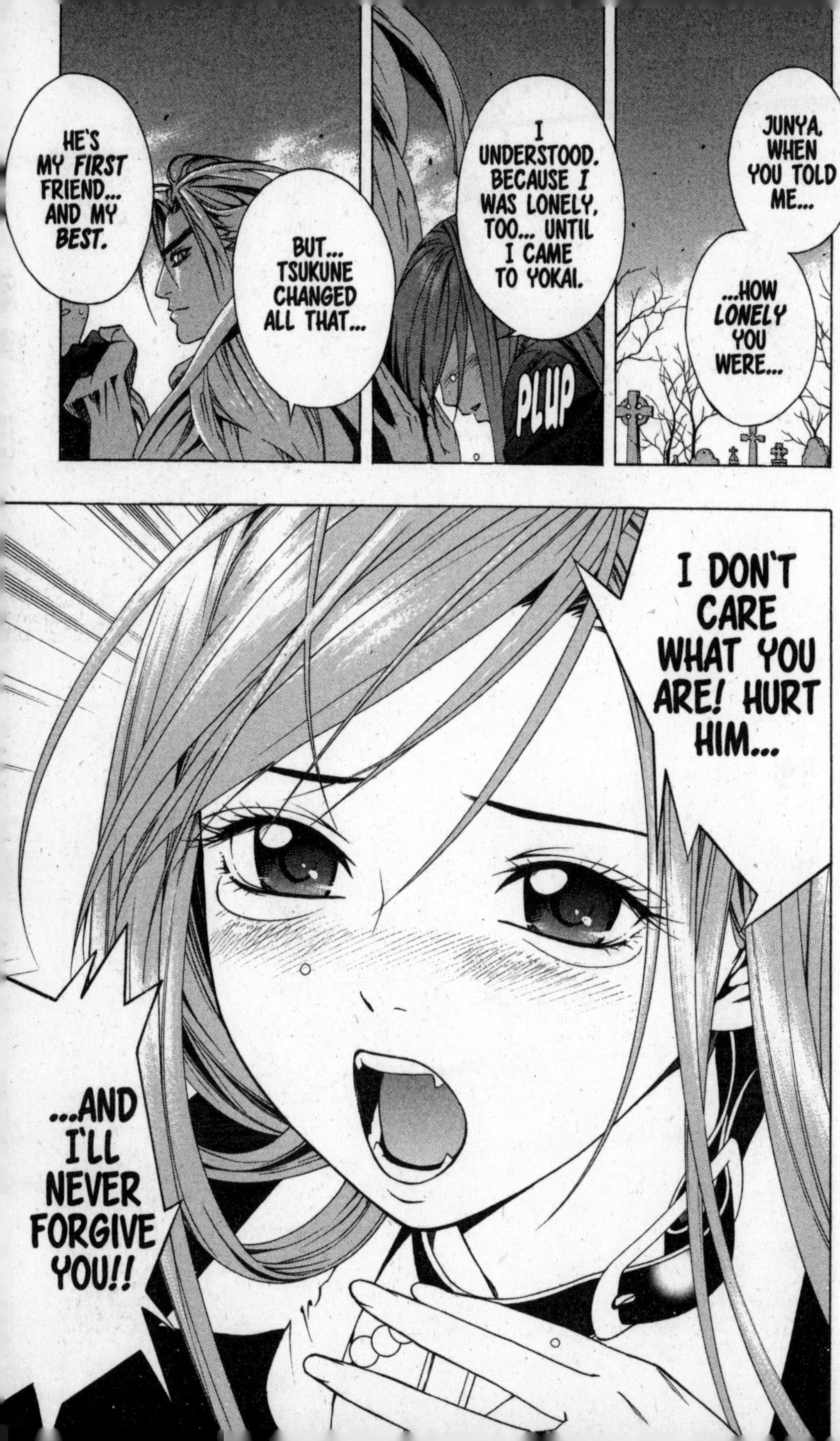
JUNYA, WHEN YOU TOLD ME...
...HOW LONELY YOU WERE...
I UNDERSTOOD. BECAUSE I WAS LONELY, TOO... UNTIL I CAME TO YOKAI.
PLUP
BUT... TSUKUNE CHANGED ALL THAT...
HE'S MY FIRST FRIEND... AND MY BEST.
I DON'T CARE WHAT YOU ARE! HURT HIM...
...AND I'LL NEVER FORGIVE YOU!!

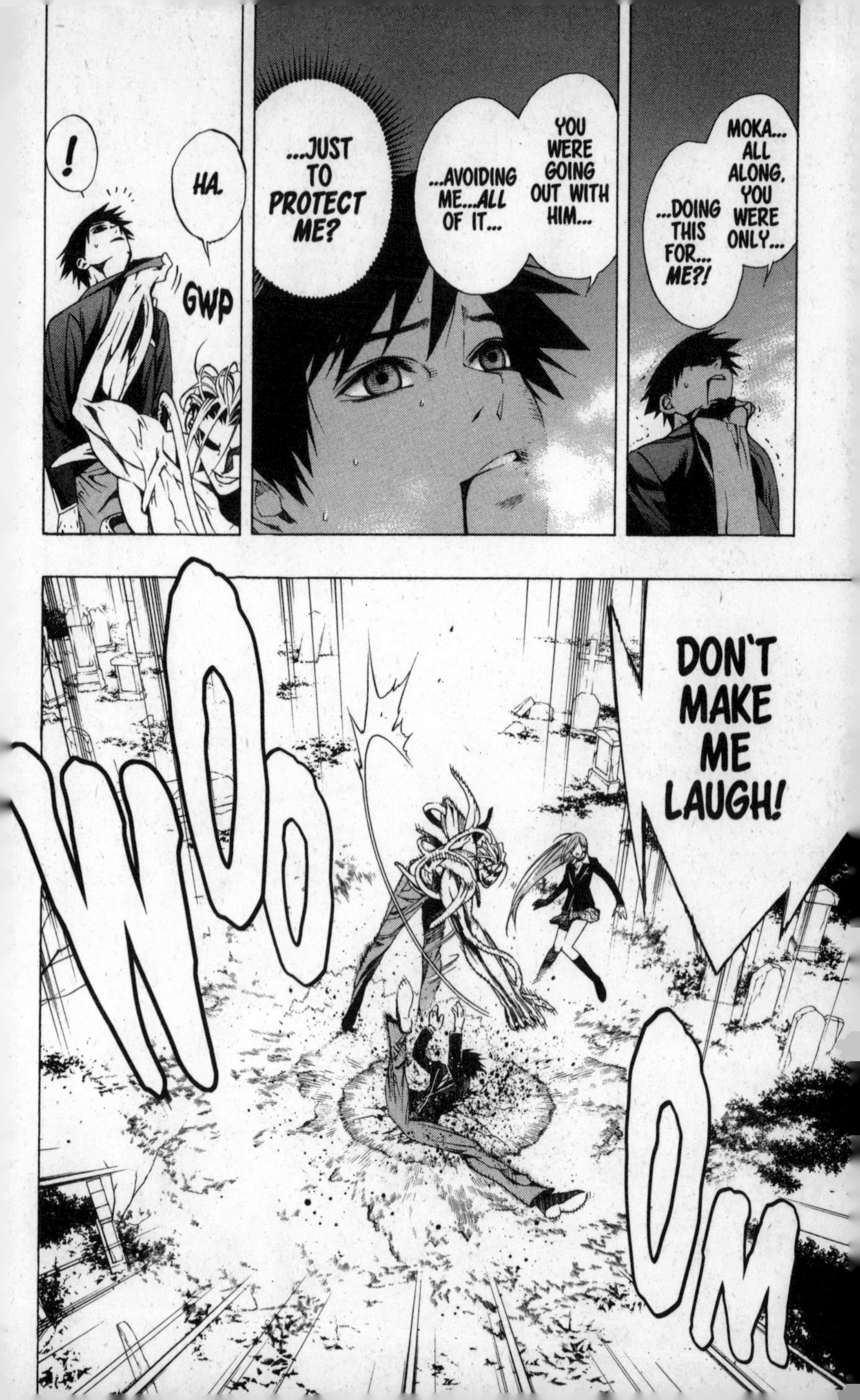

MOKA... ALL ALONG, YOU WERE ONLY...
...DOING THIS FOR... ME?!
YOU WERE GOING OUT WITH HIM...
...AVOIDING ME...ALL OF IT...
...JUST TO PROTECT ME?
!
HA.
GWP
DON'T MAKE ME LAUGH!
WOOOOM

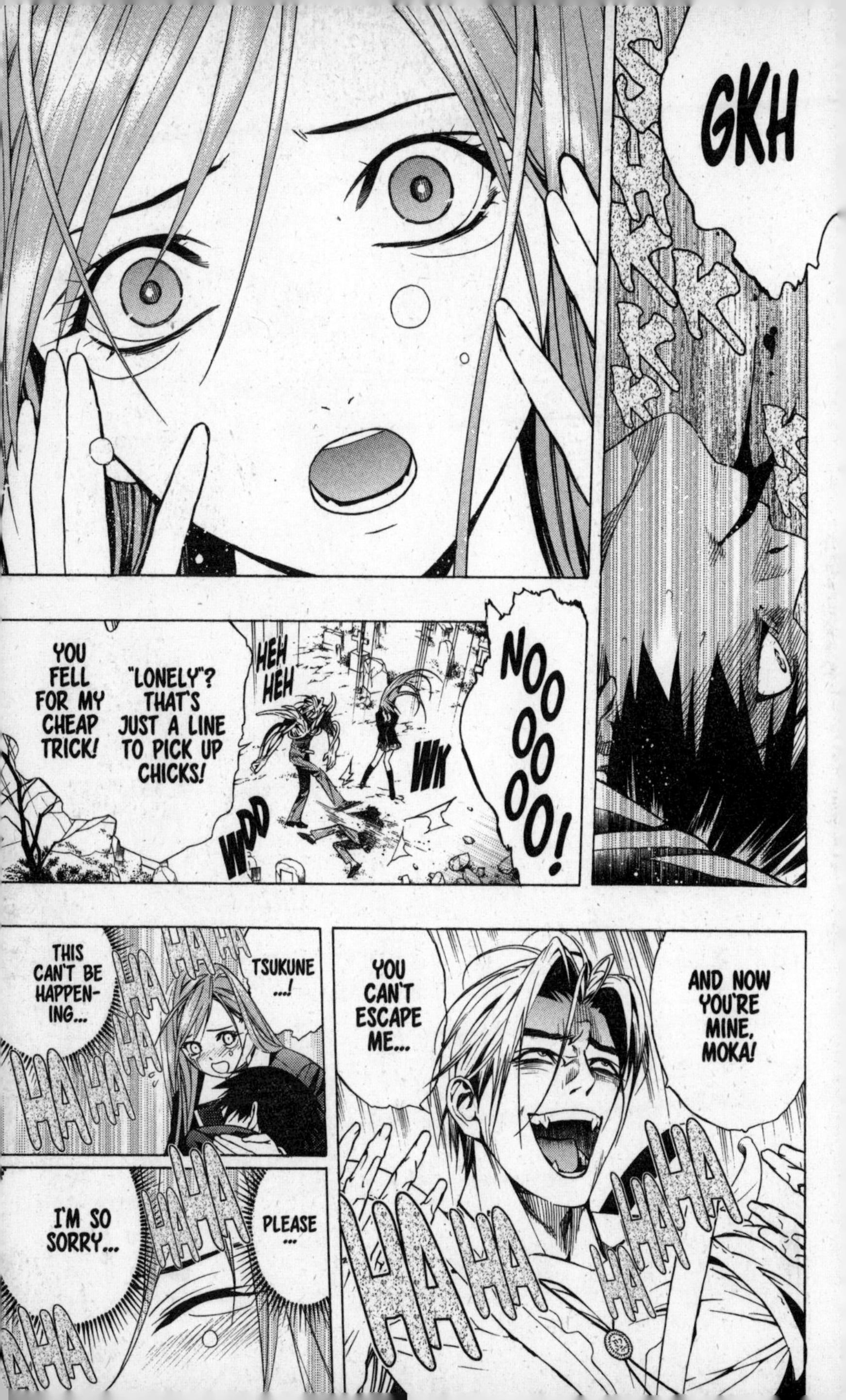
GKH
NOOOOOOOOO!
HEH HEH
"LONELY"? THAT'S JUST A LINE TO PICK UP CHICKS!
YOU FELL FOR MY CHEAP TRICK!
WK
WDD
AND NOW YOU'RE MINE, MOKA!
YOU CAN'T ESCAPE ME...
HAHAHA
HAHAHA
TSUKUNE ...!
THIS CAN'T BE HAPPENING...
HAHAHAHA
PLEASE ...
I'M SO SORRY...
HAHA

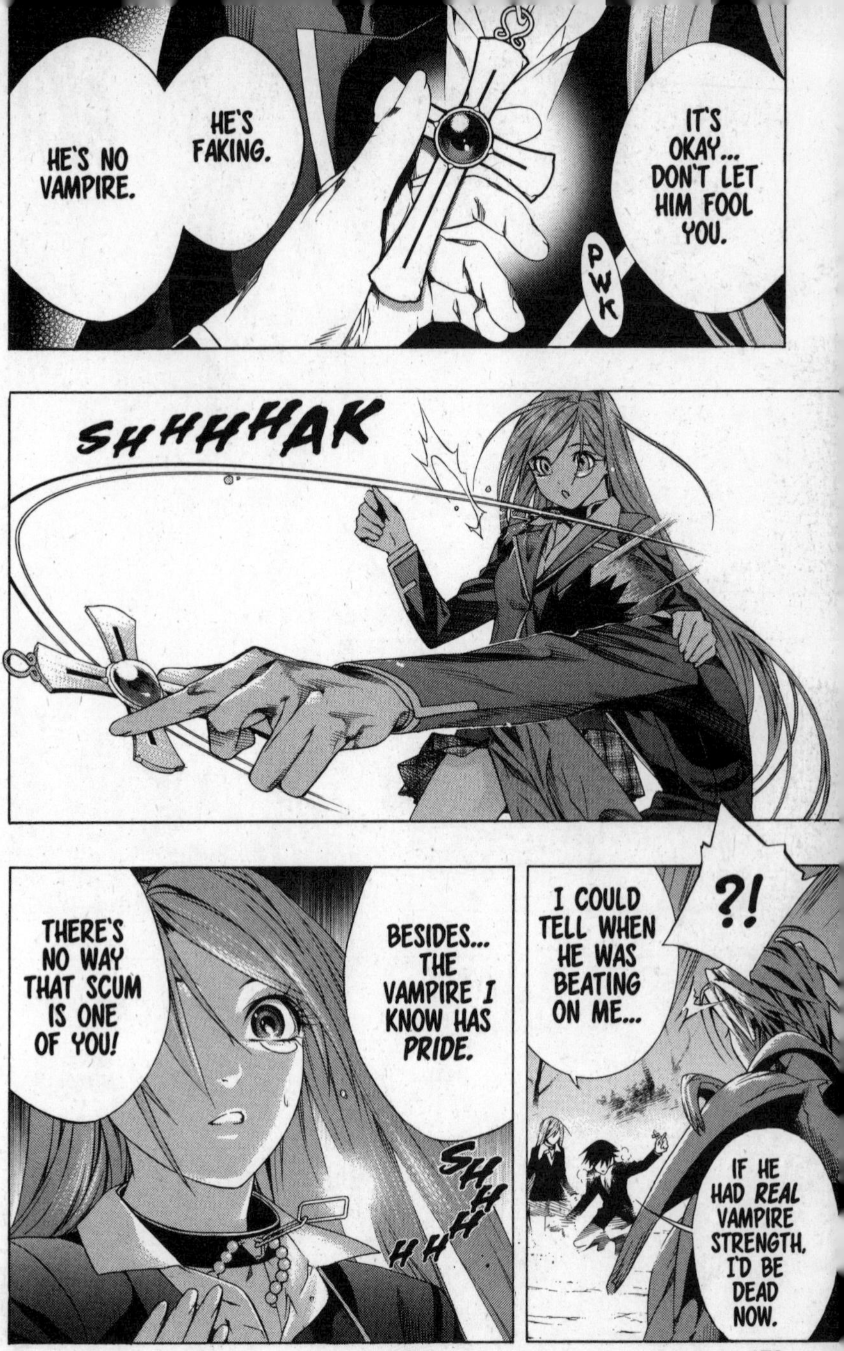
IT'S OKAY... DON'T LET HIM FOOL YOU.
PWK
HE'S FAKING.
HE'S NO VAMPIRE.
SHHHHAK
?!
I COULD TELL WHEN HE WAS BEATING ON ME...
IF HE HAD REAL VAMPIRE STRENGTH, I'D BE DEAD NOW.
BESIDES... THE VAMPIRE I KNOW HAS PRIDE.
THERE'S NO WAY THAT SCUM IS ONE OF YOU!
SHHHHHH

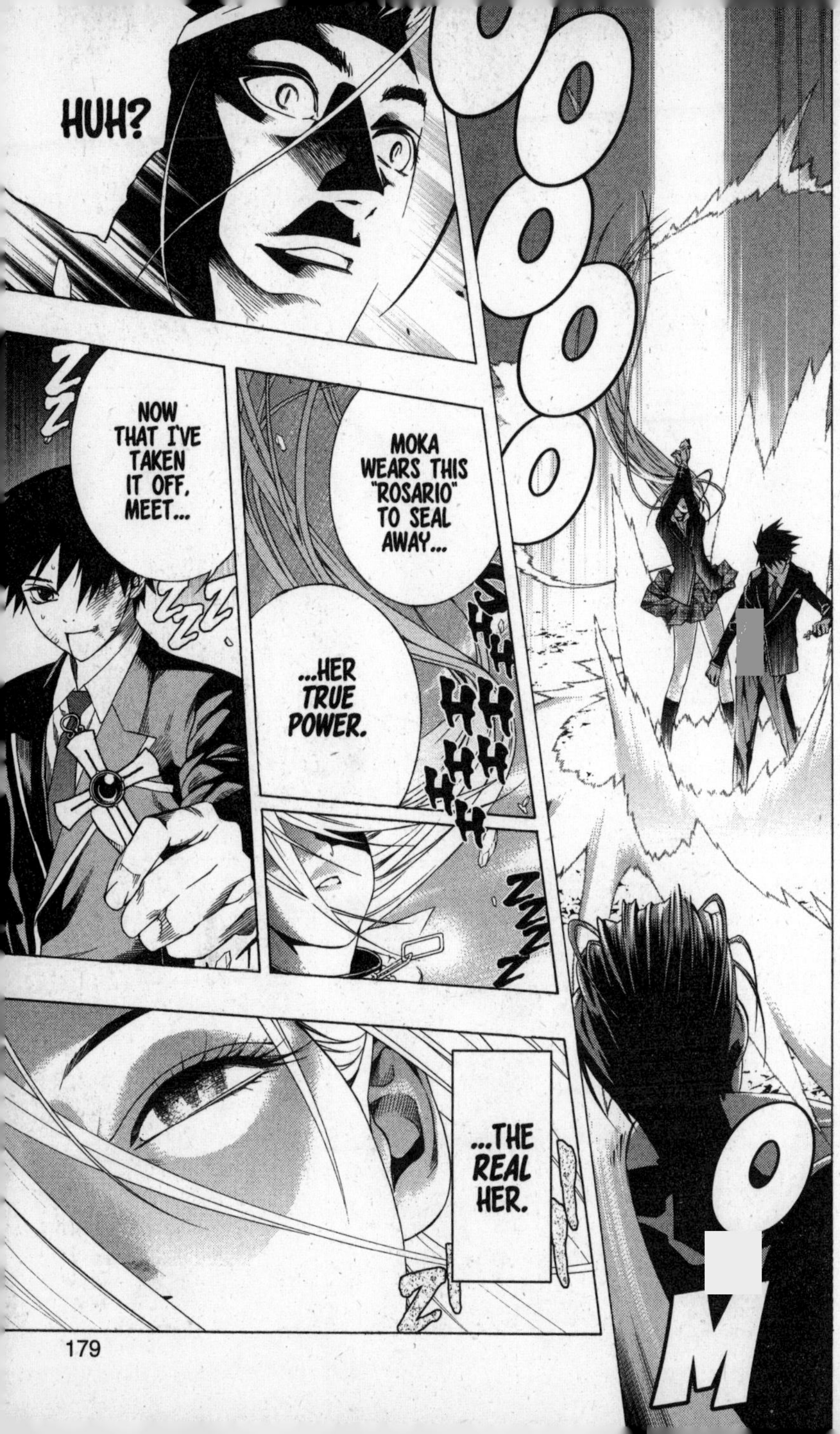
OOOOOOOOO
OM
HUH?
MOKA WEARS THIS "ROSARIO" TO SEAL AWAY...
...HER TRUE POWER.
SHHHHHHHHHH
NOW THAT I'VE TAKEN IT OFF, MEET...
ZZ
ZZZ
ZZZZZ
...THE REAL HER.

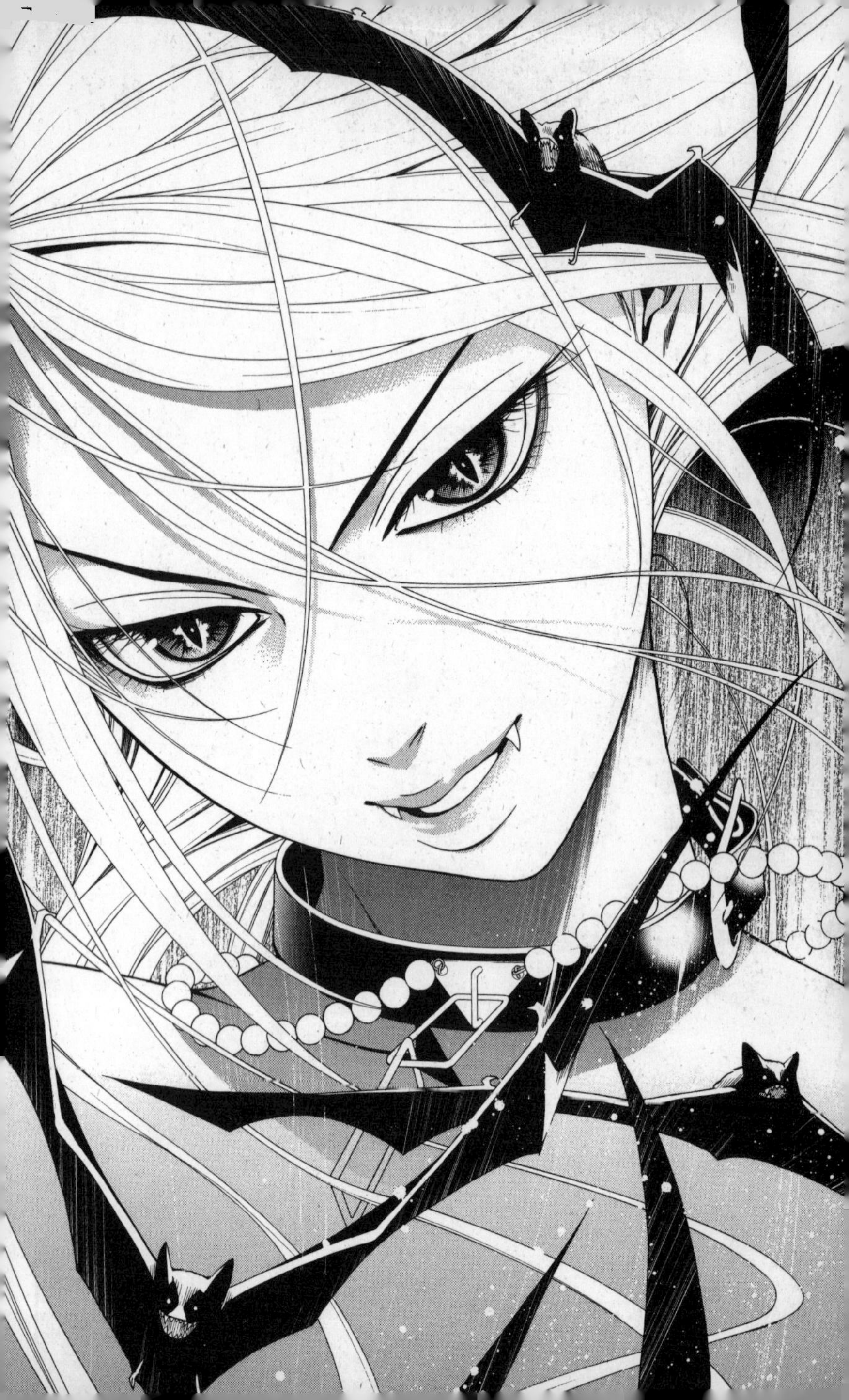

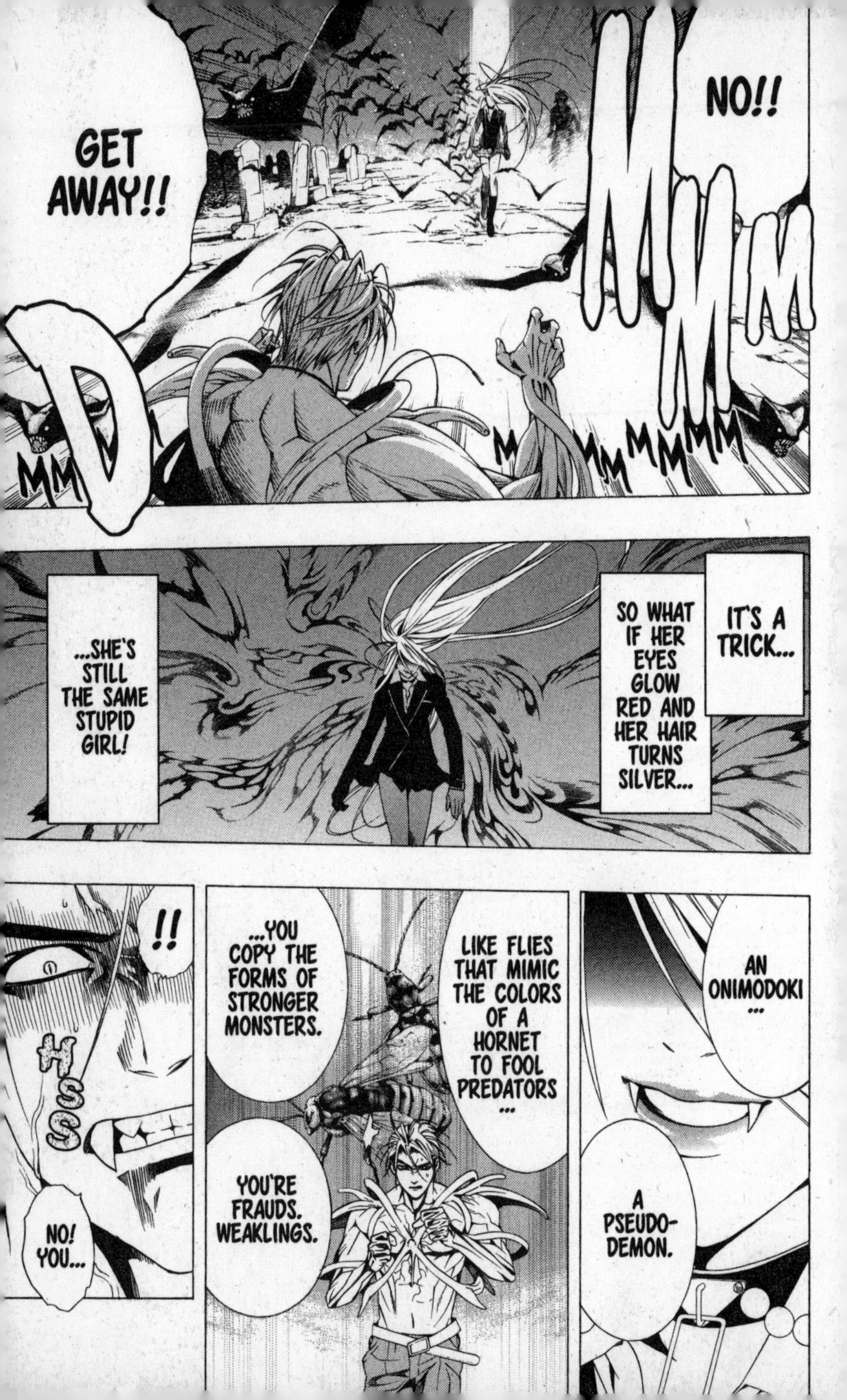
NO!!
MMMM
GET AWAY!!
DMM
MMMMMMM
IT'S A TRICK...
SO WHAT IF HER EYES GLOW RED AND HER HAIR TURNS SILVER...
...SHE'S STILL THE SAME STUPID GIRL!
AN ONIMODOKI...
A PSEUDO-DEMON.
LIKE FLIES THAT MIMIC THE COLORS OF A HORNET TO FOOL PREDATORS...
...YOU COPY THE FORMS OF STRONGER MONSTERS.
YOU'RE FRAUDS. WEAKLINGS.
!!
HSS
NO! YOU...

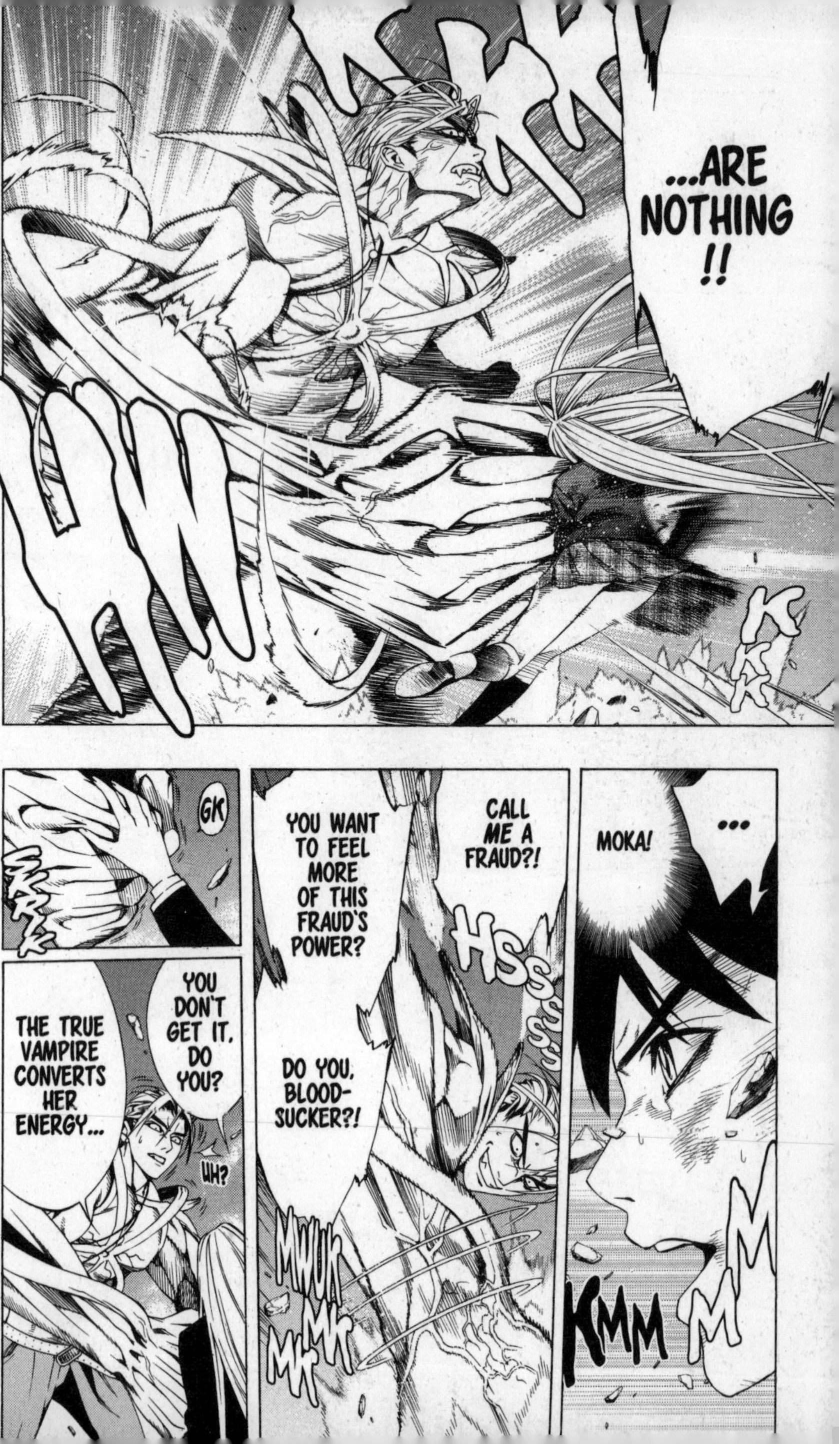
...ARE NOTHING !!
...
MOKA!
KMM
CALL ME A FRAUD?!
YOU WANT TO FEEL MORE OF THIS FRAUD'S POWER?
HSSSSS
DO YOU, BLOOD-SUCKER?!
GK
YOU DON'T GET IT, DO YOU?
UH?
THE TRUE VAMPIRE CONVERTS HER ENERGY...

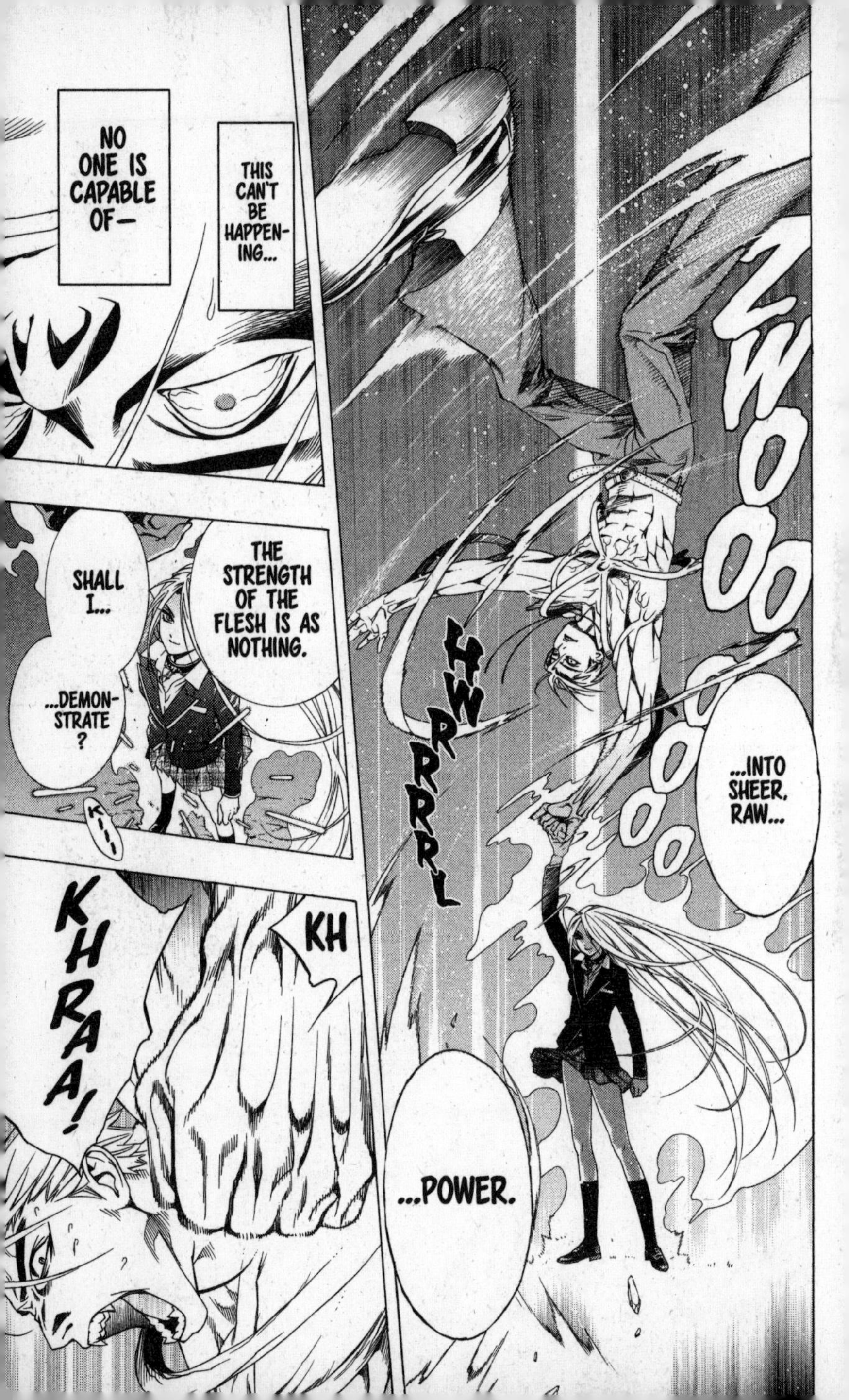
WOOOOOOOOOO
HWRRRRL
...INTO SHEER, RAW...
...POWER.
THIS CAN'T BE HAPPENING...
NO ONE IS CAPABLE OF—
THE STRENGTH OF THE FLESH IS AS NOTHING.
SHALL I...
...DEMONSTRATE?
KIII
KH
KHRAA!

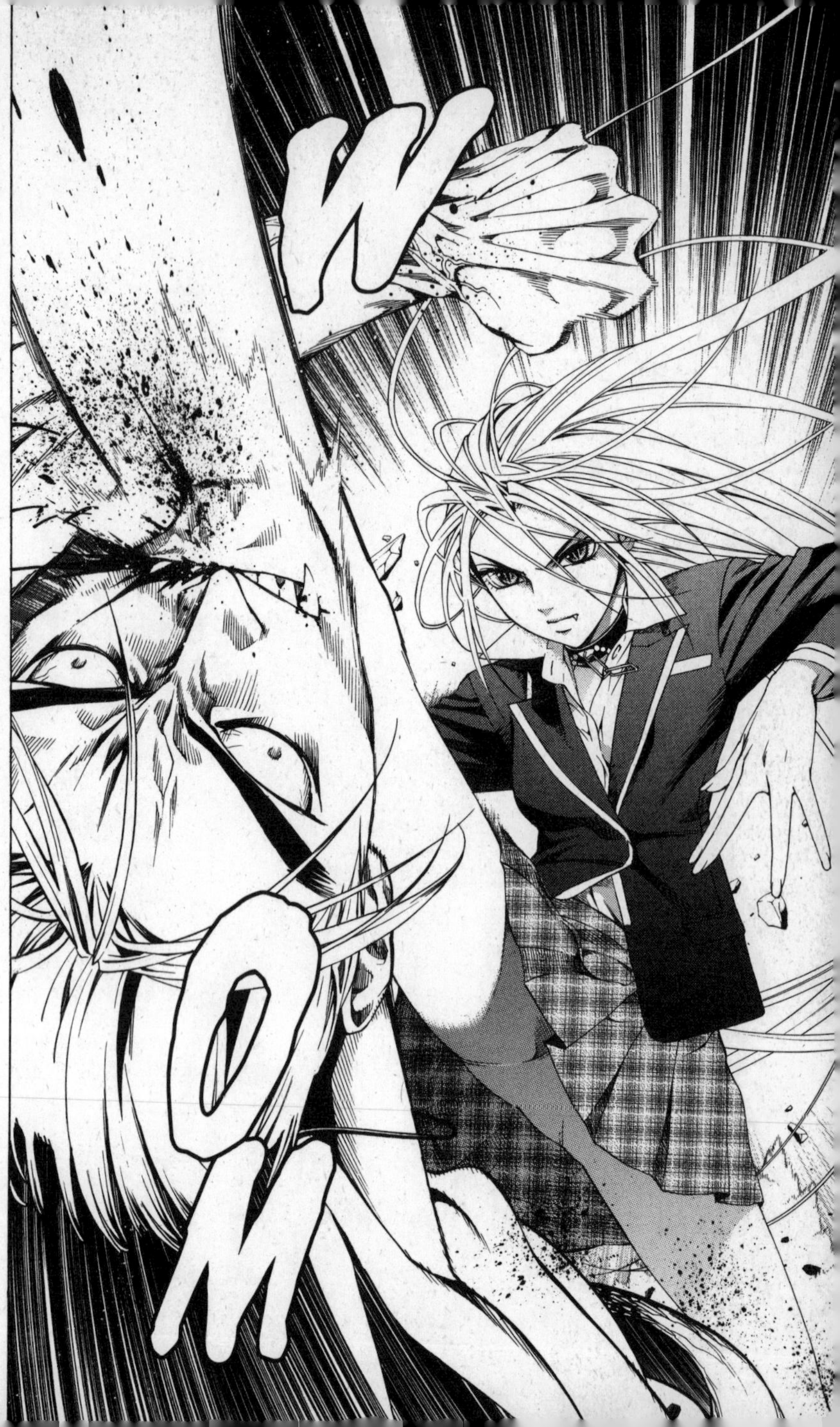
WOM

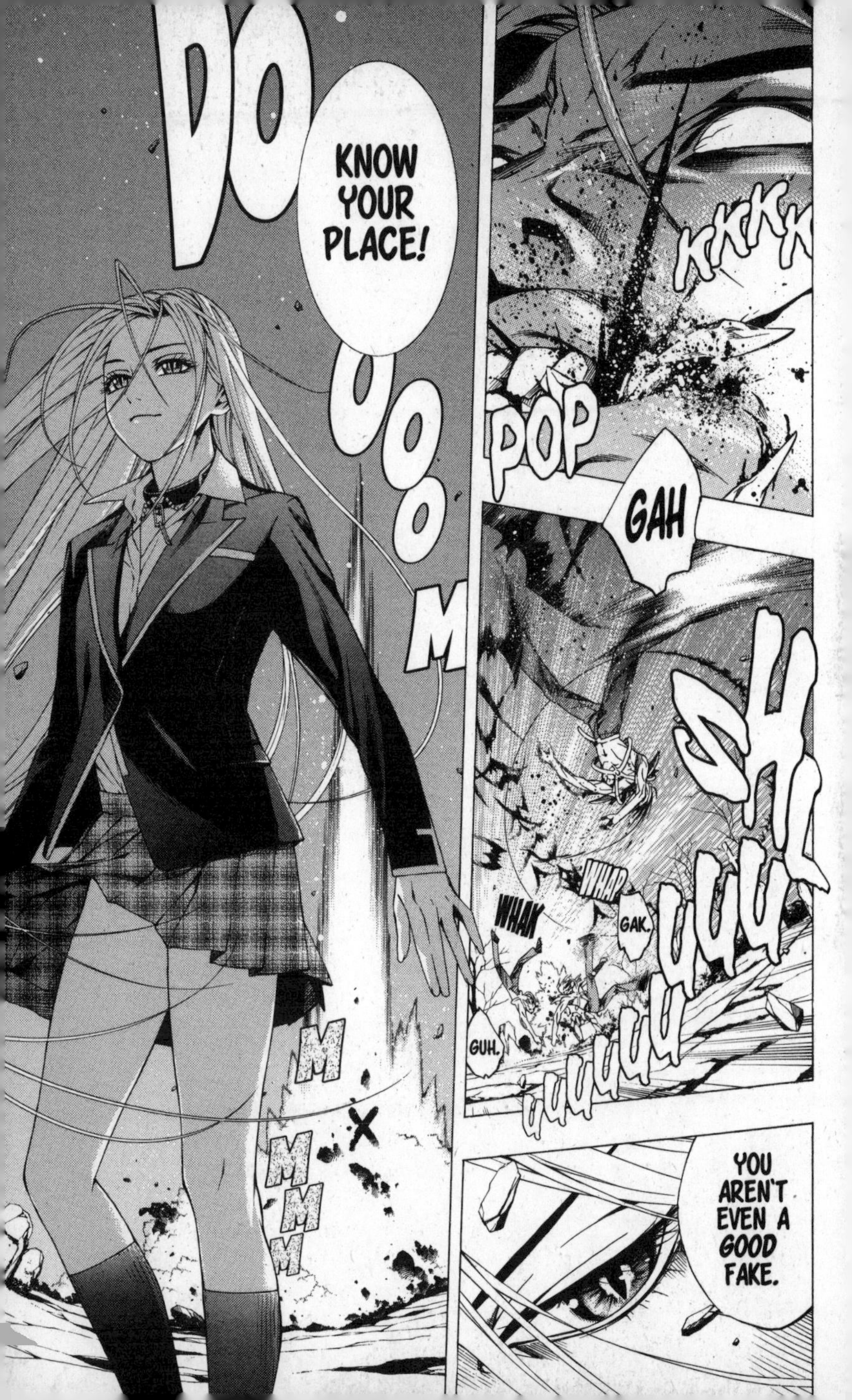
KKKKK
POP
GAH
SHUUUUUUUUU
WHAP
WHAK
GAK.
GUH.
YOU AREN'T EVEN A GOOD FAKE.
DOOOOM
KNOW YOUR PLACE!
MMMMM

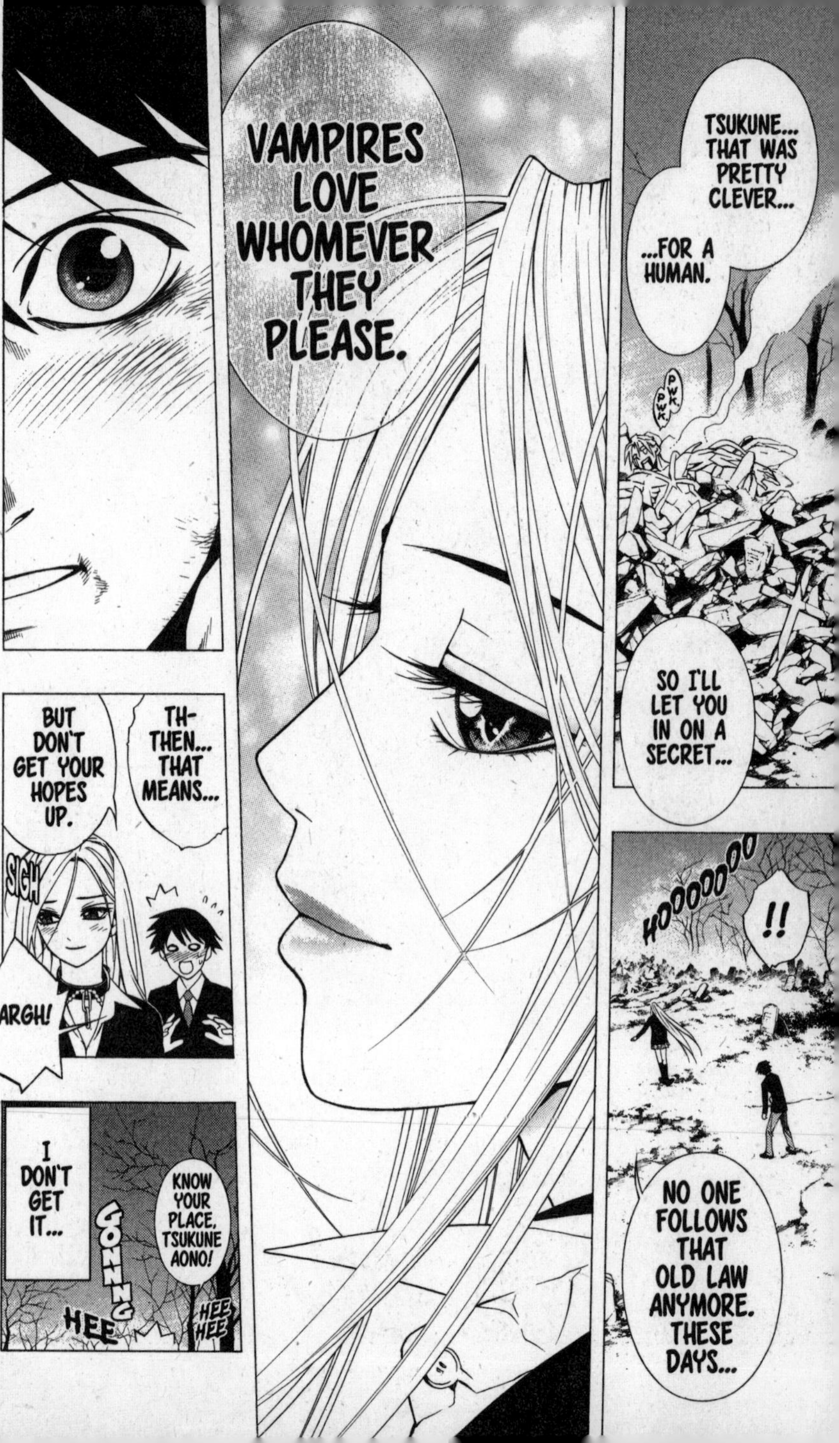
TSUKUNE... THAT WAS PRETTY CLEVER...
...FOR A HUMAN.
PWK, PWK.
SO I'LL LET YOU IN ON A SECRET...
HOOOOOOOO
!!
NO ONE FOLLOWS THAT OLD LAW ANYMORE. THESE DAYS...
VAMPIRES LOVE WHOMEVER THEY PLEASE.
TH-THEN... THAT MEANS...
BUT DON'T GET YOUR HOPES UP.
SIGH
ARGH!
KNOW YOUR PLACE, TSUKUNE AONO!
I DON'T GET IT...
GONNNG
HEE HEE
HEE HEE

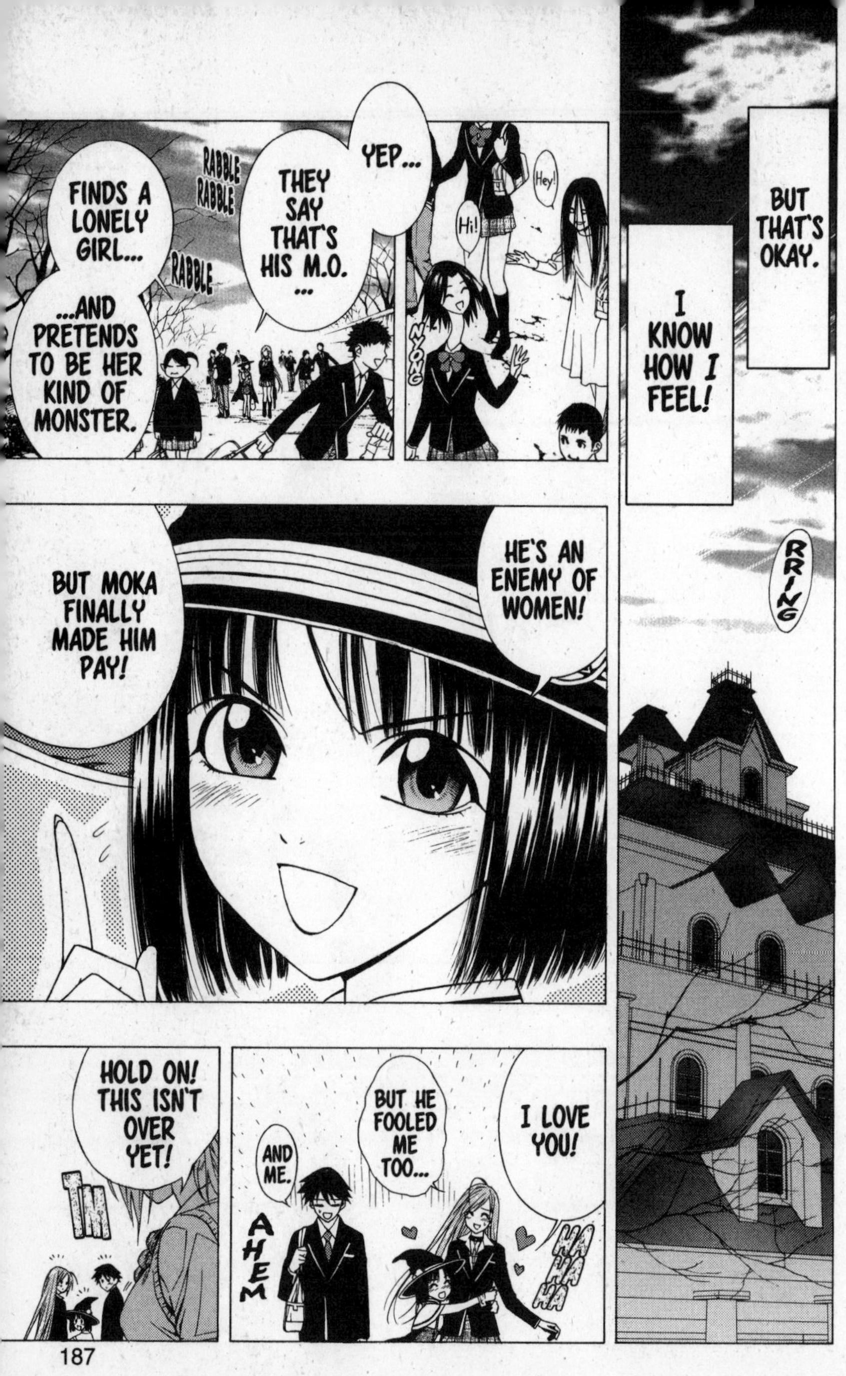
BUT THAT'S OKAY.
I KNOW HOW I FEEL!
RRING
Hey!
Hi!
NYONG
YEP...
THEY SAY THAT'S HIS M.O. ...
RABBLE RABBLE
FINDS A LONELY GIRL...
RABBLE
...AND PRETENDS TO BE HER KIND OF MONSTER.
HE'S AN ENEMY OF WOMEN!
BUT MOKA FINALLY MADE HIM PAY!
I LOVE YOU!
HA HA HA HA
BUT HE FOOLED ME TOO...
AND ME.
AHEM
HOLD ON! THIS ISN'T OVER YET!

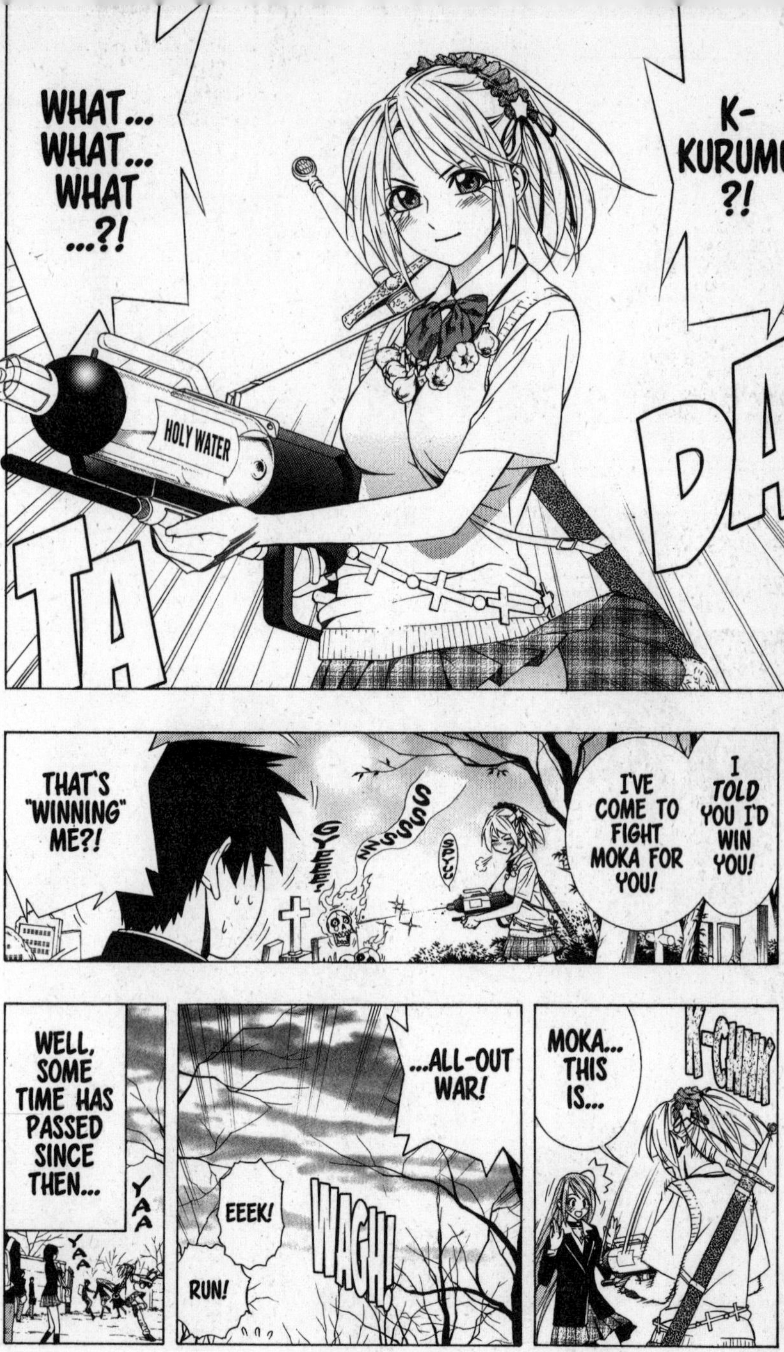
K-
KURUMU?!
WHAT... WHAT... WHAT...?!
HOLY WATER
DA
TA
I TOLD YOU I'D WIN YOU!
I'VE COME TO FIGHT MOKA FOR YOU!
THAT'S "WINNING" ME?!
MOKA... THIS IS...
...ALL-OUT WAR!
WAGH!
EEEK!
RUN!
WELL, SOME TIME HAS PASSED SINCE THEN...
YAA
YAA

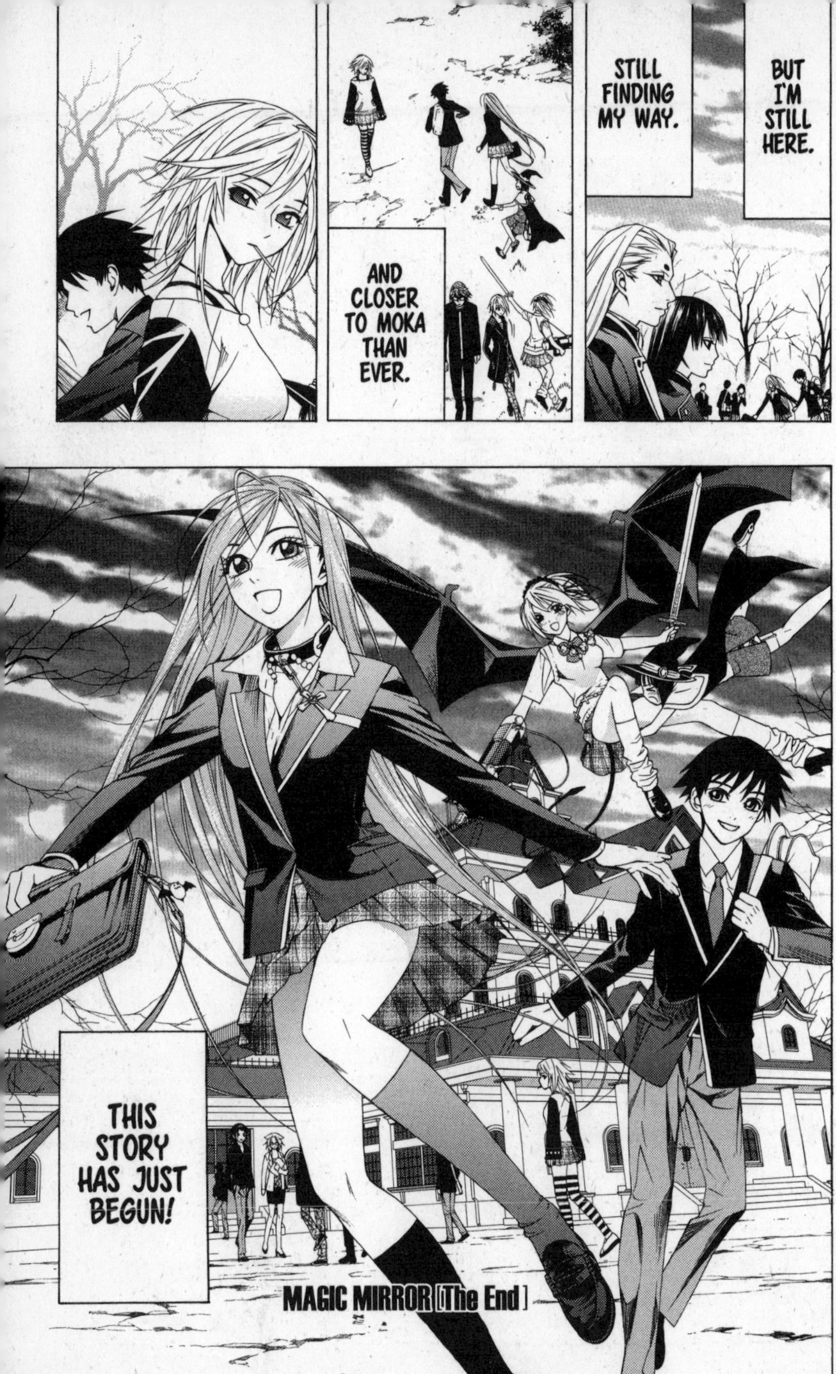
BUT I'M STILL HERE.
STILL FINDING MY WAY.
AND CLOSER TO MOKA THAN EVER.
THIS STORY HAS JUST BEGUN!
MAGIC MIRROR [The End]

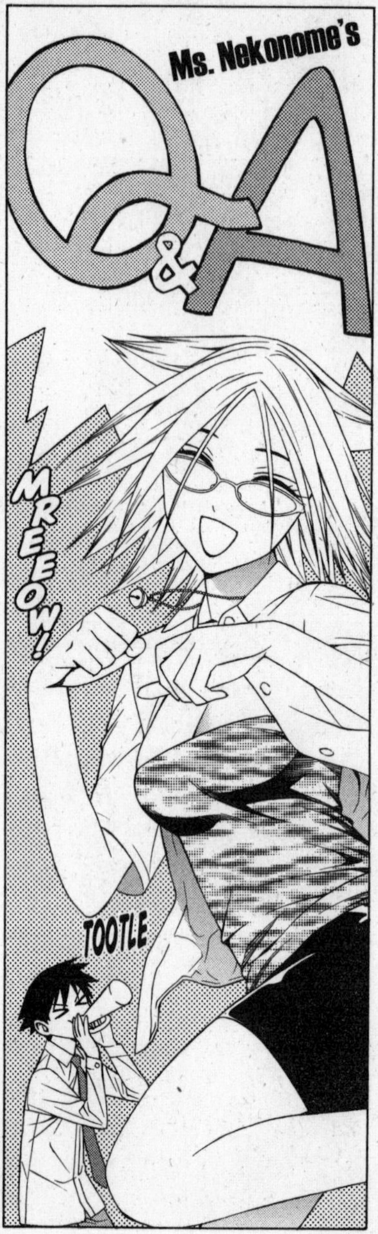
Ms. Nekonome's
Q&A
MREEOW!
TOOTLE

ROSARIO + VAMPIRE

Meaningless End-of-Volume Theater

X

•Tell Us, Ms. Nekonome!•

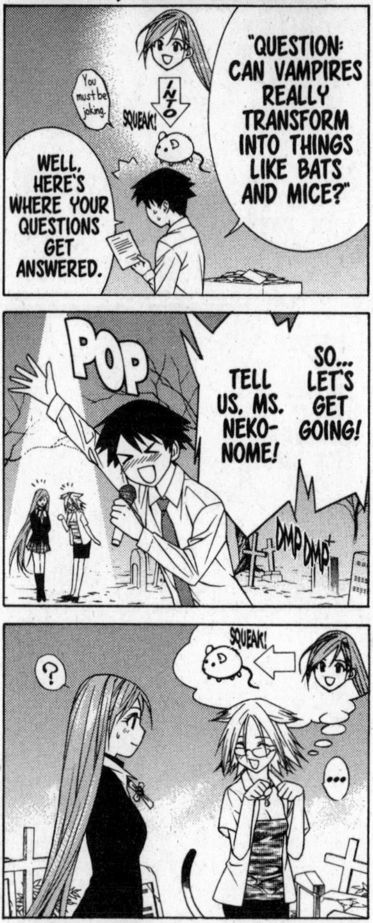
"QUESTION: CAN VAMPIRES REALLY TRANSFORM INTO THINGS LIKE BATS AND MICE?"
INTO
SQUEAK!
You must be joking.
WELL, HERE'S WHERE YOUR QUESTIONS GET ANSWERED.
SO... LET'S GET GOING!
TELL US, MS. NEKO-NOME!
POP
DMP DMP
SQUEAK!
?
...
SQUEAK!
MEW
CHMP
I CAN'T TRANS-FORM, OKAY?!
DROOL
BRR BRR
So you can't eat me!

•Test It, Ms. Nekonome!•

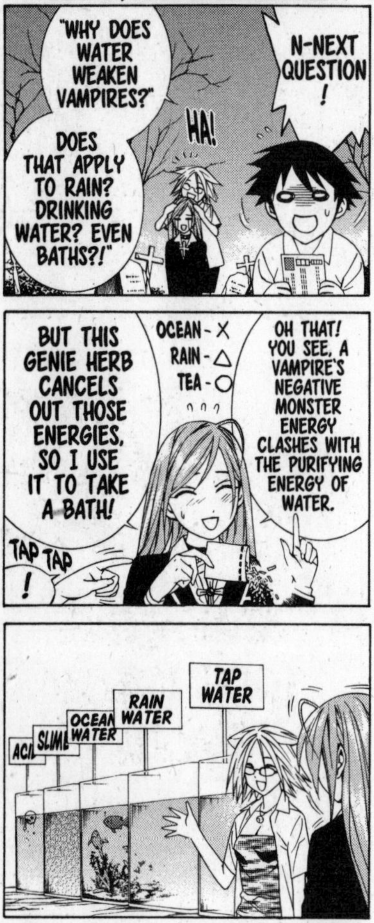
N-NEXT QUESTION!
"WHY DOES WATER WEAKEN VAMPIRES?"
HA!
DOES THAT APPLY TO RAIN? DRINKING WATER? EVEN BATHS?!"
OH THAT! YOU SEE, A VAMPIRE'S NEGATIVE MONSTER ENERGY CLASHES WITH THE PURIFYING ENERGY OF WATER.
OCEAN - X
RAIN - △
TEA - O
BUT THIS GENIE HERB CANCELS OUT THOSE ENERGIES, SO I USE IT TO TAKE A BATH!
TAP TAP!
TAP WATER
RAIN WATER
OCEAN WATER
SLIME
ACI
WE NEED TO TEST THEM ALL!
AND KILL ME?!
WAIT!
BLUP BLUP
ACID

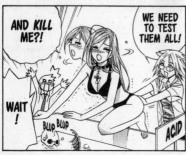

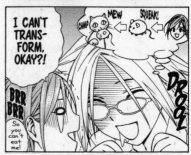

•The Most Popular Question•

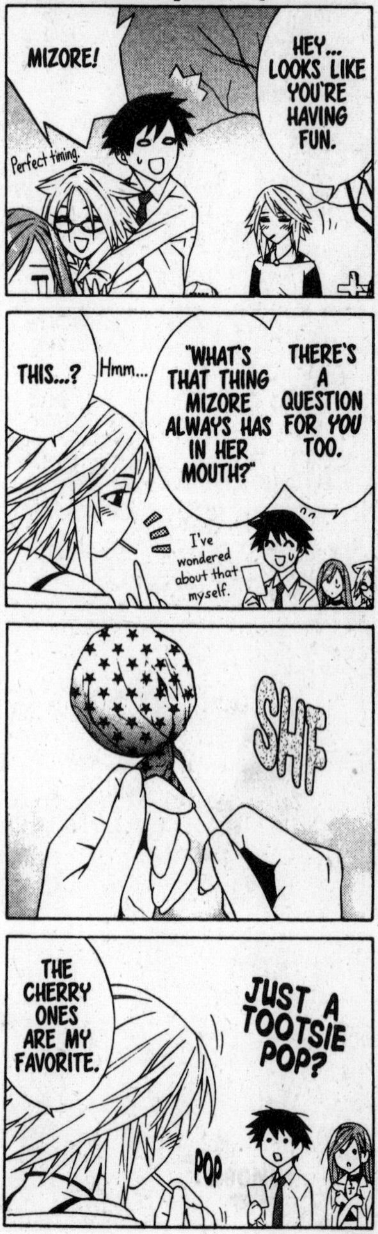
HEY... LOOKS LIKE YOU'RE HAVING FUN.
MIZORE!
Perfect timing.
THERE'S A QUESTION FOR *YOU* TOO.
"WHAT'S THAT THING MIZORE ALWAYS HAS IN HER MOUTH?"
Hmm...
THIS...?
I've wondered about that myself.
SHF
JUST A TOOTSIE POP?
THE CHERRY ONES ARE MY FAVORITE.
POP

• Don't Get It •

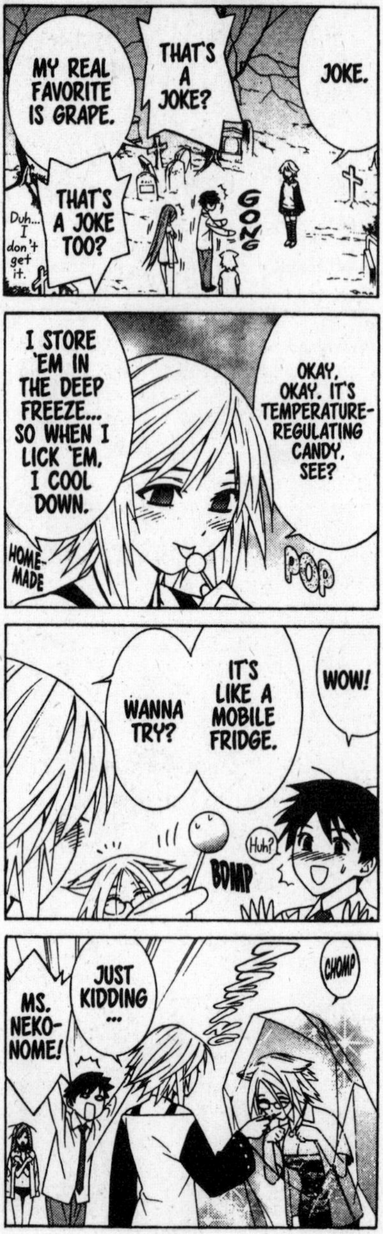
JOKE.
THAT'S A JOKE?
MY REAL FAVORITE IS GRAPE.
GONG
THAT'S A JOKE TOO?
Duh... I don't get it.
OKAY, OKAY. IT'S TEMPERATURE-REGULATING CANDY, SEE?
I STORE 'EM IN THE DEEP FREEZE... SO WHEN I LICK 'EM, I COOL DOWN.
POP
HOME-MADE
WOW!
IT'S LIKE A MOBILE FRIDGE.
WANNA TRY?
Huh?
BDMP
CHOMP
JUST KIDDING ...
MS. NEKO-NOME!

• Yukari Q&A •

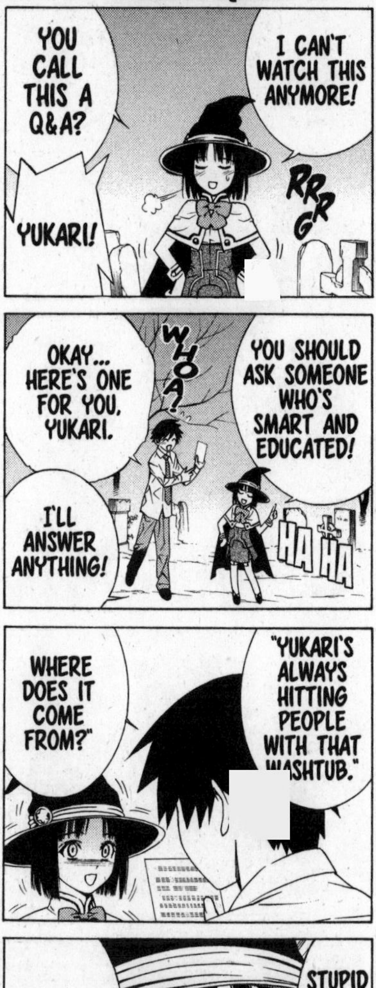
I CAN'T WATCH THIS ANYMORE!
RRRG
YOU CALL THIS A Q&A?
YUKARI!
YOU SHOULD ASK SOMEONE WHO'S SMART AND EDUCATED!
WHOA!
OKAY... HERE'S ONE FOR YOU, YUKARI.
HA HA
I'LL ANSWER ANYTHING!
"YUKARI'S ALWAYS HITTING PEOPLE WITH THAT WASHTUB."
WHERE DOES IT COME FROM?"
STUPID QUES-TION!
OBVIOUSLY!

• Three Heads Are Better Than One •

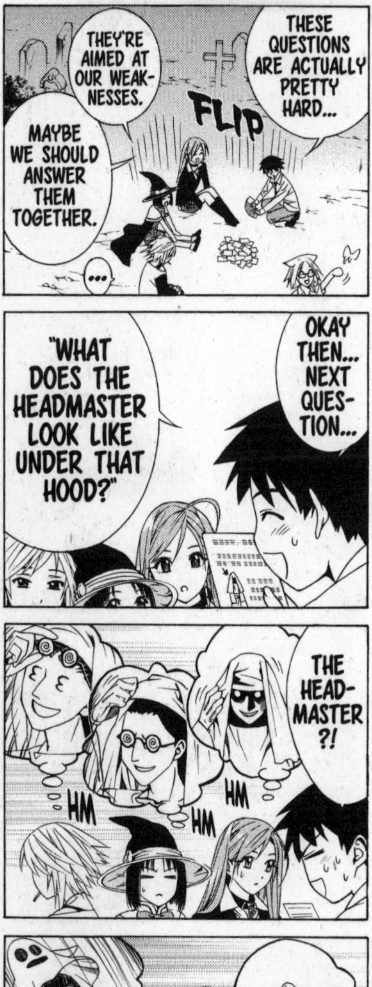
THESE QUESTIONS ARE ACTUALLY PRETTY HARD...
FLIP
THEY'RE AIMED AT OUR WEAK-NESSES.
MAYBE WE SHOULD ANSWER THEM TOGETHER.
...
OKAY THEN... NEXT QUES-TION...
"WHAT DOES THE HEADMASTER LOOK LIKE UNDER THAT HOOD?"
THE HEAD-MASTER?!
HM
HM
HM
HM
HM
EEP!
HM

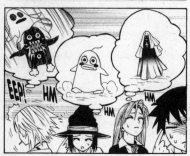

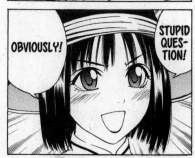

• Entreaty •

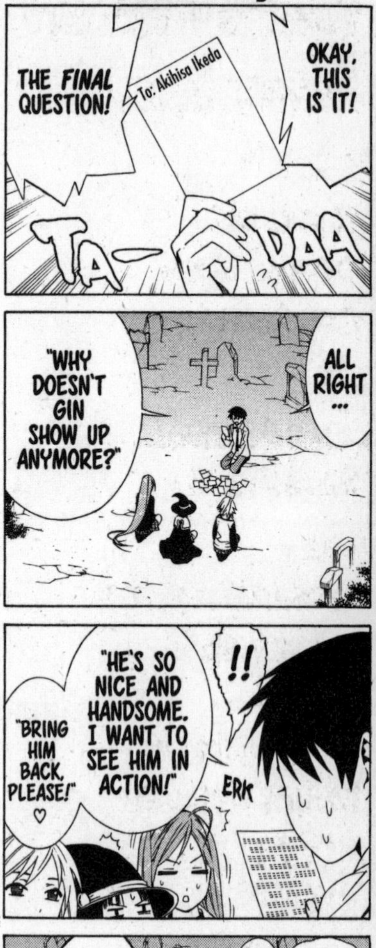
OKAY, THIS IS IT!
To: Akihisa Ikeda
THE FINAL QUESTION!
TA- DAA
ALL RIGHT...
"WHY DOESN'T GIN SHOW UP ANYMORE?"
!!
"HE'S SO NICE AND HANDSOME. I WANT TO SEE HIM IN ACTION!"
ERK
"BRING HIM BACK, PLEASE!" ♡
WOW... I GUESS EVEN GIN HAS FANS...
Good for him!
"SINCERELY, GIN MORIOKA"
WELL... ONE FAN, ANYWAY...

• The Leader Vanishes •

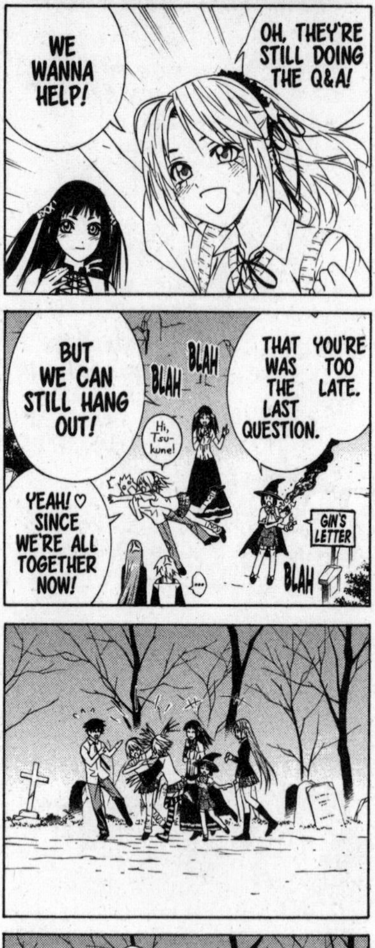
OH, THEY'RE STILL DOING THE Q&A!
WE WANNA HELP!
YOU'RE TOO LATE.
THAT WAS THE LAST QUESTION.
BLAH
BLAH
BUT WE CAN STILL HANG OUT!
Hi, Tsukune!
GIN'S LETTER
BLAH
YEAH! ♡ SINCE WE'RE ALL TOGETHER NOW!
...
HEY!
WHAT HAPPENED TO MS. NEKONOME?

Please send questions and fan letters to ➡ Rosario+Vampire Fan Mail, VIZ Media, P.O. Box 77010, San Francisco, CA 94107

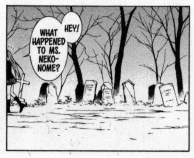

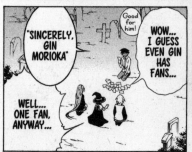

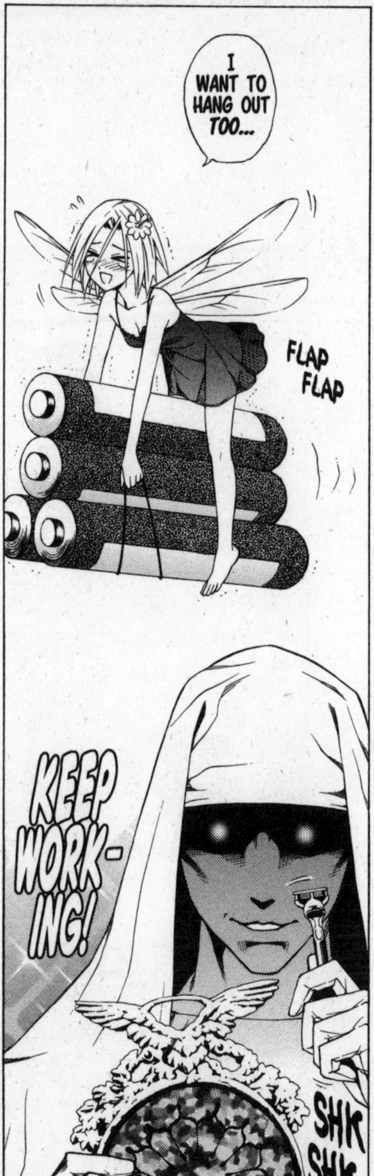
I WANT TO HANG OUT TOO...
FLAP FLAP
KEEP WORK-ING!
SHK SHK

Rosario + Vampire

Akihisa Ikeda

• Staff •

Makoto Saito
Takafumi Okubo
Kenji Tashiro

• Help •

Yoshiaki Sukeno
Kanata Tanaka

• CG •

Takaharu Yoshizawa
Akihisa Ikeda

• Editing •

Tomonori Sumiya
Makoto Watanabe

• Comic •

Kenju Noro

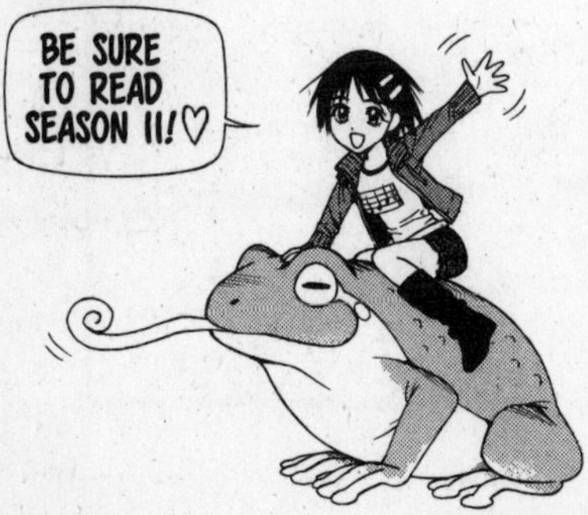
BE SURE TO READ SEASON II! ♡

CRYPT SHEET FOR SEASON II, VOL. 1: MAGICAL FRUIT

TEST 1

When confronted with a man-eating (and monster-eating) magical fruit...

a. toot

b. jam

c. harvest

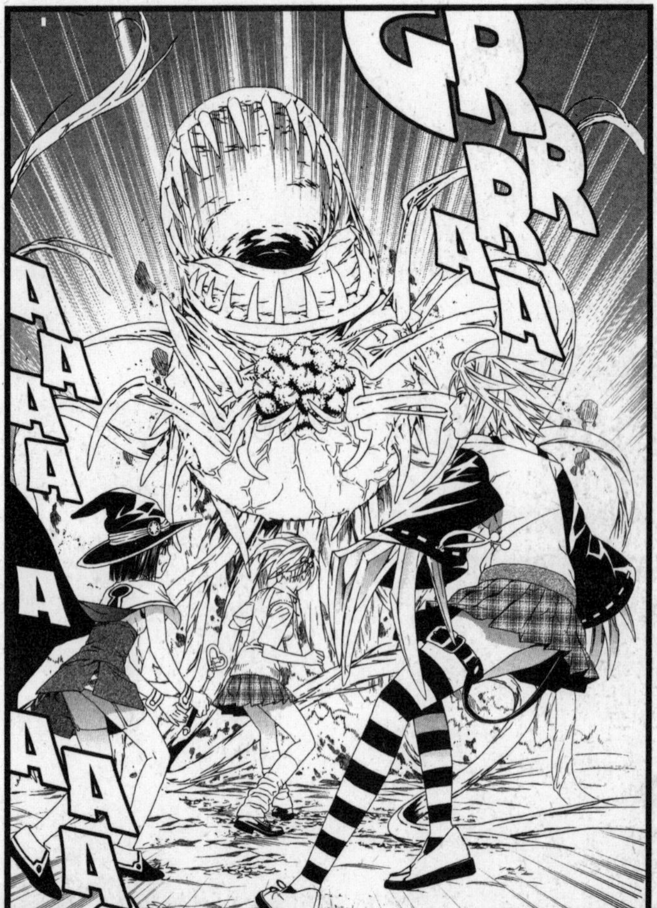
GRRRAAA
AAAAAAAAAA

AVAILABLE APRIL 2010!

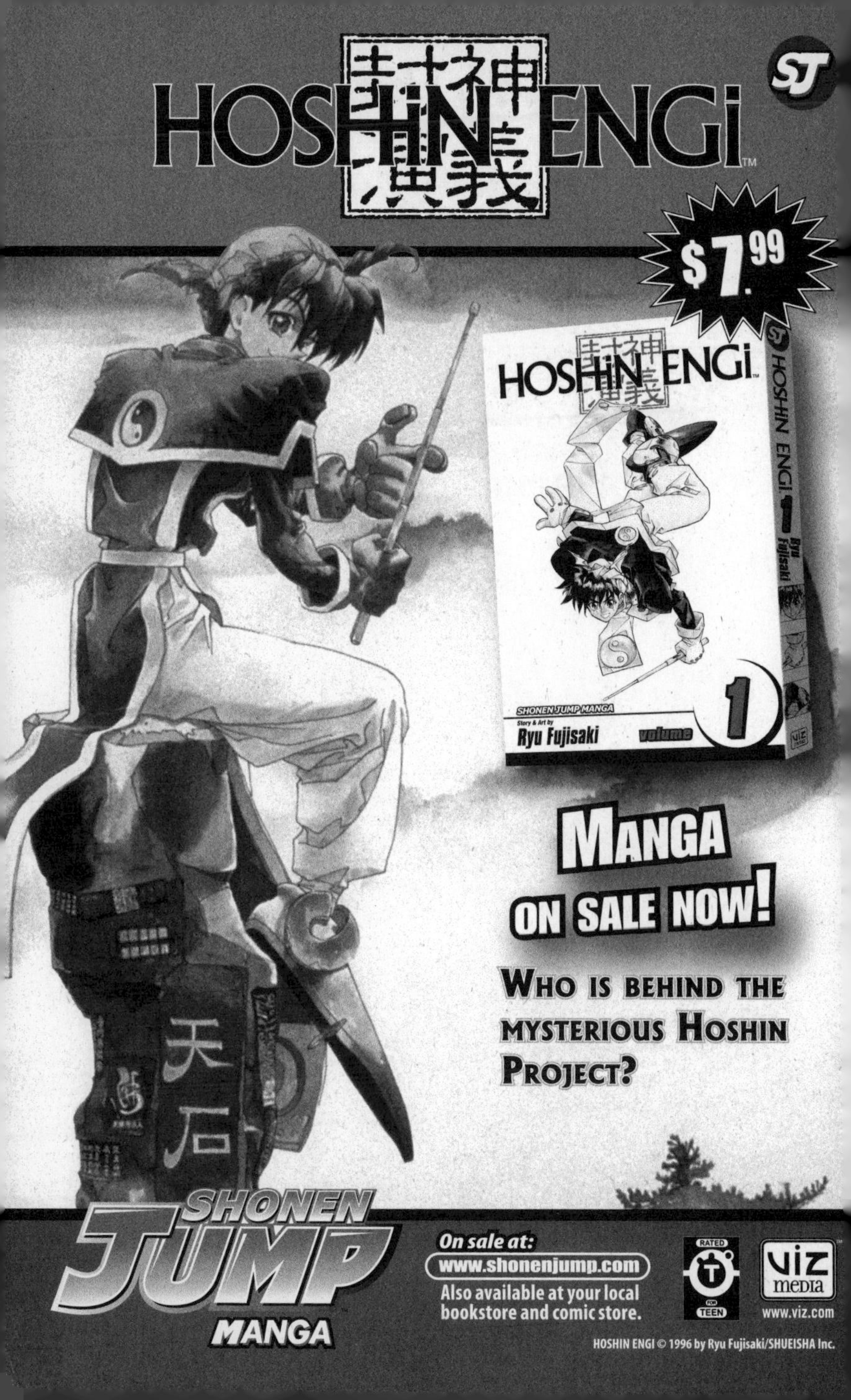
HOSHIN ENGI™
封神演義
SJ
$7.99
HOSHIN ENGI
SHONEN JUMP MANGA
Story & Art by
Ryu Fujisaki
volume 1
MANGA
ON SALE NOW!
WHO IS BEHIND THE MYSTERIOUS HOSHIN PROJECT?
SHONEN JUMP MANGA
On sale at:
www.shonenjump.com
Also available at your local bookstore and comic store.
RATED T FOR TEEN
VIZ media
www.viz.com
HOSHIN ENGI © 1996 by Ryu Fujisaki/SHUEISHA Inc.